May 17

Be Like the Fox

Be Like the Fox

Machiavelli's Lifelong Quest for Freedom

ERICA BENNER

W. W. Norton & Company
Independent Publishers Since 1923
New York • London

For information about permission to reproduce selections from this book, write to
Permissions, W. W. Norton & Company, Inc., 500 Fifth Avenue, New York, NY 10110

For information about special discounts for bulk purchases, please contact
W. W. Norton Special Sales at specialsales@wwnorton.com or 800-233-4830

Manufacturing by Berryville Graphics
Book design by Jouve (UK), Milton Keanes
Production manager: Phil Hofius

ISBN 978-0-393-60972-1

W. W. Norton & Company, Inc.,
500 Fifth Avenue, New York, N.Y. 10110
www.wwnorton.com

W. W. Norton & Company Ltd.,
15 Carlisle Street, London W1D 3BS

1 2 3 4 5 6 7 8 9 0

Contents

Dramatis Personae

Machiavelli Household

Niccolò Machiavelli, Second Chancellor of the Florentine Republic from 1498 to 1512; also a poet, playwright, historian and political writer

Bernardo and Bartolommea Machiavelli, his parents

Primavera, Margherita and Totto Machiavelli, Niccolò's sisters and brother

Marietta (Corsini) Machiavelli, Niccolò's wife

Bernardo, Ludovico, Piero, Guido, Baccina and Totto Machiavelli, their children

Nencia, Bartolommea Machiavelli's servant girl

Nicolò di Alessandro Machiavelli, Bernardo Machiavelli's younger cousin and neighbour

Machiavelli's Friends

Biagio Buonaccorsi, Niccolò's loyal coadjutor in the Chancery

Agostino Vespucci, another office-mate, a member of the patrician Vespucci family, connoisseur of fine art and publisher of Machiavelli's first published work

Filippo Casavecchia, another colleague and close friend

Francesco Vettori, a leading patrician who holds many political posts in the republic and under Medici rule, and one of Machiavelli's most intimate correspondents

The Orti Oricellari circle: Cosimo Rucellai (grandson of Bernardo), Zanobi Buondelmonti, Luigi Alamanni, Battista della Palla

Francesco Guicciardini, a lawyer, historian, and leading political figure under the Medici government after 1512

Jacopo Falconetti, a wealthy businessman of humble origins who hosts a spectacular production of Machiavelli's play *Mandragola*

Barbera Salutati Raffacani, a young singer and musician with whom Machiavelli is enamoured in his later years

The House of Medici

Lorenzo, known as il Magnifico, Florence's political leader from 1469 to 1492

Giuliano, Lorenzo's younger brother, murdered in the Pazzi conspiracy of 1478

Lorenzo's sons

Piero, Lorenzo's eldest son and heir; Florence's leader from 1492 to 1494

Giovanni, who became **Pope Leo X** in 1513

Giuliano, later Duke of Nemours

Piero's children

Lorenzo di Piero, later Duke of Urbino and leader of Florence

Clarice, who marries Filippo Strozzi

Others

Alfonsina Orsini de' Medici, Piero's Naples-born wife and Regent of Florence from 1515 to 1519

Giulio de' Medici, son of the murdered Giuliano, who became **Pope Clement VII** in 1523

Alessandro and Ippolito de' Medici, sons, respectively, of Lorenzo di Piero and Giuliano di Piero

Dramatis Personae

Other Protagonists in Florence

The family Pazzi, leaders of a conspiracy against the Medici in 1478

Bartolomeo Scala, Florentine Chancellor under the Medici and Bernardo Machiavelli's close friend

Girolamo Savonarola, a Dominican friar from Ferrara whose popular sermons and prophecies give him great authority in Florence

Bernardo Rucellai, a patrician opponent of popular government and founder of the Orti Oricellari gardens, where Machiavelli would take part in discussions that inspired his *Discourses* and *Art of War*

Messer Guidantonio Vespucci, a famous patrician lawyer and Rucellai's political ally

Tommaso Soderini, a patrician elder statesman in the early years of Lorenzo il Magnifico's government

Soderini's sons

Paoloantonio Soderini, a supporter of popular government and of Savonarola

Piero Soderini, elected Florence's first Gonfalonier (Standard-bearer) for Life in 1502

Francesco Soderini, Bishop of Volterra and later Cardinal, one of Machiavelli's early political mentors

Others

Paolo Vitelli, a renowned Italian mercenary, captain of Florence's military forces from 1498 to 1499

Filippo Strozzi ('the younger'), scion of the wealthy Strozzi family, married to Clarice de' Medici

ix

Outside Florence

The Italians

Caterina Sforza Riario, ruler of Forlì and Imola in the Romagna, Florence's closest Italian ally

The Pisan people, who rebel against Florentine rule in 1494 and engage Florence in a draining war

Vitellozzo Vitelli, Paolo Vitelli's brother and second-in-command, later allied with Cesare Borgia

The French

King Charles VIII, whose armies pass through Italy and linger in Florence in 1494

King Louis XII, Charles's successor, the Florentine republic's most important foreign defender

Cardinal Georges d'Amboise, King Louis's chief counsellor

Florimond Robertet, another of King Louis's advisers

King François I, Louis's successor

Non-Florentine popes and their relatives

Pope Sixtus IV, born Francesco della Rovere, thought to have been behind the Pazzi conspiracy in Florence

Pope Alexander VI, born Rodrigo Borgia, the subject of much gossip concerning his nepotism and other corruptions

Cesare Borgia, his son, appointed captain of the papal troops by his father and given the French title Duc de Valentinois

Pope Julius II, born Giuliano della Rovere, popularly known as *il Papa terribile* (the fearsome pope) for his impetuous and warlike disposition

N

GERMAN EMPIRE

Lyon

Bozen

Trent

Milan

DUCHY
OF
MILAN

Venice

VENETIAN REPUBLIC

OTTOMAN
EMPIRE

FRANCE

GENOA

MODENA

Ferrara

Bologna

Ravenna

Imola

Faenza

Forlì

Cesena

Adriatic Sea

LUCCA

Prato

Pisa

Florence

Urbino

REPUBLIC OF FLORENCE

Volterra

Arezzo

PAPAL

Perugia

Ragusa

SIENA

STATES

KINGDOM OF NAPLES

Rome

Ostia

Naples

Tyrrhenian
Sea

Mediterranean Sea

0   50   100 miles

0   100   200 km

Italy in the late fifteenth century

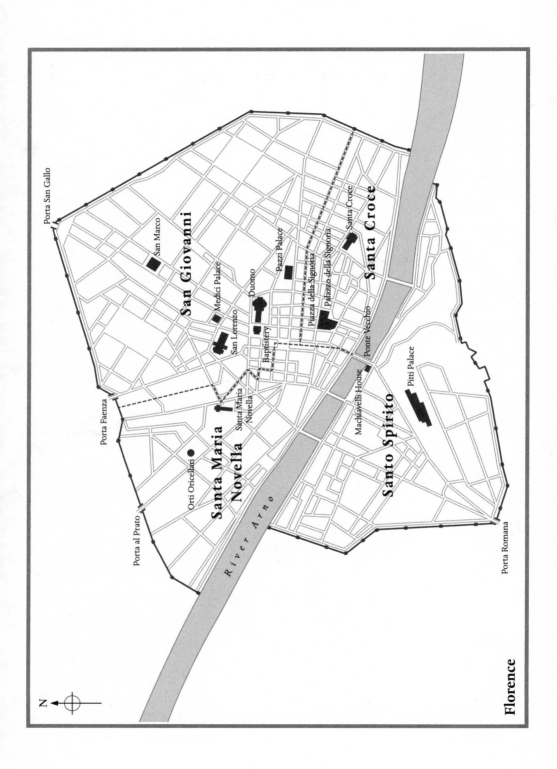

Porta San Gallo

San Marco

San Giovanni

Medici Palace

San Lorenzo

Duomo

Baptistery

Pazzi Palace

Piazza della Signoria

Palazzo della Signoria

Santa Croce

Santa Croce

Ponte Vecchio

Machiavelli House

Pitti Palace

Santo Spirito

Santa Maria Novella

Santa Maria Novella

Orti Oricellari

Porta Faenza

Porta al Prato

River Arno

Porta Romana

N

Florence

Preface

In the winter of 1538, an Englishman living in Italy travelled to Florence.[1] Cardinal Reginald Pole was a devout adherent of the Church of Rome at a time when the English Reformation threatened to tear the Church apart. He had fled into self-imposed exile from his native shores after opposing King Henry VIII's divorce from Catherine of Aragon, and settled in Italy.

Along with his other business in Florence, Pole had a personal mission. About a decade before this journey, he'd had a conversation with Thomas Cromwell, a man of low origins who now served as the king's most intimate counsellor. Cromwell had stopped at nothing – or so it seemed to Pole – to indulge Henry's lusts and blasphemies. It was this ambitious adviser who, Pole believed, had masterminded the monarch's divorce, put England in a state of war with the Church, had priests and noblemen murdered – and had always found some righteous pretext to colour these deeds. Contemplating the evils that had driven him from his homeland, Pole longed to get his hands on a book about statecraft that Cromwell had praised when they'd met. The book's author was a citizen of Florence. He had died over ten years previously, so Pole could not meet him in person. But if the cardinal could read that book, it might help him better understand Cromwell's mind and Henry's actions, and thereby make sense of what was happening to his poor England.

On acquiring a copy, Pole began to read with fascination, then with growing horror. 'I had scarcely begun to read the book,' he later wrote, 'when I recognized the finger of Satan, though it bore the name of a human author and was written in a discernibly human style.' The Florentine's text laid bare all the doctrines that seemed to guide Cromwell's policies. Princes, it said, should build their states on fear rather than love. Since they live in a world teeming with lies and violence, they have no choice but to practise duplicity. Indeed, the prince who best knows how to deceive will be the most successful. In short, Pole declared, the book Cromwell so admired is full of 'things that stink of Satan's every wickedness'. Its author is clearly 'an enemy of the human race'. The book that so appalled Cardinal Pole was the *Prince,* and the name of its author Niccolò Machiavelli.

Aghast and intrigued, Pole was determined to find out more about the man who could write such things. Machiavelli, it transpired, had at one time caused a good deal of trouble for Florence's own princely family, the Medici. In 1512, a year before Machiavelli wrote his most notorious work, the new Medici government had ejected him from the civil-service posts he'd held for nearly fifteen years, then imprisoned and tortured him on suspicion of plotting to overthrow the principality. These fragments of biography must have come up when Pole asked his Florentine hosts about their compatriot. For, he wrote, when he told them his thoughts about the book, they excused the author, 'answering the charge with the same argument that Machiavelli himself had offered when they had confronted him'.

Machiavelli's reply, the Florentines said, had been that not everything in the *Prince* expressed his own opinions. Rather, he'd written what he thought would please a prince, particularly the Medici prince to whom he dedicated the slender volume: Lorenzo di Piero de' Medici, a young man with tyrannical leanings. But, Pole's unnamed hosts continued, Machiavelli's aim wasn't just to flatter his way into favour: he had a more sinister purpose. This wiliest of writers had no illusions about the utility of his cynical teachings. In fact, he was sure that any prince who put them into practice would soon arouse popular hatred and self-destruct. And this, said Pole's Florentine friends, was precisely what Machiavelli wanted. His design 'was to write for a tyrant those things that are pleasing to tyrants, bringing about in this way, if he could, the tyrant's self-willed and swift downfall'. In other words, the book's most shocking advice was ironic. Its author wore the mask of a helpful adviser, all the while knowing the folly of his own advice, hoping to ensnare rulers and drag them to their ruin.

This explanation made sense of something that had bothered Pole while reading the *Prince*. Though Machiavelli was clearly a man of uncommon intelligence, some of his maxims seemed to show, as the cardinal put it, a 'crass stupidity'. It seemed obvious to Pole that a prince who wins power through fear won't achieve security for himself or his state. The *Prince* claimed to put hard political facts ahead of moral ideals. But as a handbook on how to secure power, its advice was flagrantly unrealistic. Machiavelli's self-proclaimed realism, his book's main selling point, was a fraud. And Thomas Cromwell, Henry VIII, and England were among its first victims. Cromwell had taken the *Prince* at face value, Pole insisted, imbibing its devilish doctrines in the belief they were highest prudence – and in doing so had walked straight into Machiavelli's trap. If the writer were alive, he'd be laughing at his handiwork. The results, though, were no laughing matter. England in 1539 was far along the road to perdition, and other Christian monarchs might soon go the way of Henry, should they or their counsellors fall under Machiavelli's spell. 'Mark this well, rulers,' Pole warned; beware of this two-faced writer. 'For it is the aim of his doctrine to act like a drug that causes princes to go mad,' making them attack their own people with 'the savagery of the lion and the wiles of the fox'.

Pole was the first of many readers to demonize Niccolò Machiavelli and associate his name with the unscrupulous practices of men like Thomas Cromwell. The *Prince* as political poison, its author as a cunning fox, Old Nick, Satan's emissary, cold-blooded destroyer of kingdoms and of true religion: these images of Machiavelli and his writings soon came to play a big role in the propaganda wars stirred up by the Reformation. The conjurors of this demonic Machiavelli were mostly men of religion, both Catholic and Protestant. The enemies they branded as Machiavelli's disciples challenged traditional relations between Church and state. Some were devout Christians like Cromwell who sought to weaken political ties with the Church of Rome. Others called for a new, more secular kind of politics.

Some of these sixteenth- and seventeenth-century challengers fought back by defending the Florentine against their opponents' smear campaign. And in this way a very different Machiavelli – this one altogether human, and humane – joined his evil double on the political stage. His champions found their undevilish Machiavelli mainly in his *Discourses* and *Florentine Histories*, much longer books than the fast-paced *Prince*.[2] This Machiavelli was a thorough-going republican, a 'eulogist of democracy'.[3] His aim was to defend the rule of law against corrupt popes and tyrants. And he sought to uphold high moral standards, not lower them to fit the gritty realities of political life. True, his morality came from ancient writers such as Livy, Plutarch and Xenophon rather than Christian Scriptures, and he loved to ridicule the empty moral platitudes of his day. But he never wanted to sever politics from morality. He simply wanted to put morality on firmer, purely human foundations.

But how could this image of a virtuous Machiavelli be squared with everything he says in the *Prince*? His defenders' answer was that the Machiavelli of the *Prince* is a master ironist, a dissimulator who offers advice that he knows to be imprudent. On this point, though in nothing else, they agreed with Cardinal Pole. But while Pole thought that Machiavelli dissimulated so that he could poison princes' minds and drive them mad, his admirers believed he did so only to unmask their deceits and their secret lusts for power.[4] When he writes that Pope Alexander VI *never did anything, or ever thought of anything, but how to deceive men,*[5] Machiavelli seems to praise the pontiff's obsessive duplicity – but really exposes his pretensions of piety. When he describes how Cesare Borgia scapegoated his own governor, having him sliced in two pieces and laid out in the piazza at Cesena with a bloody knife close by, Machiavelli gives readers an unforgettable image of how far princes will go to hold on to power – showing that the writer's true intention in the *Prince* was to expose the perversities of princely rule.⁶ His purpose was to warn people who live in free republics about the risks they face if they entrust their welfare to one man.⁷ If Machiavelli's writing horrified priests and monarchists, this was because no one else had so daringly stripped away the veneer of moralism they used to hide their tricks.⁸

~

When I first started writing about Machiavelli, over a decade ago, I knew little about these early polemics. Like most present-day readers, I assumed that the *Prince*'s author was a pragmatist and a patriot. Recent scholarship told me, over and over, that he was devoted to the salvation of his city, Florence, and his country, Italy, at a time when they were being torn apart by war and civil war. If he sometimes excused violence and hypocrisy, he did so for good, patriotic ends.

But the more I read, the more I found myself questioning this picture. I began to notice that Machiavelli's writings were extremely ambiguous. They seemed to speak in different voices at different times, saying very different things. In one breath he'd praise the ancient Romans for using two-faced means to create their vast empire. Then he'd say, almost by-the-by, that these policies sparked ferocious resistance and fuelled bitter rivalries inside Rome, rivalries that eventually drove the republic to its ruin. In the *Prince*, he seems to applaud men who break their oaths at will, caring little for good faith or justice. But he also says – in a passage most scholars pass over without comment – that *victories are never secure without some respect, especially for justice*. Turning to his *Discourses*, I'd seize on a tough-talking statement about ends justifying unjust means: surely this was the true Machiavelli speaking? But then, a few lines on, there'd be a dramatic example showing the exact opposite: that unjust means tend to ruin good ends, including the salvation of one's country.⁹

For every cynical Machiavellian argument I encountered, I'd come across two or three other arguments that clashed with it. The cynical arguments are louder, and more thrillingly unconventional. But the reasons Machiavelli gives for them are often illogical, or just feeble. At times it sounds like he's parodying cheap rhetorical sleights of hand, the kind one often hears coming from the mouths of politicians and their spin-doctors. But he gives much more powerful reasons for actions we don't normally think of as Machiavellian. Know your own limits. Don't try to win every battle. Treat other people with respect so you can get them on your side and keep them there; observe justice with enemies as well as friends; always uphold the rule of law. These are a few of Machiavelli's less notorious but more closely argued maxims.

Like Cardinal Pole – whose comments I hadn't yet read – I soon began to doubt that Machiavelli believed every piece of his own advice. Several years after writing the *Prince*, he wrote to a close friend that *for a long time I have not said what I believed, nor do I ever believe what I say. And if sometimes I do happen to tell the truth, I hide it among so many lies that it is hard to find.*[10] I sensed that the political wisdom he held to be truest wasn't encapsulated in eye-catching maxims like 'It's better to be feared than loved.' With statements like these, he seemed to want to get under his readers' skin: to irritate them, tease them, make them think and think again about the examples he set before them. As I laboured to figure him out, I began to feel the way Machiavelli says he felt while reading a rather convoluted letter from his friend Francesco Vettori. *Your letter*, he wrote to Vettori, *dismayed me: its organization, its countless lines of reasoning . . . entangled me in such a way that at first I was bewildered and confused.* But then, *as I became more familiar with it, the same thing happened to me as it did to the fox when he saw the lion* in one of Aesop's fables. *The first time, he almost died of fright; the second, he stopped behind a clump of bushes to take a look; the third, he chatted with him.*[11]

After conversing with Machiavelli for many years, I've come to think that his early defenders understood him better than we do today. If we read all his works – which include political and military writings, histories, personal letters, diplomatic dispatches, poems, and plays – the main voice that comes through, with remarkable consistency, is quite unlike any of the Machiavellian ones we've come to expect. And the more we read, the more obvious it is that

Machiavelli enjoyed using his writing to put on a variety of masks, to play with different voices. We shouldn't forget that he was a brilliant dramatist, not just a student of politics. In his own lifetime he became famous not as a political writer – the *Prince* and *Discourses* were published only after his death in 1527 – but for his play *Mandragola*, a blistering satire of corrupt morals in Florence. Like an actor in one of his plays, Machiavelli assumed diverse voices and personas, allowing him to engage with different audiences without offending them. Yet the man behind the various masks was no chameleon, adapting to whatever the times and the men in power might demand. As his closest friends knew well, and as I try to show in this book, no one was less likely to compromise what he believed in.

In trying to make sense of Machiavelli's ambiguities, I've found it helpful to place him squarely in his world, among his family, friends, colleagues and compatriots, to hear how they talked to each other, how they joked, what they took seriously, what they could or could not say to certain people. Though Machiavelli wrote for all times, he also wrote, in the first instance, for particular audiences. His entire adult life was absorbed with politics, even when he was banned from political office. And in politics, he was above all a reformer: a man who wanted to persuade specific individuals or groups – political leaders, young men from Florence's upper classes, the Florentine public at large, popes, princes from other Italian cities – to change their ways of thinking and acting. With some of these audiences he could speak frankly; with others he had to be more guarded. His diplomatic correspondence gives us a vivid impression of Machiavelli's talents in the fine, dangerous art of political persuasion. As a civil servant who had to deal with kings, countesses, popes, and Florentine patricians, he learned how to tread carefully, speak in the right register to particular people, to criticize without seeming to do so. It's not surprising that he used some of these skills in composing his *Prince*, and other works.

Machiavelli and his contemporaries' writings offer a wealth of material that have helped me to reconstruct their conversational world. But since my aim was to depict an unfamiliar Machiavelli – one who uses irony to defend high moral standards and the rule of law – I wanted to do this in a way that would let readers judge the evidence for themselves. I wanted them to experience, as directly as possible, Machiavelli's language, his patterns of writing, speaking, thinking and judging: in short, to let him speak for himself. Hearing how consistent he is from youth to old age, through all the triumphs and catastrophes of his life, readers might start to see Machiavelli as some of his early admirers saw him. And instead of having to take my word for it, they'd have plenty of evidence from which to make up their own mind.

So in what follows I present events, as far as possible, from Machiavelli's point of view, a view constructed from a wide range of his writings. One way I do this is to weave Machiavelli's own words into my narrative of his life and times, so that we hear him commenting on events. Another is through the occasional use of dialogue. Though this transgresses the usual biographical conventions, the materials at hand made it seem a natural way to show my protagonist in his element. Machiavelli loved a good conversation, and he could talk to anybody: his letters recount exchanges with friends and enemies, with millers and blacksmiths at his local tavern, and with the great male and female princes of his day. Other sources, too – the diaries of his father, Bernardo, letters from friends, minutes of Florentine political meetings that read like high drama – provide detailed accounts of conversations among my dramatis personae. What more straightforward way to evoke their ways of speaking to each other, their ways of joking, criticizing, and dissimulating, than by turning some of their reported speech into direct speech?[12] These conversations are all closely based on original sources, indicated in the endnotes, so that, if they wish, readers can consult them for themselves. I've sometimes condensed or slightly paraphrased the original, but I have not changed the main sense or wording. While most of the dialogues are drawn from direct reported speech, in a few cases I've constructed them from letters or other writings, and I explain in the notes how I've used the sources in question.

A sense of drama pervades almost everything Machiavelli wrote. When he writes to his superiors in government about his tense negotiations with the French king Louis XII, Caterina Sforza, or Cesare Borgia, he does much more than report, 'They said this, and I replied that.' He makes readers sense his interlocutors' moods, imagine their expressions and gestures, wonder about their hidden thoughts. They become characters on a stage where he, Niccolò Machiavelli, probes their minds, sizes them up, tries to conceal his misgivings, or holds back his irritation for diplomacy's sake. In retelling these reported exchanges, I've given my own interpretation of what they tell us about Machiavelli's opinions and feelings, as indeed any biographer must who tries to reconstruct a subject's perspective from their writings.

The subject matter of Machiavelli's writings is wonderfully varied, ranging from personal feelings to politics and religion. Though his conversations arose from the particular events he lived through, they address questions that stir as much heated discussion today as they did five hundred years ago. Why are people so easily taken in by misleading rhetoric and good appearances? What's the point of education? Why should winners care about justice? What is true greatness? When should you fight to the death for your beliefs, and when should you stop fighting? How can people be free in a world dominated by a few great powers and by gross inequalities?

The questions Machiavelli asks, and the answers he gives, are often surprising. When we listen to his own voice, instead of trusting too much in his 'Machiavellian' reputation, we begin to see a strong character, irrepressibly friendly yet often at odds with his fellow citizens, with a steely determination to change the corrupt world he lived in – and a belief that any individual, however weak or downtrodden, could do their bit to change things for the better. Throughout his life, he urged people to see themselves as free agents who could always hope to influence the course of events. 'Never give up' is a characteristic piece of Machiavelli's – though not textbook Machiavellian – advice. He spent his many years fighting against great odds to defend the fragile freedom of his native Florence. No Florentine – perhaps no one anywhere in his day – worked harder for the cause of republican freedom than Niccolò Machiavelli. His intense commitment sets him apart from many of his contemporaries, who preferred to seek personal success and safety under a princely government than try to recover a freer way of life at considerable personal risk. Thanks to his talent for laughing at himself, no matter how bad things got – and they often got very bad – the story of his struggles for freedom never descends into total bleakness. Towards the end of his life, in a characteristic mood of self-mocking grandiloquence, Machiavelli signed a letter to his friend Francesco Guicciardini: *Niccolò Machiavelli: Historical writer, Comic writer, Tragic writer.*[13] I hope the portrait painted in the following pages will bring out all these sides of my much-misunderstood subject.

The Importance of Good Faith

One late-October day in 1475 Bartolommea Machiavelli goes to church, accompanied by her serving girl Nencia.[1] Standing to Bartolommea's left, Nencia looks pale, her face fuller than usual. She struggles to stand up straight again after kneeling in prayer.

'Are you feeling ill?' Bartolommea asks.

'I'm fine,' Nencia insists. Her eyes evade her mistress's.

Back at home, Bartolommea finds her husband, Bernardo, in his study. She has long since given up trying to take him to Mass, except on Easter Sunday and a few other feast days when the whole family goes together: their daughters Primavera and Margherita, the new baby, Totto, and six-year-old Niccolò. While the faithful hear sermons and take Holy Communion, Bernardo communes at home with his own blessed spirits: the spirits of dead men, pagans. Men who grew wise not by kneeling before priests or praying for divine voices to guide them, but by investigating things they had some chance of understanding by themselves, natural and human things.

Now his wife finds him beavering away over a pile of leather-bound volumes and papers, including the first ten books of Titus Livy's histories of Rome, not copied by hand like older manuscripts but printed on one of Florence's few printing presses. Books are expensive, and Bernardo is always short of money. But he dearly wants his own copy of Livy, so offers to make the index for the printer, Nikolas the German, if he can keep the books he works from. A Herculean task, but one Bernardo tackles with his usual determination; he spends hours on end in his study. Nearly fifty years later, his eldest son would pass as many hours with his father's ancient companion Livy, sometimes closing himself into this same room in Florence, sometimes retreating to his study in the family's country house. Here, with the memory of Bernardo's learning and hardships to spur him on, Niccolò Machiavelli would compose his 142 *Discourses* – short, essay-like conversation pieces – on the same ten books of Livy's histories that his father had acquired through his labours. And before that surrounded by many of the same books Bernardo has in his library, he would compose his *Prince*.[2]

'I think,' Bartolommea says in low tones so their children can't hear, 'that Nencia might be pregnant.'

Bernardo listens attentively while his wife recites the evidence. As a trained lawyer entitled to use the professional title *Messer*, he needs a strong case before taking things further. When Bartolommea finishes, he says: 'Say and do whatever it takes to get the truth out of the girl. Use sweet talk or threats, if you have to. We need to settle this matter soon, before we have a scandal on our hands.'

Bartolommea knows her husband's favoured methods. Bernardo has one of the best legal minds of his generation. No one in Florence is better at cutting straight to the heart of a problem, or at resolving a dispute without provoking messy recriminations.[3] That evening she gives him a full report of her interrogations. She'd taken the girl into a quiet room where, worn down by her mistress's skilful battery of pleas and threats, the distraught Nencia admitted that she is with child, and that the father is Nicolò di Alessandro Machiavelli, Bernardo's cousin and their closest neighbour.

Bernardo is mortified. Cousin Nicolò is in his late twenties and a married father. The two families' residences face each other across a narrow courtyard, part of the housing complex for the extended family known as the Machiavelli palazzo.

Give the girl a day or two, Bernardo advises his wife. Then, together with Bartolommea's brother Giovanni Nelli, they interview the weeping Nencia again to see if a few anxious days might have made her change her story. She repeats what she'd said before. Bernardo's cousin is the father.

Bernardo later records their interview, word for word, in his *ricordi.* Some of these Florentine men's diaries make gripping reading. They describe the great political crises of the day, terrifying eclipses of sun or moon, the births of two-headed sheep and monster-babies, spectacles performed on feast days, strange, extravagant gifts presented to Florence's leading men by Eastern grandees. Bernardo jots down much blander fare. Bartolommea paid so many florins for six yards of linen for children's clothes. I sold two barrels of wine from my farm to a local merchant. My son Niccolò has started learning the abacus. I borrowed Cicero's *On Duties* from a priest at Santa Croce. Today I gave it back. But this is one of those family crises – it will not be the last – that needs to be put on record, in some detail, lest it blow up and need outside arbitration. Bernardo wants to keep the trouble in the family.

To get his cousin to own up and do the right thing, subtler methods of interrogation would be needed than those Bernardo and his fellow prosecutors had used with Nencia. Cousin Nicolò fancies himself a man of business, one who knows this world and how to use other people to serve his ends. Since men like that are convinced that honesty is a virtue for weaklings, Bernardo would have to trap him by appealing to his self-interest, and nothing more. His older son would become a master of this kind of argument. According to Niccolò Machiavelli, one should assume that most people care more about their own gains than about doing the decent thing. So instead of haranguing them with pious sermons or moral outrage, show them why it's in their own selfish interests to take responsibility for mistakes or stick to their agreements. A few years before writing the *Prince*, in his capacity as Florence's envoy to Perugia, he would lecture that city's two-faced ruler Gianpaolo Baglioni on *the value and importance of good faith*. If Baglioni violated his agreement to fight for Florence, Niccolò tells him, the whole world would *charge him with ingratitude and bad faith, and would regard him as a stumbling horse that nobody would ride for fear of getting his neck broken*.[4]

Bernardo Machiavelli appeals to the same precept to rein in his philandering relative. He knows that his cousin's dreams of success are tied up in a network of potentially lucrative contacts through his wife's family. He has a lot to lose if his little slip of the loins generates an ugly scandal. So Bernardo waits a few days. Then in the evening, knowing his relative's usual routine, he runs into cousin Nicolò crossing the Ponte Vecchio on his way home. Bernardo gestures that he has something rather delicate to tell him.

'Our serving girl Nencia is pregnant,' he says. 'And,' he adds in neutral tones, 'she says you're the father.'

Cousin Nicolò doesn't protest innocence. 'Ah, Bernardo!' he exclaims. 'I've wanted to tell you about this for months, but didn't know how.' He tries to throw the blame on a friend who, he claims, had once stayed in his house while he and his family were away in the country.

Bernardo decides to play along. 'Well,' he says, in a low, despairing voice, 'whoever the father is, he obviously despises me. If I felt aggrieved before, now I feel even more insulted, since you tell me that this happened right next to my own house, within our common walls, among such close relatives, women, children – almost under my very eyes! But why on earth,' he goes on, 'would that young friend of yours want to smear my honour like this? I can't imagine why he, or his father and family, have such a low opinion of me that they could treat me so shabbily.'

These words have the effect Bernardo had hoped for. His cousin looks distinctly rattled at the implication that his friend's father, a respected doctor, and his other male relations might now be dragged into the quagmire. The family of the accused has powerful connections in the city. If false allegations are made against one of their own, the slanderer could face serious consequences.

'I was wrong not to tell you sooner,' cousin Nicolò concedes. 'But' – his tones are now plaintive – 'I have a wife and two sisters under my roof. Think what hell they'd give me, Bernardo, if they knew that an acquaintance of mine had deflowered an unmarried virgin in their own house!'

Bernardo leaves him to ponder his options. A few days later Nicolò comes to his older cousin's house, looking pleased with himself: he has thought of a solution. Maybe it's best, he says, not to mention the whole thing to his friend, Nencia's alleged seducer, at all. 'That man is such an imbecile, we'd be wasting our time if we tried to get anything out of him. So I've decided to take care of things myself.' He offers to give Bernardo money to pay for the girl's dowry so that a good husband can be found for her.

Not an admission of guilt, to be sure. But at least this means he'd take full financial responsibility. An agreement to this effect is signed and sealed between the two Machiavelli cousins, with only one other relative as witness – Bernardo states this in his *ricordi* – *so that the matter would not be revealed.*

Contracts, informal agreements, reciprocal duties, and promises, written or spoken, are the sinews of any common human life, and they play a very large role in Bernardo's daily existence. He had inherited a few small farms outside the city, as well as a tavern in the village of Sant' Andrea in Percussina, near San Casciano; he supports his family by leasing these properties and claiming half their modest proceeds. His agreements with tenants are lengthy and detailed. *Today I hired two brothers for a term of five years to cultivate the olive groves, reed banks and vineyards.* The tenants are obliged to pay local taxes; to hire good labourers and procure sheep and pigs; and to pay the landlord *two capons each year, and ten eggs in the month of November on the vigil of San Giovanni.* Instead of using formal contracts written up by a notary, Bernardo simply writes down the terms of their bargain in his personal diaries and has the new tenants sign their agreement in his book.

Bernardo Machiavelli hardly ever practises law, but his family's livelihood depends on an endless string of such agreements, signed and honoured. Promises hold his world together, and that of most villagers and ordinary city-dwellers. They have to trust people to keep their promises most of the time; if they did not, it would be too risky to sell, buy or borrow anything. Even friends and close relatives make written notes of what they owe each other, in case someone forgets. Notaries – including, on rare occasions,

Bernardo – are used for drawing up and witnessing signatures on contracts for permanent transferrals of large properties, such as wills. They are less often employed for small-scale sales or fixed-term transactions like leasing small farms. Notaries charge fees, which all but the very wealthy prefer to avoid. It can be even more expensive to have recourse to public courts of arbitration, and more injurious to people's reputations, if a case involves charges of theft or other illicit conduct. Consequently, Florentines and their neighbours in the countryside have evolved an impressive variety of informal techniques for settling disputes.

If Bernardo's example teaches Niccolò some of the negotiating skills he would need in later life, it also shows him how to hold people to their promises. A month before seven-year-old Niccolò starts school, his father's diaries record a drawn-out skirmish with a local butcher, Romolo Cecchi, who refused to pay in full for nine lambs he'd purchased from one of Bernardo's farms.[5] Bernardo accompanies his tenant farmer to the butcher's shop and extracts a promise of full payment. But then Romolo keeps avoiding him, or showing up late to their appointments without the money, full of pompous excuses: 'I had to go to a meeting at my butchers' guild; I'm one of the new consuls. So I forgot to get the money from the bank.' But Bernardo Machiavelli is a stubborn man, and he is never more obstinate than in refusing to let people get away with lying, cheating or theft. He tracks down an acquaintance from a well-connected family of merchants from Romolo's city district, and together they confront the butcher with the prospect that his little games of hide-and-seek might sully his good name in local business networks. A grudging Romolo finally pays up. Niccolò inherits his father's stubbornness, and his impatience with people who break promises, contracts, and public laws. As he would tell Perugia's ruler Baglioni, nothing is less prudent than to get a name for bad faith; and nothing sets a worse example in public life, he writes in his *Discourses, than to make a law and not observe it.*[6]

2

Take Nothing on Authority

Through much of his elder son's boyhood, Bernardo Machiavelli divides his time between his farms in Sant' Andrea – dealing with tenants and their troubles in the same restrained, judicious way that he dealt with cousin Nicolò and the elusive butcher – and steeped in Roman histories, writing up his index of Livy. A long, long alphabetical list of ancient names, Greek, Roman, Carthaginian, Syrian: Agis and Cleomenes, Camillus and Fabius Maximus, Hannibal and Hasdrubal, Nabis, several Scipios, Tarquinius, Rome's last king, and Romulus, its first. Years later, Niccolò Machiavelli's books would breathe new life into some of these names. His accounts of their bearers' exploits usually have provocative undertones, challenging conventional ideas about who should be accounted history's heroes or scoundrels, winners or losers.

Romulus, Romolo the butcher's namesake, is widely celebrated as the founder of Rome. Yet Machiavelli recalls that Romulus made his eponymous city a kingdom with himself as top man, not a republic; he had his brother, Remus, killed so that he could rule alone. Machiavelli then considers this action from two sides. On the one hand, anyone who wants to found a new city from scratch will find it far easier if he has quasi-tyrannical powers. On the other hand, as long as kings ruled Rome, its government was unstable. And no wonder: discords never cease in states where one man stands alone at the helm, since every ambitious patrician, entrepreneur, and soldier wants to be supreme leader. Eventually, the Romans came to their senses, got rid of their kings and created that wonderful work of political art, the republic. In his *Discourses* Niccolò notes that *republics are far more observant of accords than princes*, and argues that

7

because of this popular governments last much longer and *make fewer errors than the prince*.[1] The Romans might have had a republic from the start, if Romulus hadn't insisted on ruling alone.

Then there is Fabius Maximus, one of Livy and Niccolò's heroes. When Hannibal of Carthage marched his armies into Italy, hoping to force the Romans to fight on his terms, Fabius refused to play his game.[2] He invented a new one, a different kind of warfare. Instead of going to meet the gargantuan African armies in pitched battle, the Roman general followed them around, harassed them and devastated crops and livestock in the countryside wherever the Carthaginians were encamped. Most Romans sneered at him. They wanted to go out and meet the invaders at any risk, not thinking of the bloodbath that would have engulfed the Italian peninsula if they did so. They called Fabius a coward, a delayer, *cunctator*. But his strategy worked. Bit by bit, he starved them, wore them down. The invaders were obliged to play by Fabius' less audacious but infinitely more effective rules.

In battles with smaller stakes, Bernardo Machiavelli's successes in pinning down his cousin and the butcher came from a Fabius-like willingness to play the long game, to pit patience against self-centred impetuosity. His son praises these qualities in the great Roman, and would emulate them himself when he had to marshal all his diplomatic skills to help his city resist Cesare Borgia's threats, or when he toiled to persuade his fellow citizens to overhaul their useless military defences, and on many other occasions. When someone's game is rotten, Niccolò often suggests – even if it looks like the main one in town, the only one where real men can prove that they are winners – don't let them force you to play it. Better to make and play by your own rules. Nothing is stupider than to sink to the level of mindlessly competitive men in hopes of beating them. You might win, but you end up as mindless as they are. Before long, someone slightly less stupid will beat you.

In May 1476, Niccolò begins lessons with a schoolmaster, Maestro Matteo, at the end of the Santa Trinità bridge. Here he learns the basics of Latin grammar and writing through the *donatello*, a hand-book composed a thousand years earlier by the Roman scholar Donatus. Highly educated Florentines can write almost as elo-quently in Latin as in their own vernacular, the language Niccolò would later call 'our Tuscan'. Made famous throughout Italy and Europe by Dante, Petrarch and Boccaccio, this Florentine branch of Italian is a marvel of creative energy. Though Niccolò learns to write good Latin, he composes all his chief works in his native tongue, thereby communicating his thoughts to a wider cross-section of readers. He has a talent for language, an intuitive feeling for its supple forms and fine shades of meaning. He delights in arranging coarse, pungent words into playful, rhyming verses. When his parents leave him and his brother alone in town with-out their usual home-cooked meals, he writes a poem addressed 'To Messer Bernardo', the only surviving exchange between father and son:

> *These fellows have lived a month or more*
> *on nuts, on figs, on beans, on dried meat,*
> *so it will be malicious and not a joke*
> *to make so long a stay up there.*

> *Just as the Fiesolan ox looks downward at the*
> *Arno, thirsty, and licks his snot,*
> *so do they at the eggs of the market-woman*
> *and at the mutton of the butcher, and at his beef.* [3]

Many Florentine fathers want their sons to study the humanities for purely pragmatic reasons, or ornamental ones. Equipped with an education in rhetoric, apt quotations in Latin – or Greek, the mark of a highbrow, expensive education – and ancient history, their sons would gain a reputation for being educated while getting on with the more serious business of buying, selling, and cutting profit-able deals. For men like Bernardo and his good friend Bartolomeo Scala, education offered a way for young men of modest background to pursue a civil-service career, working in Chancery offices, perhaps rising to become Chancellor, as had the low-born Scala.

But education is far more to them, and to Niccolò, than a means to a career. Some Florentines treat ancient texts as a source of moral bearings, more relevant to their lives than the pieties taught in church. Bernardo is one of these. Chancellor Scala makes Bernardo the principal interlocutor in an animated dialogue on the laws – the only source we have, apart from his own diaries, on the elder Machiavelli's personality and opinions. Messer Bernardo Machiavelli appears in Scala's dialogue as a passionate admirer of Plato, whose works are just becoming available in Marsilio Ficino's Latin translations.[4] For Bernardo and other secular-minded intellectuals, the best ancient historians and philosophers are more alive and have more practical value than most contemporary writers. What makes them great is that they pose and explore, with clarity unmatched by their successors, the most basic, perennial questions about how best to organize our shared human life. How can we make political orders that last long while keeping citizens safe and satisfied? What makes people, whether leaders or ordinary citizens, act in ways that corrupt the political orders they inhabit? And how can citizens learn to spot the early warning signs of corruption so that it can be cured before the poison kills?

Though these questions come from ancient Athens or Rome, they speak no less directly to Florentine anxieties in these times, when wealth, pedigree and sheer ruthlessness seem to carry more authority than the laws. The writers who pose them offer no easy answers. The Roman Livy and the Greek Thucydides in their histories, and Plato in his philosophical dialogues, consider them from many angles. Their depictions of human nature are at once exhilarating and unflattering. They show how much human intelligence can do to raise the quality of life – and how our carelessness, greed, or self-crippling doubt can bring fragile man-made orders crashing down on our unprotected heads. But these ancient writers don't present themselves as experts who lecture readers on matters of right and wrong. Their histories and dialogues portray the drama of political life without saying at every step: this was well done, that a disaster; this speech was wise and truthful, that one packed with cunningly hidden agendas. By withholding their own views, or merely hinting at them, they force readers to think for themselves, to become better judges of the political rhetoric that assails them from all sides in the political marketplace, especially in democracies but also under princes.

Sooner or later, Niccolò falls deeply in love with these traditions of writing. He reveres his favourite ancients' devotion to human welfare across time and space; their valiant efforts to step back from the partisan quarrels of their times and see merits and failures on all sides; their desire not just to make a name for themselves while they lived – an inferior kind of glory – but to leave behind something that would help their fellow humans long after their own death. He comes to share their ideal of what education is for: to form self-trusting minds that question everything, taking nothing on others' authority, and seek to understand by themselves. *It is good*, he declares in his *Discourses, to reason about everything* – to *defend any opinion with reasons, without using either authority or force for it.*[5] From his earliest writings to his last, Niccolò is a compulsive questioner. Whenever his contemporaries take an opinion for granted, he demands clear evidence and good reasons for it, and urges others to do the same. Florentines and other Italians have long used hired mercenaries to fight wars for them, not believing that their own peoples can be trusted to bear arms: Machiavelli questions that belief. Popular governments, most ancient writers and contemporary savants say, are less stable than aristocratic or princely rule: he demolishes that opinion, even though its defenders claim to found it on centuries' worth of experience. *Whoever seeks to act according to others*, he later tells his more convention-bound friend Francesco Vettori, *will accomplish nothing, because no two men who think alike can be found.*[6] And people who don't trust their own judgement make bad defenders of freedom; they rush too quickly into the arms of power-greedy men who are all too happy to judge things for them.

During his life's deepest crisis, Niccolò finds that conversation with his long-deceased friends is the ultimate anti-depressant. In *the courts of the ancients,* he writes to Vettori in 1513, *I nourish myself on that food that alone is mine and for which I was born;* he is *unashamed to converse with them, and they, out of their human kindness, answer me.* In their company he forgets all his own sufferings, his wounded pride, the poverty inflicted on him by recent events in Florence. He fears nothing with them, even death. *I transfer myself into them completely.*[7] Their examples and reflections are never out of date because, as Niccolò observes in his *Discourses,* human beings are always and everywhere essentially the same animal, with the same drives and abilities, and weaknesses and self-destructive tendencies. *In all cities and in all peoples there are the same desires and the same humours, and there always have been.* It should therefore be easy for anyone who *examines past things diligently to foresee future things in every republic, and to take the remedies for them that were used by the ancients.* But since most readers and those who govern fail to see the same patterns of behaviour in different times, always imagining that their times and problems are unique, *it follows that there are always the same scandals in every time.*[8]

3

Do Not Be Deceived by False Glory

While Bernardo Machiavelli waged small battles for decency in his personal and economic transactions, setting one kind of example to his son, Florence's leaders and their sons exemplified very different standards of conduct. In the masterwork of his later years, the *Florentine Histories*, Niccolò remembers the city's atmosphere in his childhood. Florence's youth at that time were *more unrestrained than usual, spending beyond bounds on dress, banquets and other similar abandonments.* Young men *consumed time and substance in games and women; they studied to appear splendid in their dress and to be clever and smart in their speech, and he who was deftest at biting the others with ridicule was held wiser and in higher esteem.* In the general scrambling for precedence, each man chased his private advantage, with no regard for public consequences. *These customs,* Niccolò claims, *were intensified by the courtiers of the Duke of Milan.*[1]

The young duke and his wife had come as the guests of Florence's newly anointed leader, twenty-two-year-old Lorenzo de' Medici. They swept into the city like conquering royalty, with a vast, preening retinue. During their stay, their courtiers strode around showing no respect, not making way for older men or ladies in the streets, almost pushing them aside without a word of apology. Public irritation turned into alarm when rumours began to emanate from the Medici Palace, where the duke and his wife were staying. *At that time,* our historian recalls, *was seen a thing never before seen in our city: this being the season of Lent, in which the Church commands that one fast by not eating meat, the duke's court, without respect to Church or God, all fed on meat.* No Florentine dared accuse Lorenzo and his household of taking part in the sacrilege. But he had done nothing to stop it.

A magnificent spectacle to honour the duke – more, critics muttered, than to honour God – was put on in the Machiavelli's district church of Santo Spirito, a few minutes' walk from their house. It represented the Apostles receiving the Holy Spirit. Machines designed by the renowned architect Filippo Brunelleschi were used to lift men and angels aloft and send them flying across the chancel, amid explosions of fireworks. Spectators were agog at this display of human ingenuity.

Straying from its mechanically charted orbit, some fast-flying object bolted down from on high and struck a row of tapers illuminating the show. And the Spirit burst forth in a fiery, righteous rage. Flames poured into the nave, where viewers stood; fire devoured the exquisite, hand-painted sets that had been built for the occasion by one of the city's best workshops. People shoved and trampled each other, trying to escape before the smoke suffocated them. Later, when priests went in to see what they could salvage, they found the altar, costly icons and sacred relics burnt to ash. Brunelleschi's penitent Mary Magdalen, a masterpiece carved out of limewood, lay black and scorched, faceless beneath the rubble. *And because the church burned down*, Niccolò writes, *as a result of the many fires that are made in such solemnities, many believed that God, angered against us, had wished to show a sign of His wrath.*

Somehow, Lorenzo managed to emerge from the trauma with his reputation unscathed. Like his grandfather Cosimo, dirt never seemed to stick to him. An immensely wealthy banker, Cosimo had been the first Medici, and the first man in Florence's history, to be acknowledged as First Citizen, an informal title borrowed from Rome's first emperors. Augustus Caesar and his immediate imperial successors called themselves *princeps*, or 'first men', while Rome was still officially a republic. This was a euphemism, if not a blatant piece of hypocrisy, since the emperors' virtually absolute power gave the lie to their claim to be merely first among equal citizens.

Cosimo's comparably ambiguous position had made him enemies. By Lorenzo's time, people had grown used to the idea that one family should have special authority, in fact if not by law. And Lorenzo was raised from infancy to continue that tradition. He was born to rule. But he was born to rule in a city that was supposed to have no rulers. The laws decreed that Florence was a city of equal citizens, a city that would tolerate no monarchs or hereditary dynasties. And no Medici, Cosimo had told his offspring, should openly defy the laws; that would only give ammunition to their adversaries. The ideal Medici leader had to seem born to rule while also seeming to think of himself as one of the people. His every move needed to project a double illusion: of natural superiority to every other citizen and a total, easy-going unawareness of that superiority.

Young Lorenzo embraced the contradiction so effortlessly that he made people forget its existence. In Niccolò Machiavelli's earliest years he was often seen strolling down the streets with his entourage, a strangely mixed crew of patrician youths and lower-born friends whose fathers Cosimo had helped to elevate. So ordinary, so affable, yet in a league of his own, above all the city's other rich powerbrokers: the Pitti, the Pazzi, the Rucellai, the Soderini. But Machiavelli would later warn his readers not to be *deceived by a false good and a false glory* into following men who *turn to tyranny*.[2] His *Prince*, *Discourses* and *Florentine Histories* were all written under Medici rule, and all these works, in different ways, convey a subtle message: beware, Florentines and readers everywhere, of placing too much hope in any one man, especially one who leads more by private wealth and charisma than by laws and prudent restraint.

With Lorenzo, the first signs of danger appeared during the war with Volterra in 1472. Niccolò, who was three years old at the time, recounts the episode in his *Florentine Histories*.[3] Perched on a peak above a sea of rolling hills, Volterra lies some fifty-four miles south-west of Florence. To reach the ancient Etruscan town, you follow a long, winding road that rises higher and higher as you approach its gates. Passing through the lower city gate, you reach a large square, overshadowed by a flat-faced edifice with its lean, crenulated tower. This is the palace of government, Palazzo dei Priori, the oldest town hall in Tuscany. It is smaller than Florence's Palazzo della Signoria, but Volterrans are proud of its seniority, and of their very ancient roots. Tensions broke out a few years after Lorenzo assumed leadership in his city. When alum deposits were discovered in the countryside around Volterra, Florentine investors eagerly bought up shares; they were backed by the Medici bank, which held a monopoly of alum in the region. The Volterrans protested that the mines should be their city's communal property. Soon their protests erupted in violence, and Florence's representatives in Volterra feared for their lives. Lorenzo summoned his councils to decide whether to declare war.

Florence's most experienced elder statesman at the time was Tommaso Soderini. His family palazzo is close to the Machiavellis' house in Santo Spirito; two of his sons, Francesco and Piero, would play a fateful role in Niccolò's life and career. Whatever we do, Machiavelli has Tommaso Soderini say in the *Histories*, we mustn't overreact. This is a matter for diplomats, not armies. And it is not *the right time to fan a flame so close that could burn down our house.* God knows we have enough subject cities in our dominions – Arezzo, Lucca, Pisa – whose peoples are itching to throw off the Florentine yoke. Remember that trite proverb: 'Better a lean truce than a fat victory.' We won't get fat with profits if we put an end to these troubles now. But we will have peace, and do what seems just to the Volterrans, who until now have always been our loyal friends.

On the other side, Lorenzo de' Medici *thought it an occasion to demonstrate how much his advice and prudence were worth.* He was very young, and keen to show who was in charge. Spurred on by *those who were envious of the authority of Messer Tommaso,* Lorenzo *decided to undertake a campaign and to punish with arms the arrogance of the Volterrans.* Private homes were plundered; the insides of churches were ripped to shreds. *For a whole day* Volterra *was robbed and overrun; neither women nor holy places were spared.*

Florentines greeted news of their victory with loud chest-thumping and fireworks. *And because it had been altogether Lorenzo's campaign,* Niccolò tells us, *he rose to very great reputation from it.* Under Medici auspices, poets trumpet, Florentia will become the next Rome, the next Eternal City. A Golden Age is dawning, and its avatar is Lorenzo.[4] The young leader himself expressed regret about the carnage, apologizing with words and money. But the deeds that followed victory were those of a remorseless conqueror. Florence's hired soldiers demolished the cathedral of St Peter and the bishop's palace. All the towers of the city's fortress were destroyed except one, which was converted into a prison, a towering symbol of subject status. Rights to the alum mines were transferred to the conquering city. No matter that on closer inspection the alum deposits turned out to be of poor quality, so that the mines were soon shut down. It had still, Lorenzo's partisans insisted, been a just war.

But Niccolò gives the last word not to the victorious prince but to the older, wiser opponent of the war on Volterra. A friend of Tommaso Soderini's, he tells us, now reproached him for advising against the war. What do you say, he demanded, now that Volterra has been vanquished? Weren't we right to seize this chance to increase our empire?

Soderini, who was *among the first citizens of Florence and by far superior to the others*, a man *whose prudence and authority were known not only in Florence but among all the princes of Italy*, responds: What you call a great victory looks to me like a loss. If you'd won over Volterra by treaty and agreement, *you would have had advantage and security from it. But since you have to hold it by force, in adverse times it will bring you weakness and trouble, and in peaceful times, loss and expense.* The Lorenzo who grows from impetuous youth into the mature leader hailed as il Magnifico remains a complex, ambivalent character in Machiavelli's *Histories*, the prime exemplar of a statesman whose talents for projecting *a false good and a false glory* might well conceal the germs of tyranny.

*

For his part, Bernardo Machiavelli keeps a distance from the increasingly corrupt world of Florentine law, and from politics. He supports his wife and children on a frugal budget. Though a landlord and the owner of a small country villa as well as the house in the city, Bernardo is far from an easy-living country squire. His farm rents are modest; so are his owner's portion of the wine, olive oil, apples, vinegar, trees for timber, sheep and other livestock. He oversees most of the sales and other farm business himself, travelling almost every week, sometimes more often, between the city and the hilly countryside around Sant' Andrea, some nine miles from Florence.

Bernardo comes from a family of old and respected landowners. The Machiavellis had owned property inside the city for at least two hundred years, perhaps more, in the Oltrarno district, near Florence's oldest bridge, the Ponte Vecchio. In the family's more prosperous days, Machiavelli men had held important public offices. Florence's moneyed elite was also its political elite, and Bernardo is part of neither. To be eligible for political office, a Florentine man has to possess a certain amount of taxable wealth; be over a certain age (usually thirty for the lesser magistracies, forty for the more important posts); and not be in arrears with his public taxes. This means that, at any given time, only a few thousand males, out of a total population of about fifty thousand men, women and children, could hold office.

Bernardo fails the last of these tests. When his father passed away soon after he was born, he was taken in and raised by an uncle, Giovanni di Buoninsegna. Most of Bernardo's inheritance – his farms, the inn in Sant' Andrea, the garden and loggia – seems to have come from this benign father figure, who died when Bernardo was a teenager. Unfortunately, the legacy seems to have included heavy debts. Bernardo's father, Niccolò, also passed on debts along with his properties. It's unclear whether the insolvency that would plague Bernardo all his life was altogether inherited, or whether he incurred fresh debts of his own in his youth. In any case, his humiliating *a specchio* status – the label given to communal debtors – means that Bernardo is barred from holding a government post. And as his heirs, his sons are also denied the right to have their names put on the city's lists of men eligible for its main magistracies. Niccolò could, and would, become a civil servant who reported to several of Florence's governing bodies. But until his family's long-standing debts were either paid off or forgiven, he could cherish no hopes of being selected as one of his city's political leaders.

Within the limits he inherited, Niccolò will try – succeeding, for a while – to become one of the city's main behind-the-scenes players. Bernardo never tries. He diligently records even the smallest family expenses in his diaries, and often goes before his district's tax officials to pay whatever he can. His tax forms state that instead of practising his potentially lucrative profession as a lawyer, Bernardo has 'no gainful employment'. Not that he lacks enthusiasm for what lawyers generally do: his diaries reveal a man who relishes negotiating disputes, securing fair agreements, and making peace. He frequently does these things gratis for friends and family. Some of his contemporaries must have wondered why Messer Machiavelli didn't use his credentials to earn a bit of money. In these times, a notary who plays his cards right could make a very comfortable living. Take on a property dispute between big merchants, or among the squabbling heirs of great bankers, and he'd soon clear his name with the tax authorities. Chancellor Scala praises Bernardo's intellect and legal knowledge to the skies. But if he's such a brilliant jurist, why does he insist on living in obscurity?

Cousin Girolamo. Older men among Florence's political class remember him well.

The Machiavelli household seldom talks of him now, but they never forget. It happened just twenty years ago, soon after Bernardo had finished his legal training. Girolamo lived with his family in the house next door, part of the Machiavellis' residential complex. He was Bernardo's second cousin, some twelve years his senior. After completing his professional education, following the same rigorous curriculum Bernardo would pursue later, Girolamo taught law and jurisprudence at the university in Florence. Soon he became one of the city's most respected legal experts. The political potentates of the day often called on him to serve as a councillor on committees dealing with sensitive political issues. When he was old enough to have his name put forward for public office, Girolamo threw himself into the political arena. He held numerous posts during the 1440s and 50s, advised the government on sensitive matters in foreign affairs, and travelled as an envoy to other Italian cities to test their loyalties to Florence. By all accounts, he was a tireless defender of his city's interests, a fair-minded judge in domestic matters. A man who kept his cool in the face of partisan hatreds and worked hard, with consummate diplomatic skill, to strike compromises between political foes.

These, as Niccolò would recall in his *Histories*, were fraught times.[5] After Cosimo de' Medici secured his leading role on Florence's political stage in 1434, he sought to control government indirectly, without sacrificing appearances of lawfulness. One of his favourite methods was to use his wealth and contacts to ensure that the lists of men eligible for city magistracies were filled with names of his supporters. To the horror of many Florentine patricians, large numbers of these loyalists came from the middling and even lower classes.[6] Grateful to Cosimo for promoting their careers, they could be counted on to defend whatever policies he preferred. By 1455, many upper-class grandees – including Cosimo's one-time partisans – had begun to rebel against the insidious presence of so many plebeians in government. Cosimo, Machiavelli tells us, pretended to stay above the fray. He continued to pose as the great protector of ordinary people's interests, the stratagem that had helped him rise to such power in the city. At the same time, when all the grandees went to Cosimo *to beg him that he be so kind as to rescue them and himself from the hands of the plebs*, he agreed to let them put forward new legislation that would restrict government to a few: to make it, that is, far more oligarchical than popular.

Girolamo Machiavelli soon emerged as a leader of the anti-oligarchic opposition, powerfully criticizing the dominant party's actions in the councils.[7] Our city, he declared, is sick from all our divisions. Citizens are split into parties of the few and the many, each bent on destroying the other. Do you seriously expect to cure the disease by making these divisions deeper? Union is what we need to cure it, and we will unite only when both parties have their fair share of power, their share of public offices and places in our councils. I blame those here who want to monopolize power for the few. You are tearing our city apart.

In a special consultation held on 28 July 1458, Girolamo and thirty others opposed the policies proposed by the party of oligarchs, led by Luca Pitti. A few days later he was arrested, accused of having improperly influenced a member of the Council to vote against the majority. Along with his brother Piero Machiavelli, Girolamo was sentenced to exile for twenty-five years on 18 August, and ordered to pay a fine of eight hundred guilders. The stiff sentence was reduced soon afterwards, though not by much: instead of being banished to Avignon, more than four hundred miles away in France, Girolamo and his family were permitted to reside anywhere they chose, so long as they were at least three hundred miles away from Florence.

If the oligarchs and Cosimo's friends thought this punishment would silence Messer Machiavelli, they were mistaken. Girolamo ignored the limits imposed by the sentence on his movements. He was soon spotted in Siena, a mere forty-three miles from his native city. Florentine spies reported that he was living in Genoa, about a hundred and forty miles away. On 29 November 1459, writes Niccolò, *Girolamo was declared a rebel for not having observed the confines of his punishment.* All his property in Florentine territory was confiscated. He tried to join other exiles who wanted to create a league of Italian cities – including Venice, Bologna, Siena, Lucca and Genoa – to go to war against Medici Florence and overthrow the regime. But *while he circulated around Italy stirring up princes against his fatherland, he was arrested in Lunigiana through the faithlessness of one of those lords.* Plots to overthrow governments, Niccolò often observes, are almost always betrayed by one of the plotters.[8]

Girolamo was hauled back to Florence, imprisoned, and tortured. Another of his brothers, Francesco, had already been imprisoned in the Stinche – that hard-faced, windowless block of stone in the middle of Florence, with air-holes so minuscule that one could almost suffocate looking at it – and beheaded earlier in the year. Girolamo died in prison in July 1460. The exact cause of death is not on record. Niccolò says only that he was *put to death*, not that he died of sickness. Giuliano de' Ricci, Niccolò's grandson, would become convinced that Girolamo had been strangled.[9]

And so the name of Machiavelli acquired its first bad odour with the Medici. Girolamo and his brothers were conspirators. Traitors. Enemies of patrician oligarchs, plotters against the government led by Cosimo de' Medici.

The first First Citizen's role was so ambiguous that the Machiavelli family couldn't confidently attribute some of their finest sons' deaths to him. Cosimo hadn't been part of the oligarchs' coup, but he did nothing to stop it or its vindictive aftermath. The oligarchic terror that followed Girolamo's banishment and death made government *unbearable and violent for the eight years it lasted. For Cosimo, now old and weary, made feeble by the condition of his body*, stayed home while *a few citizens* – a few, that is, of the already rich and powerful – *plundered the city*. The oligarchs' leader, Luca Pitti, Machiavelli notes, *was made a knight as a reward for all his hard work for the benefit of the republic*. Cosimo, he implies, had let Pitti and other patricians do his work for him.

Messer Luca *was richly bestowed with presents* from the government and from Cosimo himself, to the tune of some 20,000 ducats. All these gifts and honours so emboldened Luca Pitti that he decided to build a new palace, outrageously grandiose by Florence's restrained republican standards. When Niccolò calls the Pitti Palace *splendid and royal*, he is not expressing awestruck admiration; on the contrary, he implies that Pitti had regal aspirations that were wholly inappropriate in a republic. His massive, sprawling palazzo, a brief stroll from the Machiavelli residence on the left bank of the Arno, *was altogether greater than any other that had been built by a private citizen until that day.* Our historian insinuates that Pitti over-taxed or pilfered funds from the Florentine dominions to help build his princely residence: *the communes and whole peoples,* Machiavelli observes wryly, *provided assistance.* Other great citizens followed his example. *If they did not build as he did,* they *were not less violent or rapacious. Thus,* even without foreign wars to destroy it, *the city was destroyed by its own citizens.*

Shortly after these events, Bernardo Machiavelli married Barto-lommea de' Nelli. She was a widow, whose first husband's family, the Benizi, were well-known Medici critics; a number of them had been exiled along with the Machiavelli brothers. Bernardo's *ricordi* mention particularly heavy tax debts calculated in 1458 – the same year Girolamo and his brothers were sentenced and exiled, the year Bernardo and Bartolommea wed. While these debts may have been part of Bernardo's legacy from his father and uncle, a favourite method of punishing critics under the Medici was to burden them, together with their suspected associates and relatives, with taxes they were unable to pay, thus barring them from inclusion on the lists of citizens eligible for office. Whether or not Bernardo suffered because of his cousins' politics, his experience of oligarchic Medici 'terror' – as Niccolò calls it – in his twenties and thirties may help explain why he steers clear of high-powered political and legal cir-cles in later life. And when he is still a boy, a new assault on Medici rule brings terrible calamities on the city, giving low-profile citi-zens like Bernardo reason to keep their heads even lower.

4

Beware of Doctors

Late morning on Sunday, 26 April 1478: High Mass is being celebrated in Florence's main cathedral, the church of Santa Maria del Fiore. Some ten thousand people have gathered under the magnificent domed arches, both foreign visitors and Florentines, of all classes. Lorenzo de' Medici enters and heads towards the seats of honour near the altar, followed by his younger brother, twenty-five-year-old Giuliano. Giuliano is beloved by the young men and women of the city, a welcome counterweight to his brother's increasingly evident authoritarian tendencies. The golden boy, his elders called him. Though not yet married, he is betrothed to the pretty Fioretta Gorini, who is eight months pregnant with his child: the future Cardinal Giulio de' Medici, with whom Niccolò Machiavelli will later have many dealings. Turning from the priest chanting at the altar, all eyes strain to see these scions of the city's leading family. Two well-dressed youths of about Giuliano's age walk beside him, squeezing him affectionately. Good friends. Knowing observers recognize them as Bernardo Bandini and Francesco Pazzi.

When Machiavelli dramatizes these moments years later, what he finds most disturbing, indeed grotesque, is the genteel hypocrisy shown by all the protagonists up to the first, furious thrust of knives.[1] Appointed to guide their victim to the scene of his murder, Francesco Pazzi and Bernardo Bandini had gone to fetch Giuliano from the Medici Palace, *and with prayers and art led him to church*, all under false colours of friendship. While pretending to give Giuliano chummy caresses, the plotters were trying to feel whether their victim carried any weapons under his cloak. *It is a thing truly worthy of memory*, Niccolò observes, *that so much hatred, and so much thought about such a transgression, could be covered up with so much heart and so much obstinacy of spirit.* For though Francesco and Bernardo escorted Giuliano to his death, *on the way and in the church they entertained him with jokes and youthful banter.* More absurdly, Giuliano and his brother knew how much the great house of Pazzi and many others in Florence and beyond – including the present pope, Sixtus IV – hated Medici rule; yet they failed to take precautions. Though aware of *the bitter spirit of the Pazzi*, they *did not fear for their lives*, convinced that if their enemies were to try to topple their regime, they'd do it through political machinations, not with violence. *And so Lorenzo and Giuliano, taking no care for their own safety, also pretended to be their friends.* A memorable lesson for an almost nine-year-old boy, if Niccolò afterwards heard talk of it, about the uses and pitfalls of feigning friendship.

An agonized groan rises from the cheerful coterie. First Bernardo *pierced the breast of Giuliano*, then Francesco Pazzi *threw himself on him, filled him with wounds, and struck him with such zeal that, blinded by the fury that transported him, he wounded himself gravely in the leg.* Machiavelli can never resist this kind of irony, so common in human affairs: when attacking others in blind fury, we tend to hurt ourselves as well.

Giuliano is dead. Onlookers had seen someone lunge at Lorenzo's neck with a knife. Then he'd vanished, surrounded by a protective swarm of associates who rushed him into the sacristy and locked it for safety. When they hear that things are quieter outside, they let Lorenzo re-emerge. He is only slightly wounded.

Within hours, word of the conspiracy has spread through Florence. Murderers, traitors. Thousands of people mob the Pazzi family's several houses. Francesco is hauled naked from his bed and hanged from a high window of the Palazzo della Signoria. Beside him dangle the corpses of the Archbishop of Pisa, and others. Jacopo Pazzi tries to flee into exile. But he is soon captured and brought back to Florence, then condemned and hanged four days after Giuliano's murder. Jacopo's body is at first interred in his ancestral sepulchre.[2] But soon afterwards, he is excommunicated, his body dug up and buried outside the walls of the city, with other outcasts from the faith. Then the gangs of filthy boys who roam Florence's streets exhume the corpse again, pummel it through the streets and make it ring the doorbell of the abandoned Pazzi Palace. Eventually growing bored with this macabre entertainment, they toss the body into the Arno River, singing 'Messer Jacopo is floating down the Arno.' The pathetic, mangled thing is seen passing under the bridges as far away as Pisa.

Niccolò Machiavelli says a good deal about conspiracies and their risks in various writings. One of the greatest risks is this: if they fail, the prince who was their target almost always *rises to greater power and many times from being a good man, becomes bad*.[3] In his rage and grief at his brother's murder, Lorenzo shows no mercy. In the space of three days, over seventy men are executed. Some are innocent. More die, with or without a trial, over the coming weeks. Armed troops now patrol the streets day and night. No one goes out after nine at night. Evenings are eerily silent.

The pally manner in which Giuliano's murderers led him to slaughter had exposed a fatal weakness in the Medici strategy of trying to look like amiable, equal citizens while acting like princes – or, as their enemies saw them, tyrants. It may seem wise to keep up appearances of republican equality. But at some point people will see through them and hate you for trying to mislead them. Or, seeing that you hide your true colours behind a paper-thin pretence and avoid hard armour, they take advantage of your faux friendliness to harm you. So if you want absolute power, it might be safer to admit the truth and act forthrightly, like a prince, a tyrant, whatever people want to call you. Then you can equip yourself with a properly armed bodyguard when you go out to the town, to meet business leaders, go to church with your family.

The Signoria – Florence's leading magistracy, composed of nine citizens, who are chosen by lot to serve rotating two-month terms – approve one for Lorenzo. From now on, he moves about town accompanied by the tramping of a dozen feet and the clanking of swords. And his smile, when he flashes it, fails to hide a grim wariness in his expression.

Florence is in collective shock, and fear. News soon goes out that Pope Sixtus, who had quarrelled openly with Lorenzo not long before, had supported – some say instigated – the Pazzi conspiracy. And now, in view of the Florentines' violent reprisals, the pope has a battery of more and less convincing pretexts for declaring war on Florence, which many suspect he wanted to do anyway. It was improper for a secular prince like Lorenzo to arrest cardinals – including a nephew of the pope's who had been in the church along with the Medici and Pazzi – or *to hang bishops, to kill, dismember, and drag around priests, and to slay the innocent and the guilty without distinction*, as Lorenzo and Giuliano's avengers had done.[4] Machiavelli's graphic account of Sixtus's official justifications quietly damns both parties at once. The pope is a hypocrite. He himself fanned the blaze he now wants to quench with war. But the Florentines really did these things, though they didn't have to. In taking such bloodthirsty revenge they danced to the pope's tune and gave him just cause to attack their city.

Helped only by Milan and lacking a standing army, the Florentines hire soldiers to do their fighting for them. Apart from a few patrician grandees sent to the field as military commissioners, the men of Florence stay home and try to carry on as usual. Every day, heralds read out the latest war news. The enemy are ransacking nearby cities in Florentine territories, burning men, women and children at the stake, or in their homes. Pitiful hordes of refugees from the smaller towns and villages pound on city gates at dawn, begging to be let in, with their wagonloads of children and shabby valuables.

And then comes the thing that people fear almost as much as enemy troops storming their walls: plague. *Il segno*, Florentines call it: the sign, the mark of death. Only two months into the war, people start dying of it. By late September the hospital of La Scala is filling up with victims of pestilence.

The sickness spreads rapidly through the city, into military camps. No one knows its causes, or how to cure it. Folk wisdom links it to solar eclipses or phases of the moon. Some of the rich believe it is spread by vile practices found among the poor.[5] When God strikes them down in their filth, He is sure, they hope, to spare the honest, industrious classes. Italy is full of doctors who understand other diseases, and apothecaries whose shops produce an astonishing array of medications, some more efficacious than others. But plague seems to mock all their scientific wisdom, both ancient and modern. Only two things are clear: it is savagely contagious, and most often fatal. Plague had devoured more than two thirds of Florence's population in the 1300s. The most reliable known treatment is isolation. As soon as someone is suspected of having contracted the plague, both doctors and government regulations advise them to quarantine themselves to avoid infecting others. Send as many people as can be spared away from your house; do not touch others if you can help it, or breathe too near their open mouths – things more easily done by the well-to-do, with their larger or multiple houses. The sick poor, crammed in tighter quarters, are harder to quarantine. Some manage to drag themselves to one of Florence's hospitals. Others, some mere children, are found cast out of their overcrowded family homes and dying on the streets.

In the warm summer months Bernardo spends more time at his villa outside the city, consulting with his tenant farmers, going with them to the village market to buy or sell food, wood, piglets. On Monday, 27 April, the day after the murder in the Duomo, he notes calmly in his *ricordi* that after some of his farm labourers sold a pair of oxen to a man in the neighbouring village, one of the animals was found to be old and worn out. Life goes on; there are always new disputes of price and quality to be settled. Farmers and landlords can still travel between the city and the countryside.

For now, too, the country feels safer than the city, even for women. But by July the rural idyll is shattered. The war is in full swing. Mercenary troops hired to fight for Florence are stationed in San Casciano, right on the Machiavellis' doorstep. With soldiers crawling all over the countryside, it is no longer safe for women to go out on their business. At the end of July Bernardo records that two male relatives of one of his farm workers *asked me if I were content to let them send their sister Sandra to Florence to stay with my wife and my children for protection. I answered that although it would cause me some hardship, to give them peace of mind I'd do it, and let her eat and drink and have a bed for nothing. Though if it pleased them, she could do a bit of service around the house.* War rages on through the winter, and the spring of the following year.

A bit of moral philosophy helps to keep Bernardo sane. In April 1479 he writes: *I went to the Arte di Porta Santa Maria to return the books I'd borrowed from the book dealer Giovanni di Francesco,* among them the *Ethics* of Aristotle and various works of Cicero. Moral philosophy is the child of war, especially civil war, wars with our fellow citizens, who in peacetime we are meant to see as friends, people like us, whose well-being helps shore up our own. When everything is a matter of life or death, people lose their bearings about right and wrong: whatever helps me and mine to win, or simply to survive, seems right enough. To people at war, survival seems to trump good and bad, just and unjust. But are they right? Even if our own side wins this time around, can we stay secure and at peace if we can't agree with the enemy that some actions are just and others wrong? Niccolò in the *Prince* thinks not: *Victories are never so clear that the winner does not have to have some respect, especially for justice.*[6]

On 30 June, while travelling back to his city house from Sant' Andrea, Bernardo feels sick. He tries to fight off the inevitable, morbid fears. Bernardo is now past fifty, too old to expect a much longer life. But he has two unmarried daughters whose futures are still unsettled, though he has invested carefully in their dowries, and two young sons who need a father's guiding hand. Reasons to live.

Arriving home, he tells Bartolommea to make up a room for his quarantine. And ask our servant, he says, to call for Buoninsegna. Buoninsegna Machiavelli is Bernardo's cousin, close to him in age, and his dearest friend. Without dining or drinking in the common rooms, Bernardo goes straight to his isolated new bed.

Buoninsegna comes and takes the matter in hand. His ailing cousin gives him a urine sample and a coin for the doctor's son. They communicate through the bars of Bernardo's bedroom window to avoid contagion. Bartolommea and fourteen-year-old Primavera wait anxiously in the front room for the doctor's visit. At least the younger children are away in the countryside with Bartolommea's brother Giovanni Nelli and his wife. Bernardo had sent them there a month earlier. He remembers their farewell: he and Bartolommea had hired a mule wagon and packed it to overflowing with food, clothing and bedding to help their relatives accommodate three extra mouths and bodies. Six bushels of wheat for the children's bread, a leg of dried mutton, two bottles each of vinegar and olive oil to follow, Bernardo had promised Giovanni, and a bit of money for wine.

Buoninsegna goes to fetch the doctor Bellabarba, Bernardo records in his diaries. Fairbeard, Dr Beauteous Beard. He has little faith in doctors at the best of times. In times of plague, the cost of plague doctors soars. They wear gloves, or don't even want to enter a patient's bedchamber, then rob you blind and seldom deliver what you pay for: a return to health. Small wonder that self-help treatises for the afflicted, and for those who fear affliction, are all the rage, printed en masse on one of the new printing presses and sold at book dealers' and apothecaries' shops. Some are cheap popular tracts, others penned by learned scholars. The philosopher Marsilio Ficino, brightest light of the intellectual circle that graces Lorenzo's household, has just written a tract claiming that people of predominantly melancholic humours – deep thinkers like himself, or Socrates – are most immune to the plague.[7] Women, being less prone to the more cerebral types of melancholia, are more at risk. An overactive imagination is the worst thing: when you worry too much about being sick, your fretful mind can't help heal your body.

Over the next weeks many doctors visit the Machiavelli house in Santo Spirito, plying an impressive variety of cures. A popular remedy for those diagnosed with pestilential fevers is a cordial made from the tiny blue flowers of borage and bugloss, ground up with sugar and mixed with other ingredients: sea coral, sandalwood, pearls, powdered gemstones, silver or gold, depending on what a patient could afford.[8] Too poor and too much the sceptic for such treatments, Bernardo submits himself to simpler ones. Herbal salves are smeared on his body, abscesses sliced open and drained. Doctors bleed him and administer bitter-tasting ruewort and electuaries, perfumed drugs mixed with honey. Each physician asks for the grossly inflated fee of a florin. A barber comes, too – members of the same guild as doctors and apothecaries, barbers are authorized to perform certain medical treatments – and applies *canterelle*, emerald-green or coal-coloured beetles, on three places on the patient's left leg.

Bernardo or the doctors must have done something right, for by August he is out of danger. But there is no time to enjoy his relief. As his symptoms wane, his other relations start to report them. First a young cousin, Guido Machiavelli, only twenty years old, asks Bernardo – still convalescing himself – to help write and notarize his will, and make arrangements for his sister Adola to get married. Next, an uncle of this Guido develops the characteristic signs of the plague. Then, saddest of all, it is Buoninsegna, in and out of Bernardo's sick-house all these weeks, never showing any concern about his own health. Bernardo pays two weavers from his neighbourhood and a peasant to witness his cousin's last will. No one else can be induced to approach so near to a man dying of plague. *And I record that on this the 5th of August 1479, the aforesaid Buoninsegna died, leaving behind two sons, Battista and Piero, and Monna Antonia his wife.*

With so many lives lost to pestilence, and the costs of war soaring, Lorenzo has nearly used up the credit he gained among the Florentines after his brother's murder. So he decides to travel to Naples to see if he can persuade King Ferrante, Pope Sixtus's chief ally in the war against Florence, to make peace. Against all expectations, Ferrante agrees, and Lorenzo returns a hero. While the war went on, there was no shortage of people who had slandered the young leader openly. *To save himself,* they said, *he had sold his fatherland,* letting towns under Florentine dominion fall to the enemy.[9] But after the success of his charm offensive in Naples, *in Florence, a city eager to speak, which judges things by results and not by advice, the reasoning turned around,* and everyone now *celebrated Lorenzo to the skies.*

But these Florentines spoke too soon, Niccolò points out. The manner of Lorenzo's peacemaking soon incites violent new collisions. Sixtus is furious that his Neapolitan allies have made friends with the Florentines, while the Venetians, who had been Florence's allies, complain that they have been left out of the negotiations. They now turn their troops against Florence, joining Pope Sixtus in his crusade to reduce the city to obedience. A good example, as Machiavelli treats it, of why it's best to judge policies by their methods and sound 'advice', not by results alone. And don't rush to proclaim any policy a great success, for often *gain is seen* and widely praised in policies at first – especially when they appear bold, surprising, risky – *even though there is the ruin of the republic concealed underneath.*[10] Soon the same Florentines who'd extolled Lorenzo as a diplomatic genius turned around again, saying that the peace he'd made had given birth to a new war.

The young First Citizen and his cronies respond to these criticisms by restricting the government to an even smaller number of men than already serve on the main councils. A new council of just seventy citizens is formed and authorized to decide on matters of great importance, replacing the larger councils that had always been consulted before. These extraordinary constitutional changes discourage any Florentines who might have hoped to end Medici rule. But they don't stop the city's enraged external enemies from issuing threats. At this moment *everyone,* Niccolò writes, *affirmed that our city had never been in such danger of losing its liberty.*

Yet, on the brink of renewed war, Florence is spared the

worst. Some say it is by a great miracle. Machiavelli calls it an accident, a fluke that has nothing to do with Florence's or her great leader's merit or prudence. Mahomet the Grand Turk had recently attacked the Greek island of Rhodes but met with obstinate popular resistance. Embarrassed and bent on some other victory, he now sails towards Italy. Attacking the city of Otranto on the south-eastern coast, he sacks it and slaughters its inhabitants, builds a fortress around the port and sends his troops on a rampage in the countryside. King Ferrante sends messengers throughout Italy and Europe to plead for help against their common enemy. No time and resources should be wasted on trifling vendettas close to home. Stand together against the infidel.

This turn of events suits the Florentines. On Machiavelli's account, it is the Turks, not Lorenzo's shrewd diplomacy, that saved the great leader's reputation. In later life Niccolò will constantly warn people to beware of quack healers who make things worse with their sweet-smelling remedies, or by *taking blood from the head. Those who promise benefit by such means*, he declares in his poem *The Ass, are always believed – from which it comes that men put such faith in doctors; it seems that this alone among the occupations feeds and lives on the ills of others.*[11] The coincidence that *medici* means 'doctors' is a gift to Florentine writers, screaming out for the kind of wickedly subtle wordplay that Niccolò loves. Some people who bear the good name of 'doctor' know next to nothing about healing. And some men who are hailed at one time as saviours of republics turn out, on closer inspection, to be their worst corrupters.

5

Have No Fear of Giants

Florentines are known throughout Europe and the Levant as masters of self-protective, ambiguous speech. After visiting Florence around this time, a Jewish mystic called Alamanno wrote, in Hebrew, that 'all Florentines' are apt to communicate contradictory messages.[1] 'They speak in two ways, by the wisdom of their voices and the action of their limbs,' their movements contradicting their words, 'lest they be guilty in their speech'. By speaking 'of hidden things and in allusions', they 'carefully guard their souls' and disguise the true contents of their hearts.

The most educated Florentines, the ones with whom Alamanno held such slippery converse, had learned something about the arts of ambiguity from ancient writers, many of them only recently rediscovered and widely studied in Western Europe. In an essay called 'How the Young Man Should Read Poetry', Plutarch, a Greek who lived under the Roman Empire – and one of Niccolò Machiavelli's favourite authors – says that young readers 'should pay close attention to whether the poet drops any hints suggesting that the sentiments he expresses are distasteful to himself'.[2]

Niccolò soon discovers these tantalizingly elusive dimensions of speech and writing. His *Discourses* set out a basic rule of thumb for reading works that seem to do nothing but adulate men of great power. *No one*, he tells us, *should deceive himself because of the glory of Caesar, hearing him especially celebrated by the writers. For those who praise him are corrupted by his fortune* and unduly impressed by the long duration of the Roman Empire, which *did not permit writers to speak freely of him*.[3] Some of humanity's greatest poems and histories, including the Roman poet Virgil's and Livy's, were penned in times when authors could be sent into exile, or worse, for even seeming to question the powers that be. But a few ancient writers, instead of going silent, discovered ingenious ways to criticize authorities and corrupt social habits 'between the lines'. *Unable to blame Caesar because of his power,* critics signalled their disapproval indirectly. Machiavelli will become one of ambiguity's greatest masters, an artist of chameleon words.

For now, after mastering the basics of Latin, he goes to study under the priest Paolo da Ronciglione, a highly regarded teacher who holds classes at the Studio, Florence's university. Ser Ronciglione also teaches the sons of some of Florence's leading families, including several of the Machiavellis' neighbours in Santo Spirito: the Capponi, Vettori, and Guicciardini. The Guicciardini boys are too young to share classes with Niccolò, but at some point he may coincide with Niccolò Capponi, son of one of the city's most energetic and outspoken statesmen, or the serious, literary-minded Francesco Vettori, both a few years younger than Bernardo's son.

However equal they might be in the classroom, there are large disparities of wealth and status between Niccolò and his friends. In a city the size of Florence, anyone can take a half-hour stroll and see where his acquaintances live. In keeping with republican tradition, most of the great new houses of patricians are built in the middle of town, not on its outskirts; they have no surrounding, gated gardens or walls like the grand houses of titled nobility in other places. Florentine palaces are not fortresses; nor, with the exception of the elephantine Pitti Palace, are they designed to overawe passers-by. Most are large, solid, square buildings that blend in well with their unremarkable environs. But they are still far grander than where the Machiavellis live, let alone poorer city dwellers. And the boys who live in them have very different career prospects. Before they are twenty, they might have travelled to London or the Levant, as an apprentice in their family's trade or an agent for their bank. After gaining a few years' experience, the city might send them as envoys to some Italian or foreign court or invite them to sit on public councils.

The fathers of Niccolò's upper-class peers are constantly on the move, serving their city as diplomats to foreign courts or as officials in its many magistracies. They are bankers and men of business who also play a large part – when their Medici First Citizens let them – in deciding when and how Florence should make war or peace, in judging criminal cases, imposing taxes, cutting backroom political deals. With the right father's support and clever use of contacts, a young man could go far fast. When still in his early twenties, Francesco Vettori, as his father's first son, is invited to step into an important post upon his father's sudden death; after a successful tenure, he is hailed as a rising political star, going on from one distinguished post to another. Niccolò Machiavelli, son of a father still struggling to pay off old family debts to the city, cannot hope for such a head start. He will have to take some other route to distinction.

Though some young men might resent this kind of comparative disadvantage, there is no shred of evidence that Niccolò does. On the contrary, one of his favourite themes is that the most praiseworthy lives and works grow out of hardship. People who face obstacles at the outset – if the obstacles aren't too cruel – have better chances of thriving later on. He calls such character-building obstacles 'necessity'.[4] The struggle to overcome great difficulties teaches people self-discipline and self-knowledge, not least knowledge of their own resources of mind and spirit, which might go untapped if they had it easy. This makes them tougher than those who have too many hereditary advantages: they are thicker-skinned against those who try to pull them down, more tolerant of the setbacks that face everyone at some time or another. In his *Prince*, Niccolò contrasts the great fortunes of his dedicatee, a young Medici princeling, to his own low and base condition. But he hints at a superior kind of greatness in his own 'little book', which contains things he *came to know and understand in so many years and with so many hardships and dangers for myself*.[5] Though wealthy and powerful men may place little value on Machiavelli's sole possession – his knowledge – at least he acquired it by his own industry and

Giants

discipline. And unlike any prince or banker, who can lose all his power and wealth overnight, Niccolò is confident that his knowledge is his for good.

At the end of 1479, the Florentine army finally leaves its camp near the Machiavellis' country house. Part of it heads south-east, towards Arezzo; another part west, towards Empoli and Pisa. Bernardo records these movements with a sense of relief. It is the only place in his diaries where he speaks directly of current affairs. He notes that some of the departing troops had been quartered in Sant' Andrea and that their captain, Piero da Cartagine, had been staying at Bernardo's house. Lorenzo's war is not over yet but, for now, it has left the Machiavellis' neighbourhood.

Still in his early thirties, Lorenzo already has deep, slanted lines that cut across his brow, captured in a terracotta bust by the sculptor Verrocchio. In a few years, he has gone from golden young leader to hardened survivor. He surrounds himself with a court of literary men and scholars unmatched anywhere in the world. The phenomenally productive Marsilio Ficino is close to finishing his Latin translations of Plato. The philologer and poet Poliziano and Chancellor Bartolomeo Scala, Bernardo's friend, are among Lorenzo's most eloquent defenders.

But Scala's doubts have been growing. Little by little, Lorenzo's legislation – some of it pushed through despite the Chancellor's cautiously expressed reservations – had been chipping away at the republic's constitution. Ever since the Pazzi conspiracy, Florentines had grown warier than ever of speaking out against these measures. There is no official censorship, no law restricting freedoms of expression. But *princes are always spoken of with a thousand fears and a thousand hesitations*, Niccolò Machiavelli would later observe.[6] People have reason to guard their tongues. Even Lorenzo's most familiar advisers speak out less freely than before. After all, an adviser to a *state held by a single man should never think of himself, but always of the prince*.[7] What's more, *he should never remember anything that does not pertain to the prince*, or even *think* too much of anything that doesn't concern the prince's personal interests. The prince, for his part, should take care to make his minister rich and keep him obligated to him, *so that he sees he cannot stand without the prince.*

Some readers assume that Machiavelli wants to recommend this kind of single-minded yes-man to political leaders. Perhaps he aspires to become one. But Scala and other ministers around Lorenzo might have smelled the deadpan irony in Niccolò's words, because they knew this type of minister all too well: they were in danger of incarnating it. While seeming to describe the kind of adviser that any ruler *should* want, Bernardo's son describes how advisers *must* behave if they work for over-controlling one-man rulers. He puts up a mirror to advisers as well as to princes, and their reflection isn't pretty. If a prince demands grovelling lapdogs as his intimate counsellors, what does that say about his judgement? The wisest ancient writers tell him to surround himself with top-notch independent minds *since*, Niccolò reminds us, *there are three kinds of brains: one that understands by itself, another that discerns what others understand, the third that understands neither by itself nor through others. The first is most excellent, the second excellent, and the third useless.*

Yet any independent-brained adviser lucky enough to work for an autocratic prince will soon be thrashing about in a spider's web of contradictory demands. On the one hand, this prince expects advisers to *speak freely and without hesitation,* on pain of making him 'upset' if they hold back. On the other, they must speak only *of those things that the prince asks about and nothing else.* Whatever the quality of their brains, advisers live in constant fear of saying too much or too little, or the wrong things at the wrong time.

Bernardo Machiavelli's diary entries end in 1487, the year Niccolò turns eighteen. For the next ten years, we have no record of either of these two Machiavellis' doings: no documents confirming whether, or what, Niccolò studied at university, no evidence of any work experience he might have gained, before his name reappears, suddenly, in two cockily defiant letters written in his very late twenties. In 1497 the Machiavellis find themselves embroiled in a quarrel over rights to the benefice of the parish church of Santa Maria di Fagna, a town just north of Florence. Their opponents are the rich and noble Pazzi, whose property and citizenship rights had been restored several years earlier. Twenty-eight-year-old Niccolò is more than ready to fight their claims. He drafts a letter to Cardinal Giovanni Lopez, who will decide the case, casting the impoverished Machiavelli clan as plucky underdogs whose resolve to fight tooth and claw for their rights makes up for what they lack in social standing. His family, he tells the cardinal with theatrical aplomb, *deem themselves in no way inferior, either in nobility, in mien, or in wealth, to those who assert that they have been named as the proprietors. Indeed, whoever might wish to weigh our house with the house of Pazzi on an accurate scale will determine ours far superior in liberality and virtue of spirit.*[8]

Here we get a first taste of Niccolò's lifelong fondness for puncturing pretensions of superiority based on mere birth and connections. In a republic of supposed political equals, everyone wants to know who stands higher and lower than them on the social ladder. Like the citizens in most republics, ancient or modern, Florentines are addicted to their pecking orders. Machiavelli's *Florentine Histories* show how their official ideal of a city without nobles was constantly undercut by the desires of some citizens to be ranked higher than others. They love to argue over which patricians should be numbered among their very greatest families, and which lower-class occupations make people belong to the *popolo* proper or the *popolo minore* (the 'lesser' people); or, descending lower still, to the plebs, or lesser plebs (*infima plebe*: plebeians of the lowest order). But the people most likely to meet with open contempt in Florence are not the down-at-heel middling classes, or even the poor, but the so-called 'new men' – arrivistes who only lately rose from nowhere to great wealth and power. Bernardo's friend Bartolomeo Scala is one such man. A miller's son from the provincial town of Colle, he had come to Florence, studied hard, and impressed Cosimo de' Medici with his erudition and desire to better himself.

Now he is Chancellor of the republic, one of the city's most important posts.

Niccolò learns early on where he and his family stand in this fastidious system of ranks. The Machiavellis are not patricians. Nor are they lesser *popolani*, men 'of the people', like the mass of Florentine citizens. They are *popolano grasso*, well-to-do people, middling-to-high bourgeoisie – in the case of Bernardo's branch on the family tree, not very high at all. Niccolò's first surviving letters show both his consciousness of his family's modest status and his refusal to be cowed by the so-called *grandi*, 'the great'. The red-blooded Machiavellis, he vows, will not stand by *to see men less worthy than ourselves, men whom we consider to be our enemies, bedecked with our spoils and boasting ignominiously of victory. If we, mere pygmies, are attacking giants*, he declares in another letter – this one in Latin – his family will prove their superior virtue of spirit by taking on *a competitor at whose nod everything is done immediately*. The Machiavelli family win the case, proving on a small scale a point Niccolò will make over and over in his writings: weak families, individuals, cities and peoples should never shy away from fighting those who put them down or take what is theirs.[9] Even if they lose some battles, their efforts do them proud, and make life harder for their oppressors.

6

How to Speak of Princes

The winter of 1491 is so cold that the Arno freezes solid. Ball games are played on it by day; at night, people make bonfires on the ice. Just north of Florence, from Fiesole to the Mugello, ice-storms tear oak and chestnut trees from their roots and break the branches of olive and fruit trees, with such a loud cracking of wood that anyone who happened to be nearby thought the world was coming to an end.[1]

Then winter starts to ebb away, and it is Carnival time again. Country people put on their best clothes and come to the city, leaving their troubles behind for a day or two; young men prowl the streets in packs, exuding carnality. Drumbeats, pipes and horns accompany parades and spectacles.

There are fewer Carnival floats than there used to be. Now Lorenzo himself plans the most elaborate spectacles and composes their scripts. Even this most irreverent of festivals has been reconfigured to revere one *padrone*. But the people love a leader who can write songs about peasants and phalluses as well as compose the highbrow poetry in Latin that circulates between great houses. One show has red-cheeked men dressed as farmers' wives hawking their country produce to Florentine ladies and telling them, in Lorenzo's words, how to eat it:

> First take the fruit in hand. Expose
> The core by pulling back the skin.
> Open your mouth and suck. For those
> Who know the way, it does not hurt at all.

Florence's leader is a real man, who has never tried to hide his private peccadilloes. He was, as Machiavelli puts it, *marvellously involved in things of Venus.*[2] But if il Magnifico can write titillating Carnival songs, so can Niccolò. At an unknown date, he writes several of them, not quite as graphic as Lorenzo's beans and cucumbers, though in the same taboo-sloughing spirit. But where the First Citizen's beefy farm lasses paint Florence as a garden of innocent, earthy delights, Niccolò's singers evoke a different kind of garden:

> *We are snake-charmers who charm by nature, ladies,*
> *and go seeking our fortune . . .*
> *We are all born with a sign underneath, and*
> *he who has the largest is the most learned.*[3]

Let the snake-charmers tell you about the ways of our native serpents, they sing, lest you trip over one unawares. One variety is especially dangerous and vicious. It chases everyone it sees from front and back, without respect for age or sex or class. Others bloat more than they bite, so to speak, and in the end won't give you much action. Then there are those that aren't at all what they seem; don't let their friendly appearances deceive you:

> *May it please you, then, to learn from us*
> *what evil these serpents can do you . . .*
> *For when you are charmed, in all places you'll sit down; and*
> *the larger the snakes you find, the more it will seem to you*
> *that you have greater luck.*

Lorenzo's amorous affairs – which often involved riding out late at night for a tryst in one of his villas outside Florence, then straggling home before dawn – had weakened his body, draining his vital juices before time. Barely into his forties, he is already a very sick man, crippled with gout and stomach troubles. He used to be seen limping across the Piazza della Signoria with his retinue, wearing a look of grim determination. As his pains worsen, he is carried in a covered litter, often escorted by twelve foreign guards who walk with swords drawn. He writes to doctors all over Italy in search of a cure. They write back.[4] Beware of cold and damp feet, of moonlight, and of the air at sunset. To ease gouty aches in the joints, get a sapphire, have it set in gold and wear it so it touches the skin on the third finger of the left hand. *Est enim divina res et miraculosa*: it is a divine thing, and miraculous. Certain medications in vogue among the rich – herbs and syrups mixed with ground-up pearls, precious gems, or gold leaf – doubtless exacerbate, or perhaps produce, the gastric disorders that wear Lorenzo down as much as the gout. Yet none of this stops him from enjoying life's small pleasures. *He delighted in facetious and pungent men and in childish games, more than would appear fitting in such a man.* Indeed, Niccolò adds, *considering both his voluptuous life and his grave life, one might see in him two different persons, joined in an almost impossible conjunction.*[5] A comment on the doubleness of Lorenzo's persona that brings out the doubleness of Machiavelli's writing, the ambiguity in his implied judgement: Lorenzo's personal doubleness might be a political achievement worthy of high praise – or a kind of unhealthy division in his being, a failure to achieve an integrated self, a failure of integrity.

As the ailing leader looks down from his window at Carnival masques below, thousands abandon the festive streets to witness a different kind of performance, worlds away from metaphorical obscenities and the reek of last night's sweat and sex and wine.

Remove from among yourselves these poems and games and taverns, and the evil fashions of women's clothes.[6]

At first the friar speaks calmly, almost tenderly, in the voice of a father who longs to embrace his prodigal children, who wants them safe back home. His words make the audience feel that they too know, in the neglected, better parts of their souls, that there is only one path to safety. **Throw out everything noxious to the health of the soul. Let everyone live for God, and not for the world. Live all in simplicity and charity.**

His fame is spreading fast. The friar from Ferrara, Frate

Girolamo. Old and young, men and women, rich, poor and middling, all are drawn at first by the buzz about his name, then by the siren voice pronouncing words they'd already heard ad nauseam from scores of other preachers but that now sound so different. This small, gaunt man makes tired platitudes pulsate with new, almost physical vigour. Unlike the others, he practises what he preaches, say his brothers at the Dominican church of San Marco. Sleeps on a hard pallet filled with straw, eats almost nothing.

Girolamo Savonarola is the son and grandson of Ferrara's court doctors, brought up among great riches. Disgusted by courtly life, he fled to the cloisters as a young man, in search of deeper truths. When later he arrived in Florence, he found a city full of people surrounded by opulence and worldly ambition, outwardly unworried by the state of their souls. Yet ever more of them attend his sermons and shed tears of remorse and desperate longing when he tells them: Go back, Florentines, to the spare, simple ways of Christ, and show others the way. The wives and sons of rich patricians, and not a few patricians themselves, keep coming back and jostling for the best seats in the congregation so that he can chide them and their kind: You merchants, you bankers, you ladies weighed down by jewels and gold. You think you can buy everything with money. You pay master painters to depict your beloved selves, your sons and daughters as saints. **Do you really believe the Virgin Mary went dressed as you paint her? Efface these figures that are painted so unchastely.** You do better to risk your lives for Christ instead of amassing riches or building your great palaces.

This champion of the poor pulls crowds from across the social spectrum. The rich, he declares, claim that the poor have only themselves to blame for their miseries. They're wrong: it's the rich who exploit the poor and make them do bad, driving them to sickness and thievery and prostitution. You think wealthy people help pull the poor up with alms and private charities? Think again. The ambitious projects of the rich impoverish the poor even more. Your great men buy land and shops from the poor at a low price, taking advantage of others' poverty to aggrandize themselves in vain shows of extravagance. **The devil uses the great to oppress the poor so the poor can't do good.**

There is no divide between educated elites and ignorant masses before Friar Girolamo's pulpit. Old women and young rogues stand side by side with lawyers and philosophers and men of letters who declare that these sermons are almost as erudite as lectures at the university. Intellectuals from Lorenzo's inner circle – Pico della Mirandola, Angelo Poliziano, Marsilio Ficino – become devoted regulars at San Marco. Gentlemen and paupers, sodomites and virgins, all are equally transfixed, conjoined by his words in mysterious fellowship. **Everyone has to die: that great master, that youth, the rich, the handsome, the strong. They are all stink and ashes.** And whose lives will leave behind the worst stench? Those who pretend to live by holy orders: those priests who, for a handful of ducats, absolve the rich from the darkest of sins, and threaten the poor with hellfire unless they hand over a week's living for indulgences. **And you, Rome, Rome!** The entire Holy City reeks of perdition.

When God allows ambition, lechery, and other vices to exist in the head of government, believe that God's scourge is near. The days of tyranny are numbered. When he speaks about heads of government, the friar names no names. His thousands of auditors are left free to speculate: is he speaking in general terms? Or does he mean our government, our tyranny, our head? Silence exudes ambiguity. Sometimes it accuses more powerfully than words.

Lorenzo lets Friar Girolamo preach what he likes. It was he who invited the Dominican to Florence in 1490. Soon Savonarola's sermons draw such large crowds that it would be imprudent to try to muzzle him. He's a good man, Pico and Poliziano assure Lorenzo. And his religious doctrines are salutary. People today do nothing but run after material things. Most are driven by necessity, but many by this unhealthy spirit of competition that infects our society like a contagious disease. Now they're all exhausted, rich and poor and those flailing about somewhere in the middle. They crave something more. A great city needs a great moral teacher, a man of God, to supplement the wisdom of its political leaders.

As the half-millennium approaches, then, Florentines are presented with two paths to salvation. One path is bound to the fortunes of the Medici family, with its expensively purchased ties to the Vatican: Lorenzo had recently married his daughter Maddalena to one of Innocent VIII's sons, then persuaded the pope to make his adolescent son Giovanni de' Medici a cardinal. It was *beyond every past example*, Niccolò Machiavelli comments wryly, that a mere boy *be brought to such rank when not yet fourteen years of age. It was a ladder enabling his house to rise to heaven*, to more than human heights.[7] The other path, Savonarola's, points in the opposite direction, away from plutocratic dynasties and great bankers' palaces and the Church of Rome, rotten to its core. Like Lorenzo's ascent to excessive power, the friar's astonishing rise in Florentine politics would leave a deep mark on Machiavelli's political thought and shape his future career.

In March 1492, sixteen-year-old Giovanni de' Medici is formally admitted into the Sacred College of Cardinals. When he rides into Florence on a donkey after receiving his red cap at Fiesole, every street and house seems to overflow with joy.[8] Banners bearing the word 'PALLE' – *palle* are the balls on the Medici coat of arms, a golden shield encrusted with five red spheres and one blue – are hung at the entryways of grand houses and in shop windows. No Florentine cardinal had ever been given such a reception before, as if he were a foreign monarch, or a pope.

> *The earth smiles where you set foot, and the air grows happy*
> *wherever the welcome sounds of your voice are heard . . .*
> *O gift of so many gods, condescend to accept me among your faithful subjects,*
> *if to have such a servant you do not scorn.*[9]

The date and addressee of Niccolò's pastoral poem are unknown. So are his reasons for writing it. It might be nothing but a youthful exercise in conventional versification, a bad imitation of Virgil or Petrarch's pastoral poetry. Or it might be a piece of grandiose ingratiation.

> *To fully praise all that beauty,*
> *it behooves us to pray for loftier talents . . .*
> *Every light before this one grows dim, as soon as we behold those looks*
> *deserving every crown and every diadem.*

Yet if the poem is addressed to a Medici, such fulsome praise seems impolitic. That family, after all, insists on upholding the fiction that they are mere First Citizens, under Lorenzo and afterwards.

> *Fierce Mars, that you might shine the more,*
> *within your generous breast enclosed a heart like that of Caesar,*
> *duke of all the other dukes . . .*
> *Juno put in private citizen's clothing a soul fit to dominate empire and*
>   *kingdoms.*

So now this divine youngster, whose command our poet longs to obey, resembles Julius Caesar, the man who destroyed the Roman republic while pretending to protect it. Caesar, who, as Machiavelli put it elsewhere, *could so blind the multitude* with his people-pleasing tricks *that it did not recognize the yoke it was putting on its own neck.*[10] Not a comparison likely to flatter the Medici, any more than the vaguely pornographic metaphors:

> *And though I have been reared in the throng of these rough shepherds,*
> *when I speak of you, much higher than my wont I fly.*
> *Yet still higher up you will see me mounting if I know that you accept my gift*
> *when I recite your praises . . .*
> *Hence it is my prayer that I, even I, O Jove divine,*
> *among so many trumpets exalting him, may be permitted*
> *to make my crude shepherd's horn resound!*

When you depart, the little plant that was flowering withers and is left in
  misery
and the air deprived of you shows grief.

Towards the end of March, soon after his son's elevation to the cardinalate, Lorenzo is carried to his villa at Careggi outside Florence, crippled with stomach pains. Then the portents of death start appearing. One of the lions kept as city mascots at the back of the government palazzo is mauled to death by the others. And on 5 April, at around eleven o'clock at night, a bolt of lightning strikes a lantern in the cupola of the church of Santa Reparata, *with such fury that a great part of the pinnacle was ruined, to the amazement and marvelling of everyone.*[11] There had been no sign of rain before, not a cloud in the clear night sky.

Three days later, at his Careggi estate, Lorenzo's friends prepare his soul for the afterlife. In his long years of premature decline, he had ample time to ponder the question that agitates the minds of every ruler who has exercised great power: What will people say about me once I'm gone? Will their praise outweigh the blame?

The question is hard to answer in Lorenzo's case, even five centuries later, because some of his obituaries read like Virgil's or Tacitus' chameleon praise for Roman emperors: they recount his deeds in words that change colour depending on your perspective. Like the ancient nobility, Machiavelli tells us, Lorenzo invested in landed property and built private family estates *that for their utility, the quality of their buildings, and their magnificence were those not of a private citizen but of a king.* If your perspective is that of a supporter of a Medici-led aristocracy or monarchy, these lines sound pleasing, appropriately reverent towards a man whose expensive properties are no more than what he and his family deserve for services rendered to their country. If you prefer a more frugal, egalitarian republic – still Florence's official civic ideal – Machiavelli's words may strike you quite differently.

Especially if you have doubts about where all that money came from. Lorenzo, as our discreet historian says – his histories were written under a later Medici government, so any criticisms had to be muted – was *very unprosperous in trade*, so that *it was required that his fatherland help him with a great sum of money*. Another historian, Niccolò's close friend Francesco Guicciardini, puts it more bluntly: 'Lorenzo availed himself of public monies to meet his own needs, which at times were very great.'[12] Neither writer calls Lorenzo an embezzler outright, but their readers, aware of the rumours, would get the insinuation.

Other notable deeds, perhaps, weigh on the other side. In times of peace, the First Citizen *kept his fatherland always in festivities: there were frequent jousts, and representations of old deeds and triumphs were to be seen; and his aim was to keep the city in abundance, the people united, and the nobility honoured*. Surely it's hard to fault these things? Indeed – particularly if you're among the honoured nobility, or among the patrician oligarchs who hope that Lorenzo's distracting entertainments would help the people forget about the freedom they'd lost under his watch.

And Niccolò's ultimate test of any one-man ruler's legacy: did his policies create a firm, well-ordered, secure state, one whose boons can survive and flower beyond his own brief lifespan? *To make himself live more securely*, Lorenzo *built many fortifications* in cities near Florence. *With stipends and pensions, he maintained his friends* in these fortress cities, knowing he could count on their arms to support him, since his money could make or break them – friends like the Baglioni in Perugia and the Vitelli in Città del Castello. A wise security policy, one might well think. But in his *Prince* and *Discourses*, Machiavelli says otherwise. If you want to maintain your state over time, the only sure way is to arm your own people and keep them satisfied; it's always safer to found yourself *not upon fortresses but upon the benevolence of men*.[13] To say that any ruler relies on fortresses is to insinuate that he doesn't, or can't, trust his own people to defend him; he relies instead on client states and friends beyond his borders.

Nevertheless, *Lorenzo was loved by fortune and by God in the highest degree, because of which all his enterprises had a prosperous end*. Unquestionably high praise, if we measure a statesman's success by the effects his actions have on his personal survival. But we might still wonder whether, when he dies, his own good fortune will stick around to prop up his country in his absence. And we might doubt that a state based on any one man's fortune can really be called secure, especially when good fortune seems to have abandoned him in his final years, letting him suffer a prolonged and agonizing early death. *In his last days he lived full of distress caused by the illness that held him marvellously afflicted. He was oppressed by intolerable stomach pain, which so racked him that in April of 1492 he died, in the fourty-fourth year of his life. And that very great disasters must arise from his death, heaven showed with many very evident signs.*

7

Recover Your Freedom

When things turn bad after a great leader's death, people tend to praise him more than ever and malign his inferior successor. But a closer look often reveals that post-mortem problems have their origins not in the successor but in the great leader, who made everyone and everything – the magistrates, the laws, foreign alliances and wars – depend so much on him that no one else could possibly fill his shoes. Before, the city had laws and institutions that held things together no matter who ruled, that lasted longer than any one mere mortal's life. Now, precisely because of the leader's personal greatness, those old laws and institutions are weak, or reduced to empty shells. After the prince dies, his subjects find themselves utterly bereft, with nothing to lean on. Nothing but his sons.

Florence's leading citizens agree to give twenty-one-year-old Piero de' Medici the same honours as his deceased father. It soon becomes clear that Piero's sense of personal entitlement goes well beyond that seen in Lorenzo, or any other Medici leader. His predecessors expected to work hard to keep their political machine well oiled; Piero takes his privileges as First Citizen for granted. Bernardo Rucellai, married to Lorenzo's sister Nannina, urges the young head of state to exercise power more moderately.[1] Rucellai enlists the help of Paoloantonio Soderini, eldest son of the Tommaso Soderini who had urged Lorenzo to exercise restraint over Volterra. When Piero's Chancellor da Bibbiena gets wind of these conversations, he gathers together a few Medici zealots who go to work on Piero in the opposite way, urging him to assert his new powers with statesmanlike vigour. Soon Piero grows suspicious of his critical relations and their associates. He begins to go sullen in their company, finding excuses not to meet them in private.

Now even some of the leading family's most devoted friends start to feel nostalgic for the genuinely republican constitution Florence had before the Medici became a de facto dynasty. They had backed Cosimo de' Medici when he claimed to stand above all the Florentines' divisions, both class and partisan, as a wise arbiter. Then Lorenzo, while accruing far more power for his family than his grandfather had done, seemed to pull off the oxymoronic feat of being both unconstitutional monarch and citizen of a republic of equals. But the truth, Niccolò Machiavelli argues in a proposal for reform written around 1520, is that the two roles cannot be combined for long.[2] Sooner or later, one must cancel out the other: either the prince must be reduced to citizen, or the First Citizen must openly become a prince. Now, with Lorenzo's smug young heir, that truth is so glaring that even Medici partisans admit it.

And whatever the shortcomings of any real-life republic – Rome, too, was man-made and therefore imperfect, Niccolò's *Discourses* tell us – they have this great advantage over hereditary principalities. In republics, dead or incompetent leaders can easily be replaced. Out of a wide pool of citizens, you can choose *infinite most virtuous princes to succeed one another*, elected, short-term 'princes' like the Roman consuls who are chosen for their seniority and experience.[3] In a dynastic princedom, citizens have no choice: the sons inherit the leadership. And in Rome or Florence or any other known city, *as the prince began to be made by succession and not by choice*, very soon the heirs *degenerate from their ancestors*.[4] If a good prince happens to come out of a ruling family, this is largely a matter of brute luck. And since the progeny of princes are spoiled by a fortune they didn't have to work for, such luck always runs out.

When the test of wills finally comes, it is provoked by an audacious move on the part of Rucellai and Paoloantonio Soderini. On behalf of their children, both patriarchs enter into secret marriage negotiations with the extraordinarily rich and ambitious Strozzi family, old rivals of the Medici. Convinced that these discussions are part of a plot to topple him, Piero breaks all personal ties with the suspected ringleaders, forces them out of their government posts, and declares them and their offspring ineligible for any such posts in future.

Among the main body of the populace, people who now have no voice in political decisions, the voices of charismatic preachers are growing louder, speaking to their fears. Friar Savonarola's latest vision is on everyone's lips.

I saw a sword over Italy, and it quivered – All of a sudden, I saw that sword turn its point downward and, with the greatest tempest and scourge, go among them and scourge them all.

I will explicate it for you. The sword that quivered – I must say this to you, Florence – is that of the King of France, which is appearing all over Italy.[5]

Even cynics soon admit that there had been a strange prescience in the friar's forebodings. France's King Charles VIII had inherited a claim to the throne of Naples through his father. By the end of 1493, word had spread all over Italy that the young king was resolved on the enterprise. Florence's ambassadors report that military preparations are underway, and appear to be on a vast scale.

First in his *Decennale* and later in the *Prince*, Machiavelli gives a self-critical diagnosis of his country's condition on the eve of the French incursion – just as, in his *Florentine Histories*, he blames the late Roman Empire's self-inflicted shambles for the barbarian invasions.[6] King Charles and his advisers had merely seized an opportunity created by two deadly flaws in Italy's then current organization. One was dynastic rule. If Italian states hadn't been ruled by family dynasties that intermarried with foreign royalty and gave them claims to Italian thrones, French or German or Spanish monarchs would lack that pretext for bringing their armies into the peninsula. The other flaw was Italy's system of military defences. If, instead of relying on paid mercenaries, the Italians had possessed better armies of their own – and sturdy alliances to help them resist common threats – no foreign army could have marched unimpeded into Italy, even the mighty French behemoth.

Thus, in 1494, the seeds are planted of what would become Machiavelli's lifelong dream of a self-armed, well-ordered Italy, with Florence showing the way. His friends affectionately deride it as one of his many extravagant pet ideas, his *fantasie*. But he never doubts that it offers the only realistic chance for Italians to save themselves from becoming the helpless prey of foreign powers.

Many ancient writers, and Machiavelli, too, observe that when tyrannical dynasties finally fall to ruin, the catalyst is often the tyrant family's own members turning against each other.[7] Some princes marry their cousins or siblings and produce weak-minded new rulers who drive the country to ruin and terrorize their nearest and dearest. Others start murdering, or are murdered by, their own kin. Wives poison their husbands, brothers strangle brothers, mothers pay assassins to stab sons through the heart. For the ancients, this recurring pattern represented the ultimate cosmic and natural justice, akin to the self-destruction of a gluttonous individual: a family that has tried to seize and scarf down every scrap of power for itself becomes bloated on its own overeating, then implodes.

In April 1494, Florentines hear rumours that Piero's second cousins Lorenzino and Giovanni di Pierfrancesco de' Medici have been detained for questioning.[8] These two brothers, nine and five years older than Piero, are well liked among middle- and lower-class Florentines; they represent a part of the Medici family widely known as the Popolani, 'the popular' branch. The story goes about that it's all a trivial matter, a brawl over some girl at a spring ball. Some say that Piero, a strong, bull-necked lad, punched cousin Giovanni in the face when he insisted on dancing with Piero's lady of choice. He and his brother had to be put under guard to prevent their followers from battling it out in public.

Whatever its immediate cause, political insiders well know that a family flare-up had long been in the offing. After their father's death in 1476, the two boys had come under the guardianship of their older cousin Lorenzo il Magnifico. A few years later, when they came of age, they accused Lorenzo of plundering their inheritance when he found himself in financial straits. Relations broke down completely in 1484, when the First Citizen secured the removal of Lorenzino's name from the lists of men eligible for city magistracies. Now, in April 1494, with the French about to descend on Italy, he and his brother are accused of conspiring with Milan's Ludovico Sforza to overthrow Piero's government.

On 4 May, visiting French ambassadors ask the Florentines to join their king's campaign or, if they would not, to allow French troops passage through Florentine territory. The Signoria assure the French of their city's devotion to the king but cite various obstacles to fulfilling his wishes, in particular a treaty that binds the Florentines to defend Naples. The king responds by ordering Florentine ambassadors out of France and expelling from Lyons the representatives of the Medici bank.

Faced with a worried, angry populace, the Signoria convene an emergency committee.[9] A few men make excuses for their leader. Piero has family ties to the King of Naples. He can hardly be expected to invite the French in to throw out his own relatives, who are, moreover, the strongest prop he has for his own tottering regime. But most think it madness to refuse safe passage to a gargantuan army when one has none to oppose it. King Charles commands the largest army in the world. Florentines have no arms of their own at all, some citizens point out, and the mercenary soldiers they pay to fight for them have no experience of the new style of French warfare. In fact, since they are not fighting for their own lands and families, they'd do anything to avoid outright battle, preferring to parry and circle, and beat up a great noise with tambourines and blow shrieking little whistles to intimidate their opponents. But monstrous cannonballs that leave thousands of mutilated bodies strewn across burnt-out fields, whole cities bathed in blood: that's what these French call war, and what Florentines face if they put their lives and property at risk for the King of Naples.

King Charles VIII enters Italy via Monginevro at the beginning of September 1494, with some 25,000 armed men. About the same number of camp followers accompany the army: cooks and doctors, grooms and military musicians, courtiers, servants carrying supplies, prostitutes and other entertainers. Nothing like it had ever been seen on Italian soil. By mid-September, the King of Naples's fleet is defeated. On 4 October, yet another round of ambassadors comes to Florence from France, offering the Signoria a last chance to put the city on the side of safety. Florentines pray for a turnaround. Yet once again their leaders give the French a vague reply, and the indignant ambassadors leave without a grant of safe conduct through Florence's territories.

When word spreads to the shops and streets, 'it was said,' one Florentine diarist reports, 'that the king now swore to let his soldiers plunder Florence.'[10] With the French at their doorstep, the Venetians hastily send an ambassador to King Charles to congratulate him on his first successes and to declare friendship. In the coming days, Florence's neighbours Siena and Lucca send friendly embassies to the foreigner. One after another, Italians are all *throwing themselves*, in a phrase Machiavelli likes to use, *into the lap* of this king who has enough forces to flatten them all, not having bothered to build up forces of their own before it was too late. For *when one foresees from afar, one can easily find a remedy* for future troubles. *But when you wait until they come close to you, the medicine is not in time, because the disease has become incurable.*[11]

On 20 October, the French conquer and sack the town of Mordano on the way from Venice to Florence, burning and massacring without mercy. By now, more Florentines than ever are ready to accept a huge foreign army in their territory if the French agree to spare their lives and property.[12] And it is starting to look as though this agreement will never be secured while the Medici hold the reins of power. Florence's streets and piazzas are littered with anonymous leaflets calling on the 'Most Christian King of France' to free the city from its yoke of tyranny. Entering Florentine dominions, the French seize several strategically important military fortresses from Florentine control: Sarzana, Sarzanello, Pietrasanta, Livorno, Pisa.

Then, without consulting the Signoria, on 26 October, Piero de' Medici travels to Pisa to meet King Charles at his camp and gives in to all the king's demands: he agrees to let Charles keep the fortresses he has taken, and promises Florentine money for Charles's expedition if he refrains from attacking the city. When the news soon comes back to Florence, it causes an uproar. With Piero away from the city, everyone begins to speak freely at last. 'How much longer can we bear with this blasted government of boys?' demands Piero Capponi, one of the city's boldest and most respected patricians.

The Signoria issue a proclamation obliging everyone in Florence to offer lodgings to French soldiers. Scouts come from the king and go around all the houses, large and small, marking with chalk those suitable for billeting. Girls are sent in haste to convents or to relatives outside the city. On 5 November, now operating without any Medici say-so, the Signoria send four ambassadors to King Charles. In a remarkable deviation from diplomatic custom, one of these envoys is neither a government man nor a native Florentine: the friar from Ferrara, Girolamo Savonarola, chosen for his authority among the populace and his renown as a true man of God, which the city's leaders hoped might weigh with the king. The ambassadors neither dissuade Charles from entering Florence nor persuade him to hand back the fortresses Piero has given him. But they do gain his promise to enter as a friend. And, for now, at least, he agrees to deal only with Florence's duly appointed representatives, not with the self-willed Piero de' Medici.

Piero rides back to Florence on 8 November. Having got wind of events in his absence, he has sweetmeats thrown from his house and doles out barrels of wine to the populace.[13] But when, the next day, he tries to enter the government palazzo with a following of armed men, the Signoria lock him out and put a guard at the doors. In the Piazza della Signoria his opponents are ringing the bells, calling men of all ages to come outside and welcome their newly won freedom.

Within an hour, the whole piazza is packed with citizens and armed men standing under the banners of their districts. A shout goes up from the streets and from men appearing at the windows of houses, and grows louder and louder: *'Popolo e Libertà! Popolo e Libertà!'* A new proclamation forbids anyone from aiding or abetting Piero de' Medici. Another states that whoever slays him would have 2,000 ducats, while young Cardinal Giovanni de' Medici's death would earn one thousand. Losing no more time, Piero and his household depart for Bologna.

On 17 November, passing through the high city gate of San Frediano near the Machiavellis' house, King Charles makes his triumphal entry into Florence.[14] Inscriptions on the arch of the gate hail him as the *Conservateur et Libérateur de nostre Liberté*. Thousands of people line the streets, lean out of windows and perch on rooftops to watch the king pass slowly through the city on horseback under a canopy, crying out, *'Viva Francia!'* On reaching the Piazza della Signoria, Charles is greeted by a float of Peace, decorated with a gigantic golden lily the height of two spears and topped with a crown of silvery palms. At midnight, he arrives at the cathedral and dismounts. Onlookers are taken aback: on foot, this great king is a very small man with a hunched back visible beneath his coat, his gait uneven. But they had all decided to adore him today, to show him such sincere devotion that he would trust the Florentines completely and desire never to do them harm. Inside the cathedral, Charles takes a solemn vow to respect the liberty of the republic. Then he heads off to the Medici Palace, where he will stay as the city's revered guest.

At first appearances, this welcoming celebration expresses the Florentines' fathomless gratitude to the French for helping them to cast off Medici tyranny. But the joyous street theatre barely masks a far more equivocal reality, perceptible to anyone who knows the protocol of such processions. For the French parade with their lances held high, a gesture characteristic of the conqueror. If this was the start of a beautiful new friendship, it was a laughably unequal one.

And the weaker party still has both freedom and empire to lose. Freedom: Piero de' Medici had been chased out, but he would soon try to return, with the help of every Italian city that Florence had ever offended. Empire: French troops still hold Pisa's fortresses and the other city fortresses that Piero had given the king. And as soon as the Pisans heard news of this change of masters, they declared themselves liberated from the Florentine yoke that had held them down for a hundred years, imploring King Charles to be their protector.

French and Swiss troops are quartered in every acceptable house; the Machiavellis' is presumably one of them. For eleven days, the city is kept on tenterhooks while King Charles enjoys Florentine hospitality. He dines in the highest style at the Palazzo della Signoria and attends local festivals and Mass, always accompanied by a troop of armed horsemen. Yet as the days pass, there is still no word on whether the king will help Florence keep out the Medici and recover Pisa. The unpleasant truth soon dawns: he wants to screw as much money from the city as he can. Protection money. While celebrating their freedom, the Florentines may merely have traded in the Medici tyranny for another yoke, a foreign one.

Then on 20 November, mere days after the king rode in, rumours fly through the city that Charles is demanding the restoration of Piero de' Medici. With over twenty thousand soldiers billeted in a city of forty thousand, liberation begins to feel like occupation. The visitors confiscate the Florentines' personal weapons and parade their own guards at night. Fearing that the king might order the sacking of the city at the least provocation, people stay quiet.

Thus you could not rejoice as you should have done
at being taken from under the yoke that

for sixty years had weighed heavy upon you,
because you saw your state laid waste;
you saw your city in great peril,
and in the French arrogance and pride.[15]

Looking back on these times a decade later, Niccolò could think of nothing more humiliating than the Florentines' helplessness during Charles's sojourn. Here were his fellow citizens, cowering behind closed shutters, waiting for foreigners to hand down a verdict on Florence's future, without even having been defeated in war.

You stood here with open mouth
to wait for someone coming from France
who would bring you manna in the desert
and would restore to you the castles
of Pisa, Pietrasanta and the other towns.[16]

The Florentines soon realize that their guests are as nervous as they are. 'In their hearts,' surmises the diarist Luca Landucci, these French soldiers 'felt a secret dread.' Whether in the Latin lingua franca or in whatever hodgepodge of French and Italian and German dialects did the job, 'they kept asking how many men Florence could dispose of; and they were told that at the sound of a bell the city would have a hundred thousand men within and without at her command.' The general populace, it seems, had been primed to exaggerate their own potential to harm their esteemed visitors, should relations take a downward turn. The Florentines might have few bargaining chips, but they did hold these troops within their city walls, and could call on loyal country people outside to help.

By the end of the first week, the collective pretence of friendship breaks down. Youths begin to mimic and taunt the hunchbacked king when he passes on the streets. A few skirmishes between locals and soldiers are calmed, but Florentines of all classes have had enough. They start preparing for a fight. Men and women gather what arms they have, stacking piles of wood at each corner so streets can be barricaded in a hurry.

On 24 November, people lock themselves indoors en masse. Some start throwing stones at French soldiers from their windows. The king stays in his lodgings at the Medici Palace, afraid to venture out to dine as usual at the government palace.

The odds are stacked too high against us, some say. They have over twenty thousand armed men and we a few rocks and bits of wood. Machiavelli answers such doubts in his *Prince*. Why did David think he stood a chance against Goliath? Because he fought for himself, from the gut, and all the harder knowing the greater strength of his enemy. And because he fought with *his own arms*, paltry as they were. When he took up the arms given him by King Saul, he felt as if his visceral fighting spirit was smothered under borrowed weapons. So he said *he would rather meet the enemy with his sling and his knife*, and with these he killed the giant.[17]

As the people prepare for whatever might come next, leading citizens gather at the Medici Palace. Flanked by his ministers and military chiefs, Charles presents a draft treaty with his demands: 200,000 ducats and the return of Piero de' Medici. Otherwise, he threatens, the city would be sacked at the sound of his trumpets.

Most of Florence's premier citizens feel trapped. If they reject the king's terms they'll have no choice but to unleash the multitude, who are preparing to defend themselves of their own accord and seem eager enough to play their part in saving the city. But more than French extortions, this prospect terrifies the city's patricians. Such, Niccolò comes to think, are Florence's glorious grandees: they'd rather pay out every last *grosso* from their banks and live as slaves than risk their soft necks in a fight. Except for one:

> The clangour of arms and of horses
> was not loud enough to keep unheard
> the voice of one capon (Cappon) *among a hundred gamecocks.*

The capon is Piero Capponi.[18] 'Since your Most Christian Majesty does not wish to make an agreement with us,' he says evenly, 'things can be settled by other means. If you sound your trumpets, we shall toll our bells.' He tears up the French treaty and walks out of the chamber.

His stunned colleagues stand by for a moment, unsure what has just happened. Then they follow.

Charles seems to have realized that a mass revolt was in the making. *'Ah Chapon, Chapon, vous êtes un Chapon mal,'* he calls after Capponi: Ah, Capponi, Capponi, you are a naughty capon! Now the king is all smiles and readiness to talk. For this outcome, Capponi would earn Niccolò's warm tribute: *One can praise him, above everything else, for this: that he alone supported what all the other citizens had abandoned, when before the king's face he tore up those articles of agreement that took away the liberty of his native city.* Capponi refused to be intimidated *by the insolence and power of the French, or by the cowardice of his fellows; and only through him it was that Florence did not live as the slave of the French.*[19]

After gruelling negotiations, Charles agrees to more moderate terms. He promises to return Pisa's and the other fortresses to the republic and to help restore the rebellious Pisans to Florence's dominion after completing his conquest of Naples. Florence is to pay him the reduced, though still hefty, sum of 120,000 gold ducats.

As for the Medici, the king remains evasive. It might be useful, his advisers tell him, to keep this sword hanging over the Florentines' heads for a while.

> So the proud king left, after he learned
> that the city, in maintaining her freedom, was united.[20]

Charles leaves Florence on 28 November. The Medici family's possessions are removed from their palazzo and auctioned off to pay their very considerable public and private debts. Bronze statues of Judith and Holofernes and David, cast by the sculptor Donatello for the Medici to advertise their republican credentials, are moved from the Medici Palace to the main square in front of the government palace.

The French are gone, and sixty years of Medici rule are over. Florentines are free again, like the Romans after they drove out the Tarquins, their last kings. They have a chance to build a republic in deed, not just in name, stronger and freer than all previous Florentine governments. Niccolò Machiavelli is still too young to play a part in laying the foundations of this new republic, and his family's debts make it pointless to dream about being elected to a city magistracy in a year or two. Yet for him this is an exhilarating moment, an opportunity for his compatriots to use their intelligence and the lessons of history to get things right, or at least better than they had been for a long time. Until now, he had never lived under a republic in which a large number of worthy men – not just Medici cronies – were free to hold office, speak their minds, and play their part in the great, messy, shared business of civil self-government. A republic where no man of any class has cause to *fear that his patrimony will be taken away*, and where he knows that his children *not only are born free and not slaves, but that they can, through their virtue, become princes.*[21] Become princes: all governments need leaders, and every well-ordered republic – like the Roman one when it was good – gives its first rank of authority to one or a few men, as the Romans gave it to their consuls. But these republican 'princes' are a different thing entirely from the offspring of family dynasties. They hold first rank for a clearly defined term and attain it *not by inheritance or deception or by violent ambition, but by free votes* and their own merits.[22]

But how, some of his compatriots are already asking, can we stand up to today's great kings if we have no one great leader of our own? Learn, Niccolò will say, from history. Great dynasties may make large gains in a short time, but they lose them just as easily, or struggle to hold on to them. Indeed, *it is seen through experience that cities have never expanded either in dominion or in riches if they have not been in freedom.*[23] The reason for this, he adds, is easy enough to understand. Princes and oligarchic governments give high offices and honours to only a few. And while they claim to give them to deserving individuals, in reality most honours are granted in exchange for political support or because of family connections. By contrast, *a free way of life*, if it is free in truth and not just in name, *proffers honours and rewards through certain honest and determinate causes*, not shady or private ones. When people believe that public honours and political authority are conferred for valid reasons that are open to scrutiny, they are unlikely to revolt against their government. And they are more likely to defend their state against home-grown and foreign enemies when they trust that everyone there can *enjoy one's things freely, without any suspicion*, without fear of arbitrary taxes or punishments.

For six decades of Medici rule, men like Bernardo Machiavelli, armed with his Livy, had kept alive the memory of that kind of *vivere libero*, or free way of life. Niccolò speaks from very personal knowledge when he says that *freedom, one knows, is often restored in a city by those who have never tasted it but who loved it only through the memories of it left to them by their fathers. And thus*, he continues, *once recovered, they preserve it with all obstinacy and at any peril.*[24] And a warning for any Florentine patricians who might already be conspiring to take away the freedom of the people who had just reclaimed it: if you consider all the advantages of a genuinely free way of life, *it is not marvellous that peoples take extraordinary revenges against those who have seized their freedom.* This happened in the Greek city of Corcyra during the Peloponnesian War. The nobility took away the people's freedom for a time. But when, later, the popular party recovered its strength, *they laid hands on all the nobility and shut them up in a prison*, and later *had them killed with many examples of cruelty*, destroying the prison roof so that the ruins fell down on the nobles and crushed them to death.[25] Niccolò can never resist shocking his readers – most of the early ones are his well-born patrician friends – with examples of power-hungry upper classes getting their comeuppance. He relates them with boyish glee, however, not in hopes that Florentines will lay violent hands on their own elites, but to warn the latter: this is what happens to freedom-killers.

But during the French king's long march towards Naples, not one but two Tuscan cities recovered their long-lost freedom: Florence from the Medici, and Pisa from Florence. Having broken free from their centuries-old chains, the Pisans show to what lengths they will go to preserve their own *libertà*. Thousands of Florentines live in Pisa: merchants, bankers, administrators and government officials, shopkeepers. After King Charles heads south towards Naples, armed Pisan gangs go to their houses and threaten to sack them. Free Pisa's newly organized police quell these threats – for now. But fears grow, and guards are called out to patrol the bridges and Florentine quarters. Florence pays armed bands to harass the country people around Pisa, reminding them who is the true master of the lands all around. The Pisans send ambassadors to the French camp to report these actions. In January 1495, two months after the first rebellion, Pisa's government expels all Florentines from its territories.

On 22 February, French troops take Naples without a siege or battle. In June, Charles passes through Pisa, having assured importunate Florentines that he will restore the rebel city at last. The entire Pisan populace comes out to greet him.[26] Men, women, and the smallest children prostrate themselves at the king's feet, weeping and crying out *Misericordia!* Have pity on us! Even the king's courtiers and armed guards are moved by these laments. His Swiss troops appoint one of their captains, a man called Salzart, to supplicate Charles. 'For the glory of the French crown and the consolation of so many of Your Majesty's loyal soldiers, do not deprive these poor Pisans of the boons that you yourself gave them. If lack of money is what induces Your Majesty to contemplate such a grave injustice,' Herr Salzart continues boldly, 'we soldiers would rather give you our silver chains and the pay and pensions we take from you.' At a ball that night, Charles is seated between two girls, the most beautiful ones there, who beguile him with further entreaties. The king is so bewildered by all this that he leaves the Pisans still in hope. Not long afterwards, however, he makes a firm pact with Florence that Pisa should be theirs. At the end of 1495, Charles's men evacuate Pisa, leaving the city to fight for freedom in whatever way it can.

But the French do not secure Pisa for the Florentines. The fledgling republic would have to do that on its own, or by paying through the nose for occasional French help.

> *So all Tuscany was in confusion; so you lost Pisa*
> *and those states the Medici family gave to the French.*[27]

Florentines had regained free government for themselves, but lost control of their Tuscan empire. In the opinion shared by a majority, the first could not compensate for the second. Pisa is the region's chief port, giving traders direct access to the sea. Beautiful, white-walled Pisa is the glittering jewel in the Florentines' imperial diadem. They could not imagine dominating Tuscany without it.

So the Florentines embark on their new life of freedom, hell-bent on eliminating the freedom of others. The terrible irony in this beginning is not lost on Niccolò Machiavelli; nor is the danger it carries for the new republic's future. Though he later works tirelessly to help his city reconquer Pisa, he worries that his countrymen are so obsessed with depriving others of their freedom that they might fail to nurture their own. Their craving for Pisa would become a poison in the new republic's lifeblood.

8

The Way to Paradise

Two decades later, Niccolò would look back on these first years of
the 1494 republic, compare them with ancient Rome's experience,
and offer these general observations about the perils any newly
liberated city must face. *Infinite examples*, he writes in the *Discourses*,
*show how difficult it is for a people used to living under a prince to preserve
its freedom* if it later becomes free. Liberation, the act of casting off
unwanted rulers, is the easy part. The hard part is to build a free
way of life out of the wreckage left over from decades of oppres-
sion. *For that people is nothing but a brute animal that, although of a
ferocious and feral nature, has always been nourished in prison and in
servitude. Left free in a field to its fate, it becomes the prey of the first one
who seeks to rechain it, not being used to feed itself and not knowing the
places where it may take refuge.*[1]

Only days after King Charles VIII leaves Florence, reports fly
through the city that French troops have butchered eleven old men
in one town over some petty misunderstanding, and ravaged the
surrounding country with fire.[2] No one trusts this king. After all
his solemn promises, he still seems to be playing games over Pisa.

Then new reports start pouring in about Piero de' Medici. After
hearing that he'd been banished for life, together with all the males
of his family, he'd travelled to the king's camp to plead for aid.
According to rumours, Charles received him favourably.

Florentines are tired of being at the mercy of boy tyrants and
foreign monarchs. They want someone to pay for the loss of Pisa,
and for French bullying. The obvious scapegoats are friends of the
Medici, the men who had egged Piero on in his unpopular policies,
and who might secretly try to help him again now. As calls for

revenge grow louder, the entire patrician class lives in dread. If you go back far enough, most of their families had supported or profited from Medici rule at some point in the past sixty years.

Then help comes from a surprising quarter.

To preserve and strengthen your city now, Florentines, you must love one another. The citizens must drop feuds and forget all past offences. God will reward your benevolence.[3]

The friar now preaches almost daily to immense gatherings, in gentler tones than before the great changes took place. At this moment, no man in Florence has more authority than this hollow-cheeked figure in plain habit. Many people believe that the real reason for King Charles's departure was not Capponi's courage or the populace's sullen rattling of sticks and rocks: it was Friar Girolamo's repeated visits to Charles during his stay in Florence, his warnings that the king was going against God's will by pressing the Florentines so hard.[4] Now the crowds at Savonarola's sermons have swollen, according to some estimates, to 13,000 or 14,000 souls. Not everyone there is moved by his appeals for clemency towards Medici partisans. But enough are. The cries for revenge soon grow less shrill.

On 2 December, bells toll to summon a *parlamento*, a gathering of all citizens, in the Piazza della Signoria, organized under their district banners, to start deliberations aimed at overhauling the entire political order. All laws passed since the beginning of Cosimo's regime in 1434 are annulled, and a provisional government is formed to run city affairs until elections can be held in January. Most of its members favour a narrowly based republic run by the wealthy few. But demands for wider participation grow daily. Some patricians, notably Paoloantonio Soderini, speak out in support of a more popular government.[5]

His chief opponent is Guidantonio Vespucci, a lawyer whose face and gestures always have the most wonderfully misleading appearance of openness. 'If the form of government proposed by Paoloantonio could easily produce security and unity,' he says, 'who but the lowest of scoundrels wouldn't want to live in a country where offices are assigned by personal merit and experience, not money or family connections? But history teaches us that the populace lacks the discretion needed to choose wise men over ignorant ones, or good policies over bad. And at this moment, when our city is so weak, it would be folly to put ourselves in the hands of those who have the least skill.'

Yet as leading citizens deliberate over the next days and weeks, those who want a narrow, patrician-led government run into an unexpected difficulty. In his now daily, packed-out sermons, Friar Girolamo takes up the themes being discussed behind closed doors and exposes them to public scrutiny. When he intends to speak more of politics than the salvation of souls, he asks the thousands of women in his congregations to stay home and let the men alone hear what he has to say. And from his pulpit, where he commands more attention than any popular speaker in Christendom, he calls for the most radical reforms Florence has seen for over a century. A new political body should be formed, he declares, from a large number of citizens, and called the Great Council. Here **one citizen will not need to look up to another; every man can consider himself the equal of any other.**[6]

Savonarola's unofficial campaign generates such irresistible popular pressure that the oligarchs have little choice but to go along with it. At the end of December, a new constitution is approved. Its centrepiece is the Great Council, modelled broadly on the main governing assembly in the aristocratic republic of Venice. But in Florence, council members are not a closed, noble caste but a collection of some 3,500 men, more than ever before in Florence's history. Since no room in the government palace is large enough to hold so many, it is resolved that a new Great Hall should be built within the government palazzo.

After the Medici are expelled, Luca Landucci records that 'to everyone who wishes to live quietly and without turmoil, this appears to be the most worthy government that Florence has ever had.'[7]

Their lives are not quiet for long. The basic elements of

Savonarola's programme please those who'd wished for a more popular yet well-ordered government. Bernardo Machiavelli and twenty-five-year-old Niccolò may well have been among its cautious admirers. When Niccolò sets out his own proposals for reforming Florence's government a quarter of a century later, he defends the Great Council and argues that the largest share of power should be given to the *generality of people.*[8]

But the friar's claims about the origins and aspirations of the new republic are another matter.[9] Savonarola preaches that the Great Council is the creation of God, not of men. The new government, he tells Florentines, must become an instrument of divine virtue. In a short time, the city, by forging a government that is more heavenly than mundane, will be filled with true religion. **The people will live amidst rejoicing and the singing of psalms. The boys and girls will be like angels.**

When founding a new republic, Niccolò writes in his *Discourses,* it's wisest *to presuppose that all men are bad, and that they always use the malignity of their spirit whenever they have the opportunity.*[10] Founders of new institutions should assume that a large part of human nature inclines most people to behave badly, at least now and then: to take more than their share of power or wealth, to profit from other people's weaknesses, to cheat, lie, betray promises. Inclinations like these can't be rooted out of our species; human nature itself cannot be reformed so that more and more people become reliably angelic. That is why prudent founders have built strong checks on human badness into their constitutions.

Savonarola's constitution is far less other-worldly than some of his rhetoric. No man in Florence understands better how power may be used and abused. He preaches the evils of tyranny, and has made sure that the new government is vigilant towards overambitious men, and towards those who might want to restore the Medici tyrants. All this, in Machiavelli's accounting, is good. But there is a flaw in the friar's programme. It assumes that, instead of simply regulating the infinite kinds of bad behaviour that disrupt or poison our common life on earth, government should seek to reshape human nature itself, taking pure, bodiless spirits as its model. This aim is unrealistic: it sets the target too high for the poor, flawed beings that most people are. It is also, to use one of Machiavelli's own words, inhuman, since crusades to build heaven on earth usually end up calling for excessively harsh means. And how, he asks, will Florentines find relief when the uphill battle against sin starts to wear us down? Even the most dogged of virtue's warriors need moments of rest. And for each vice you send packing, ten others sprout up in its place.

When this war without end gets too hard, come take refuge in our Company of Pleasure.[11] We offer members a change of air, lest they suffocate from an excess of piety out there in the streets. We're not the most exclusive of clubs; we believe that one should embrace all sorts of people in brotherly love, or sisterly. And we're not, it must be admitted, all that hard on sin. But we do have Company Rules, signed and settled by common agreement, which are most punctiliously enforced:

No man younger than thirty can be of the said Company. The women can be of any age.

The Company shall have a Head, man or woman as it may be, to hold office for eight days. Of the men, the first Head shall be he who has the longer nose, and so in succession; and of the women, she who has the smallest feet, also in succession [the nose and feet being known to correspond inversely to the size of each sex's private parts].

The Company's Members shall always speak badly of each other, and if any strangers stumble into their midst, they will reveal all each other's faults without hesitation.

In order that each may have his opportunity, it is enacted that each man and each woman shall sleep the one without his wife and the other without her husband at least fifteen days every month, under the penalty that husband and wife shall sleep together two months without intermission.

Niccolò's *Articles for a Company of Pleasure* – date of composition unknown – parody the verbose and prudish charters of religious confraternities. The confraternity is a venerable institution in

Florence and elsewhere in Christian Europe, run entirely by lay-men from all walks of life. Some are philanthropic: they raise money to feed the poor, fund orphanages and hospitals, or provide solace to prisoners. Others, known as flagellant confraternities, are less involved with the wider community. Their members seek to repent of their own and society's sins by means of ritual chanting, self-flagellation and sermons they write and deliver themselves.[12] Bernardo Machiavelli belongs to a flagellant organization called the Company of Piety, which meets at the oratory of San Girolamo, on the left bank of the Arno. When Niccolò was eleven, he'd joined the youth branch of his father's confraternity; at twenty-four, in 1493, he moved to the adult organization.

So he writes as an insider. His *Articles* preserve the forms of confraternal statutes but invert their content. Where religious confraternities admit men only, Machiavelli's Company of Pleasure welcomes women as well. The avowed purposes of the former are devotion, penitence, and good works; the sole aim of the latter is to indulge its members' desires for pleasure, not least for sexual titilla-tion. Where a Company of Piety would exhort members to mutual respect and sincerity of heart, no conduct incurs more dreadful penalties in Niccolò's Pleasure Company than honest dealing or straight talking, whether about oneself or anything else. Vainglori-ous pretence reaps the highest rewards, as it often does in the everyday life of laymen and of priests. And it is resolved *that no one is ever to show by external signs the thoughts in his mind; rather, the con-trary shall be done, and he who best knows how to pretend or to tell lies merits most commendation.*

Machiavelli's other writings are full of similar inversions of saintly pieties. His comedy *Mandragola* has a two-faced friar excus-ing his own lies and cupidity with absurdly elaborate, high-minded pretexts. His comic fable *Belfagor* goes in the other direction: it pre-sents all the Princes of Hell as lovers of truth and justice and as sticklers for correct procedure in their councils. Even their master, Pluto, who has absolute powers over the other devils, refrains from exercising them *since*, as Niccolò has him say, *it is the highest prudence for those who are most powerful to be most subject to the laws and to esteem the judgement of others.*[13] Devils who respect the rule of law are worth more, perhaps, than the angels, the priests or the popes who flout it.

But whether he paints devils as models of rectitude or men of angelic ambitions as rogues, the target of Machiavelli's satire is sanctimony: hypocritical or impossible claims to be holy or moral. His message isn't that all moral standards should be lowered, but only those that seek to raise human beings to superhuman perfection.

At the height of Savonarola's influence, in 1495–7, Niccolò most likely attends lectures at the university in Florence, becoming friendly with several men who would soon be his colleagues in the Florentine Chancery. The up-and-coming classical scholar Marcello Virgilio Adriani, who helps Niccolò secure his first political post as Second Chancellor to the Republic; Agostino Vespucci, a lover of fine modern art and nephew of Savonarola's arch-enemy Messer Guidantonio; the camp, generous-hearted Filippo Casavecchia.[14] These young men are steeped in ancient writings, Greek and Latin, and share a secular turn of mind. Most are at an age when, if not already married, they are expected to wed and become heads of household within the next five years or so: thirty to thirty-one is the average age of marriage for Florentine men of the middling to upper classes. These men gamble, throw wine-sodden parties, read and compose obscene verses, visit women of dubious repute. Be ready, one friend writes to the absent Niccolò, for some action when you get back to Florence, *for she is waiting for you with open figs, and stands at her window like a hawk, you know who I'm talking about!*[15] Niccolò seems to have been on particularly intimate terms with a courtesan known as La Riccia, Curly Lady, with whom he is later accused, anonymously, of committing the unmentionable vice; though most sodomy charges were brought against male-on-male intercourse, Florentine laws also punish it when one or both parties were female.

At an unknown date, but probably not long after joining the Company of Piety, he accepts an invitation to deliver a sermon on penitence to another confraternity, the Company of Charity.[16]

'Consider all the benefits we get from God,' Niccolò tells his brethren from the pulpit, 'and how much punishment man deserves when he perverts the use of these things and turns them towards evil. That tongue made to glorify God blasphemes Him; that mouth, through which he must be fed, he makes into a sewer, and a passageway for satisfying the appetite and the belly with delicate and superfluous food, for lust and many other dissipations. *Saints! O mercy!*'

If any of his companions in what Savonarola calls sin heard Machiavelli preach, they must have admired his mastery of puritanical language. He invokes St Francis and St Jerome (Girolamo, Savonarola's namesake), how they would roll in thorns and tear their breasts with a stone in order to restrain their flesh and take from it the means for driving them to sin. So far, the same wrenching, emotional fare served up by most flagellant sermons.

'And yet,' Niccolò goes on, 'how useful are the scourge and whiplash? The rigours of such vengeance would make it impossible to save anyone. And again, it is not enough to repent and to weep. One must also prepare oneself by means of actions opposed to the sin.'

To correct our sins towards God and man, he tells his congregation, we need not whips or thorns or tears, but charity. 'This word means more than giving alms to the poor, raising money for orphanages and hospitals, or finding confessors for men condemned to death. True charity is being friendly to your neighbour, helping him in need, patiently tolerating his faults, consoling him in his tribulations. Charity involves teaching the ignorant, advising him who errs, helping the good, and punishing evil. This, my Fathers and Brothers, is the only thing that guides our souls to heaven. It is the only thing that has more worth than all the other virtues of men.'

All this has much in common with certain ancient understandings of religion that focus on this-worldly conduct towards one's fellow humans rather than on the afterlife, or on the purity of individual souls. Since human weaknesses are part of our God-given make-up, the preacher suggests next, what sense is there in beating people up if they fall into them now and then?

'Those who rush to judge others harshly, being impatient with human flaws, lack charity. A generous God does not rejoice in ferreting out every human error.' *Charity is patient, and kindly. It does not delight in the wicked man, but meditates upon him. This is that celestial garment in which we must be clad if we are to be admitted to the marriage feast of our Emperor Jesus Christ in the kingdom of heaven!*

The language and imagery are irreproachably Christian. The speaker says not a word to raise devout eyebrows; towards the end he even turns up the volume on his evangelical rhetoric. Yet his sermon sets out common ground that the secular-minded, even the pagan, can share with at least some of their more pious fellow humans. It treats outward actions as more important than inner spirituality, and the considerate treatment of others as the best way to heaven – whatever the word 'heaven' may signify to you. This is typical Machiavelli: while seeming to share his audience's idioms and purposes, whether holy or unholy, he quietly pushes the conversation in a direction he deems more reasonable – less polemical, less extreme, and more sensitive to what is both difficult and decent about our shared humanity. He ends his performance with a flourish in the best tradition of his flagellant brethren, declaiming:

'We are deceived by lust, involved in transgressions, and enmeshed by the snares of sin and find ourselves in the hands of the Devil. Hence, to get out of it, we must resort to penitence and cry out with David: Have mercy on me, oh God! and with St Peter weep bitterly, and for all the faults we have committed feel shame

'And repent and know clearly
that what delights the world is a short dream.'

All this, again, delivered in perfect Christian-flagellant idiom – except the last words. They come not from the mouth of a saint or the Prophet David, but from his fellow-poet Petrarch, who, though a devout Christian, had done more than any other man to revive the pagan culture of the ancients.[17] The lines come from the first of

Petrarch's *Sonnets*. Their theme is the very earthly love of a young man pining away for a married, and therefore unavailable, woman. The poet repents for his 'fault' of romantic self-indulgence, for wallowing in endless woes of frustrated desire. He seeks 'pity, and forgiveness, for all the varied ways in which I talk and weep'.

An older Niccolò would express similar feelings of helpless embarrassment in his loves. He would surely have sympathized with Petrarch's young lover. With the poet's voice, he calls on his brethren to remember their own youthful passions and shames. Is love sin if it cannot receive the sacrament of marriage, or procreate? Does this exquisite suffering of mind and flesh deserve the whip and the pillory? Sometimes it produces works of great beauty that console us and raise our thoughts above ourselves. Be careful, my brothers, what you call mortal sin and how you punish it.

Machiavelli would never be a conventional Christian – if he considered his beliefs as Christian at all. Like his father, he observes religious traditions for the sake of family and community: he joins confraternities, baptizes his children, accepts last confession, and occasionally donates money to churches. But his beliefs have little in common with most Florentines' intense Christianity, with its cults of saints and adoration of the man-god Christ. The figure of Christ makes precious few appearances in Machiavelli's writings. When he does appear, it is as the founder of a well-intentioned yet unworldly religion whose followers soon corrupted his teachings with their sectarian brawls.[18]

Niccolò's preferred religion is one without what he calls 'sects', a word he uses – always scathingly – for disputatious club-like groupings, political or religious. The worst religious sects are those whose members claim to possess the truth about *things natural and supernatural* that *we do not have* and perhaps never can.[19] But if we cannot learn how to behave from God's commands because human minds are too feeble to access such commands, or even to know whether they exist, this doesn't mean that there are no well-founded moral standards at all. For Niccolò, the main truths that pertain to a suitably human-sized religion have to do with correct behaviour towards other people, with morality.[20] This is why, as he insists in his sermon on penitence, charitable conduct towards one's fellow man is the best way to repent of human faults. Unchanging, universal moral truths can be worked out through a close study of human interactions and reflections on human nature. History is an especially good aid to this study; drama, poetry and fables are others. It needs no special education or intellectual skills to undertake it. We are all students of morality in our way, every day asking whether and why our own and others' actions deserve praise or blame. As for whether there is a God who created and oversees human life, Machiavelli does not claim to know one way or another. At most he implies that, if our own judicious reasoning tells us that certain actions deserve praise and others blame, it is also reasonable to believe that some higher power underwrites those judgements.

But if moral truths are to penetrate people's minds and move them from within, individuals need to come to them in their own way, at their own speed, following their own reason and conscience rather than the self-righteous doctrines of sects or prophets. *I believe,* Niccolò writes to a friend in 1506, *that just as Nature has created men with different faces, so she has created them with different intellects and imaginations. As a result, each man behaves according to his own intellect and imagination,* and believes or does not believe in higher powers, according to his own mind.[21] There is room for worshipful awe of transcendent powers in Machiavelli's religion: sometimes he calls them 'God', sometimes 'the gods', sometimes 'the heavens'. But when men claim to know more about those powers' purposes than our human shortcomings allow us to know, they overstep a line – and flirt with disaster by acting, or encouraging others to act, on presumptive knowledge that is no knowledge at all.

Why, Niccolò would later ask, did tens of thousands of Florentines rush to throw all their hopes into one threadbare friar's lap, make him master of their minds, make every political decision depend on his words?[22] No one could say it was because the people are naturally credulous and full of superstition. Unlettered plebs are hardly alone in venerating Savonarola as a prophet sent to guide Florence out of the wilderness. Some of the city's most brilliant men, the likes of Pico della Mirandola and Marsilio Ficino – you can't find men of greater learning anywhere in the world – have become his ardent disciples. Bartolomeo Scala has joined the friar's partisans, along with Paoloantonio Soderini and hundreds of other sophisticated men. *The people of Florence do not appear to themselves as ignorant or coarse*, Niccolò observes. A mischievous understatement: in fact, they boast about their business shrewdness and native wit and education, their ability to see through clouds of rhetoric in the courtroom and halls of government. *Nonetheless, they were persuaded by Friar Girolamo Savonarola that he spoke with God. I do not*, our writer adds with a touch of mock-politeness, *wish to judge whether this is true or not, because one should speak with reverence of such a man. But I do say that an infinite number believed him without having seen anything extraordinary to make them believe him.*

Savonarola's sermons already count for more than political debate. Prophecies prevail over evidence; terrifying visions trump reasoned arguments. Florence relies for its defences on one friar and his prophecies. But *a city based on good laws and good orders has no necessity, as have others, for the virtue of a single man to maintain it.*[23] If Lorenzo was a tyrant, one must wonder about Savonarola. He already wields more power than any elected magistrate, directing everything from behind the scenes through his devoted partisans in the magistracies and the Great Council. As long as the people keep leaning on him, they would never learn how to reason for themselves about internal and external defence.

Now exiled in Rome, Piero and Cardinal Giovanni de' Medici make sure that their agents and allies bombard the pope with reports of Savonarola's audacities. He has cast an evil spell over the Florentines, they say, making them change their government into a tyranny of heretics. And he blasphemes by pretending to be a prophet, God's chosen mouthpiece. It is a grave sin for any man to claim such an office for himself, an office near to that of angels.

On 21 July 1495, the friar receives an invitation from Pope

Alexander VI to pay him a visit in the Vatican.[24] We have heard, the pope writes, that you have a most extraordinary gift of being able to foretell future things by divine revelation. It would please us if you would come here to tell us more about this ability.

The letter could not appear friendlier. But Savonarola and his colleagues immediately recognize it for what it is: an order that will brook no refusal, addressed to a friar famous throughout Europe for his vehement denunciations of corruption in the Church. Friar Girolamo had prudently avoided naming names when he castigated the prelates in Rome whose simony, nepotism, and fornications were the root of all the vices in Christendom. But he had also avoided calling Lorenzo a tyrant while he lived, though everyone knew whom he meant; the same was true now. And even if he could ignore the implied personal offence, the pope knows that Savonarola's unheard-of popularity makes him a dangerous role model for other renegade clergy, who could use the pulpit to attack the authority of the papacy.

Savonarola writes back with the most profuse apologies, pleading persistent fevers, dysentery, and stomach ailments as the main cause preventing His Holiness's humble servant from doing whatever would gratify him. Besides which, he adds, his friends and brothers at San Marco have urged him not to travel abroad; they fear for his life. In September, another letter from the pope arrives in Florence. This time there is no pretence of goodwill: Friar Savonarola is accused point-blank of propagating heresies and schisms under cover of a 'feigned simplicity'. He is therefore forbidden to preach for whatever period is needed to complete an inquiry into his teachings.

For 120 days, from mid-October 1495 to 11 February 1496, Savonarola does not preach. He uses the time to write treatises on government and on matters of the spirit; his followers copy them or have them printed, and they are widely read. For the Florentines, whether they support the friar's works or oppose them, this state of affairs is a nerve-wracking limbo. Sceptics are growing angrier. *Questo fratuccio ci fa capitare male*, they say: this friarling will bring us evil.[25] On 1 January 1496, French castellans give the Pisan fortresses back to the Pisans. So now, the friar's critics rage, the results of all his divinely inspired diplomacy are clear as day – the French king never meant to keep his promises, he's been stringing us along! A mob surrounds the entrance of San Marco, screaming, 'This pig of a monk, we'll burn the house over his head!'

All this is music to the ears of those Florentines who want to silence Savonarola. In public and in government consultations, Guidantonio Vespucci and Bernardo Rucellai take care to speak respectfully of the city's revered visionary. But behind the scenes they orchestrate a smear campaign. Keep up pressure on the pope. Make sure word gets to Rome that, even now, while he's forbidden to preach, Savonarola spreads heretical lies and makes himself de facto leader of a political party here. He'll not stop until he's greater than the pope himself; perhaps he wants to usurp his Holy Seat. And tens of thousands can testify that he makes wild claims for his own prophetic powers: **Believe me, Florence. You have heard with your ears not me but God. You say I am crazy? But you ought to believe, because you have already seen a great many of the things I have preached here verified.**[26] The deaths of Lorenzo de' Medici and Pope Innocent; the city's recent change of government.

In February 1496, Pope Alexander gives his permission for Savonarola to preach again. Carnival festivities begin soon after. Florentines scarcely recognize their old pagan street-feast. On corners where gangs used to fleece passers-by, polluting their ears with curses if they refused to pay a toll to pass, one now sees boys chanting hymns with crosses in their hands, requesting alms for the poor. Everyone dresses according to strict codes passed in the Great Council. Boys' hair must be cut short around the ear. French-style men's purses, all the rage, have been banned.

Every corner of the Duomo is packed for the friar's cycle of Lenten sermons. The period of banning has made him even more of a celebrity. With his strangely electrifying presence, Savonarola again proves himself a master of the religious theatre so beloved by

Florentines.[27] High stands are erected in the churches where he preaches and lined with a host of children whose ethereal singing echoes through the vault and reaches towards the heavens. On Palm Sunday, he musters a procession of boys and girls, thousands of them, from all ranks of Florentine society, some as young as five years old, all dressed in purest dove-white with olive wreaths on their heads. They move slowly through the streets, holding little red crosses and olive branches, singing the glory of Christ. Their numbers and discipline are mind-boggling. Even his critics grudgingly admit that there is something miraculous here: it seems impossible that merely human means could bring about such a change in the city's shameless boys. His colleagues from San Marco order their child-cadres to help them build a Bonfire of Vanities: an octagonal pyramid ninety feet high erected with scaffolding, then laden with objects gathered from houses and unwary strollers by patrols of boys. Luxuriously bound books by Petrarch and Virgil are consigned to flame; so are statues of half-clad Roman and Florentine women sculpted by Donatello and other great masters. Gunpowder is placed beneath the edifice, making it boom and sparkle like fireworks as heaps of vanities go to ash.

Florence's bawdy ancient revelries are being twisted into something frightening. The friar's opponents hound Ricciardo Becchi, Florentine ambassador to the pope, with charges they want him to convey to His Holiness. *Savonarola's sermons continue to insult the papacy and the whole Curia*, Becchi tells Alexander in March.[28] *The whole world should know that Friar Girolamo and children now govern Florence. Citizens are afraid of them; they lack the courage to speak up or propose measures against the friar's will.* Niccolò and his dice-playing, abomination-seeking friends no doubt agree with the last of these complaints. These cleaned-up persecutors of all earthly pleasures are worse than the old gangs that used to torment pedestrians on dark alleys, low-life who'd hawk their little backsides to any pot-bellied banker for a few *grossi*. The friar's boys bear down like buzzards on pretty women, practically skinning them alive. Now there is drabness where there used to be colour. No poetry is safe, no great art, none of the joyful lusts of spring. Meanwhile, the plague is back. The Great Council elects four citizens to try to contain it by sanitary measures and medical advice, and to assist the poor who fall sick. In April, Florentines hear that it had rained blood over two gates in nearby Siena. And now a new disease is spreading fast, called 'French boils' because French troops had brought it into Italy: syphilis. Since doctors have no idea how to treat it, their remedies often make it worse.

At the end of April the following year, city heralds make a frightening announcement: Piero de' Medici is at Siena with a large body of soldiers, and planning an attack with the help of Florence's enemies. Guards are placed around the walls throughout the night. On 28 April 1497, he arrives at Fonte di San Gaggio on the outskirts of the city with 2,000 men on foot and horseback. Leading citizens take up their swords and go out to the gate of San Piero Gattolino. A few hours later, at around five in the afternoon, news flies through the streets that the Medici party had turned back. Relief, but the threat of their return still seems imminent.

And there is still no peace for Savonarola. He now finds himself besieged by vigilantes inside Florence who smear dirt on his pulpit and disrupt his sermons, and by further attempts to shut him down issuing from Rome. A papal bull is read out in every quarter of Florence. Friar Girolamo is declared excommunicate and summoned to meet the pope straightaway. No one may give him aid, or go to hear him speak, on pain of excommunication.

Then, in early August, as people continue to die from plague, from infectious fevers and heat exhaustion, more news: someone has admitted under torture to plotting to return Piero de' Medici and his brothers to Florence. The men fingered as co-conspirators include five highly respected citizens, among them the young and popular Lorenzo Tornabuoni and the septuagenarian Bernardo del Nero, a close political friend of the oligarch powerbrokers Bernardo Rucellai and Guidantonio Vespucci. The five are arrested and accused of crimes against the state. On 17 August, after a discussion lasting from morning to midnight, a court dominated by Savonarola's followers condemns the prisoners to death.[29]

The friar's opponents are convinced that Savonarola's supporters want to destroy del Nero because he'd been at the head of the anti-Savonarolan party. 'How can they think of killing men of such quality, when no real harm was done in the end?' an anguished Bernardo Rucellai explodes. At a meeting of some 200 citizens formed to discuss the case, Guidantonio Vespucci mobilizes his peerless legal and rhetorical skills on behalf of the condemned.

'Let us remember,' he urges, 'that we have here in Florence a law of appeal. It states that any citizen condemned to death for political reasons should have the right to appeal to the Great Council. This law was originally proposed and pushed through by Friar Girolamo Savonarola himself.' His partisans would find it hard to refuse the Five an appeal according to their friar's own law.

'So,' retorts Francesco Valori, leader of the pro-Savonarolan party, 'now the friends of these traitors are invoking the same law of appeal they called outrageous when we proposed it, saying it was madness to submit matters of treason to an assembly of ignorant donkeys!' The debate is taken to the Signoria, where discussions soon degenerate into a brawl. 'Either the convicted men die, or I do!' shouts Valori. Another Savonarola partisan shoves the moderate Piero Guicciardini towards the high window of the government palazzo and seems close to tossing him out. At the final vote, appeal is denied. That same evening, the condemned men are given confession and decapitated in the courtyard of the Bargello prison.

The summary execution casts a black cloud over the young republic. When Machiavelli later discusses the events that led to it, his dismay at its supporters' lack of foresight is audible. *I do not believe,* he declares, *that anything can set a more wicked example in a republic than to make a law and not observe it, and so much the more as it is not observed by him who made it.*[30] He illustrates this maxim with the case at hand. *Florence after '94 had been reordered in its state by the aid of Friar Girolamo Savonarola. He had a law made so that one could appeal to the people* – the citizens assembled in the Great Council – *from sentences of treason* passed by the Signoria. Savonarola *urged this law for a long time and obtained it with the greatest difficulty.* When soon afterwards these five citizens were condemned to death by the Signoria and asked to appeal, *they were not allowed to, and the law was not observed.*

This, for Niccolò, was a fatal political error that *took away more reputation from the friar* than anything else. The episode showed that there was one law for Savonarola's friends, another for his enemies. It proved that, far from rising above the muck of partisan strife, he was as contaminated by it as his worldly detractors. The only hope for managing such strife is for members of every party and sect to obey the same laws and apply them impartially. If a law is generally useful, it ought to be applied in every case without exception. If the friar's law of appeal was not generally useful, *he should not have had it passed.* When it was not applied in this case, Machiavelli notes, people immediately began to accuse Savonarola and his partisans of hypocrisy. His silence on the matter *after the law had been broken* made manifest the friar's *ambitious and partisan spirit and brought him very much disapproval.* And henceforth he could add to the already long list of people who wanted his downfall – oligarchs who hated the Great Council, or proponents of a more secular republic – anyone whose friends or relatives had been executed without appeal, and those who cared about the strict impartiality of the laws.

By the summer of 1497, Savonarola is preaching again, in defiance of the pope's orders. Yet the ranks of his devotees are diminishing, many of them terrified of excommunication if they are seen near him. His enemies are growing more pugnacious. In February 1498, a new festive company whose members call themselves Compagnacci, 'the bad comrades', launch a battle to reconquer Carnival for the pagans.[31] Parades of cross-bearing children are joined by men in outrageous drag who howl: 'Carnival is forced to flee the city where everyone has become a friar!' A gang of toughs pelts the friar's angels with stones; one of them grabs a red cross from a boy's hand and smashes it. 'Take their crosses!' they all start screaming. 'Throw them in the Arno!'

Sometime during the same month, Florence's ambassador to the pope, Ricciardo Becchi, contacts Niccolò Machiavelli. We do not know how they came to know each other, only that by early 1498 Niccolò has decided to throw his hat into the political ring: he stands as a candidate for First Secretary of the Signoria. Perhaps because of his anti-Savonarolan leanings, he fails to win the necessary votes. But to be considered for such a post, he would need some powerful supporters in government circles.

Now, probably backed by other critics of Savonarola's politics, Becchi enlists Machiavelli's talents in debunking illusions to help the anti-Savonarolan cause. Becchi had never had much sympathy for Savonarola's crusade; by now, he had lost all patience with the friar's rebellion against papal authority. He knows what serious trouble is brewing for Florence inside the Vatican and beyond. Piero de' Medici's envoys and foreign allies are deep in talks with Pope Alexander VI about how to rid the city of its false prophet. The most efficacious way, some of the pope's advisers propose, would be to use arms to return the Medici to their homeland.

Among Niccolò's many reasons to join anti-Savonarolan forces, this one may be decisive. His activities seem to have been low-key: mainly gathering information to help Becchi assess Friar Girolamo's state of mind, on the one hand, and popular feelings towards him on the other. In brazen defiance of his excommunication, Savonarola has been delivering sermons at the Duomo for the Carnival season. Machiavelli goes to church several times in late February and early March and reports what he hears to Ambassador Becchi.[32] His own hopes of a political career might well depend on Savonarola's declining fortunes.

On the Sunday of Carnival, he joins the nervous crowd pouring into the cathedral. At the end of the sermon, the friar invites the whole congregation to come to his own church of San Marco on Carnival Day to take Communion with him. 'I will pray to God,' he says, 'that if what I predict does not come from Him on high, He might display a very clear sign of it. Indeed,' he goes on, '**when you see me holding the Sacrament in my hand at Communion, pray, every one of you,**

85

make a fervid plea to the Lord that if this work does not come from Him, He will send a fire to consume me in Hell.'[33]

Niccolò later sits down to write all this in his letter to Becchi. He is unimpressed by the preacher's histrionics, smelling in them the calculations of a demagogue. To him, the friar's prayers and prophecies are nothing but self-serving rhetorical manipulations, which he, at least, sees straight through. 'Some say he asked for a sign,' he tells Becchi, 'in order to unite his partisans and strengthen their defence of him. It seems he fears that the new Signoria, whose names have been chosen but not yet made public, might be filled with his opponents.' A new Signoria consisting of nine men, together with a head of government, the Gonfalonier of Justice, are chosen by lot every two months; most of Florence's other magistracies have somewhat longer six- or eight-month terms. For the past three years, the Signoria had often been packed with Savonarola's friends, who'd defended him against the pope and let him preach despite the interdictions. If the new government came out overwhelmingly hostile, Niccolò suggests, the friar's game might be up.

Savonarola *delineated two ranks of people: one that soldiered under God, that is, himself and his adherents; the other, under the Devil, that is, his adversaries.* Here is a feature of Savonarola's recent sermons that Niccolò finds catastrophic for Florence: his rhetoric, at first used for civil peace, has over time become ferociously divisive. He splits the whole city into the good and the wicked, into angels and demons, locked in a holy and potentially deadly struggle for the city's soul. Now that he's declared open war, what room is there for seeking common ground? It's us against them, and someone – half the city – must lose.

In order to weaken his adversaries further, Savonarola *pointed out that our discords might cause a tyrant to rise up who would bring down our houses and waste our land.* Another cheap orator's trick, the easiest way to get a mob's jaws drooling for a fight: scaremongering. Take my side and attack now, or your houses and land will be sacked. How helpful in a republic where civil decency still has the feeblest of roots! *He made so much of this,* Niccolò says with a wink at his comrade-in-arms Becchi, *that people speculated publicly about someone who is about as close to being a tyrant as you are to Heaven.*

The hotter the rhetoric, the colder Niccolò grows. He is young, pleased with his own sharp, lively brain, in whose company it is impossible to be bored with this world. There are still a few independent minds in Florence, although, like independents everywhere, they need lion-like ferocity to survive. He doesn't want his city to fall further under the sway of people who expect the Florentines to succumb to conjurer's tricks and unreal hopes of paradise on earth. He stands back from the heat and the roiling crowd and analyses the friar's rhetoric with clinical detachment. Many of his contemporaries who study classic rhetorical techniques – those who become highly paid lawyers or hold important public offices – do so with a view to using them as weapons to win legal and political battles. Niccolò is just as interested in exposing rhetorical tricks and sleights of hand.

And now, in his twenty-ninth year, he will show Ambassador Becchi and whoever else might read his report how well he can read hidden motives and spot manipulations behind the most accomplished oratory – talents that Florence's political leaders might put to some good use.

A few weeks after Niccolò attended Savonarola's incendiary sermons, the friar's fellow priest at San Marco, Domenico da Pescia, issues an extraordinary challenge to a Franciscan brother from Santa Croce who had been castigating Friar Girolamo in his sermons. 'Shall we,' da Pescia demands, 'put your slanders to the test? Let us both walk through the fire to see which of us holds the truth!'[34]

News of the friars' war spreads fast, even to the countryside. On 29 March, a delegation of friars comes to the government palazzo to inform the authorities of their holy duel and request moral and logistical support. A meeting is called to discuss the matter.[35]

'A depraved and adulterous people looks for miraculous signs,' quips Guidantonio Vespucci, quoting the Apostle Matthew. 'We should prevail on these friars to try some less homicidal sort of test.'

But others urge that they should be allowed to go ahead. If these friars walk through fire, someone says, they'll die. If they die, the city can finally be united. So let the thing proceed.

Two platforms are erected in front of the Palazzo della Signoria: one for Signori and leading citizens, the other for the warring friars. The latter is some twenty-seven yards long, lined with a low wall of unbaked bricks. Logs are stacked on either side to just over a yard's height; twigs and brushwood are stuffed around them. All this wood is saturated with inflammable oil, resin, spirits and gunpowder. A Dominican friar is to enter at one end of the crackling inferno, a Franciscan at the other.

On 7 April, at the appointed hour, two processions arrive in the Piazza della Signoria. First the Franciscans come and proceed to the Loggia de' Signori, which has been divided in the middle to accommodate both groups of adversaries. Then, with great pomp, come some 250 Dominicans, followed by Friar Domenico and Girolamo Savonarola, who holds a crucifix and a Eucharist. A crowd trails behind them with torches and tapers, singing psalms. After they say Mass, the people – all men, for women and children have been forbidden to come – wait for the spectacle to begin. Personal weapons have been banned from the square, but the Signoria's troops stand guard with swords and spears. The government has further authorized a group of anti-Savonarolan Compagnacci to guard one side of the piazza, while a company of 300 soldiers raised by the friar's supporters is posted near the Dominican side of the loggia. All foreigners other than hired soldiers have been ordered to leave Florence for the occasion. Whatever the outcome of the friars' war, the city's enemies will be looking for any excuse to exploit it for their own ends.

With the thick crowd held back by soldiers, most spectators are too far away to hear or see much; they strain to catch a glimpse of the protagonists. Hours pass. Those who can see far enough spread the word that groups of friars from both sides keep going in and out of the Palazzo della Signoria. The delay, it transpires, has been caused by disputes between the friars about their proper attire for performing a trial by fire. Out in the piazza, people start to grow impatient. Each side's supporters complain that their opponent is trying to get out of it. Coward, they growl. Fraud.

And then comes the rain. A storm pounds the log-heaped platform with hailstones. The drenched throng barely budges. 'You see,' cry out Savonarola's faithful, 'a clear sign from God that Friar Girolamo is truly a holy prophet!' 'A sign,' others shoot back, 'that he uses witchcraft or some other dark powers to stop a trial that will prove him a charlatan.' At last the Signoria rise to go inside the government palazzo and the crowd disperses.

The diarist Luca Landucci, a stalwart defender of Savonarola to the last, was among the crowds of expectant men in the piazza. The Dominicans' anticlimactic departure, he reports, 'caused great perturbance among the people, who had almost lost faith in the prophet'. Savonarola's enemies leap at the chance to vilify him and taunt his followers. On the walk home to San Marco, though surrounded by a guard of municipal and private troops, the friar is subjected to violent abuse. Here, Niccolò Machiavelli will point out in his *Prince*, lies the problem for anyone who relies on prophecies to win supporters. Like others who rise to great authority without the benefit of public office or an army, Savonarola *was ruined in his new orders as soon as the multitude began not to believe in them, and he had no way to hold firm those who had believed nor for making unbelievers believe*.[36] A few days later, Florentines learn that France's King Charles VIII, whom Savonarola had once proclaimed the God-sent liberator of Florence, had died on that same day. Friar Girolamo had not predicted that death. But he had been anticipating his own for a long time.

Countless travails had weighed heavily on Florentines since the French came in 1494. But as Niccolò's *Decennale* says about the events of that year, in a direct address to 'you' Florentines:

> *that which to many was far more distressing*
> *and made for disunion, was that school*

under whose sign your city lay.
I speak of that great Savonarola who, inspired by divine virtue,
kept you tightly rapt with his word.
But since many feared to see their country ruined, little by little,
under his prophetic teaching,
no ground for your reunion could be discovered,
unless his light divine either continued to increase
or was extinguished by a greater fire.[37]

On Palm Sunday, the day after the fireless trial of friars, Savonarola's enemies enter the churches and assume thuggish postures behind rows of praying women. They strike the backs of their seats and spit curses. *Andate con Dio, piagnonacci!* they bellow at the terrified matrons: 'Go with God, you weeping, wailing hags!' Trying to flee, many faithful are struck and wounded.

Soon the whole city is up in arms. The Compagnacci lead a mob to the convent of San Marco. More and more men and children join them on the way, grabbing stones to hurl at the fraudster friar and his accomplices. Savonarola's steadfast friends from the populace, women and men, including Landucci, are in the church there; the diarist records that if he'd not managed to escape through the cloister, the attackers might well have killed him.[38] Town criers now issue a proclamation: the government will pay 1,000 ducats to anyone who captures Savonarola and delivers him to the authorities.

Suddenly, the game has changed. Yesterday, government troops shielded Friar Girolamo on his walk home; now, he and his loyal disciples can no longer count on official protection. His once vociferous champions among the populace bite their tongues, in fear of their lives. His leading partisans try to go into hiding.

At around six in the evening, a group of men swarm into the Piazza della Signoria. They rush to the Valori palazzo, home of the Savonarola partisans' leader, and begin pillaging and burning. Peering out from an upstairs window, Valori's wife is struck by an arrow shot from a crossbow and dies on the spot. His children and their nursemaids too are injured in the raid. Francesco Valori himself is tracked down and, approached from behind, struck with a bill-hook that splits open his skull. His killers are relatives of the men who, at Valori's impassioned urgings, had been summarily executed eight months before.

The mob then turn to sack the house of Paoloantonio Soderini. On Machiavelli's account, the assailants find Paoloantonio's younger brother at home. Francesco Soderini, a respected man of the cloth and the Bishop of Volterra, would soon become Niccolò's chief political mentor.[39] *Having heard the noise and seen the disturbance,* Francesco stayed calm. He *at once put on his most honourable clothes and over them the episcopal rochet,* the short garment worn for certain functions by dignitaries of the Church. Protected by this ecclesiastical armour, he *put himself against those who were armed, and with presence and with words stopped them. That affair,* writes Niccolò some twenty-five years after the event, *was noted and celebrated through all the city for many days.* Valori's murderers are never tried or arrested. A general amnesty declared later that month pardons all crimes committed on the bloody days of 8–9 April 1498.

At around two in the morning on the ninth, after the friars of San Marco had put up a brave defence against their attackers, Savonarola, Domenico da Pescia, and their associate Friar Silvestro Maruffi are arrested and taken into custody. The magistracies of the Ten of War and Eight of Security – bodies in charge, respectively, of Florence's military matters and its internal and external defence – are re-elected in the Great Council and filled with men trusted by the anti-Savonarolan leadership.

Then a council is convened to decide whether and how to interrogate Savonarola and his two associates.[40] 'Our city,' Bernardo Rucellai reminds colleagues, 'is very weak. Its seduction by the friar has left us without friends in Italy nor outside. So we should examine these friars with the greatest diligence. But also bear in mind,' he adds, 'what might ensue if Friar Girolamo confesses that he intrigued against the city with many citizens, not just a few friars.'

This has the desired effect. Rucellai insinuates that anyone who had ever defended Savonarola might easily fall under suspicion. Some such men had already left the city for their safety; others are here in the room. So they keep silent while their fellow citizens call on the government to interrogate the three friars 'with every possible licence'. They have lied and deceived our people for years, several say. Do whatever it takes to squeeze them now. No one dares to call for a fair trial. Savonarola's friends had denied his enemies the right of appeal less than a year before. Now his enemies would deny him the full benefit of the law.

Once Florence's saviour, now Savonarola is to be made its scapegoat – for Pisa, for French perfidy, for Florence's isolation in Italy, for Piero de' Medici's constant machinations; for all of the city's self-mutilating dissensions. Friar Girolamo is put to several bouts of the *strappado,* the same torture machine that will be used to interrogate Niccolò Machiavelli almost fifteen years later. The examinee's arms are lashed behind his back with a strap tied to a crane-like machine that jerks his whole body up above ground, wrenching his arms from their sockets. Eventually, the friar pleads for mercy and confesses to whatever charges his interrogators want to pin on him.

Some points in his confession are purely religious in nature, sins rather than crimes in civil law. He has tried to foster a schism in the Church. He has lied to all the people about being a God-sent prophet, saying and doing everything not for God's eternal glory but for his own worldly ambitions. By making these confessions public, the new government hopes to administer a shocking dose of their version of reality to the whole city, purging believers of their illusions. Parts of them are read out to the Great Council, to the heartbreaking distress of Savonarola's devotees. 'I was present,' Luca Landucci writes in his diaries, 'when the statement was read. My heart was grieved to see such an edifice fall to the ground, having been founded on a lie. Florence had been expecting a New Jerusalem, from which would issue just laws and splendour and an example of righteous living.'

But if they want to dispose of the friar once and for all, and to do it in Florence, not Rome, the anti-Savonarolans need to build a criminal case in civil law as well. So they persuade Savonarola to confess that all his activities in Florence were aimed at gradually taking complete control of the city's governing organs. He was leader of a conspiracy whose sole purpose was to make himself great. He had formed the nucleus of a secret and illegal political party based in San Marco. He had used spies to obtain political secrets. By supporting the creation of a private army for his own protection, he had shown that he was prepared to use arms against his adversaries and, eventually, against the state. And he had conspired with foreign princes in hopes of creating a new universal Council of the Church in rebellion against Rome.

What sentence could these crimes possibly deserve except death? But should the other two friars receive the same punishment as their ringleader, or should the city's new secular leadership show mercy? At a meeting called to discuss these questions, most leading citizens – those who aren't still outside Florence, fearing further vengeful attacks – call for distinctions to be made against those who committed crimes with malicious intent and those who thought they were doing good. Apply the laws severely to the former, they urge. Towards the others, use temperance and show humane mercy, *umanità*.

Guidantonio Vespucci and Bernardo Rucellai are of a different opinion. 'Those who say the laws should be observed speak well,' says Vespucci. 'But our laws are unclear about how to ascertain greater or lesser degrees of guilt in cases of treason. Since I don't know how to distinguish between one and the others, I say either condemn all the perpetrators, or give them all absolution.'

This view prevails, and Savonarola and his two colleagues are hanged on 23 May. Friar Girolamo is forty-five years old at his death. The bodies are then burnt at the stake in the Piazza della Signoria. Gunpowder is mixed in the flames to produce a fearsome noise of explosions and cracking. Government authorities order the executioners to stir the ashes more thoroughly than usual, so that no scrap of flesh or cloth remains which could be made an object of future veneration.

For all his distaste for Savonarola's methods, it is doubtful that Niccolò Machiavelli agreed with the partisan and questionably legal tactics of the friar's chief opponents.

> *What is most pernicious is to see how the promoters and princes of parties give a decent appearance to their aims with a pious word. For always, though they are all enemies of freedom, they oppress it under colour of defending the state either of the optimates or of the people. For the prize they desire to win is not the glory of having liberated the city, but the satisfaction of having overcome others and usurped the principality of the city. Having been led to this point, there is nothing so unjust, so cruel, or so mean that they don't dare to do it.*[41]

Niccolò knew that men like Vespucci and Rucellai wanted to bring back a government of patricians and diminish, or get rid of, the Great Council. Their vision of redemptive unity was thoroughly partisan, its terms decided by a few great men and imposed on the *popolo* by intimidation and mob rule, the latter orchestrated by mainly upper-class Compagnacci. Such union never lasts long; and Florence had not heard the last of Savonarola's chastened supporters.

But for now, Niccolò benefits from the death of open Savonarolan politics. Three weeks later, on 19 June, amid rioting throughout the city, he is elected to his first public post. He is now Second Chancellor of the Republic, replacing a deposed follower of Savonarola. On 14 July, he wins a further appointment as Secretary to the Ten of War. Over the next fourteen years, from the ages of twenty-nine to forty-three, he plays an increasingly important role in looking after the republic's external affairs and military security. It will soon prove impossible for Machiavelli to avoid being pulled into Florence's brutally partisan politics.

9

So Blinded Are You by Present Greed

It is July 1499, a year and one month since Niccolò joined the Chancery. He is about to travel north and east to the Romagna on the second diplomatic assignment of his career; the first was a brief mission to the coastal city of Piombino in November 1498.[1] *Commission given to Niccolò Machiavelli to Their Excellencies the Lady of Forlì and the Lord Ottaviano her firstborn son.*

What outrageous good fortune, colleagues tease him. Soon Niccolò will be sipping wine with Countess Caterina, twittering sweet nothings in her ear. 'Bring me back a likeness of Her Majesty,' begs Biagio Buonaccorsi, 'one of those portraits on a sheet of paper that they sell over there. You can buy them cheap from one of those hawkers who hang around the city walls. And if you send it by messenger, roll it up so the folds don't spoil it.'[2]

Biagio is one of Niccolò's coadjutors in the Second Chancery. He misses the Second Chancellor terribly when he goes away for longer than a few days. In Machiavelli's absence, the job of checking on Biagio and his office-mates' progress falls to one Antonio della Valle, coadjutor to the professorial First Chancellor, Marcello Virgilio Adriani. Ser Antonio's chip-on-shoulder power-games are legendary among Chancery assistants and clerks. With no Niccolò around, he swaggers into the office every morning and persecutes the younger assistants in their sober black robes. *May he have bloody shit in his arsehole*, Biagio vents in a letter to his friend.[3] Whenever you're away, Niccolò, Ser Antonio and all the other magnificences here are always bawling me out for no good reason at all. *So I'll keep begging and praying for you to come back. I just want to return to my place, writing alongside you.*

Despite these young men's grand titles, their jobs mostly involve writing letters. Hundreds, sometimes thousands, of letters a year. They go to meetings, endless meetings, of the Signoria and the Ten of War and special consultations on pressing matters of state, and scribble down detailed minutes of what every speaker says, trying to write as legibly as possible. Biagio's calligraphy always wins high praise from his superiors, but he wants to be remembered for more than his good handwriting. He keeps his own *ricordi* where, along-side family matters, he chronicles political events in Florence and Italy. One day, he hopes to polish it all up as a proper history of Florence, as seen from the privileged perspective of the Chancery. He also writes poetry, a more intimate and sentimental sort than Niccolò's, expressing his feelings about his beloved wife, Lessandra, in life and after her premature death.[4]

Niccolò's other coadjutor, Agostino Vespucci – cousin of the more famous Amerigo, who gave his name to the New World, and nephew of Messer Guidantonio – is easily bored by the grubbiness of politics. Whereas Biagio and Niccolò immerse themselves in it, hoping to draw lessons they can write down for the benefit of their countrymen and to their own glory, Agostino distracts himself from his day job by visiting private collections of fine art, jotting down his observations in the margins of whatever book he happens to be carrying around that day. He will later be remembered for identifying the mystery model of Leonardo da Vinci's *Mona Lisa* as Lisa del Giaconda, a discovery he notes in the margins of Cicero's *Letters* in 1503. Poor Biagio, he writes to Niccolò. He's like the well-meaning Protesilaus in Homer: the first man to jump off the Greek ships at Troy, and the first to get killed.[5] Sheltered by his patrician family name, Agostino can afford not to take seriously men like della Valle, with their popular or recent peasant origins; social rank trumps official rank. While Ser Antonio's tantrums make Biagio cringe behind the heap of portfolios on his desk, Agostino merely stares at their office superior as if he were a stray farm animal that has somehow wandered into the city and, stumbling into the refined halls of government, panicked and run amuck.

Niccolò, for his part, has a wonderfully haughty contempt for playground politics in the office. The assistants who work under him include older men with long experience in the job and recent, younger hires like Agostino and Biagio. Unless official protocol or age calls for differentiation, he treats everyone as an equal. And he has a talent for deflating pretensions with only a delicate hint of malice. Come now, Biagio – what do you expect from people whose greatest joy in life is to be called Most Excellent Assistant to the First Chancellor and the like? Such men have to seize crumbs of glory while they can, because once they're dead, no one will remember them.

So Biagio, who is too much in awe of people he knows don't deserve it, clings to Niccolò's side in his first year on the job. In return, he defends his superior's interests whenever he is away. Not long after Niccolò leaves for the court of Caterina Sforza, Biagio warns him about a colleague who, having heard certain important men praise the Second Chancellor's letters, now comes to the office every day to sniff around and try to undermine him with gossip. *But you can take it for granted*, says Biagio, *that I answered him in such a way that he doesn't say such things to me any more.* Agostino feels his colleague's absence, too. The office gang are only half alive when you're gone, he tells Niccolò, in self-mockingly grandiose Latin. *For your amusing, urbane, and pleasant conversation, while it echoes about our ears, relieves, cheers and refreshes us, who are spent and flagging from endless work.*[6]

The city of Forlì, where Countess Sforza is now holding court, lies about fifty miles north-east of Florence. Caterina Sforza is one of Italy's living legends, and one of the peninsula's most ferocious rulers. She was born the illegitimate daughter of Galeazzo Maria Sforza, the Duke of Milan whose visit to Florence in 1471 had indirectly caused the fire that burned down the Church of Santo Spirito near Machiavelli's house. At the age of ten, she married Girolamo Riario, nephew of Pope Sixtus IV. Or perhaps he was really the pope's son: writing later, Niccolò couldn't resist noting that Sixtus had two boys in his household, one of them Girolamo, *who, according to what everyone believed, were his sons; nonetheless, he cloaked them under other, more decent names*, as popes and other great men are wont to do.[7] Through marrying Riario, Caterina acquired the titles of Lady of Imola and Countess of Forlì. After Riario was killed in a conspiracy, she ruled in place of her son Ottaviano, who was still very young. Then she fell in love with one of her stable grooms, Giacomo Feo, and married him in secret. He, too, was murdered in a conspiracy. Her third husband was Giovanni di Pierfrancesco of the Popolani branch of the Medici, who died – this time of natural causes – in 1498. This conjugal connection with the pro-republican branch of the Medici had sealed firm bonds of friendship between Florence and the cities of Imola and Forlì. Since a law of 1494 forbade Florentine citizens to marry foreign women who were rulers, or of any ruler's bloodline – people remembered that Lorenzo and Piero's noble Orsini wives had brought in un-republican manners and unsettling dynastic ties – Caterina, her children, and her descendants had been made citizens of Florence so that she could marry Giovanni.

As a girl, Caterina had often been taken hunting by her father. Her education, he insisted, should include training in arms as well as in Latin and poetry, as befitted any child of a celebrated *condottiero*. When she was twenty, and seven months pregnant, she had donned full military armour and crossed the Tiber on horseback, commanding her husband Girolamo Riario's troops to occupy the papal fortress of Castel Sant' Angelo. At Pope Sixtus's death his nephew, afraid that a hostile new pontiff would strip him of his noble titles and seize his property, hoped to force the conclave of cardinals to leave him his possessions in Imola and Forlì. With Caterina's help, they did. When Riario was assassinated, the plotters seized the count's young widow and her children – she had six at the time, including the then nine-year-old Ottaviano – and locked them up. But taking the fortress of Forlì proved harder than they had expected. The castellan and his men, loyal to their countess, refused to hand it over to the usurpers. Terrified that their popular support would evaporate, the conspirators begged Caterina to persuade her men to give it up. I'll do my best, she told them. But you'll have to let me into the fortress to talk to them, alone. As a pledge of my good faith, I leave you all my children as hostages.

Her husband's assassins let her into the fortress. And *as soon as she was inside*, in Niccolò's words, *she threatened the conspirators with death and every kind of punishment in revenge for her husband. And when they threatened to kill her children*, she yanked up her skirts in defiance and *showed them her genital parts, saying: I have the means for making more of them!*[8]

The conspiracy collapsed; Caterina's children were left shaken but alive. *Then the countess, having retaken the state, avenged her husband's death with every kind of cruelty*. She had everyone involved in the plot thrown into prison, along with the pope's governor and other clergymen whom she held in suspicion. The women of the conspirators' families were rounded up and put into custody. Then the countess ordered her men to sack and burn the houses of the imprisoned and to distribute their property to the poor.

At first, Caterina tried to win popularity by keeping taxes low, knowing that the onerous duties on land and goods levied by her late husband had made him dangerous enemies. But after her second husband was murdered in a plot that had aimed to kill her as well, she again took harsh revenge and began to govern with an iron fist. She didn't seem to mind that, for all her high repute abroad and among her own plebs, the nobles and middle classes of Forlì and Imola hated her pitiless ways and the high taxes she slapped on them to fund her ambitious building projects and defence needs. And her defence needs were growing all the time, in part because of threats from outside, but also because so many of her own people were waiting for the right moment to depose her.

Having heard all these reports, some good and some bad, Niccolò is keen to meet the famous countess and to find out what her neighbours and subjects say about her government. Here is his first opportunity to make a close-up study of a princely ruler who does not, like the Medici, pretend to be nothing more than first among equal citizens. Caterina Sforza is a fully fledged prince, a ruler with a regal title who has the power to make, bend, and break laws almost at will.⁹ The fact that Niccolò's object of study happens to be a beautiful woman only adds spice to his assignment.

And it might well need spicing up, since on paper this mission is spectacularly unthrilling. A year earlier, the Florentines had hired the countess's son, nineteen-year-old Ottaviano Riario, as a mercenary captain to help fight the campaign to recover Pisa. He had terminated his contract after only a short stint, claiming he'd been underpaid. But now, only months later, his mother wants the Florentines to engage Ottaviano's services again, on the same terms as before. Niccolò's official brief is to ooze Florentine goodwill while offering Ottaviano a much lower salary.

The trip to Caterina's court at Forlì takes him a few days on horseback, and longer in July than in the cooler months, when travellers needn't break their journey to avoid the baking midday sun. Even the leathery-skinned mule drivers at the watering stations complain; their poor beasts look parched and faint. Mercifully, Niccolò has instructions to do a stopover in Castrocaro, a town some six miles from Forlì. The place is easy to spot from a distance: a mass of crumpled rock sprouting incongruously out of the soft, rolling landscape, an old fortress glowering down from the cliff; below it, a haze of sandstone houses and church towers clinging to hillsides. Here, the north-eastern edge of Florence's Tuscan empire borders the chaotic province of Romagna. Once controlled by the popes in Rome, Romagna's cities – Bologna, Modena, Forlì, Imola, Cesena, Faenza – have a habit of rebelling against papal authority. The Florentines had purchased Castrocaro from Pope Boniface IX in 1394, for the modest sum of 18,000 thousand gold florins.

Though its population is small, the border town is important for Florence's security. Niccolò's first business is to make an inventory of the military supplies stored in its fortress. He counts iron balls, inspects the saltpetre, and keeps an eagle eye on the castellan's men to make sure they don't cheat while weighing the gunpowder. Then he turns to another piece of business, this one not written down in his official instructions, due to its sensitive nature, though to Niccolò it seems more interesting than little Ottaviano Riario's pay package. The Signoria and the Ten of War want him to find out more about a quarrel that has been brewing here in Castrocaro, where Florence's dominions rub up against those of Caterina Sforza. For several years now, a truce had been upheld in an old vendetta between two factions, led by the Naldi and Corbizi families. Worried that new disturbances in the town might weaken their border defences, the Florentines want Niccolò to interview a local man, Ser Guerrino del Bello, whom they suspect of involvement in the quarrel.

Niccolò goes to Guerrino del Bello's house to make enquiries. He is out, but his elderly father, Bello del Bello, invites his Florentine visitor inside and offers to answer whatever questions he might have. He leads Niccolò into a cool room, simply but rather elegantly furnished. They exchange the usual courtesies and complain about the scorching heat; a serving girl brings a carafe of wine. Once they are seated, Niccolò gets straight to the purpose of his visit.[10]

'From what I understand,' he begins amiably, 'it seems your son had a number of friends and relatives dining here the other night when our Florentine commander came around. He had intelligence that some of the guests might be conniving with the Naldi to make trouble. His report says that Ser Guerrino barred the door and refused to let the police take these men from his house.'

The old man nods. 'I'll make no excuses for my son,' he replies. 'He disobeyed orders. But he considers that the Florentine police captain behaved inhumanely in demanding that he should send away four of his friends and relatives in the night.'

Niccolò understands. To say that he behaved inhumanely means that he wanted the host to violate unwritten laws of hospitality, laws that men like Bello consider part of basic human decency.

'My son believed his loyalty was so well known,' the elder Bello continues, 'that no one could ever doubt it, let alone suspect him of trying to injure the Florentines. He's always made a point of freely inviting his friends around, even in our earlier times of trouble.'

Niccolò watches his host closely while keeping his gaze frank, trusting, and respectful of his host's superior years. Bello looks straight at him; he speaks naturally. After bidding him a warm farewell, Niccolò takes a stroll to the main town church. The priest, Father Farragano, comes out to meet him.

Niccolò mentions that he's just had a chat with Bello del Bello. 'Ah!' Farragano exclaims, 'an excellent man. And his son Guerrino is the very image of his father.'

With further gentle probing, Niccolò's first impressions are strengthened. *This Bello*, he writes in his dispatch a few days later, *according to what I learn from the priest Farragano and from other inhabitants of this place, is a worthy and peaceful man who has never openly taken sides with either party. He has been more a mediator of peace than a disseminator of troubles.* The Florentines should lay off Ser Guerrino, Machiavelli recommends. In fact, they should avoid making too much of this alleged plot to reignite the old vendetta, which, as far as he can tell, has been cooked up by a couple of isolated mischief-makers. The most dangerous thing his investigations uncover is a bit of head-butting inside the Corbizi faction over who should be leader after the death of their last chief. *But unless someone deliberately stimulates this feeling*, Secretary Machiavelli judges, *it is not likely to produce any bad results.* On the contrary, *it seems to me that the people are very united, and that there is no open enmity between any of its inhabitants.* And for Niccolò, the people are the real foundation of any state's safety.[11] If the general populace is content, rulers should leave well enough alone and avoid overreacting to the first rumours of turmoil.

But something still bothers him. Who's spreading these new rumours, after such a long truce? He asks further discreet questions when he dines with Florentine officials and a few local dignitaries, and later on the last stretch of the road to Forlì. And he soon discovers that the people of Castrocaro are worried. They worry not just that the powder keg of Corbizi–Naldi hatreds might blow up again. Locals are afraid, Niccolò tells his superiors, that the Naldi faction's ringleaders might try to stir up trouble *with the help of the Lady Caterina*, behind Florentine backs. *For although this*

Lady is on terms of friendship with your Lordships, the locals neither hold her in regard nor trust her. Thus they remain in a constant state of anxiety, both the town and country people. Only yesterday, he relates, some fifteen or twenty of Caterina's own crossbowmen robbed a house and wounded three men, carrying one off with them. This violence happened not in Caterina's dominions but in Florentine territory near Castrocaro. It seems she was sending out gangs of raiders to attack her good neighbours across the border. *Similar outrages are committed every day. And it was only yesterday,* Niccolò continues, *that a number of country people complained to me, saying: 'Our lords the Florentines have abandoned us! They have too many other things on their hands.'* It is part of Niccolò's job to let the people back home sense the mood wherever he travels, to hear the voices of people whose concerns affect their own security. *Your Lordships will doubtless, with your great prudence, take such measures in this matter as the honour of our republic demands, and as will give satisfaction to these your most faithful subjects.*

But why would Countess Sforza play such games now, at the very moment when she's seeking even closer ties with Florence? Apart from her relatives in Milan, the Florentines are the countess' closest allies. If Niccolò had been ambivalent about this mission before, now his curiosity was fully aroused. The lady prince he was about to meet was not only Italy's greatest warrior and a good-looking woman; she might have a sinister side that this Florentine Signoria didn't know about. This new information about her underhand dealings, if it wasn't just rumour or smear, could make Niccolò's dealings with Caterina more interesting than he'd expected.

At daybreak, Niccolò rides the remaining short stretch to Forlì. Having presented his credentials to the helmeted guards at the city walls, he proceeds to the palace. Her Excellency has other business, says the well-dressed gentleman who screens her visitors. Come back later. His accent sounds Florentine.

So Niccolò has a look around. He dips into snaking side alleys where the sun's blaze can't reach, and follows the shade to another quadrangle. The clattering of hooves on cobblestones, the clank of armour; hoarse shouts in dialects he can barely make out. Over lunch, Niccolò goes over his letters of assignment from the Signoria and recalls the advice more experienced diplomats had been keen to pass on to the fresh-faced Secretary. Each of these princely courts, even the pettiest, has its own protocols for an audience with its local excellency or magnificence. Some self-important official will inform you of them in the waiting room. Generally speaking, the pettier the magnificence, the more pomp and ceremony one must observe when granted the privilege of entering his or her presence.

While on his first, even less thrilling mission to the city of Piombino, Niccolò had already worked out the two essential, unwritten rules of Florentine diplomacy. One: give them words, good words, be a veritable fountain bubbling over with sweet words; but use every industry to avoid offering them deeds. Two: have at the tip of your tongue a ready arsenal of excuses for not spending money. We Florentines are already overstretched with all our necessities of war and defence; our bigger and stronger allies, that is to say the French, would be angry if we were to give you a single florin; in any case, our Great Council, which as you know is the sovereign voice of our republic, refuses to grant the Signoria another florin for the necessities of war, or even a *grosso*; everyone fears a popular revolt if we keep pressing the people with taxes to pay for whatever you foreign chieftains demand from us.

When he is finally given his audience that afternoon, Niccolò gets a surprise. Instead of the usual gaggle of courtiers who hover around thrones trying to impress or intimidate visitors, Countess Caterina has invited only one man to their negotiations.[12] And he is not one of her own personal advisers, but Messer Giovanni da Casale, the Duke of Milan's chargé d'affaires.

Niccolò quickly grasps the situation. In trying to renew Ottaviano's contract at full pay, his mother's bargaining ploy will play Florentine interests against Milan's. If you don't accept my terms, Caterina will insinuate, I'll get even closer to Milan. And you know Duke Ludovico might not always work for your good.

Indeed. Only weeks earlier, the Signoria had dithered over an urgent request from Ludovico Sforza, Caterina's uncle, for a defensive alliance against France. The new French king, Louis XII, was preparing to attack the north Italian duchy, which he claimed as his through his grandmother, a daughter of Milanese dukes. With the Florentines still clinging to French apron strings and suspicious of Ludovico's tricks, Caterina could pressure them by threatening to follow her uncle's lead, perhaps even turning against her old friends in Florence if he urged it. Casale's presence speaks volumes for the countess. His master is her relative; she would always have the Milanese Sforzas on her side. The Florentines, on the other hand, have no one in Italy more reliable than Caterina.

'My Lordships the Signoria of Florence,' Niccolò begins, after genuflecting in the correct manner, 'earnestly await the time when they may show how much they value those who have loyally served our republic and shared its varying fortunes, as Her Excellency has always done.' These elaborate preliminaries are followed by even more elaborate circumlocutions concerning Ottaviano's contract. Though Her Ladyship's request to renew it gives rise to certain difficulties for my Lordships, for the sake of such a treasured friendship the latter agree to hire him again as their captain. But since Signor Ottaviano broke off his earlier contract before time, we had to engage other men-at-arms. So our budget prevents us from offering the same conditions as before; and, to speak frankly, we have no urgent need of another captain at present. 'But out of the great affection my Lordships have for Your Excellency, and because of her great merits, they offer to engage her son for not more than 10,000 ducats for this year.'

In person, as in her widely circulating portraits, the thirty-six-year-old countess is undoubtedly attractive. But at this moment she wears an expression so steely that even Niccolò, a ready victim of feminine charms, almost forgets she is a woman. 'Your Florentine Lordships' words,' she says, in a voice neither unpleasant nor pleasant, 'have always given me satisfaction. But their actions have often displeased me. The compensation I've received from them has always fallen short of the value of my services. Nevertheless,' she continues, 'knowing that your illustrious republic is grateful by nature, I can't believe that they would show themselves ungrateful to one who had for a great while done more for Florence than any of your other allies.'

Niccolò offers a modest bow. She exchanges an inaudible word or two with Casale, then signals that their very short session is over. 'Since it seems your Signoria have considered their offer most prudently, we too need time to consider our reply.'

'My Lordships,' Niccolò hastens to interject, 'wrote to ask Your Ladyship if you might supply us with some cannonballs and saltpetre.'

'I have neither,' she says coldly, 'and am myself greatly in need of both.'

Later that day, while trying to cool off at his lodgings after this first bout of genteel haggling, Niccolò has a visit from the countess's First Secretary. Now the real bargaining begins: now they are free to mention pecuniary and political details that are far too grubby to be discussed in the prince's presence.

'My Ladyship,' says her man, 'has received better offers from other cities for Ottaviano's services. In fact, this very morning she had a letter from the Duke of Milan. He writes that, since she hasn't reached agreeable terms with the Florentines, it might be wise to send her son to work for his relatives.' He does not need to add: to fight against the French, your lords and masters. 'She remains in doubt about what to do, as it seems disgraceful for her and Signor Ottaviano to accept your present offer. In fact, she's quite at a loss, being under obligations to the Duke of Milan both by blood and by the innumerable benefits she's received from that prince.'

Niccolò gives the non-committal replies that are expected in the first round of talks. But despite his misgivings about the raids into Florentine territory that seem to be made with her approval, he decides to give Caterina Sforza the benefit of the doubt – for now. He writes home that, from what he hears, her intentions towards

Florence are good. If there's anyone they should mistrust, it's the Milanese and this minister from Milan Casale, who seems to rule everything. Perhaps he's the one ordering the cross-border raids. On the other hand, the countess is no one's puppet. Niccolò wants to find out more.

The next day he has another audience. 'I have nothing new to say to you,' she tells him. Her manner is still severe, but more courteous than before. Of course, he understands that she needs time to examine the Florentine offer. But since he is here, and since she has said she lacks artillery balls and saltpetre, might he ask whether she could spare any gunpowder or men to help her neighbours recover Pisa?

'I have very little powder,' she says. 'But I'll see what we can do about that, and about the saltpetre. As for troops, these I have. Your Lordships are welcome to hire some part of them, but only if they send money to pay them immediately. These are soldiers, hard men and greedy. They tolerate no delay.'

So they are getting somewhere, creeping forward: I give you something you want, now you give. She seems transparent, and demands transparency in return. She sees through Florentine smooth talk and says so outright, instead of wasting time trying to match it. Her Ladyship wants actions now, Niccolò writes to the Signoria, and won't be taken in by pleasantries. *And I truly believe that if Your Lordships were to make some acknowledgement to the countess for past services, or increase the compensation under the new arrangement, you will be sure to preserve her friendship.* He advises them to raise the offer for Ottaviano's pay from 10,000 to 12,000 ducats. *That's my opinion, though I may be mistaken.*

Some of his city's bankers and businessmen have no idea of the value of steady, lasting friendship; with them, everything is reduced to a question of saving money. To hell with long-term consequences, with simple common sense. But the surest way to win esteem, Niccolò writes in the *Prince*, is to be *a true friend and a true enemy.* That man or state will be most secure who *without any hesitation discloses himself in support of someone against another.* If you act like a lukewarm or fair-weather friend, you can hardly expect your friends to step up for you when you need favours. And when you're as weak as Florence, you can ill afford to have only half-hearted friends, friends as unreliable as yourselves. *I have often known such ambiguity to hurt public actions,* he will later remark, *with harm and shame for our republic.*[13] Our great Florentine profiteers are shocked when no one trusts their republic of skinflints, men who'd do anything to dodge long-term commitments to save a few ducats. What Countess Sforza wants is small enough. And Niccolò is beginning to suspect that she has more urgent need of Florentine friendship than she's letting on.

Now he waits for his leaders' reply. He had written to his office-mates about his first days in Forlì; speedy messengers soon bring him their letters. Biagio: I'm delighted, though not astonished, to learn from your letter that Lady Caterina has made you such a pet. *Of course I have no doubt at all that Her Excellency is doing you as much honour, and is as happy to see you, as you write.*

Not forgetting his promise to Biagio, Niccolò ambles out to the piazza, where rows of vendors stand hawking pictures of their local celebrity. Men scurry about the square cordoning off the edges. Some kind of spectacle is about to begin. A crowd gathers behind the barrier. Then a flourish of trumpets and a quick-march roll of drums, and hundreds of men burst into the piazza. Five hundred of Caterina's best infantrymen put on a fine show, displaying their weapons, marching and turning in perfect step. Their plumed commander, it seems, is a Naldi, one of the clan the Florentines suspect of troublemaking around their borders. They are about to go north to Milan to help defend Duke Ludovico, together with fifty crossbowmen who perform an equally impressive muster. To Niccolò's untrained eye, they look like top-notch, disciplined troops. Later, he asks around and hears that Caterina herself oversees their training and command. It seems Countess Sforza Riario is a close student of military arts, not just a fierce fighter; she understands the need for careful training, for order. By themselves, ferocity and stubbornness get you only so far.[14]

But well-rounded military skills are not enough to make a good prince. Niccolò has seen and heard enough to doubt that Caterina has the political skills to match her martial prowess. Her government is unpopular. People complain, though not too openly, that she continues to harass suspected critics with extraordinary taxes, and worse. The countrypeople don't trust her to protect them in the event of war, should she side too closely with Milan against France. Her fortresses are strong and loyal, and that is something: everyone remembers how, when enemies tried to foment an uprising against her husband all those years ago, his wife had the good fortune to be saved by fleeing to her fortress. But would she always be so lucky, even if a powerful foreigner came along and promised to help her people get rid of her? *Not fortresses but the will of men keeps princes in their states*, and Niccolò can't help blaming *anyone who, trusting in fortresses, thinks little of being hated by the people*.[15]

A few days later, at last, a letter arrives from the Signoria. They agree to up their offer for engagement to 12,000 ducats from 10,000. Niccolò rushes to the palace to give the countess the good news.

Caterina says she is satisfied and accepts this new offer. But now she comes out with a much larger request. 'In order to justify sending Signor Ottaviano into Your Lordships' service,' she says, 'and to give my government more credit, I should prefer that the Florentines formally bind themselves to defend the integrity of my dominions. While of course I trust that Your Lordships would do this without any formal obligation or alliance, as they have ever done, I greatly desire such a formal undertaking, for the sake of my honour. I am sure they will not refuse me in this.'

After a moment's astonishment, Niccolò understands what's behind it all – her original request to renew the cancelled contract, the rigorous military drills, the glint of swords on the streets, her courtiers' shifty gazes and nervous tones. She doesn't really care much about her honour, though she keeps invoking it like a mantra. She cares even less who will pay Ottaviano more, Florence or Milan. What she wants is to keep her state, because she fears she is about to lose it. And the threat doesn't come from France. King Louis wants Milan, not the provincial statelets of Forlì and Imola.

Valentino. The name no one utters out loud to the envoy from Florence, though he kept hearing it as he stood among the throngs watching the muster, muttered below the drumbeat. Pope Alexander's bastard son. Nothing is certain yet, but there have been reports from Rome that the pope is contemplating a new crusade on behalf of Holy Mother Church. But instead of sending troops bearing crucifixes towards Jerusalem, Alexander VI wants to send his son Cesare a few days north to the Romagna, to reclaim its rebel cities for the papacy.

All Christendom has heard of Cesare Borgia. His father had made him a cardinal at eighteen, alongside Giovanni de' Medici, who is the same age. A few years later, when the pope's older son, Juan, was found murdered, suspicions fell on the young Cardinal Borgia his brother, though no one was ever charged with the crime.

Then, a year ago, at the age of twenty-three, Cesare traded in his ecclesiastical robes for the sword. A shocking thing: no man on record had ever given up his cardinal's hat. He wanted to be a soldier, a captain of great armies. And then, as if the universe itself were eager to gratify his every wish, all the higher powers that seemed to matter made his wish come true. On the same day that he abandoned the red, France's King Louis XII awarded him the noble title Duc de Valentinois. Not for anything Cesare had done, but in exchange for his father's agreement to annul the king's marriage to the allegedly hideous and barren sister of the deceased Charles VIII. Now, armed mightily by Pope Alexander and the grateful French king, Valentino – as the Italians liked to call Cesare – would swoop down on the Romagna like a ravening beast and make mincemeat of its present rulers. Caterina Sforza would doubtless be among his first victims.

Here in Forlì, no one speaks of these things to Niccolò. His bosses in Florence do not mention the pope's enterprise in the letters they send him. They hope, of course, that Alexander's plans to conquer the Romagna will dry up and blow away, like the greasy ashes from Savonarola's pyre. For if they go ahead, Florence will soon be living again in daily dread.

Niccolò has heard enough panic-mongering rumours in his life. His sceptical reflexes tell him to avoid exaggerating threats that have barely begun to materialize. But from all he has heard about this pope and seen in his policies, it seems reasonable to expect that he won't stop at Romagna. If Cesare Borgia sends his Franco-papal army against Caterina, Florence might be next.

But for now they keep up the diplomatic fiction that there is no threat from Rome. Alexander is the most reverend protector of all Italy and Christendom and of humankind, and Caterina Sforza has fear of no man, not even the Vicar of Christ. 'I am sure,' Niccolò replies to her, 'that a formal alliance between Your Ladyship and my republic is superfluous, for the reasons you yourself have alleged. And as you must know, I have no authority to conclude such an agreement.'

'Then write to Your Lordships and ask them to give you those powers.' This comes from Caterina's secretary. 'As soon as possible.'

He already knows what the Signoria will say. Of course we can't give Secretary Machiavelli the authority to make an alliance. He's a young civil servant of no particular family. We'll find someone more important to send to discuss the countess' proposal.

The truth is, the Florentines are afraid to take sides in any stand-off between Caterina Sforza and the pope, especially while the French king supports Alexander's designs and offers the pope's son his own troops. Niccolò returns home with a bad taste in his mouth. After all his efforts, nothing has been settled. His government's reluctance to commit Florence to Caterina's defence seems ungrateful and short-sighted. But what else can you expect from men who reduce matters of public safety to a series of short-term business transactions?

As Niccolò set off towards Forlì in July 1499, the Florentines were preparing to launch an all-out assault on Pisa. Their captain, Paolo Vitelli, had encamped outside the city walls with his formidable army of mercenaries.

Vitelli is renowned throughout Italy and beyond as the best captain on the market, the star mercenary of his generation. He comes from a family of famous *condottiere*, professional soldiers, long-faced and big-boned, fighters to the core. His father had ennobled himself and his progeny by seizing the city of Città di Castello with the Florentines' support. Now everyone wants Paolo Vitelli, and he knows it. Italy's shabbily armed princes and rich, war-shy republics like Venice and Florence pay through the nose for his services. Though his appearance is brief, Captain Vitelli will play a fatally important part in the drama of Florence's 1494 republic as seen through Machiavelli's eyes. If the struggle to conquer Pisa shows how dangerous it is for republics to assault others' freedoms, the Vitelli episode comes to epitomize, for Machiavelli, the disastrous policy of depending on hired mercenary captains to do one's fighting.

No one doubts Paolo Vitelli's experience and phenomenal energy. His men fulfil all his orders with the most admirable discipline, inflicting heavy casualties on the Pisans in the countryside and towns that lie between the warring cities. But Vitelli's strategies draw as much criticism in Florence as his unheard-of stipend.[16] After several months of fighting the Pisans in 1498, he had advised the Signoria that it would be forbiddingly hard to capture Pisa by siege alone. The city has strong walls, he said. Its friends keep it well supplied with artillery, food and other necessaries. Above all, it is full of good fighters armed with adamantine resolve. It would be better to attack and occupy neighbouring towns and try to control the countryside, surrounding the Pisans with enemy bastions and preventing their friends from sending aid. The people inside the city's walls would soon realize that they were being strangled, give up hope and surrender of their own accord.

These opinions met with public dismay. Most Florentines wanted Vitelli to attack Pisa directly, putting the city under siege. That way, they imagined, the campaign would be over fairly soon, incurring less expense than a war of attrition. Some members of the Signoria and the Ten tried to dissuade Vitelli, pointing out that the people yearned for a quick end to this war and feared the soaring expenses. Vitelli replied that, in his opinion, he knew a bit more about how to fight and win wars than the Florentine populace. The Signoria might, of course, save a great deal of money by asking their Great Council to draw up a strategy and appoint some shopkeeper to command whatever local men they might dredge from the sewers.

He set to work on his plans in the summer of 1498. Though his troops succeeded in taking some key towns, rumours of Vitelli's knavery began to spread. The man is too cocksure; he shows no respect for our commissioners or anyone else. Or worse: he's probably in league with the Venetians, or with the Duke of Milan, who want this war to drag on and on and ruin us.

Whether or not these last apprehensions had any truth in them, Niccolò later points out, people would have had good reasons to worry about Vitelli's good faith even if he were the most honest man in the world.[17] However trustworthy any individual mercenary might be, the nature of his job makes him suspect to his employers. Since he isn't native to the country he fights for, he has neither love of it nor any other stake in its victory. His only motive to fight well is a salary, which he receives even if he loses. And a man who soldiers for pay will be tempted to take more money on the side from third parties who might not want his employers to win.

But a worse suspicion stalks hired captains. If they win, they might turn around with their victorious army and seize their employers' state. Recent Italian history offered some disquieting examples. Florentines had not forgotten that the founder of Milan's Sforza dynasty, Countess Caterina's grandfather Francesco, began as a mercenary hired by the Milanese to fight the Venetians. Having defeated them, he used his troops to conquer Milan and make himself duke. And now the Florentines have Paolo Vitelli, *a most prudent man* of *very great reputation* who has no hope of gaining their trust whatever he might do.[18] If he fails to capture Pisa, they'll suspect that someone paid him to fail. If he succeeds, they'll be at his mercy, since they have no troops of their own. Either way, as Niccolò will soon be pointing out to anyone who'll listen, the whole mercenary business puts the city in deep danger.

And while Florentines pay foreigners to fight for them, their enemies prepare to fight for themselves and their own. The Pisans' resolve and self-belief, Niccolò observes, put their would-be conquerors to shame.[19] Pisan memories of former freedom are long, and carry all the tenderness and bitterness of a lost great love. Wealthy Pisa once held more than fifty thousand souls, more than Florence had at the same time.[20] By 1494, after a hundred years of subjection, the population numbered only around ten thousand. And now all Pisa's shops have shut down; the thriving harbour city has been turned into a garrison.[21] Every inhabitant who has passed infancy either bears arms or is in training to bear them. Tradesmen, lawyers, professors, doctors and priests have fled into exile. Some work from abroad for the cause of resistance, writing letters and pamphlets, travelling as envoys to all the courts of Europe, channelling funds in and out of foreign banks. Any who express a desire to reach an accord with Florence are hounded out of town as traitors, or killed.

Yet if the city's wealthy and middle-class population was depleted after it became free, refugees fleeing from the surrounding country have made up the lost numbers. One count taken in the summer of 1499 estimates that Pisa had more than seven thousand men and women who were ready and active in combat. The incoming countrypeople make the fight for Pisa's freedom tougher, more implacable, giving it the character of an ancient family vendetta writ large. These farmers want revenge. In the five years since liberation, Florentine troops have been razing their crops and their houses. They have butchered their sons, raped their wives and daughters. *Whoever becomes patron of a city accustomed to living free and does not destroy it*, declares Niccolò in one of the warmest passages in his reputedly cold-blooded *Prince*, *should expect to be destroyed by it. For it always has as a refuge in rebellion the name of liberty and its own ancient orders that are never forgotten, either through length of time or because of benefits received.*[22]

No one in Florence wants to reduce Pisa to char and rubble, as the Romans reduced Carthage and Corinth. Florentines have had enough bad publicity; and it is better to possess a rich and vibrant subject city than a desert. Yet no one wants to admit that the wisest course, the only one that will save Florence the ever-escalating costs and terrors of war, might be to let the Pisans live free. Niccolò is only a civil servant; no one asks his opinion about grave matters of state security. But in a piece dated around this time, an imagined oration delivered to some unspecified Florentine assembly, he subtly criticizes current policies. You Florentines, his nameless speaker declares in his *Discourse on Pisa*, have never considered sending an embassy to the Pisans, or made even the smallest overtures to discuss terms.[23] *Given your unbending spirit, you cannot expect the Pisans to come voluntarily under your yoke.* By refusing to try diplomacy, you leave yourselves no choice but to use force and fight them to the end, because that is how they will fight you. But don't deceive yourselves, the speaker warns: the fight will be ugly, and your own freedom and safety will be compromised on the way to the total victory you seek.

The siege begins on 1 August 1499, when Niccolò is just back from Forlì. By now, the entire populace of Pisa is organized into military companies. The piazza is filled with streaming banners in the colours of each district. Under them, men and women of every status, priests of rival orders and children exercise and test their weapons. Chroniclers lavish special praise on the women of the popular classes and the countryside, trained in their own squadrons with a *capitania* at their head, for setting a brave example of martial spirit that is emulated by their patrician superiors.

But a week into the stand-off, Vitelli's forces start battering down the wall beside the fortress tower of Stampace in the south. The time had come for the Pisans to fight to their death. Priests lead a solemn procession from one end of the city to the other. Then, having prayed to the Virgin for succour, the Pisans take up their swords and lances, rocks and bricks, and go to fight for the tower of Stampace.

At daybreak on 10 August, when the Pisans are off guard, a contingent of Vitelli's troops attacks. Soon the defenders are being slaughtered or driven back into the city. When the shell-shocked populace gathers again, a long, terrible howl of female protest meets their Gonfalonier's proposal to call off the campaign.

In Florence, people flood the streets and squares, shouting, embracing each other. In his dual capacities as Second Chancellor and Secretary to the Ten of War, Niccolò attends a flurry of meetings called to decide the city's next steps.[24] 'Captain Vitelli seems to have made Pisa return to the dominion of our Republic,' announces Florence's current Gonfalonier. 'So let us start thinking about what terms we as victors should impose.' On 24 August, Our Lady of Impruneta is carried in procession to the church of San Felice. For centuries, Florentines had revered this painted icon representing the mother of God, calling on its talismanic powers in times of crisis. On the road outside Florence, the twig of an olive branch gets caught on a star on Our Lady's mantle: a portent of peace.[25] The next day, Chancellor Marcello Adriani presents a detailed report on the present, very healthy state of provisions and supplies needed to secure the conquest.

But four days later, alarming letters arrive from Florence's military commissioners at the camp outside Pisa. The whole infantry has come down with some deadly fever, and sickness is spreading fast. One sick commissioner is brought back home, two other leading citizens are sent to replace him. All die within the week. On 4 September, the Florentines order Vitelli to lift camp and halt the campaign.

People are furious. The government is beleaguered with questions it cannot answer: how could this be happening, when everything seemed to be going Florence's way? And why, before sickness struck, had Vitelli's men not surged into Pisa and occupied the city?

The captain's defenders claim that he had good reasons for holding back. His troops were short of artillery; they could hope for fewer casualties and a quicker victory if they waited for new supplies. Then sickness swept through camp, Vitelli lacked enough able-bodied soldiers to carry on, and then took ill himself.

This was not good enough for people whose high hopes had collapsed overnight. Florentine commissioners now claim to have heard rumours that Vitelli had undertaken to serve the Duke of Milan while still under contract to Florence. If this was true, it amounted to a gross breach of contract. At best, it meant that Vitelli had been greedy in hoping to double his present salary. At worst – again, if true – Ludovico Sforza was paying him to deprive the Florentines of victory and prolong the war.

At last, Vitelli's enemies approach the Gonfalonier Giovachino Guasconi and two other leading magistrates, one of them Nicolò di Alessandro Machiavelli, Bernardo's cousin and neighbour who, in his youth, had allegedly impregnated the serving girl Nencia. Now close to fifty, he is a respected citizen and a prior of the city. We are convinced, Bernardo Rucellai tells him and the others, that Vitelli is guilty and should be punished. Pretending that they want to discuss a reorganization of the army, the Signoria summon the captain to a meeting in Cascina, to the east of Pisa, on 30 September. He is arrested and taken to Florence.

Vitelli is imprisoned for one night in the Palazzo Vecchio. The following day, 1 October, a council of eighty men discuss the 'universal belief that he acted wretchedly', in Gonfalonier Guasconi's words. The council's records are full of incriminating hearsay and contradictory reports. Some say the captain wanted to go ahead with the siege but was suddenly assailed by fever. Others report that his brother and second-in-command, Vitellozzo, had been seen, in disguise, at meetings with Piero de' Medici. They still have no evidence; nothing but rumours. No matter. The majority agree that Paolo Vitelli must have committed some treasonous crime, though they are unsure what it is. He is examined under torture that same day. Witnesses report that he bore the pain quietly and confessed nothing, though the tortures were intensified with his every denial. Nonetheless, the examining committee sentence him to immediate death by beheading. Vitelli's head is stuck on a spear outside the government palazzo, a flaming torch beside it for all to see.

The news is greeted with outrage throughout Italy. Some Florentines are reeling, too. Biagio Buonaccorsi records in his diary that *after various torments our captain was decapitated, although he had not confessed to anything that showed a lack of faith. And such was the end of Paolo Vitelli, an excellent man in his office and in the Pisan campaign.*[26] The Signoria receive reports of angry protests in Lucca, the city in Florence's dominions that had been doing most to help Pisa. A letter sent from Lucca's Chancery Secretary to a Pisan dignitary is intercepted. It lands, among a heap of other suspect communications, on Secretary Machiavelli's desk.

His response is a tour de force of acid indignation.[27] 'I am amazed,' he writes to the Luccan Secretary, 'that a man so serious as you and holding a post as important as yours could swallow and spread so many vicious calumnies against Florence. *I thank you for congratulating your Pisan contact about the glory that, in your judgement, they have won and the opprobrium that has redounded to us.* It pleases you to peddle the lie, worthy of the vilest slanderers, that Paolo Vitelli had lent our city money, so the Florentines decided to murder him to avoid having to repay him. *Are you not aware, you poor man* [Niccolò can do an excellent put-down] *that this completely exonerates our city and accuses Paolo?* If Vitelli had lent us money, he was a scoundrel, since he could have come by such money only by illicit means, *by graft given him so he would do the wrong thing.* Whether he did not wish to complete the offensive against Pisa, being corrupted by Florence's enemies, or whether he could not do it because of incompetence, *infinite evils to our campaign arose through his fault, and so one or the other error, or both together, deserve infinite punishment.*'

As Secretary to the Ten and the Republic, Machiavelli is duty-bound to defend his government's actions. But this withering official letter betrays private misgivings that would grow and grow in his mind. What, after all, was the exact charge – the legal ground – that was supposed to justify Vitelli's execution? No one, including Niccolò, knows exactly what Vitelli did or is supposed to have done, because there had been no formal accusations, no examination of evidence, no trial, and no confession, not even a trumped-up one. Just a summary judgement passed by an ad hoc committee after an inconclusive bout of torture and a few hours of frantic deliberations.

If Niccolò suppresses his unease now, his later writings admit that Florence's critics were right about one thing. Gossip and mere suspicion, not laws or evidence, had convicted Vitelli. His death sentence was based on calumnies – unfounded accusations that use *neither witnesses nor any other specific corroboration to prove them*.[28] While one is used to hearing people *calumniated in piazzas and in loggias*, calumny should have no place in public councils and courts of law. This, Niccolò insists in his *Discourses*, is one of the most indispensable pillars of any well-ordered state. Calumniators, whose poisoned tongues injure men without proof, had already brought much ill to Florence, and would bring more: people said of one individual that he pilfered public money, of another that he was too ambitious, *of another* – he does not name these victims of calumny, but any contemporary reader would recognize the allusion – *that he had not won a military campaign because he had been corrupted*. A man who fell victim to his enemies' slanders had no chance to defend himself, *because there were no procedures in that Florentine republic to enable him to do it*. If there had been, *the infinite scandals that occurred* in Florence *would not have occurred*.

And even if Vitelli had been tried and found guilty of corruption or some other fault, was it wise to punish him with death? Look, Niccolò writes in his *Discourses*, at what Titus Livy says about the Romans.[29] While their republic was still in good health, they never punished captains by dubiously legal means, or punished them for errors committed through ignorance. No: the Romans *were more merciful and more hesitant in their punishment than other republics*. Even if a captain brought them trouble through malice, *they punished him humanely*, with fines of money. Why: because they believed that the leaders of armies worked best with *a free and ready spirit,* without having to fear the loss of their heads at the first suspicion of error or misconduct. Livy's wise Romans *did not wish to add new difficulties and dangers to a thing in itself difficult and dangerous, since they thought that if they added them, no one would ever work virtuously.* But *another republic,* Machiavelli writes – a far less prudent one near at hand – *would have punished those captains with the capital penalty.*

Then again, the Romans could adopt this policy because they had their own armies. Their captains were Roman citizens, subject to Roman laws and Roman penalties. If judges found a captain guilty of some grave offence and he failed to pay his fine, they could confiscate his property or send him into exile. That other, unnamed republic resorts to harsh and arbitrary punishments because it has no other way to penalize mercenary captains. Mercenaries are not Florentine citizens, so most of their property, their castles or great houses, their flush bank accounts, lie where the short arm of Florentine law cannot reach.

In that case, apologists for Vitelli's killing might well say: then the Florentines had no choice but to do as they did. Niccolò replies: only if we Florentines have no choice but to depend on hired foreigners for our military defence. But we do have a choice; there are better alternatives. The Romans had them, here in Italy. Florence and other young republics used to have their own citizen militias. They dissolved them only later, when the rich tradesmen who came to dominate the city decided that they had better things to do than fight for their city's freedom, and that they could not trust the people to be trained in arms. But look where this policy has brought us. The whole Vitelli scandal, with the stench of premature decay it leaves hovering over Florence's legal orders, could have been avoided if the city had captains drawn from among its own citizens. And an army of its own, placed under strict civilian controls.

He doesn't yet know what a mere Secretary like himself, a man without a great name or high connections, can do to make this idea become reality. He does know that if nothing is done soon to overhaul Florence's sorry defences, the republic will bleed to death from its self-inflicted wounds. In the space of two years, there have been three high-profile cases of crimes against the state – the five pro-Medici plotters who were denied their right to appeal, Savonarola, and now Vitelli – each prosecuted by more dubious means than the previous one. In each case, the prosecutors had pleaded the excuse of necessity. They were dealing with people who posed a manifest threat to the republic; when faced with such threats, they claimed, one can't worry too much about ordinary legal procedures or the rights of defendants. Niccolò repudiates these excuses. He recalls a case in ancient Rome where, citing the necessity of state security, the Romans denied a man called Appius Claudius the appeal to which the laws entitled him. Appius' *criminal life*, Niccolò concedes, *merited every punishment. Nonetheless, it was hardly a civil thing to violate the laws.* For if ignoring legal procedures *may do good* in one particular case, *nonetheless the example does ill.* And *if one sets up a habit of breaking the* [legal and political] *orders for the sake of good, then later, under that colouring, they are broken for ill.*[30]

In other words, no matter how serious someone's crimes, exceptional punishments that violate the laws set a corrupting precedent. First one exception is made to the general command to obey the laws, then another – and soon the laws look toothless, or like the mere instruments of partisan interests. Then no one respects or sees reason to obey them. That, according to Machiavelli, is how civility dies; it is how even great cities like Rome fell from greatness.

Whatever the Florentines might do or fail to do to stop the rot, the death of a superstar captain like Vitelli is another blot on their young republic's inglorious chronicles. It would not be forgotten, or forgiven. Florence's old rivals would keep looking for ways to turn the scandal against the city, which now has a lethal new enemy in Vitellozzo Vitelli: he has vowed to use his and brother's excellent troops to harm Florence and help her enemies. The Medici and their accomplices in Venice and Rome, not to mention the pope's son Cesare, will be rubbing their hands with glee.

IO

Build Dykes and Dams

At the end of June 1500, Swiss and French troops march towards Pisa. King Louis XII has ordered a siege of that city in fulfilment of his treaty with Florence, and hopes of final victory are high. Secretary Machiavelli is to accompany the city's war commissioners to the camp at Pisa.

This new mission comes at a bad time. His father has just died. Bartolommea Machiavelli had died some years before; the circumstances of both parents' deaths are unknown. Bernardo Machiavelli expected so little for himself from this world of genteel hypocrites and fraudsters, but raised his sons to confront it with their eyes wide open, standing firm on their principles, as he had done, and ignoring slights from the mighty. If the portrait of Bernardo painted in Bartolomeo Scala's dialogue is accurate, he venerated the laws too much to profit from his profession in times when people invoked or flouted legal codes as it pleased them. And when Niccolò and Totto were grown men, perhaps shortly before he died he sent them birds from the farm in Sant' Andrea so that the poor bachelors would not starve. His older son thanked his father in verse and playfully honoured his selflessness:

> At the end of the play then, my Messer Bernardo,
> you will buy ducks and geese and will not eat them.[1]

Still mourning his loss with his family, Niccolò prepares to go to Pisa. This is his most important mission so far. With the city's neighbours under pressure from Pope Alexander's armies, captained by his son, Florentines badly need to strengthen their brittle

122

alliance with France. They hope that the joint French–Florentine campaign at Pisa will smooth their relations and help secure firm guarantees of French protection from the looming Borgia menace. Cesare Borgia's early successes in the Romagna seem to be feeding rather than satisfying his appetites for conquest. At the end of 1499, on the eve of the new millennium, Florentines had heard that the fortress of Forlì had fallen to Borgia. Caterina Sforza had been there to the last, fighting alongside five hundred men who were garrisoned there; all were slain except the former countess, who was taken prisoner and carried to Rome. Pope Alexander staged a superb triumphal parade for his new Caesar on his return to Rome.[2] Cesare wore a black velvet cloak reaching to his knees, with a collar of simple and severe design. He made a short speech in Spanish, or perhaps it was Catalan – most chroniclers couldn't tell the difference – to thank the pope for deeming him worthy of such an honour. The dead Paolo Vitelli's brother Vitellozzo marched with him, trailing behind ambassadors from France, England and other countries, and those of Florence and the rest of Italy.

At around the same time, the Signoria had received an envoy from the pope's son, demanding that the Florentines give him whatever gunpowder they possessed. In the deliberations that followed, everyone was of the same mind. The most defiant speaker was a younger brother of Paoloantonio Soderini. 'Let us refuse entirely this request for gunpowder,' Piero Soderini urged.[3] He had recently served as Florence's ambassador in France and had good relations with the king and his court. 'I say we send new ambassadors to King Louis. Impress on him that his own new state in Milan will soon be at risk if he doesn't put a rein on these Borgia ambitions.'

Now, in the summer of 1500, with Duke Cesare Borgia as their new neighbour in the east, the Florentines think more than ever of how to recover their dominions to the south and east. King Louis is sworn to help retrieve Pisa. But he wants Florence to pay for the Swiss troops who will do this for him. His ambassadors have been complaining that the Florentines are behind in paying their portion of the troops surrounding the rebel city. And now Louis wants more money, 12,000 ducats, to pay more Swiss to guard newly captured Milan.[4] Secretary Machiavelli's task is to do what he can to appease the French at the camp near Pisa, to temporize, put them off until the city can afford to pay.

On reaching the camp, Niccolò and his travelling companions almost immediately sense trouble.[5] The Florentine commissioners who've come with him, Francesco della Casa and Luca degli Albizzi, receive no courtesy from the soldiers who stand guard, or those who show them to their quarters. Dishevelled, red-faced men crouch outside their tents, gabbling in the odd Latinate cadences of alpine German, occasionally in some coarse strain of French. Niccolò and his superiors have scarcely settled in when officers report to them from Seigneur de Beaumont, the French captain of this new Pisa campaign. Bad feelings are running high among the Swiss and Gascon troops, they say. The men claim that the Florentines haven't paid their wages.

Niccolò goes with Luca degli Albizzi and della Casa to dine with Beaumont. He is an easy-going nobleman with impeccable manners and military credentials, appointed to his post at the request of Piero Soderini and other Florentines who'd met him on embassies to France. He assures the guests that he'll keep doing his best to appease the men, confident that the Florentines will do their part to the same end. 'It might help,' he suggests tactfully, 'if you could provide them with more drink. The men have sufficient bread, but they complain about a shortage of wine. I expect some of their discontents and ours will be relieved if their cups are kept full.'

Secretary Machiavelli knows nothing of soldiering, except what he has read in his father's Livy, Caesar's commentaries on his wars with Gaul, and perhaps other well-known Roman histories and books on military strategy: Frontinus, Vegetius. This reading is enough, however, to make him wonder whether Beaumont can be in earnest. More wine, as a remedy for ill-disciplined troops? According to the ancients, this sort of pampering in the armies was among the main causes that drove Rome to ruin. Captains seeking to win favour among their soldiers spoiled them with liberal pay and plunder. When Roman virtue was at its height, good captains did the contrary: they punished any disorder among their men with the severest penalties.[6] Perhaps Niccolò had misunderstood the remark – their dinner conversation was in a bewildering melange of Tuscan, French and Latin – or Seigneur Beaumont's high-aristocratic sense of humour. But after dinner, Luca degli Albizzi, who understands more French than he does, asks him to write straight away to Florence's war commissioner in Cascina to ask for several large barrels.

Nevertheless, within a few days the Gascon troops mutiny and abandon the camp, leaving behind heaps of stinking rubbish and stealing weapons and provisions. Then the Swiss start disobeying orders. When French officers tell them to stand guard, they spit on the ground and slouch about near their tents, feigning deafness to the signal calling them to their daily exercises.

One morning a group of heavily armed Swiss come to Luca degli Albizzi's tent. Niccolò is there, taking a letter. 'My men,' says their leader in a language not quite French or Latin, 'that is, 130 of us from the company of Captain Antonius Buner, were in your city's employ some months ago and were never paid. We are here to demand that you pay us now.'

Luca deals with them most graciously. 'I'm afraid I know nothing of this,' he replies, 'and have no authority to deal with it. But if you would kindly appoint two representatives, I'll give them letters stating your case. Then you may submit the matter to my Signoria yourselves, and settle with them direct.'

Niccolò doesn't catch every word that follows, but registers the exceedingly abusive tone in his subsequent report. A few French officers drift into the tent, then shrink back into the shadows when they see what's happening. Niccolò stands near Luca, trying to look unruffled, but feels helpless; with his muscle-free frame and thin, milky-white face, he is possibly the least terrifying presence ever to face a phalanx of armed *Svizzeri*.

When the Swiss storm out, the Frenchmen start fluttering around Luca with anxious chirps and clucks, bringing fresh water to cool him down. Captain Beaumont visits the tent to convey his deepest regrets. He seems more depressed than angered by the outrage,

Niccolò observes, as though he thoroughly expected it. 'Quite frankly,' Beaumont says, 'I don't know what to do.' The idea that a captain might have various ways to keep his troops in line, even if they are mercenaries and wild with greed, never seems to cross the French captain's mind. He politely reminds the Florentines that his army is still in urgent need of weapons, especially long lances, cuirasses, bucklers and ammunition. 'I have only a few more barrels of powder,' he says, 'and am owed other necessities by your Signoria.'

Luca is badly shaken. 'I may have to start thinking about my own safety and request leave to go home,' he tells Niccolò when the Frenchmen have left. 'Between you and me, I'm not certain our friend Beaumont is up to this job. This entire camp is in chaos, and he does little but regret it, or point the finger at us. He says we should have built a bridge over the River Osole, but failed. Well, we failed because the French didn't provide us with an escort to guard the building, though they agreed to do it. We gave them more than double the munitions they asked for, but where are they now? Stolen, wasted, maybe sent secretly to the enemy? And there's always someone from Lucca lurking about camp. Those Judases tell the French they're our loyal subjects, but the whole world knows they run covert operations to help the Pisans. I've said these things to Beaumont, but he just keeps expressing more regrets.'

Niccolò has been snooping around in his time off and had some interesting chats with other Florentines in the camp. Some told him that while the French held the mouth of the Arno, they kept letting munitions and other provisions reach Pisa by the river; they even let troops get in by boat. The new head of Pisa's infantry, Tarlatino of Città di Castello – a friend of Vitellozzo and Paolo Vitelli – had entered Pisa that way with his men. Someone on the French side, it seemed, could not be trusted.

In the early afternoon the following day, some hundred Swiss soldiers come to Luca's quarters as he, Francesco della Casa and Niccolò are at work. They demand back-pay for their entire company, swearing that they won't leave until satisfied. Again, Luca promises to intercede with the Signoria in Florence.

But the men's leaders will have none of it. After a lengthy argument, in which Luca's heroic efforts to stay calm seem to make the Swiss angrier and angrier, two of them hoist him up by the armpits and carry him off.

Niccolò writes an urgent dispatch to Florence and sends it off by express courier. Not long afterwards, poor Luca also writes to the Signoria: *I fear I may be in the last hour of my life; I feel abandoned by all, like one forsaken and lost.* The Swiss are holding him hostage, threatening him with their halberds. *I am trying to raise the money myself,* Luca writes, *as none is forthcoming from Florence. I've sent men to ask for a loan from Florentines who live nearby.* His relatives beg the government to do something.

In the end, after promising to get his captors their money, Luca is released after just a day and a night in Swiss custody. But they were a frightening day and night for the middle-aged patrician, who is used to gentler treatment. On hearing of the disastrous state of Beaumont's camp, the Signoria and General Council are appalled.

King Louis XII wants to carry on with the siege. The Signoria receive a letter from him. *Very dear friends,* it says, *we have only now been informed of the great disorders, etc. And inasmuch as, besides the injury it has caused you, it touches our honour and reputation, we are absolutely determined to remedy what has occurred in such a manner as to maintain our power and authority.*

Fair words, followed by offers to furnish fresh troops for the siege on the same terms as before. But the Florentines have lost faith in troops they get on hire from the French. These new ones might mutiny again, or join with the mutinous Swiss and Gascons, who are still on Florentine territory. But they are suspicious above all of other Italians. It's our old enemies who put these foreigners up to these tricks, people say. The Swiss must have been paid by the Sienese or Venetians or Genoans, or by some rich Pisan exile or the Medici, to kidnap our commissioner and harass us.

So with the politest possible excuses, the Signoria decide to turn down the king's offer to go ahead with the siege of Pisa. They are aware that Louis will blame the Florentines for the whole humiliating episode, and for wasting his time and money; his agents are already hissing as much in His Majesty's ear. It would be best if the king were to hear their side of the story from two men who witnessed the events in camp: Luca degli Albizzi's fellow commissioner Francesco della Casa and Secretary Niccolò Machiavelli.

This new assignment could not have come at a worse time for Niccolò. He had just lost his father, and now his widowed sister, Primavera, has taken ill. He and Totto fear she might not live out the summer, when the city air seethes with bad humours. Their family's financial affairs are in a mess: there are notaries to consult and pay for sorting through Bernardo's legacy, priests to be paid for the funeral and burial arrangements, contracts with tenants at the farms and the country tavern to be confirmed or renewed. Bernardo had looked after such banal practicalities up to the last, leaving his sons to pursue their careers. Now Niccolò is head of their small family, with his younger sister and mother dead for some years, brother Totto still in his early twenties and finding his way in the world. Totto talks of going into foreign trade with some friends; how wonderful if he would make a success of it and help pay off the old family debts. For now, Niccolò has to leave him to deal alone with all the notaries and tenants and priests, and to visit Primavera and her young son. It won't be long, he assures his brother and ailing sister. They say we should be back after a week or two.

Niccolò and Francesco depart for France on 18 July 1500. Della Casa is older by a few years, and not bad company. His family is not from one of the great houses and he is not much wealthier than Niccolò, but he is assigned the senior rank of the two envoys and paid a higher salary: eight lire a day compared to Niccolò's four. On the way, they pass through the Romagna, stopping over in Bologna.[7] That city's de facto ruling family, the Bentivogli, have appealed to Florence to help them arm themselves against their new neighbour Cesare Borgia. After offering the usual Florentine sedative of empty good words, they travel westward towards Asti and Turin, then cross into France and head for Lyons, where the king is holding his court. The king depends on dozens of provincial barons and smaller lords for his authority and armed forces. Louis XII, like Charles VIII and other monarchs in their times, maintains his supporters by travelling continuously around his realm, addressing local concerns on the spot. If a foreigner has business with a French king, he must be ready to follow a moving court, sometimes over long distances, in a country that sprawls from the Mediterranean to the Atlantic.

The Florentine travellers have little pleasure on the road. There is the heat, the constant need of water for horses and men, servants who ride with them but make themselves less and less useful the further they travel from Florence. Crossing into French territory somewhere near Maurienne, the lodgings become more ramshackle, though the food is tasty. The following day, however, Niccolò's stomach is so upset that he has to forgo further culinary adventures for the rest of the trip. And they still have days to go before reaching Lyons. Days of nausea bouncing up and down on a horse in blistering heat, gnats hurling themselves into one's eyes. Nights of fitful dozing on hard couches, unable to block out the squeaks and scrabbling of rodents. One morning, Niccolò finds his new boots nibbled and full of droppings. The sack carrying his clothes, the ones he bought to wear at the king's court, has been gnawed through and occupied by several families of mice. This time he loses his temper and shouts at his servant, who is supposed to look after his clothing and other belongings. The man should have known, at least, to put the boots on a high shelf instead of on the ground. He makes sure to mention all these mishaps in his *Notes for One Going as Ambassador to France*, telling his reader to especially beware of the food and the mice. *Although this is a small thing and ridiculous*, he writes, *still I speak from experience*.

Worse is to come. At some point, probably soon after they enter France, something forces the envoys to stop and delay their onward journey. Niccolò and Francesco report this 'unforeseen accident' in their co-signed letters to the Signoria, but do not say what happened.[8] They say only that they will have to replace everything they brought with them from Florence: clothes, horses and servants. Perhaps they were robbed on the road; perhaps the insolent servants ran off with their horses and personal effects. In any case, on 26 July they arrive in Lyons denuded of their belongings – only to be told that the royal court has already moved on to another provincial town.

This is terrible news: it means that the two unseasoned envoys might have far more on their plates than they anticipated. Had they not been delayed, they would have gone to court in the company of one or both of Florence's two ambassadors in Lyons, patricians who are on good terms with the king and his advisers. They would have smoothed the way for their visiting countrymen, managed any awkwardness, and undertaken whatever practical negotiations might flow from their meetings. Now, it seems, they will have to defend their city's actions to the French all on their own. They have urgent need of money, and not just to pay for new horses and clothing. Anyone who seeks an audience with the French king, or any prince in Christendom, has to pay a whole flotilla of men to open the golden doors in proper style. Porters, liveried servants, buglers, pipers, tambourine players and mace-bearers.

Niccolò uses the last florins left from his monthly salary to pay a courier going to Florence. He writes to Totto and Biagio, and to the Signoria and the Ten. Please, he entreats his employers, raise my envoy's salary to the same level as Francesco's. Since I incur the same expenses as he, *it seems to me beyond all human and divine reason that I should not have the same emoluments. If the expenses I incur seem to Your Lordships too great, then I would observe that either they are quite as useful as Francesco's, or the twenty ducats allowed to me per month are simply thrown away. If you think the latter is the case, then I beg Your Lordships to recall me. If not, I trust you will take such measures that I may not ruin myself.* These two weeks I have already spent forty ducats of my own, two months' salary, and have asked my brother to make an advance of seventy more. Instead of the usual *Servitor,* he signs the letter *Humilissimus servitor,* Your most humble servant, Niccolò Machiavelli.

After a painfully slow ride on their wretched nags, the only animals they could find for sale in Lyons, Niccolò and della Casa arrive at the small city of Nevers. It is 7 August, and some sort of summer fever rages in the countryside all around. The innkeepers are blasé about it. There's been no sickness in this house this year, they swear. But pestilential fevers have already carried off several members of Niccolò's family. Totto writes that Primavera lies very close to death, and now her young son, Giovanni, is sick with the same illness.

The envoys had been advised to consult first with Cardinal Georges d'Amboise, King Louis's most trusted counsellor and Florence's chief intermediary in France. 'When you meet the cardinal,' one of the Florentine ambassadors had warned them in Lyons, 'never, ever try to argue about any point on which you see he's formed a definite judgement. If you find him set upon any course, whether you like it or not, approve it most heartily. For in the end you'll have to conform to His Eminence's will.' They go straight to d'Amboise's chambers and present themselves as well as they can, apologizing that they lack formal letters of introduction from their Signoria. 'We put ourselves in Your Eminence's hands,' declares Francesco, according to formula, 'as our government's sole protector, in whom Our Lordships have the utmost confidence.'

'If you're here to talk about what happened at the camp at Pisa,' the cardinal replies impatiently, 'we consider that an old affair. But let us go together to His Majesty the King.'

D'Amboise is around forty, a decade older than Niccolò. His bony nose and narrow face give the first impression of a lean man. But when he rises from his desk, a magnificent portly belly bulges out from his red robes.

The king has been napping after dinner, but soon calls them to audience in the presence of d'Amboise, the French general Robertet and several Italians who had been at the camp when Luca degli Albizzi was taken hostage.

Francesco does most of their introductions, in Latin. Niccolò has noticed that even Beaumont and d'Amboise, and other aristocratic Frenchmen, speak the ancient lingua franca with odd accents and even odder grammar. *They are enemies of the language of the Romans, and of their fame,* he later scribbles down along with other pithy observations concerning 'The Nature of the French' (*De natura*

Gallorum).⁹ His travelling companion recounts the Florentines' version of the regrettable events in camp. He prudently avoids accusing any Italians of treachery, as the principal suspects are there in the room. Then it is Niccolò's turn to give his account, as chief witness of the brutal and infamous kidnap of the Florentine commissioner.

The king listens and replies in courteous tones. He is a few years younger than the cardinal and, by nature or by study, has the look of a man determined to show the world that he takes his responsibilities very seriously indeed – that he is not like his cousin Charles VIII, a young man in too much of a hurry, a king who freely gave his word and just as freely broke it.

Then d'Amboise speaks. 'That carrying off of your commissioner was of course unpleasant. But the Swiss, you know, are in the habit of practising such extortions; that's what happens if you have them in your hire. Otherwise, the failure of the enterprise was down as much to your Signoria's faults as to those of the king's army.'

The Florentine envoys try to protest, but the king cuts them short. 'There's nothing to be gained by discussing past events. Now that you're here, we should find a way to go forward with the Pisan campaign. I trust the Florentines have no intention of backing off from it, after all I've done for them.'

Francesco replies, 'We have no orders on that point, not being full ambassadors but only witnesses to the unfortunate events at Pisa. But in our opinion, the people of Florence have grown so weary of war, and feel so worn down by ill fortune and numerous enemies, that they've lost all confidence and lack the strength to launch another campaign. But,' he says in a more upbeat tone, 'once Your Majesty has restored Pisa into Florentine hands, so that we see a certain reward for all our expenses, we're confident that our Signoria will justly and amply compensate Your Majesty for your efforts.'

At these words, the Florentine envoys report home that afternoon, *the king and other persons present all began to cry out.* 'What, do you expect the king to make your Pisan war for you, at his own expense?'

'You realize,' says Louis, 'that if I should decide that I want Pisa for myself, not to mention several other towns in Tuscany, I can have and keep them. Of course,' he continues frigidly, 'I intend to meet our treaty obligations to return Pisa to your authority.' But don't forget, his tone insinuates, who has the power here. 'Write to your Signoria that we need an urgent reply on these matters.'

But of course he's pressing us hard, thinks Niccolò. He knows that there is a powerful faction of oligarchs and closet Medici supporters in Florence that hopes to scrap the French alliance. When Louis sent troops to assert his claims in Milan, we prevaricated over which side to back, instead of coming out as his unswerving friends. Why should he be disposed to do us any favours now, *knowing that the Florentines had come forcibly and not willingly into his friendship?*[10] Our dread of commitment will end up costing us money and pride, and perhaps a good part of our dominions.

That same day, the court packs up and heads toward Montargis. Florence's hapless envoys trudge reluctantly after it. They are moving further and further north and west, further from home than Niccolò has ever been. Several weeks' journey away from his sister and nephew, whom he may never see again, and from the family duties he has dropped in his young brother's lap.

After settling in at their new lodgings, he and Francesco hold a meeting with Cardinal d'Amboise, who presents them with a long list of complaints. 'Everyone here is shocked by your suggestion that the king should recover Pisa at his expense,' the cardinal tells them. 'His Majesty is now so displeased with your Signoria that I really don't see anyone at court here who can remain your friend, or support your interests.'

So it seems the cardinal himself, their only protector, has decided to wash his hands of the Florentines as well, after their one brief audience with the king. The bewildered young envoys can do nothing but write again to the Signoria, urging them to send a full ambassador so that they may flee from this Gallic hell.

They wait. Days stretch into weeks. They write home again: *We have neither the means nor the credit of our own that would permit us to maintain ourselves here for months, unlike so many other ambassadors* of great private means. Every sou goes on dreary lodgings, cheap food, and a woman they hire to cook greasy meals. They don't even have enough to send regular letters by courier. The Signoria will blame them: the envoys were told to write constantly about anything that might be useful for the Florentines, even if it has no direct bearing on the matter at hand. Even the slightest thing might be important.

Niccolò enjoys casual intelligence-gathering. If he had more money to post dispatches, he'd gladly do more. When abroad, as he later advises a compatriot going as ambassador to Spain, find out all you can not just about that country but also about events in Italy.[11] *But since some of the things you pick up may be true and some false but probable, you need to weigh them in your judgement. From those that have most likeness to the truth you can profit, and the others you can neglect.* Prudent diplomats keep a daily record of what they've learned. Then, after taking time to examine different reports and rumours, after eight or ten days *form it into a letter, selecting from the whole mass the part that seems more reasonable.* So Niccolò makes it his business to sniff out anything he can – he has nothing better to do here – starting with Italian affairs. This court is crawling with Italians, all courting French goodwill and French forces with varying degrees of obsequiousness. An emissary of Vitellozzo Vitelli's is here, he writes to the Signoria, spreading reports that Vitellozzo is about to inflict some gruesome revenge on the Florentines for his brother's death, whenever the pope and his son finally declare war on our city. Pope Alexander's ambassadors are here, too, pressing the king to authorize ever-wider conquests for Cesare. The king toys with him, so that these Borgias don't think they can become his equals in power. Most people here say the king considers that he's done enough already by helping them take Forlì and Imola from the countess. Yet for now, he keeps up His Holiness's hopes.

Niccolò has never seen so many different breeds of Italians in one place. Poor, exquisitely tailored beggars swanning about the court of the foreign invader, whom all seek to gratify more than they'd ever dream of gratifying each other. Each is convinced that any other Italian state's gain must be to their loss. So here they all are, bowing and scraping all over France, *more enslaved than the Hebrews, more servile than the Persians, more dispersed than the Athenians, without a head, without order, beaten, despoiled, torn, pillaged and having endured every sort of ruin.*[12]

How did they get here? According to his poem *On Ambition: From Ambition come those wounds that have killed the Italian provinces.*[13] Italians complain about foreign barbarians tormenting them, though they pave the way for their armies with their own quarrels and disorders. *If one considers those lords in Italy who have lost their states in our times,* Niccolò writes in his *Prince – like the King of Naples, the Duke of Milan and others – one will find in them a common defect as to arms.*[14] And this defect is not just in princes; the Florentine republic has it, too. All come running to this French king because he has a strong army of his own, drawn from all the far-flung regions of his kingdom, from Burgundy and Gascony, Normandy and Brittany. Italians don't even have proper armies in their separate cities and dominions. And none let this daring thought cross their minds: that they might combine their forces for more than a few months or a year, in a lasting collaboration, so that one might speak of an Italian army as one speaks of a French one. God forbid that Florentines should ever fight alongside Venetian canal-slime.

Yet if you put these habitual hatreds aside, Italy is not so different from France. *Though there may be some disparity of language* among the various French duchies and baronies, *nonetheless the customs are similar.*[15] If only Italians had the political imagination to forge new orders among themselves, orders that would give birth to a confederated Italian army as big as France's, without a kingdom or a king. For *fortune demonstrates her power where virtue has not been ordered to resist her, and therefore turns her impetus where she knows that dykes and dams have not been made to contain her. And if you consider Italy, you will see a country without dams and without any dyke.*[16]

At the end of August, the court has moved from Montargis to Melun, just south of Paris. The Florentine envoys are fast losing hope of getting home before winter. They still have no agreement from the Signoria to pay for the Swiss, and no firm promise that the city will send proper ambassadors. They try again to approach Cardinal d'Amboise, who spurns their earnest pleas to reopen negotiations. So, returning to their lodgings, they write more dispatches. So far their tone has been respectful, but now, Niccolò decides, they have every reason to be impertinent. Their illustrious Signoria have stranded them here without adequate pay or the smallest crumb of hope to feed the city's French patrons. *According to our judgement*, he writes home, *Your Lordships ought to satisfy the demands to pay the Swiss, or you will have to defend yourselves against the anger His Majesty will feel against you.* Until then, no one wants to see our faces. *These French use a very different language about all these things from what you do, and view them with another eye altogether. For they are blinded by their power and their immediate advantage, and respect only those who are either well armed, or prepared to pay.* Since the Florentines have no arms, we must have an open purse. *They call you Ser Nihilo, and baptize your uselessness discord among yourselves. Our mission here is evidently not agreeable to them, and our rank and quality insufficient to save a sinking cause. If Your Lordships really hope to maintain relations with this court, we deem it absolutely indispensable to send fresh ambassadors here.* They keep hearing that this important man or that has been fingered for the job. But each appointee-apparent finds some excuse to wriggle out. So, month after month, no one comes.

Back in Florence, Totto has been waging a full-scale campaign to increase his brother's pathetic allowance.[17] In early September, Niccolò receives a letter saying that his salary has been raised to parity with Francesco's. *I chased after them for fifteen straight days*, Totto writes, *both morning and evening*, rallying the support of Luca degli Albizzi and several magistrates who think well of Niccolò's abilities.

Small consolations in the desert. Biagio has been asked to read out his dispatches to the Signoria and the Ten, who commend them most highly. *I took extreme pleasure from this and strove adroitly to confirm that opinion with a few words*, Biagio reports. He sends other news, not so good. Florence has lost more towns and bastions around Pisa; Pistoia has been in great upheaval. Another colleague,

Andrea di Romolo, adds a note to Biagio's letter telling Niccolò to come home soon, they've been having quite a few parties over at Biagio's house after work, even the tyrannical Ser Antonio has come along to some; he seems to lighten up when they tease him about needing a woman *to warm him up or give him exercise on the seesaw.* Speaking of women, Biagio and I have seen yours pining away for you at her open window, at that house of fine delicacies along the Arno by the Grazie. But if she loses patience during your long absence, don't worry, by God – *we shall find other stings for you, at least if you haven't become too Frenchified.*

Unlikely. Around this time, Niccolò jots down a few dyspeptic aphorisms about his less than friendly hosts.

The French are more eager for money than for blood.

In adversity they are abject, and in prosperity insolent. If you can resist the fury of their first onslaught, you will find them depressed and so entirely discouraged, that they become cowardly like women.[18]

These words apply mainly to the great barons and cardinals one has the pleasure to meet in court, and the great captains one meets on the battlefield. Yet whatever distaste he has acquired for French *gentiluomini* – who are at least as bad as their Italian counterparts – he has also gained a grudging respect for their organizational skills. This peripatetic court is a marvel of good French order. Niccolò takes notes of this, as of everything: Italians, or at least Florentines, might learn a thing or two. The king keeps four hundred archers, including a hundred Scotsmen. His foot guard is composed of a hundred Germans who wear doublet and hose of the king's livery. Thirty-two fourriers wear king's livery; their job is to provide lodgings for the moving court, and they do this so efficiently that all the vast numbers of people in court find their lodgings fully arranged on their arrival in a new place, down to the women of pleasure. To remove any cause for complaint from lodger or proprietor, they have a tariff of set prices which apply to all, and fix the price of a room at one sou a day, specifying that each room must contain a bed and a couch. Every guest pays a set fee per day for linen, vinegar, and other condiments. Linen must be changed at least twice a week. Chambers must be kept clean, beds properly made.

He is vaguely amused that, of all the great powers in the world, the French fear one that has long since posed little threat to anyone, and at present has no military discipline to speak of.

> *France fears the English, because she remembers the incursions and devastations by the latter, so that the very name of English is a terror to the people.*

On the other hand:

> *France has nothing to fear from the side of Italy, because there is not in all Italy a prince capable of assaulting France, and Italy herself is not united, as she was in the time of the Romans.*

In early September, Francesco della Casa comes down with fever and travels north to Paris for treatment. Alone, desolate, and fearing that sickness might attack him next, Niccolò needles the Signoria with the likely fallout of their negligence. His Majesty's irritation at you has now been so increased, he writes in his and Francesco's names, that *it has encouraged a number of your enemies to propose various measures that would be adverse to your interests. These propositions have all found favour with the king.* The other day they discussed in counsel whether to accept a Pisan offer to surrender to the French, on condition that they would not be subjected again to Florence. For *since His Majesty's dissatisfaction with you has become manifest, everyone seeks to injure your cause.* Soon you'll have to give up Pisa altogether, and think only how to protect yourselves at home. Indeed, *there are intrigues afoot to induce the king to take Pisa for himself, and then to form a state out of the surrounding territories,* including many cities Your Lordships rule at present. The Pisans offer the French vast sums of money to betray you, promising to pay immediately. Your Lordships will forgive us *if we have expressed ourselves too boldly; it was because we preferred to harm ourselves by thus erring than, by not writing, to risk failing in our duty to our republic.*

The court is moving south-west now, past Orléans and towards Blois. On 25 September, Niccolò decides that since his government has dropped him in the middle of France with nothing to do but be snubbed, he'll have to take action of his own accord. Hearing that Cardinal d'Amboise is riding in from Melun, he jumps on his horse and rides out to meet the great man at the hostel where he is to lodge overnight. The cardinal might soften if he sees that this young Florentine has gone out of his way to talk to him, to catch him when he isn't at court, burdened with everyone else's business.

D'Amboise has already retired when Niccolò reaches the inn, so he finds a cheap room nearby and stays the night. The next day, he accosts the cardinal on the road, using *the most suitable and affectionate words that occurred to me*, he assures his employers. He speaks movingly of the sad condition Florence finds itself in at present. He recalls all the help his city gave the king when he conquered Milan, and begs the cardinal to *persist in persuading His Majesty to treat you like his own children*, who might err sometimes but still require protection. If grovelling is what these French want, he resolves, I shall grovel, and get home at last. *Wait for the Florentine ambassadors*, he urges d'Amboise, *and don't listen to evil tongues.*

The cardinal remains sceptical. '*Dixisti, verum est* – it's true that you say so. But we shall all be dead before these ambassadors come.' Then he adds, with the slightest twinkle of appeasement, '*Sed conabimur ut alii prius moriantur* – we will endeavour, though, that others shall die before.'

And so, bumping along on horseback, the Frenchman and a Florentine finally talk again. Cardinal d'Amboise showers the young Secretary with the usual reproaches about Florentine misconduct. But Niccolò's show of initiative and boyish humility has opened a door. No doubt he conveys to the cardinal, without quite saying so openly, that he is almost as frustrated with his bosses as are the French; that he is writing almost daily, badgering them with the direst warnings, telling them to pay the Swiss; that in the meantime their enemies are intriguing, goading the king to make his own state in the very heart of Florentine territories, *so that Your Lordships would be forced to come to His Majesty with chains around your necks and lay a carte blanche at his feet.* And the Florentines have more cause to fear every day, for the pope's army is drawing closer, and no one knows where it will turn next. *The king concedes everything to the pontiff, unwilling to oppose his unbridled desires. The well-known, insatiable rapacity of the pope* will one day come against you if you don't do better with this king.[19]

From Blois, the court moves further west, through Angers towards Nantes. How, Niccolò marvels, have I come all this way north to the Atlantic seaboard, when they told me it would be a week or two, just a quick nip over to the south-eastern border? His friends, those who remember him after all this time, try to cheer him up. *Your letter,* Agostino writes in his usual mock-pompous Latin, *which reached me three days ago, although in Etruscan,*[20] *was nevertheless very welcome, for it came from Machiavelli and from Blois, a very distant region and, as the poet says, almost from another world.* Nantes and Brittany are even more alien. The countrypeople speak a language that sounds nothing like French or Latin. The post sometimes takes weeks to reach this furthest edge of the continent.

And when it comes, the news is sad. *This is the year of our misfortunes,* writes Totto. Primavera has died, and now her son Giovanni lies at death's door. Niccolò has tried to be a good uncle to his thirteen-year-old nephew since the boy's father passed away. Now he begs, pleads, for leave to come home, even if just for one month. After that he will willingly return to France, or go to any other place his government might wish to send him. *The necessity for me to be in Florence is so urgent that I do not wish to be wanting to myself. For, as you are aware, my father died a month before my departure, and since then I have lost a sister. And my private affairs are so unsettled and without order that my property is going to waste.* Totto and their friends have tried to get his discharge, and a bit more money, but this time they got nowhere. *It seemed to me,* writes Totto, that this Signoria are playing *a game to make you endure hardship there.*

But why would they want to torture him? At first it seemed obvious enough: the Signoria thought they could temporize with France by dumping their problems in the laps of two young envoys, men of modest background and few connections. If the king complained, the Florentine government could blame these amateurs for failing in their duties. By now, though, that game had long been up. The king and his advisers know it is up to the Signoria to send them full ambassadors, or not. Niccolò begins to wonder whether someone in the government or Chancery offices might want to hurt him personally, to force him out of his job, out of enmity towards him or his supporters or to create an opening for someone else's protégé. Agostino has hinted as much.[21] *Return as soon as you can, return post-haste, I pray,* he writes in his frothily melodramatic style; but he means it. *Someone very high up, who loves you particularly, has implied that unless you are here you may lose your place in the palace altogether.*

For a Florentine far from home, alone and in fear of his job, with no money to spare for warm boots and a good woollen coat, a rainy November in north-western France promises nothing but gloom. There are only two remedies: write down anything of interest, and make a few friends among one's fellow court-rats. *Because courts always include different kinds of gossipmongers alert to find out what is going on,* he realizes, *you will profit by making all of them your friends, so that from each one you can learn something.*[22] The more he can learn, the more he can help himself, and his city at the same time.

Once he decides to mingle with other Italians at court, Niccolò finds it easy to make the kinds of friends-cum-informants every good diplomat needs in abundance. He enjoys a good party with wine and women; he knows when to be discreet, and when not to be. *A man who wants others to tell him what they know must tell them what he knows, because the best means for getting information is to give it. Men who see that they can also get something are eager to tell him what they know.*

His strategy of using the Borgia bugbear to terrify the Signoria into action seems to be working, for they finally agree to pay the king for his refractory Swiss. But knowing that most of his superiors have no interest in a thirty-one-year-old Secretary's opinion, and that some of them want any excuse to replace him with their cronies, he resorts to indirect persuasive tactics. *Because to put your judgement in your own mouth might be offensive*, he later advises another diplomat, *use such words as these: 'Considering, then, everything about which I have written, prudent men here judge that the outcome will be such and such.'* Or invent a 'very prudent and well-informed' source that supplies you with intelligence and advice, so that it doesn't seem to come from you alone. His dispatches are now full of an anonymous new friend who feeds him 'secret information about the pope'. A great plot is underway, he tells Niccolò, and Niccolò tells his Signoria, to ruin your republic. The pope's ambassador has instructions to propose that the king should restore Piero de' Medici to power in Florence. Cardinal Giovanni de' Medici is constantly supplicating Alexander to do this. The ambassador promises that a Medici government would be entirely in the king's pocket, but who knows what an alliance of pope and Medici would do?

The Borgia card can be played both ways, to alarm the French as well as the Florentines and push them towards each other. Fear might be the only thing that can reunite the estranged allies. He can do them both a favour. *Upon hearing all this, which seemed to me a plot worthy of our Most Holy Father the Pope, I resolved to say something to His Eminence d'Amboise about it.* They have now turned eastward again and have stopped in Tours. On 21 November, four full months since he left Florence, Niccolò pays a visit to Cardinal d'Amboise.

The cardinal has grown indulgent towards this odd young Florentine, who has no air of inherited greatness yet speaks boldly, with the confidence of sound judgement rather than of birth or rank. 'His Majesty,' says Niccolò, 'ought to be careful not to let anyone destroy his friends in Italy.'

He and the cardinal are now on terms that permit the younger man to proffer this kind of advice without causing offence. His Eminence seems mildly entertained, in fact, by the workings of the envoy's mind. Everything done in the present, by the French king or the Florentines, reminds him of something done before by the Romans or the Macedonians.

'It would be best,' Niccolò now suggests – omitting 'for His Majesty', which might be too direct – 'to adopt the practice of all sovereigns who want to establish power in a foreign province. This is to weaken the powerful, conciliate the subjected, and sustain their friends.'

D'Amboise listens, pretending to be more bemused than intrigued. 'Above all, one should beware of letting other great sovereigns exercise an equal share of power in that province.' Niccolò slows down, letting the cardinal connect his general rule to present particulars. 'And in the province of Italy, those who might rival the French in power are not the Florentines, who are manifestly not great, but others who have always sought to dominate all the Italians.'[23]

Cardinal d'Amboise waits to see if his visitor will name these others whose Italian ambitions rival those of the French. He does not. It is one thing to cast direct aspersions on the Sienese or the Venetians, another to appear to be stirring up trouble between His Holiness the Pope and his French allies, especially when speaking to a man of the cloth. But Niccolò has done his research among the busybodies in court. They say that Georges d'Amboise has set his heart on becoming the next pope. He and the incumbent Alexander do not, by all reports, share the warmest of brotherly loves.

'The king,' the cardinal replies brusquely, 'is prudent in the highest degree. His ears are long, but his belief is short. He isn't such a fool as to fall prey to any Italian's cunning.' He stresses 'Italian's'; they both know of whom they speak, and the pope is not Italian. 'But since you seem to be brimming over with advice for His Majesty, I advise you to deliver it yourself.'

A few days later, Niccolò has his audience. 'If My Lordships have still not answered Your Majesty exactly as you would wish,' he begins, 'this is owing to the heavy expenses they are forced to pay, having the victorious army of Cesare Borgia on their borders. Borgia constantly threatens to assail Florence, not with his own forces, but with Your Majesty's. And he constantly boasts of being so supported, which will produce very bad effects unless Your Majesty puts a stop to it.'

The king replies with reassuring alacrity. 'But we've written to our lieutenants in Italy, in duplicate, that if Cesare Borgia should attempt anything against the Florentines or the Bolognese, they should march at once against him. On this point, you may rest in perfect security.'

Niccolò can't be sure whether his appeal to the king's ambitions might have the desired effect. If Louis wants to be uncontested arbiter of Italian affairs, he is a fool to have given this pope and his son the power to challenge him. For his part, Niccolò wishes Italians were free of both evils, of popes and foreign powers that seek to dominate them all. But since they've let themselves be saddled with both, they must choose between evils. And the choice for Florence is clear as day. A few weeks later, in the middle of December, a full Florentine ambassador arrives at court, and Niccolò is released from his five-month-long purgatory. A vast quantity of snow has fallen in Florence, his faithful correspondents tell him. No one here remembers a snow that stayed on the roofs and ground for so long without turning to slush. The boys have made many snow-lions.[24]

The next year brings the city more fears from outside. In April 1501, Faenza in the Romagna falls to Cesare Borgia's forces, and his armies start swarming around Bologna. But since the king still withholds his support for an assault on that city, Cesare flexes his muscles on other prey. First, he attacks Piombino, south of Pisa. Then he surges further south and captures Capua, with the help of a local citizen called Fabrizio. After Fabrizio lets Borgia's soldiers into town, they slay him and proceed to kill some three thousand men at arms, noblemen and citizens, priests and monks and nuns in churches and monasteries.[25] Whatever women they find they treat without mercy.

Lacking the shelter of city walls, countrypeople all over Italy have never been more terrified. When the French came through with their tens of thousands of troops and cannons in '94, at least they – eventually – kept to their agreements, or found some plausible pretext for breaking them. Cesare Borgia hardly bothers to feign respect for accords. He breaks all the rules of fair dealing whenever it suits him, with his Most Holy Father's blessing. And he has as his henchman Vitellozzo Vitelli, all on fire to avenge his brother Paolo's summary execution and make every Florentine suffer. Throughout the spring and summer, papal troops make raids into Florentine territories, cutting down corn, setting crops and farms on fire, stealing livestock. In May, they set up quarters only a few miles from Florence.

The Signoria publish proclamations: every house must keep a light burning at the windows all night, to deter attackers. Shopkeepers must clear out their shelves and hide their goods at home.[26] Florence now has more ambassadors in France than ever, working day and night to persuade King Louis that a formal defence treaty would be in both their countries' interests. In the winter of 1502, moved by a belated avalanche of Florentine goodwill and mounting evidence that Cesare Borgia respects no boundaries approved by men or God, the king at last signs an agreement to defend the city and provide it with six thousand cavalry. In exchange, Florence will pay him 40,000 ducats for three years.

Then, at one in the morning on 4 June, a messenger arouses the Signoria from their sleep with devastating news. Arezzo, one of the principal cities in Florence's dominions, has rebelled in favour of Borgia and his allies. Other rebellions follow, in Sansepolcro and Anghiari, Casentino and the Mugello. Their instigator is the republic's arch-nemesis, Vitellozzo Vitelli. Now the truth is irresistible: Florence's little Tuscan empire is collapsing, piece by piece. Gangs of young men go about blaming the patrician-led government, saying it should have stood up to the pope's bastard son before he stripped Florence of half its territories. Pictures of gallows appear on the houses of leading magistrates.

The Signoria send Bishop Francesco Soderini to talk to Borgia. Niccolò Machiavelli accompanies him to Urbino, where Cesare's troops have recently deposed that city's lord, Duke Guidobaldo

145

Montefeltro. On 27 June, the Signoria convoke a meeting of some four hundred citizens to consider a letter from Bishop Soderini, written in the hand and spirit of Machiavelli. Cesare Borgia intends to change our form of government, it says, if we don't give him further money and promises of loyalty. *If you don't want to be my friends*, Borgia had told Florence's envoys, *you may try to be my enemies.*[27] He wants a reply within four days.

And suddenly, under pressure from Borgia's armies, Florentines start debating a momentous change in their government. The Signoria and Gonfalonier of Justice had always been elected for mere two-month terms. This made the republic look weak and inconstant in the eyes of foreign princes. In Venice, a city governed by men drawn exclusively from old aristocratic families, they have a head called a Doge, elected for life. Venetian doges are not unconstitutional princes like the Medici; their powers are strictly defined by law, so that they cannot easily make themselves or their offspring tyrants. At the end of August, a vote is passed in the Great Council: the Gonfalonier will henceforth be appointed for life. When elections are held on 21 September, Piero Soderini is declared the winner.

Brother of Machiavelli's friend Bishop Francesco Soderini, the new Gonfalonier is fifty-one years old and in good health; he might well enjoy a long tenure as the most powerful fully legal head of government in Florence's republican history. The King of France sends letters congratulating the city on its excellent choice; Louis knows Soderini well as a strong champion of the French alliance. The general populace too, on the whole, are content. Soderini has always defended the Great Council against its detractors, and worked hard to mediate between the city's popular and oligarchic factions.

But some citizens are less happy. Bernardo Rucellai had long nursed a bitter enmity towards Piero Soderini. After the election he withdraws completely from public life, refusing to take part in consultations or to have his name drawn for magistracies.[28] He spends his days writing histories, commissioning statues and ordering exotic plants for the garden beside his villa. This garden, the Orti

Oricellari, soon becomes the site of vibrant discussions about literature, history and philosophy. Bernardo presides over them as if he were holding court. Some come to suspect that he uses these meetings to spew venom about the new Gonfalonier and the republic, or even to plot the return of the Medici.

August 1501 brings a happy occasion: a wedding. Niccolò is getting married. While he was stranded in France after Bernardo died, friends talked to other friends and to Totto, and found a suitable candidate to espouse the new head of the Machiavelli household. Like so many Florentine couplings, theirs is securely enmeshed in a web of neighbourhood ties. Marietta Corsini is a Santo Spirito girl from a less exalted branch of the patrician Corsini family. She seems old-fashioned and strong-willed. Somehow, the bridegroom and Totto find money for the priests, for the notaries, for a wedding jacket and her dress; then more for a pauper's banquet afterwards, with a few family and friends. In a short time, Niccolò's responsibilities have multiplied several times over: he will have to look after the country properties and city house, as well as a new family and a job he takes well beyond his official duties. But once Bernardo was gone, everyone expected it. He expects it of himself.

Marietta is young, some twelve to fifteen years younger than her new husband. Her marriage takes place at one of the most frightening times Florentines have ever faced, better only than the black years of plague that wiped out two thirds of the populace some 150 years before. And her new husband is one of the officers responsible for the city's safety. From now on, he'd have to satisfy a wife as well as his political masters – and Marietta has no qualms about demanding her fair share of her husband's time. Don't worry, Agostino tells him. If you find you've had enough of marriage, just wait for the pope to visit Florence. *If His Beatitude should come there, you and others might want some dispensation, either to take or to leave your wives. And you will get it out of the kindness of his heart, provided your hand is loaded with money.*[29]

II

Fortune Loves Impetuous Young Men

In early October 1502, Niccolò departs for the Romagna. I'll be eight days away, he tells Marietta. No more. Cesare Borgia is on the move again, threatening Florence more directly than ever. At yet another crisis meeting called in September, leading citizens had resolved to send some 'man of good quality' to Borgia's new court as soon as it could be arranged, *under the pretext of congratulating him on his recent conquests and requesting safe conduct for our merchants through his lands on their way to the Levant. Let this person gauge Borgia's intentions towards us, as far as he can, and try to keep him off our backs.*[1] Niccolò Machiavelli, someone had suggested.

He has already had dealings with Borgia, when he went to Urbino with Bishop Francesco Soderini that summer, faithfully reporting Borgia's own words in their dispatches. The bishop supports this choice. Secretary Machiavelli is a shrewd judge of men, not easily taken in by nimble tongues or impressed by push-over victories. He'd soon size up Borgia's nature and let his superiors know if there is some way to manage it.

At the meetings with Cesare in Urbino, he'd stood quietly at Bishop Soderini's elbow in that great gilded hall, in a palace and city that Cesare had just stolen by treachery. He had mustered all his powers of concentration to store every word in his mind, so that he might have an accurate record of what was said when he and the bishop sat down to write their dispatches. 'I know very well,' Borgia had said, 'that your city isn't well disposed towards me. On the contrary, you revile me as an assassin.'[2]

The bishop had denied this, but the young duke, almost half the age of his Florentine interlocutor, had smiled sagely and narrowed his small eyes. 'I know very well,' he'd said again – Cesare often uses that phrase – 'that you are prudent and will understand me, so I'll put this in few words. I don't like this government of yours and can't put any faith in it. It will have to be changed so that I can make your city observe whatever promises it makes me. Because if it doesn't, you'll understand very soon that I won't let things go on as they are.'

Big words, uttered at the moment when his fortunes were at a peak, when all Italy went pale at the euphonious name of Valentino, as Italians call Cesare Borgia, Duke of Valentinois. Yet now, just three months later, his erstwhile allies are rebelling: the great Orsini of Rome, Vitellozzo Vitelli, Siena's lord Pandolfo Petrucci, Gianpaolo Baglioni of Perugia, Oliverotto da Fermo. Fearing that the duplicitous Cesare and his father might soon turn their conquering designs against them, they had arranged a secret meeting at Magione, near Perugia, to plot their counter-moves, and invited the Florentines to join their anti-Borgia league.

But because of their hatred against the Vitelli and the Orsini, the Florentines not merely did not join them but sent Niccolò Machiavelli, their Secretary, to offer Borgia asylum and aid against these new enemies of his.[3] In this rare reference to himself, Niccolò's irritation at the decision is palpable. Of course, his official offers of assistance to Borgia were meant merely to buy time and hold off an attack on Florence. Nevertheless, he implies that his government missed a golden opportunity to stand up to the bully who had terrorized their neighbourhood for three years.

The pope's once invincible son is the weakest he has been in his short career. For once, he needs the Florentines' goodwill almost as much as they need his. This time, Niccolò anticipates, there would be no grovelling. If this duke – as people impressed by big titles call him, even when protocols don't require it[4] – if Cesare Borgia wants to reach terms with Florence, let him say why we should put the slightest faith in his words.

Niccolò is determined to study Cesare more closely than anyone in Florence has yet had the chance to do. He will find out the numbers and disposition of troops that remain loyal to the pope's son, if there are any new defections in the wake of his allies' revolt, and whether the French still seem disposed to support him. But he also wants to know more of the man behind the diabolical reputation, of the son apart from the father. He would later advise envoys to princely courts that they should *observe the nature of the man: whether he rules for himself or lets himself be ruled; whether he is stingy or liberal; whether he loves war or peace; whether desire for glory or any other passion moves him, whether the people love him.*[5] Every gossip-monger in Italy thinks he knows Cesare's motives, but they haven't talked to him. *What men does he keep about him? How much sway do they have over him, how often does he change them, can they be bribed?* Might his intentions be changed? Can he be weaned away from the pope's bad influence? Is he his own man or merely his father's creature? If his father were no longer pope – if, that is, he were to die in the course of nature, or in one of the more sinister modes that bring death to many popes – would Cesare still pose a threat to Florence or to anyone else?

Some princes, like King Louis XII, are open books; they tend to speak their minds, leaving double-talk and dextrous feats of cunning to their advisers. Cesare Borgia is not one of those. *This lord is very solitary and secretive*, men around him had told Niccolò at Urbino. Cesare knows well that people only pretend to trust him, that they hate his Catalan father and wish him gone by any means. He knows that older statesmen and ecclesiastics think he, Cesare, knows a thing or two about war but nothing about statesmanship or the human mind, which is why he insists too much that he knows such things. He lets them see that he sees through their pretences of friendship, see that he is always on his guard. A Florentine envoy would gain nothing through flattery or false promises of devotion. As a general rule, Niccolò by now knows well, envoys produce better results *by being liberal and honest, not avaricious and two-faced, and by not being held to believe one thing and say another. This matter is very important; there are men who, through being clever and two-faced, have so completely lost the trust of a prince that they have never afterwards been able to negotiate with him.* It is all the more important when one has to deal with a suspicious ruler like Cesare Borgia.

So Secretary Machiavelli will not dissemble his feelings any more than professional diplomacy requires. Cesare will trust him more, and thus show more of his own true feelings and intentions, if Niccolò speaks to him as one prudent man of state to another, each fully aware of their mutual mistrust. But still: *One needs to be a fox to recognize snares, and a lion to frighten the wolves.*

Folklore, and many Roman writers – Cicero, Horace, Juvenal – treat foxes as creatures of fraud.[6] If they're right, then Borgia, father and son, are the quintessential foxes of their times. Pope Alexander VI *never did anything*, Niccolò will later remark, *nor ever thought of anything but how to deceive men. There never was a man with greater efficacy in asserting a thing, and affirming it with greater oaths, who observed it less.* Though Cesare still has some way to go to match his father's skills, he, too, is already *a very skilful dissembler.*[7]

But fraud aimed at taking advantage of others is a distinctively human talent. Real foxes, the ones with fur and tail, have nothing to teach men about lying or cheating, even to trap their small prey. Their talent, which so few humans have, is to *recognize snares*, and avoid being trapped. This is the faculty an envoy needs to learn from the fox, especially when he comes face to face with a prince who is a master of deception. To defend oneself against Borgia cunning, the kind of cunning that ensnares and devours, one needs a very different kind of vulpine guile: the kind that sees through ruses, decent words or sacred oaths. If this Borgia prince is one kind of fox, the aggressive anthropomorphized kind, Niccolò will be the other kind, truer to the nature of the animal he imitates: defensive in its ends, and armed with mental agility rather than physical weapons.

Arriving in Imola on 7 October, the Florentine envoy hears sensational news: Cesare's former allies have retaken Urbino for Duke Guidobaldo. The city had fallen easily into their hands, as the citizens revolted of their own accord, having no desire to be the subjects of Cesare or the pope. Now Cesare will have more need than ever to keep the Florentines from throwing in their lot with the traitors. Niccolò rushes at once to the palace, not stopping to change out of his travelling clothes.

He enters the same hall of audience where, not long before, Caterina Sforza had held urgent conferences with her Milanese advisers about how to ward off the Borgia menace. Now this and many other palatial halls are Cesare's. The Secretary presents his credentials.[8] Cesare receives him cordially, acknowledging their previous brief acquaintance. As per instructions, Niccolò starts by speaking of the renegade allies and his government's desire to remain on good terms with the duke and the Church. 'My Signoria,' he says, 'regard all friends of France as their own allies.'

Cesare thanks the Florentines for their demonstrations of amity. 'I have always,' he avers, 'wanted the friendship of Your Lordships. If I haven't attained it, this is more through the malignity of others than through any cause of my own.'

Niccolò has heard this line before. The raids on Florentine territory and the rebellions of Arezzo and other Florentine towns were Vitellozzo Vitelli's doing. Cesare himself had been shocked when he heard what wanton mischief his ally had made. At Urbino in June, Bishop Soderini had pressed him further – but Vitellozzo is your man, why couldn't you control him? 'It's true that he's my man,' Cesare had replied defensively, 'but he meddled with your affairs in Arezzo without my knowledge. Vitellozzo has his private vendetta with you because you killed his brother.' That didn't, of course, answer the question of why a captain had so little control over one of his *condottiere* that Vitellozzo could get away with so many things that Cesare claimed appalled him.

But now, having had time to think further under the shock of unexpected loss, the pope's son seems to have worked out a more convincing response. 'I'm going to tell you, Signor Secretary, what I've never told anybody until now. It concerns my plans to come with my army to Florence.'

Niccolò listens attentively, playing along with his host's surprising show of confidentiality. Whether the cause is the downturn in his fortunes or Niccolò's lower rank and comparative youth – the two men are only about seven years apart in age – Cesare seems distinctly warmer than at his audience with Bishop Soderini.

'Let me tell you how hard I tried to resist all those moves towards Florence, which were entirely against my will. Ever since we took Faenza and attempted Bologna, Vitellozzo and the Orsini kept nagging at me to return to Rome by taking the road through Florence. I refused, because His Holiness the pope instructed me otherwise. When I announced our decision to my men, Vitellozzo threw himself at my feet, begging me to take that road. I tell you. He swore on his knees that he'd do no violence to your city or to the surrounding countryside. Even so, I wouldn't stoop to do what he and the others begged of me. But they kept on at me with so many prayers and pleas that I finally gave in. But only when I had their solemn pledge that your country should not be violated and the return of the Medici not be discussed.'

When he has to, Niccolò notes, this famously guarded Duke Valentino can talk. He speaks in Italian, his mother's Roman tongue, but at the speed of lightning, like a Spaniard. Excuses stream seamlessly from his mouth. He knows that when someone has reason to doubt you, you can win their trust only by letting them scrutinize the details of your case, by talking freely as if you have nothing to hide. It seems he has often had to talk his way out of others' suspicions, probably since boyhood.

'As I still wanted to draw some fruit from my approach to Florence,' he rattles on, 'I jumped at the opportunity to try to make friends with your republic.' His excuses keep coming. He had never let Piero de' Medici enter his camp. Many times, the Orsini and Vitellozzo had asked his permission to attack Florence or Pistoia, but he had never consented. 'On the contrary, with a thousand protests I made them understand that I'd fight them if they caused you any trouble.' He'd ordered Vitellozzo to withdraw from Arezzo, even gone with his own troops to the Vitelli stronghold at Città di Castello to threaten him. 'This, if you want to know the truth, is the cause of Vitellozzo's ill humour towards me.' As for the Orsini, who'd approached Florence with the rebel allies' request to join their cause, someone must have spread reports that the pope was planning to deprive the Orsini of their estates. 'So they joined that gathering of losers at Magione. But their defection proves only that they're even greater idiots than I already thought, since they choose a moment to injure me when the King of France is back in Italy, and His Holiness the pope is still alive. The king and the pope have kindled such a fire under me that all the water my enemies can command won't quench it.'

These last words leave a deep imprint in Niccolò's mind. If one or both sources of the blaze were removed, would Cesare's flame splutter and die?

Excuses made, Borgia moves on to make his requests, or rather his offers, since he still talks as if he has the undisputed upper hand vis-à-vis the Florentines. 'If I haven't been able to make proper amends for my allies' bad behaviour, it's because your Signoria still haven't paid me the stipend we arranged at our meetings.' Now is the time for them to pay up and make friends with him, sealing their friendship with a formal treaty. But if the Signoria were to postpone reaching terms again and, in the meantime, he were to patch things up with the Orsini, the chance would be gone. And since the Orsini would not be satisfied unless he agreed to reinstate the Medici, Florence would be exposed to the same jealousies and difficulties as before.

Niccolò expresses great interest in the suggestion of a treaty, and tries to probe further. But Cesare offers no details on what it might look like. *Although His Excellency manifested a great desire that a treaty between yourselves and him should be promptly concluded*, the Secretary writes to his government, *notwithstanding all my efforts to get at his deeper thoughts and come to particulars, he always avoided the subject with generalities.* As a subtle reminder to Cesare that his current position is in some upheaval, Niccolò asks how his former allies had managed to take Urbino from him so quickly.

'I don't care much about that,' he replies. 'I haven't yet forgotten how to reconquer Urbino, if it is really lost for now.' Then he adds,

'My being so clement, and having little esteem for those things, has done me harm.'

What he has little esteem for, Niccolò surmises, is the grunt work of trying to build up support among new subjects; winning hearts and minds. He has far more interest in military action, conquests. Winning battles and acquiring states, he esteems, and knows how to do. Maintaining states and victories is another matter. *Those who have suddenly become princes* quickly lose their states unless *they have so much virtue that they know immediately how to prepare to keep what fortune has placed in their laps.*[9] Cesare did not know how to keep Urbino. He did not know how to hold on to his allies, who now threaten his whole precarious new state. He is young; perhaps he could learn. Though one almost never sees men of such limitless ambitions acquire the qualities of a statesman: the industry, the foresight, the patience, the understanding of how to deal with people so that they willingly support your power.

Niccolò leaves the audience chamber with the distinct sense that Cesare is badly shaken by the recent turn in his fortunes, which until now had seemed to fly ever higher upwards. He says he is confident of winning again, but he talks too much and too excitedly. The Florentine Secretary has to be careful about how he conveys this judgement in his dispatch. Cesare and the pope will be so nervous now that they will intercept and check letters sent out from Romagna, even more than usual.

Niccolò decides to give his government Cesare's long disquisition *in full, not only its substance, but his very words, so that Your Lordships may better judge it all.* He will make them hear Cesare's voice as if they had been in the hall at Imola with him, hear him tell how Vitellozzo and the Orsini pushed him towards Florence against his will, not realizing that by blaming them he makes himself look weak and malleable. Some of Florence's great leaders are too dim to understand how much weakness this Borgia duke betrays through his self-justifications. But Bishop Soderini, or some other prudent person, will help them read the message between the lines. Hearing Cesare unwittingly indict himself, they should grasp the gist: either Cesare is lying and gladly turned a blind eye to his allies' moves against Florence, or he tells the truth and tried hard to stop them, which means he is an ineffectual leader. Either way, his explanations give Florentines no good reason to invest hopes of safety in him.

The streets of Imola are restless. Niccolò hears that some of Cesare's own troops have been threatening rebellion. *We see all his enemies armed*, he writes home, *and ready at any moment to ignite a general conflagration.* And the local people are all thoroughgoing Romagnole patriots *and have been badly treated by this lord, who has always favoured his soldiers more than the locals.* For all their bravado, Cesare and his advisers are palpably on edge. If the renegade allies move swiftly, they might yet invade the whole Romagna and leave the Borgias' princely aspirations in tatters. Now is the moment Florentines have been praying for.

But if Cesare himself is weak, he could still rely on his very strong friends and relatives. Two days after Niccolò's first audience, the duke summons him with news that Louis XII has promised him troops for an attempt on Bologna. 'You see now, Secretary,' he says, 'just imagine how many more troops I could have from France for my future campaigns! Tell your Signoria that I'm far from abandoning my own case. I should be glad to count Your Lordships among my friends, if they are prompt in giving me their understanding. And if they don't, I'll leave them aside, and even if I had water up to the throat I'd talk no more of friendship with them.'

The following days bring more good news for Cesare. Acting on their own initiative – indeed, against Cesare's express orders to withdraw – two of his best Spanish captains, Hugo de Cardona and Miguel de Corella, seize control over several towns that were under attack from the turncoat allies. Another stroke of luck for the beleaguered young duke, rather than the fruit of his prudent designs. When Niccolò goes to see him on 12 October, Cesare greets him joyfully, declaring, 'See what bad fortune visits men who revolt against me?' He is on a high. Vitellozzo is scorched with fever, he chuckles, Paolo Orsini covered with scurvy and scratching his bloody scabs. The Orsini are already begging the pope's forgiveness. Cesare's star is still on the rise.

From all Niccolò has seen and heard in Imola, Cesare's power depends a great deal on flukes of fortune, and not much at all on his own far-sighted plans. Yes, he keeps getting new troops from France. But he can't rely on his own captains or soldiers – even those who are loyal, so far – to obey his orders. He has the men and horses and artillery to seize and intimidate cities, but not, it seems, the political skills needed to win over conquered peoples. Does he have what it takes to build a lasting state in the middle of Italy, or anywhere? This, for Machiavelli, is the real test of any statesman's quality: his virtue. And while good fortune can help you conquer states, *virtù* is what lets you hold them securely.

Cesare's secretary Agapito trumpets his master's green and virile fortune. With the remarkable reversal of his fortunes over the past few days, he tells Niccolò, my duke *is covered in glory, exceedingly fortunate, and used to winning.* The Florentine Signoria and anyone with half a brain should, he implies, want to jump on the wheel with Cesare and share what they can of Goddess Fortuna's bounties, lavished on her pet. *Yet,* as Machiavelli writes in his 'Tercets on Fortune',

> *you cannot trust yourself to her or hope to escape*
> *her hard bite, her hard blows, impetuous and cruel,*
> *because while you are whirled about by the rim of a wheel*
> *that for the moment is happy and good,*
> *she is wont to reverse its course in mid-circle.*[10]

More fool Agapito, if he does not realize that no one should entrust their safety to a man who depends on fortune. When people say a man is fortunate, they mean that good things happen to him regardless of his own merits or plans. Fortune is sheer arbitrariness: it is the good or the bad that people experience without deserving one or the other. Cesare was fortunate in acquiring his state in Romagna because, without much hard work of his own, he got it through his father in exchange for favours to the king. Now, with his allies in revolt, he is fortunate again – without doing anything to deserve it, he'll be rescued from his rebels by troops from France and ill-begotten money from the Vatican treasury. But King Louis might yet go cold on him; he has gone hot and cold before. And popes don't last for ever. If anything, they tend to die more suddenly and mysteriously than men who are not popes, and leave any states they found *with roots so few and so weak that they wither at the first wind.*[11]

Cesare's courtiers might exult in their master's fortune, in the fire sent from France and Rome that keeps his spirits hot and cannonballs flying. But when Niccolò hears that this or any lord is fortune's darling – or when he writes it in his dispatches or poems or books – the words 'fortune' and 'fortunate' warn more than they praise. A very fortunate man is a man whose success you can't trust, a man you shouldn't bet on. You can trust success that arises from someone's hard work, intelligence, resourcefulness, and deep understanding of human nature – qualities Niccolò will come to associate with 'virtue' in its fullest sense. So far, Cesare has exhibited little of these qualities. He hasn't needed them. That's the trouble with relying on fortune: you get so used to winning with *the arms of others*, with the weapons or money that other people hand you on a plate, that you never develop the qualities needed to stand on your own two feet; you never put in the labours needed to build up *your own arms*. You get spoiled, and if one day your benefactors pull out or depart this world, all your successes can come crashing down overnight.[12]

As he ponders Cesare's career until now, a series of contrasts starts to take shape in Niccolò's mind. States, or any kind of power over other people, *are acquired either with the arms of others or with one's own, either by fortune or by virtue.*[13] People call virtue those qualities that deserve praise, whether in general or in relation to a specific activity: spiritedness and physical courage are a large part of a military captain's virtue, but not of a wool merchant's. Cesare is undoubtedly spirited and brave in battle. But he will need to nurture other qualities – and soon – if he hopes to keep his state. One essential quality of a true, virtuous leader, Niccolò stresses in his

Prince, is self-reliance. Virtuous statesmen succeed through their own discipline, foresight, organizational skills and demonstrated merits. Fortune-dependent people, on the other hand, succeed by means of others' arms and money. And *Cesare Borgia*, the *Prince* tells its readers, *acquired his state through the fortune of his father* and with the help of foreign arms. Another quality found in excellent leaders is patience. *Those who become princes by the paths of virtue* come to power with difficulty, *but hold it with ease*, having worked hard to win supporters by proving that they can be trusted to govern well.[14] *Those who become princes solely by fortune* have it much easier at first, rising to power *with little trouble*. But when the time comes to consolidate their newfound power, then *all the difficulties arise*, since these impetuous high-flyers seldom take the time to build up solid foundations for their state. Because of this, princes of fortune tend to be moody, fickle in their policies, even manic – now acting as if nothing could stop them, then losing all confidence at the first failure, as if failure weren't a normal part of life. Virtuous leaders are far steadier, more trustworthy. They refuse to become arrogant with success or dejected with failure and, if their luck changes for better or for worse, *they do not vary but always keep their spirit firm*, showing that *fortune does not have power over them*.[15]

It might still be possible for the pope's fortunate son to develop some of the qualities of a virtuous statesman. If he doesn't, the last act of this tumultuous Borgia drama is easy to foresee, for the fortune-reliant tend to fall as fast and as dramatically as they rise. They are all dizzying heights and disastrous, crushing lows. If you hark back to ancient times:

> *Caesar and Alexander you will see among those who were happy while*
>   *alive . . .*
> *Yet nevertheless the coveted harbour one of the two failed to reach,*
>   *and the other, covered with wounds, in his enemy's shadow was slain.*[16]

Ten days after their first meeting, on 17 October, Cesare sends for Niccolò. 'I have a letter from one of my agents,' he says. 'It says the

Orsini will gladly come back to me' – his expression is grave, as if
he's still wrestling with a tempting offer – 'if I agree to attack either
Venice or Florence. You see, Secretary, what good faith I show you
in sharing this with you! I do so, of course, only because I believe
that your Signoria will come cheerfully to be my friends and allies.'

Niccolò has begun to compile a list of Cesare's pressure tactics,
in descending order of friendliness. This one is near the top of the
list; no need to worry too much, yet. He thanks him for his magnanimity in sharing this information.

Over the next days, he writes home, *I continue to do my utmost to
win His Excellency's confidence and to be allowed to talk familiarly with
him*. The Secretary's dispatches often report very long conversations in which *the duke said nothing of any importance*. At times,
Cesare seems to want to appear easy-going and guileless, to coun-
teract his reputation as a devious fox. At other times, his one-way
gabbling starts to feel like a trap, a stranglehold of hot air that swirls
and coils around his prey until they can't speak, can hardly breathe,
can't flee from the domineering, empty force of his noise. He especially likes to give his enemies, the ones who were so recently his
friends, a good roasting. 'I don't mean to brag, Secretary, but what
hopes can they have? Just compare what we are, and what they are.
As for that Vitellozzo Vitelli to whom they've given such great reputation, ha!' he laughs out loud. 'He constantly gets out of things by
whining that he suffers from the French disease. All he's fit for is to
devastate defenceless countries and practise treachery.'

Cesare must know that this is more or less what people say about
him. Or perhaps he is less artful than most people assume. Sometimes he says these things calmly, Niccolò notes, but sometimes
in raw anger that he makes no effort to control. As if he, offspring
of that master deceiver in the Vatican and himself no mean liar,
is truly shocked, wounded even, that anyone would betray him –
he who has so much promise and so much power behind him. In
these moments, Niccolò is almost moved to pity. How hard life
can become for those who start off winning too easily, with too
much help.

But though Cesare natters on about his enemies and how he sees through their tricks, Niccolò can get nothing from him or anyone else about his plans to attack or reconcile with them. *In this court things that are meant to be kept silent are never mentioned to us*, he tells the Signoria, whose letters keep hectoring him for meatier intelligence. *Everything is carried on with a wonderful secrecy.* He has heard sotto voce reports, though he can't confirm them, that Borgia's Spanish troops have suffered heavy defeats around Urbino.

One day Cesare calls him in with a demand: 'Tell your government to send ten squadrons of cavalry to my assistance. And tell them I'm ready to conclude an indissoluble alliance with them, from which they'll derive all the advantages of my support and my fortune.'

Niccolò conveys this message to his bosses in Florence. I doubt that I can do any more here, he tells them. It would be better if you sent a full ambassador in my place, someone of greater weight and reputation, someone known here to be on good terms with the French. I should very much like to return home, *for my private interests there are going to ruin.* Biagio has had a letter from Marietta's brother asking when his vagrant brother-in-law will be back. *She says she does not want to write herself, and she is making a big fuss, and she's hurt because you promised her you would stay eight days and no more. So come back, in the name of the devil, so the womb doesn't suffer.* Biagio sends his wife, Lessandra, to look in on the abandoned Signora Machiavelli, who had recently given birth to the couple's first child, a daughter called Primerana. Somehow, through her bouts of fury, Marietta had managed to order a new doublet for her husband, which Biagio will try to have sent. Ser Antonio della Valle is on a rampage again; Niccolò's office-mates curse him for letting tyranny take over through his long absence. *So you see*, scolds Agostino, *where that spirit of yours, so eager for riding, wandering, and roaming about, has got us. I wish that no one but you were standing beside me and was my superior in the Chancery, even if you dared to do all the things that poisonous viper does. Biagio, likewise, besides hating you on account of such things, blabbers on, reviles you with insults, damning and cursing you, reckoning all things worthless without you.* How well Florentines can blame through praise and send tender embraces through abuse.

At the end of October, Niccolò hears on good authority that Cesare and his allies are about to reunite. Their reconciliation, Secretary Machiavelli fears, might be fatal for the Florentine republic: Cesare might finally give in to Orsini pleas to put their Medici relatives back in Florence. The pope's son stokes the Secretary's anxieties by insinuating that this might be part of their secret plan, at the same time swearing high and low, 'I'll never permit your city to be wronged. Not even a single hair.'

Yet the more public talk Niccolò hears of peace between Cesare and his faithless allies, the more he also hears the duke's ministers disparage the traitors in private. *On the one hand,* he reports in his latest dispatch home, *they talk of a treaty of amity; on the other, they prepare for war.* He sounds out one of Cesare's more talkative bodyguards. 'From all I'm hearing,' this man tells him, 'the duke wants to take revenge on those who imperilled his state. He's not serious about a reconciliation.'

In a short time, Cesare recovers Urbino. Then, urged by the French to curb his ambitions, he promises to hold back from further conquests. Niccolò tries to sound cautiously optimistic. Perhaps, he writes home, *this duke is now teaching himself to restrain his desires, and knows that Fortune does not let him win all of them.* And now, at a court in a town overrun by soldiers, where since October all the talk had been of French troops and papal bank accounts, one hears of measures taken to construct a new state. A court of justice is being set up in Cesena for Cesare's new duchy of Romagna, headed by a Messer Antonio del Monte – *a most learned and virtuous man,* Niccolò assures his Signoria.

In his *Prince*, written ten years after his mission to Cesare, Niccolò will tell princes what they need to do to secure their newly acquired states. Cesare is not the only prince he has in mind when he formulates the following maxims. But to Niccolò he is a textbook case of a new prince whose state must remain weak, without roots or branches, unless he understands very quickly *how to prepare what fortune has placed in his lap* by building the essential foundations of any stable state.[17] *The principal foundations all states have are good laws and good arms.*[18] Until now, Cesare has cared only about arms, and the arms he had proved to be neither good nor his own. Now at last he will have a well-staffed court of law in his capital city. He plans to send its head as a papal emissary to offer a pardon to all the inhabitants of Urbino and other rebellious cities. *A prince can never secure himself against a hostile people, for they are too many.* Cesare's standing with the local population is unsteady, to say the least. Of course, people who hated the old rulers he toppled will lionize him as their liberator for a short while. But if he does nothing more to improve their lives, he'll soon lose their favour. Now he appoints one of his most able Spanish lieutenants, Ramiro de Lorco, as governor of the Romagna. Ramiro has an eagle eye for breaches in defence, and a reputation among his troops for being hard on slackers and mutineers. If anyone can silence conspirators and make citizens in Romagna's rich towns pay their taxes to Rome, de Lorco is the man. *A prince should not care about the infamy of cruelty* – if people call it 'cruel' to punish those who don't pay their taxes or who break other laws. Such bellyachers are used to states whose princes are too weak or corrupt to enforce penalties against all violaters, including their friends. Niccolò's virtuous prince has no time for these complaints. Perhaps, under the tutelage of his older and wiser advisers, Duke Cesare would absorb similar maxims.

Prudent princes, we read in the *Prince*, know that they need to win the trust of both subjects and allies. To win trust, they need to behave consistently and avoid a reputation for fickleness or hypocrisy. Niccolò doubts whether Cesare's temperament will allow him to grasp that *men are never so indecent as to betray your good faith when you've observed it towards them.*[19] A man used to winning spectacular victories through one set of methods must find it hard – very hard – to change those methods. To organize a state well *presupposes a good man*, a man who keeps his word and applies the same rigorous standards to punish lawbreakers, whether friends or foes; while becoming a prince by violence *presupposes a bad man*. And *it very rarely happens that someone good wishes to become prince by bad ways, even though his end is good* – or *that someone wicked, having become prince, wishes to work well*, and indeed *that it will ever occur to his mind to use well the authority that he has acquired badly*.[20] If Cesare is one of those rare men who can learn very quickly how to change his so far dangerous course, not just in word but in deed, his virtue will shine through soon enough. If not, it will soon be too late.

It does not escape Niccolò's notice that Cesare still holds secret meetings with all the enemies of his restored allies. *No one really knows what course he will take, for it is difficult to penetrate his designs and to know him. If we judge by the facts themselves and by what the duke himself or his first minister says, we cannot but foresee ill for those who were lately his adversaries.* The treaties are clear, but ambiguity seems to reign more completely than ever at Cesare's court. It is wearing Niccolò down. His requests for audiences get nowhere now. Florence has lost Cesare's interest. The Signoria keep complaining that their envoy writes too few letters, keeping them in darkness. He replies in tones he knows some of them will call arrogant: I've told you how secretive this duke has been lately, and *to avoid writing mere fancies and reveries, one must study matters well and take time. I endeavour to spend my time profitably. I may not easily get an audience with him, because he lives only to advance what is useful to him, or seems so, without placing faith in anyone else.* Niccolò entreats his masters, again, to let him come home. *Apart from seeing that I can be of no use to our republic here, my bodily health has suffered much. For two days I had a violent fever, and feel altogether unwell.* Marietta often sends to the Chancery for news of him, his colleagues report, asking when he will come home.

For almost two weeks, Niccolò struggles to drag himself from his hostel bed in the mornings. He feels hot and cold in turn, coughs up phlegm. After ten days without speaking to Cesare, he decides to try again, while he can still move about. This time, he is granted an audience straight away. It is 5 December, two months since he left Florence. They talk for a full hour, mostly about trivial matters. How the duke holds Florentine interests close to his heart. The capture of Pisa – now that would be the most glorious thing any captain could accomplish! And Lucca, that den of Judases who keep helping the Pisans in their war against Florence – a city full of riches. Pistoia. Siena.

Ancient historians and philosophers likened the appetite for limitless conquests to a potentially fatal addiction. Herodotus' Persians, Thucydides' and Plato's Athenians, Livy's and Tacitus' Romans: all acquired far-flung empires in a short time, then choked to death from overeating. Once whole peoples or individuals become accustomed to swallowing up more than is necessary to live well, they find that they can scarcely live at all without consuming more, though they know it might kill them. Perhaps Cesare is trying hard to break his old habits, goaded by the King of France and a few prudent advisers. Or maybe he has not changed at all. Shortly afterwards, Niccolò imagines a speech delivered to the Signoria in Florence. The speaker, perhaps himself, expresses freely what it would be incautious for an envoy to say in his dispatches. *Anybody who has observed the duke sees that he has never planned to lay his foundation on Italian friendships.* All his actions make it plain that he wants to build a large state for himself in the middle of Italy, and will of necessity soon turn to conquer Tuscany. *It remains now to see if time will accommodate his efforts to colour his designs.*[21]

Niccolò had asked his friends to scour local booksellers' for a copy of Plutarch's *Lives of Illustrious Greeks and Romans*.[22] It is full of famous men brought down to earth and examined from all angles, humanely yet unsparingly, painted from the whole polychrome palette of greater and lesser human virtues and failings. Some, not unlike Cesare, seem to win every battle they pick and, if they falter for a bit, to come out even better after a short setback. Fortune loves them. They have no scruples, no respect for others' freedom or for written or unwritten laws. They do not need them: since fortune works for them, they don't need to know how to make men do so. Or so they come to think. Biagio writes that he's tried to find the *Lives* in Florence, but there were none for sale. Be patient: I'm about to write to Venice to see if someone has them there. *To tell you the truth, you can rot in hell for asking for so many things.*

Borgia has decided to travel from Imola to his new state's capital of Cesena in the east, near the coast. Niccolò is obliged to follow. *I do not go with a good will*, he tells his political bosses, *for I am by no means well, and have but seven ducats left in my purse* and am forced to borrow a few ducats from this man or that. Troops – Gascon, German, Swiss, all sorts of motley French – clog the road along the way. Niccolò's servants complain that they push everyone else aside in the evening dash to find food and lodgings. There are hundreds of them, maybe more, marching in bad order, menacing the locals, harassing women, stealing hens and geese. The duke is taking all his French troops with him to Cesena, one of Cesare's men says. His whole army.

This news gives rise to a buzz of speculation among the travelling envoys. What on earth can he be planning to do with so many soldiers? Why should a ruler need all these heavily armed men to travel about his own realm? One could only conclude – and Niccolò does – that Cesare means somehow to use them against Paolo Orsini and Vitellozzo Vitelli and the other men who nearly deprived him of his state, men who are now his signed and sworn allies, an alliance blessed by Cesare's father, the pope.

But the aim astonishes him less than the chosen means. If you're a new prince over subjects who don't yet trust you, is it wise to take hundreds of ill-disciplined soldiers and let them tramp across your subjects' fields, into their towns and taverns? Niccolò marvels at the forbearance of the people of Imola, who had put up with all these foreign troops and their rough behaviour for months, and endured shortages of food and other necessaries, for Cesare's soldiers *consumed everything, to the very stones.* A few run-ins with locals occur shortly after they reach Cesena. Here even more than at Imola, the duke and his troops *live according to their own pleasure, and not that of the persons who lodge them.*

A prince has little cause to fear for his state *if the people show good-will to him. But if they are hostile and bear hatred for him, he should fear everything and everyone. And well-ordered states and wise princes have thought out with all diligence how to satisfy the people and keep them content, because this is one of the most important matters that concern a prince.*[23] In the corrupt days of Rome's decline, when the ancient virtuous republic had been torn apart by men who all wanted to rule as emperor, princes had to please the soldiers more than the people, because the soldiers could do more harm to them than the people. But *now it is necessary for all princes except the Turk and the Sultan to satisfy the people rather than the soldiers, because the people can do more than the soldiers.*

Cesare behaves like a despot in a time and a country where despots face constant conspiracies and rebellions. If his advisers try to warn him that he should control his men or risk alienating wary subjects, he ignores them. Instead of reining in his soldiers, he indulges them, freely handing out money to the infantry and men-at-arms. Just like his namesake and hero, Julius Caesar.[24]

On 20 December, Niccolò is at court when a crowd of French officers burst into the waiting room before Cesare's hall of audience. They chatter fast and loudly; their faces and gesticulations look angry. Soon they disappear into the chamber.

Niccolò goes at once to the well-appointed lodgings of one of his friendlier French contacts, the Baron di Bierra. 'The king has ordered all French men and troops to leave here,' the baron tells him. It seems that several French officers had been assaulted by countrypeople around Cesena, and decided that they were no longer safe here. 'The countryside is growing hostile to Duke Borgia,' other French officers tell Niccolò, 'being burdened with so many soldiers.'

Cesare might be a speedy conqueror, but he is proving, again, a slow learner of political art. First, his tightest allies turn on him;

then his French troops, the main source of his overbearing pride and strength, abandon him. He keeps insisting that now his power is secure, now his state has very good foundations. But he has a knack for spoiling whatever hopeful beginnings his friends help him build. He seems unable to grasp one of the first rules of politics: if you don't give people reasons to trust you, they won't support you. And without other people's support, all your castles and princely titles rest on mud. Above all *for a prince it is necessary to have the people friendly; otherwise he has no remedy in adversity.*[25]

No one seems to know what Cesare wants or is able to do next. Niccolò can only report back to Florence that, as of 23 December, *he is not abandoning any plan made so far.* Even without the French he still has a thick host of troops, mostly Swiss and Germans, on the move. On the other hand, in a matter of days, *he has lost more than half his forces and two thirds of his reputation; and it is believed that he will not be able to do many things that he gave signs of earlier and that were thought possible.* His enemies wait eagerly for him to tumble further. Their agents prowl about the Romagna, stirring up popular resentments against Duke Borgia. They do not have to work hard.

But Cesare has his ways of fighting back. In the same dispatch, Niccolò reports that Messer Ramiro de Lorco, Cesare's governor in charge of ordering political affairs in the whole duchy of Romagna, has been confined in a dungeon at Cesena on his master's orders. *There are guesses here that he will sacrifice him to the local people, who have a very strong desire for it.* By now, everyone in the Romagna seems to have some grievance against their new prince, his troops, or his agents. Messer Ramiro has won a reputation for cruelty, whether deserved or not.[26] And Cesare needs a scapegoat to quiet the unrest. He orders a trial, presided over by the excellent Messer Antonio del Monte. Only three days later, on 26 December, Niccolò witnesses and reports the outcome. *Messer Ramiro this morning was found in two pieces on the public square, where he still is; and all the people have been able to see him. Nobody feels sure of the cause of death, except that so it has pleased the prince, who shows that he can make and unmake men as he likes.*

Whatever legal proceedings had started were never completed. There had been no sentencing, no public statement of reasons for the killing, no pretence that Cesare's new state cared about transparent justice or the rule of law, that this was a lawful execution rather than an extrajudicial murder. The court's distinguished president seems to have been shunted aside. In his later, more literary accounts Niccolò would add a piece of wood and a bloody knife at the scene, placing them beside the mutilated corpse.[27] *The ferocity of this spectacle left the people at once satisfied and stupefied.* The Romagnoles wanted some satisfaction for the harshness and disorders they endured under Cesare's short rule, but this was beyond their expectations. This prince can make and unmake men as he likes. He will give the people what they want, and terrify them at the same time. His theatrical coup in the piazza was either a stroke of rare political genius or the desperate act of a new ruler in deep trouble. Niccolò plays with its ambiguity when he describes it in his *Prince*; he lets readers judge for themselves. For now, he writes to the Signoria and lets them judge whether his words swoon with admiration or ooze scepticism. Duke Cesare *exhibits an unheard-of fortune, a spirit and a more than human confidence that he can attain everything he desires.* He remains very secretive; no one but he seems to know what his next move will be. His secretaries keep telling Niccolò, with more than a little frustration, that he does not tell them any of his plans up to the minute when he wants them to execute it. *Hence I beg of Your Lordships to excuse me and not impute it to my negligence if I do not satisfy you with information, because most of the time I do not even satisfy myself.*

A few days later, 31 December: at last, Cesare reveals the main purpose of his excessively well-armed journey across his state. In a later, dramatic account of the events – his 'Description of the Method used by Duke Valentino . . . [at Sinigaglia]' – Niccolò recalls Cesare's attempts to negotiate with his wayward allies over Urbino and other towns they'd taken for him. *Being a very skilful dissembler, he strove to make them believe that they were moving against a man who intended what he took to become theirs, and that it was enough for him to have the title of prince.* Meanwhile, he kept increasing his own armies and acquired five hundred new French lancers. And *although he was now so strong that he could revenge himself on his enemies in open war, nevertheless he decided that to deceive them would be a more secure and useful method.* So while his advisers worked to secure treaties with them, Cesare waited for a suitable occasion to carry out his secret vengeance.

In the last days of December, the Orsini, Vitellozzo and their cohorts had captured the town of Sinigaglia on the Adriatic coast for Cesare, who decided – apparently without consulting his main advisers – to go there with his troops, *saying he wished to avail himself of the weapons and the counsels of his friends.* On the thirty-first, he entered the town and met Vitellozzo, Paolo and the Duke of Gravina Orsini, and Oliverotto da Fermo. Niccolò's drama has Vitellozzo *unarmed, in a cloak lined with green, and very disconsolate, as though he were aware* of what would come next. *The duke welcomed them with a pleasant face* and went with them to a room in the headquarters they had taken in his name. Here Borgia had his soldiers seize and imprison his allies, then plundered all their troops, who were waiting outside the town. Manifestos were published throughout the Romagna, proclaiming, 'The traitors are captured!'

That same night, Cesare summoned Secretary Machiavelli. *With the most serene air in the world,* Niccolò reports in his dispatches, *he expressed to me his delight at his success.* Then he spoke affectionately of the Florentine republic and how he desired its friendship, provided the Signoria reciprocated his feelings. 'Ask Your Lordships to rejoice with me,' he orders. 'Tell them to send cavalry to assist my assaults on Città di Castello and Perugia. They have no reason now to fear or mistrust me, as you can see, since I'm well provided with troops and your enemies are my prisoners. Oh – and I have a particular wish that your leaders will help ensure that the Duke of Urbino is arrested, in case he should try to take refuge in Florentine territory.'

Cesare's flirtation with the *virtuoso* methods of state-building and diplomacy had barely lasted a month. The next day, 1 January, Niccolò hears that Vitellozzo Vitelli and Oliverotto da Fermo had been strangled in the night. Paolo and Gravina di Orsini were left alive, until the duke learned that Pope Alexander had arrested their relative Cardinal Giambattista Orsini at Rome. He died in Castel Sant' Angelo on 22 February, probably poisoned on Cesare's or his father's orders.

Now the new Caesar turns towards Perugia and Siena, cities ruled by two of his remaining friends-turned-enemies, Gianpaolo Baglioni and Pandolfo Petrucci. Niccolò follows. On the road, he sees what's left of Cesare's army, in a terrible condition. Any man able to find the flimsiest cover to sleep under thinks himself fortunate. There is so much snow, and there are so many road robberies in the countryside, that couriers refuse to carry letters.

Cesare sends for Niccolò several times in the second week of January, asking him to persuade the Signoria to assist him in driving Pandolfo from Siena. That man and his city are Florence's bitterest rivals, he points out. Surely your Signoria would be nothing but pleased to help make himself, their friend the Duke of Romagna, lord of Siena? And, he adds with some passion, 'It is well to deceive those who themselves have been masters of treachery.'

He spoke with so much animation, Niccolò reports, *that if one could believe that he was as true as he says, we might rest assured. Nevertheless, the experience of others makes one fear for oneself.* Siena is in Tuscany, some forty-five miles south of Florence. Cesare's present state of Romagna lies to the north of both; Florence occupies the tempting middle ground between Cesare and Pandolfo. *What I infer from all this,* writes Niccolò, *is that when the duke has carried out his enterprise against Siena, he will think that the opportunity he has planned and waited for has at last come.* The opportunity, that is, to turn his armies on Florence.

A week later, rumours spread through Rome and Florence that Borgia's troops had captured Chiusi, Pienza, and other places in Siennese territory. In one town, it was said that they found only two old men and all the old women, the rest having fled.[28] The duke's men strung the women up by their arms and lit fires under their feet, hoping to make them confess where the citizens had hidden their wealth. Refusing, they died. Soldiers then ransacked houses, tearing down roofs and beams, breaking through doors, splitting open casks to spill wine everywhere, then set everything on fire.

Late in January, the Florentine Secretary's pleas are heard at last: a full ambassador joins the court, and Niccolò is back home by the end of the month. By springtime, the city lives again in daily fear. Yes, Vitellozzo is dead, and the French king has gone cool on Cesare's enterprises. But now the pope and his son are shopping for troops and support from Spain, whose king is keen to compete with the French for spoils in Italy.

Leading citizens urge the government to prepare for an impending attack on Florence.[29] Some insist hopefully that the pope has promised to spare the city. Others recall that when it comes to Papa Borgia, those who lack trust find themselves less deceived. Piero Soderini, the Gonfalonier for Life, issues stern calls for calm. 'We've fresh cavalry and infantry,' he says, 'which have raised people's spirits. And spirits must remain high.' But by the middle of August, the city's defences are still sorely lacking. Now Cesare is at our frontiers, wail patricians in the councils, and still the Great Council kicks and howls whenever we ask for more money. We must appeal to the King of France, push the people to vote for more taxes, have recourse to God!

What they don't yet know, but hear only days after the event, is that Pope Alexander is dead. He had died on 18 August, of unconfirmed causes.

Pope Borgia goes unmourned, even in the Vatican. According to the papal notary, neither priests nor anyone else attended to his body, and a gang of labourers cracked blasphemous jokes about the deceased as they pummelled his bloated, discoloured corpse into the coffin.[30] When he died, Niccolò's *Decennale* will eulogize, *slain by Heaven* for his sins,

> *the soul of the glorious Alexander, that it might have rest, departed*
> *to the blessed spirits;*
> *his sacred footsteps were followed by his three dear and intimate*
> *handmaids:*
> *Luxury, Simony, Cruelty.*[31]

Now, it seems, Cesare's fortune must turn. Within days, Urbino, Faenza, Piombino are rising against him. The new pope, Pius III, supports Cesare's state and confirms him as captain of the papal army. The goddess Fortuna smiles on Cesare again – for twenty-six days. Then Pius dies, after one of the briefest papacies in the Church's history, and on 1 November another man is elected pope: Giuliano della Rovere, Alexander's fiercest enemy. He calls himself Julius II. Before the election, Cesare had struck a bargain with his father's old nemesis. He would induce the cardinals who had been created or heavily bribed by his father to support della Rovere in the electoral conclave. In exchange, Julius would leave Cesare lord of Romagna, permitting him to try to recover his recently lost territories.

Niccolò travels to Rome for Julius's coronation. He has never been less eager to travel. Marietta is on the verge of giving birth to their second child, and berates him terribly for leaving her in this condition. Biagio writes that *Marietta is cursing God, and feels she has thrown away both her body and her possessions. For your own sake, arrange for her to have her dowry like other women, otherwise we won't hear the end of it.* Biagio is being half playful, but only half. The hostels around Rome reek of some deadly contagion; each traveller Niccolò meets seems to know men who arrived there in perfect health then collapsed the next day.[32]

He soon reports back to the Signoria that His Excellency the Duke of Romagna seems more confident than ever of accomplishing his grand designs, which presumably include gaining control over Florence and its dominions. On 4 November, he writes that Borgia has taken up residence in the papal palace, along with some fifty retainers. Pope Julius has made him many great promises. Cesare seems to put faith in them.

Yet some observers believe that he's in for a surprise. Julius finds it convenient to keep feeding his hopes for the present. But the new pope's hatred of the Borgias is notorious, and it seems inconceivable that Julius would quickly forget the ten years of exile he endured under Alexander. *The duke meanwhile,* Niccolò writes home, *allows himself to be carried away by his rash confidence, believing that the word of others is more to be relied on than his own.* That's another thing about fortune-dependent types: they tend to think that they're the only shrewd operators in the room. They can easily deceive others, but never be deceived. So Julius

> *fed him with many hopes;*
> *and the duke believed he would find in another such pity*
> *as never he knew himself.*[33]

Meanwhile, the great infant duchy of Romagna is disintegrating fast, and all Rome is talking about it. Since the pope's death, Imola's fortress has fallen. The Venetians are attacking Faenza. Cesare might secure all the papal promises in the world that he can keep his state, but he now has almost no state left to keep. On 6 November, Niccolò goes to his quarters, hoping to be the first to bring him the latest bad news of his losses. It seems he is, for Cesare grows agitated when he hears it.

'You Florentines in that republic of yours, you've always been my enemies, whatever you pretended. Believe me, Secretary Machiavelli, you'll soon see your republic ruined, and then it'll be my turn to laugh.'

He rails on at his habitual impressive length, but with greater vehemence. *I tried to calm him down,* Niccolò tells his Signoria, *and as skilfully as I could got away from him, which seemed to take a thousand years.* He goes to see Gonfalonier Soderini's brother Francesco, lately elevated from bishop to cardinal, and finds him dining with Cardinal d'Amboise, who had been Julius's rival in the recent papal election. D'Amboise's aristocratic nose quivers angrily as he listens to Niccolò's account of his meeting. 'Up to now, God has never left any sin unpunished,' he growls. 'He won't leave that rogue's sins in peace either!' A majority of the cardinals, they tell Niccolò, is determined to put the cities of Romagna into the hands of either the papacy or the King of France.

Yet Cesare keeps trying to raise soldiers to retake his lost territories. He complains about the French and about everybody, blaming the king and the Florentines and the Venetians for his bad luck. The new pope, he seems sure, will fulfil his promise to make him general of the Holy Church at his coronation ceremony. Perhaps Cesare is variable by nature, Niccolò remarks in his dispatches. Or perhaps he behaves like this because *these blows from Fortune have stunned him and, since he is unaccustomed to receive them, his mind is addled.* Another cardinal said *he believed the duke out of his mind, confused and irresolute.*

At Cardinal Soderini's bidding, Niccolò seeks audience with the new pope to discuss Florentine concerns about Borgia. He reads Julius parts of letters he has had from the Signoria, explaining why the city has refrained from granting the duke safe conduct through its dominions, despite Cesare's repeated requests.

'That's good,' Julius says, inclining his head in a significant manner. From this, Niccolò infers, *it will be seen that His Holiness thought it an eternity before he could get rid of the duke,* and would not oppose anything the Florentines or anyone else might do against Cesare. Later, several cardinals intimate that Julius has plans to lock Duke Borgia up in the Castel Sant' Angelo when he can find a suitable pretext. On 23 November, Niccolò hears that the pope has put Cesare under arrest. He would later be sent to Spain as a prisoner of Ferdinand of Aragon.

Throughout the tense stand-off between Julius and Cesare, Niccolò worries about his family. Marietta is due to give birth any day, writes Biagio; she is still too angry with her husband to write herself. *If it were not for the fact that my own boy has been very ill, I would have sent my Lessandra to visit her. She will go as soon as she can, and you will be informed of everything, my most reverend chief.* Then Niccolò comes down with fever. He fears that this time he will go the way of his parents and his two sisters, carried off by pestilence. He broods and broods, feeling sure that death is breathing down his neck, before he's had time to do anything worthy of memory. The more he dwells on his sweats and coughing and the colour of his expectorations, the less anguish he feels over what Marietta or his children might be suffering far away, where he is helpless to relieve or comfort them.

When he is more certain than ever that his whole body will soon break out in hideous black boils, letters arrive.[34] One is from Totto. Niccolò had written to prepare him for his probable demise, entreating him to look after Marietta like a sister. Pull yourself together, writes his younger brother. *These worries crop up a few times every year for anyone who travels about.* Working in foreign trade, Totto knows a little more about travel than Niccolò. Keep your good spirits, and have it in your mind *that there is no way you are going to be ill.* Another letter in the same vein from Marietta's stepfather Piero del Nero: *After all those times I've spoken, eaten or slept with infected people, I should have died twenty times. I'd be tempted to say that you are not Niccolò, if you are so overwhelmed and lose heart over a thing that happens to a man a hundred times in his life.*

I'm teasing you, says del Nero, *because you need it – try to be a man.* And anyway, he adds towards the end, here's some good news to cheer us both up: you have had a son. And there was never a finer little sprog, or a livelier one.

Niccolò forgets all his miseries. A son, a namesake for his father, Bernardo. He tears open more letters. Congratulations pour from the pages, washing away all his imagined sprouting boils. *Truly your Madonna Marietta did not cheat on you, for the lad is your spitting image,* gushes another friend. 'Leonardo da Vinci could not have done a better portrait.' And Biagio: *Both baby and Marietta are fine, thank God. It's true that she lives in great distress about this absence of yours. Good Lord, there is no way to get her to calm down and take comfort!*

Her plague-free husband writes, teasing her for being so upset. Emboldened by the news from home but certain he won't be allowed back any time soon, Niccolò asks his bosses for more money. I had no idea how expensive everything is here in Rome, he says, but let me tell you how it is. In addition to daily expenses, *I've had to pay eighteen ducats for a mule, and for a velvet suit eighteen more. For a Spanish cloak they took eleven ducats from me, for an overcoat ten. That makes seventy ducats I've had to spend for necessaries Your Lordships require of my work. I am living at a hostelry that costs ten carlini daily for myself, two servants and the aforementioned mule. At my age men labour to get ahead, not to fall behind.*

After a long, letterless huff, Marietta writes back, the only letter we have in her hand, addressed 'To the notable Niccolò di Messer Bernardo Machiavelli in Rome, In the name of God'.[35]

My dearest Niccolò. You make fun of me, but you are not right to. You know very well how happy I am when you are not there; and all the more so now that I have been told that there is so much disease down there, for I find no rest either day or night. That is the happiness I get from the baby.

Marietta can do irony, too. What happiness to hear how much sickness threatens my husband, how much more to be kept up all night by his mewling infant!

For now the baby is well, he looks like you. He is white as snow, but his head looks like black velvet, and he is hairy like you. Since he looks like you, he is beautiful to me. And he is so lively he seems to have been in the world for a year; he opened his eyes when he was scarcely born and filled the whole house with noise. Remember to come back home. Nothing else. God be with you, and keep you. I am sending you a doublet and two shirts and two kerchiefs and a towel, which I am sewing for you.

12

How to Win

Towards the end of 1504, in his poem *Decennale*, Niccolò stands back and surveys Italy's hectic political biography over the past decade. He is thirty-five, a father of young children and a functionary who helps implement life-and-death decisions about foreign and defence policy, but whose hereditary insolvency bars him from sitting on the magistracies that make those decisions. Yet he cannot help scrutinizing the decisions others make and noticing how often they fail to get to the root of problems, so that they soon wind up repeating them.

He writes his poem in the form of a direct address to his fellow citizens, speaking throughout of what 'you' Florentines did or failed to do to make yourselves safer since 1494. By 1504, Vitellozzo, Pope Alexander, and Piero de' Medici – who early that January had drowned in battle – were all dead. Cesare Borgia was as good as dead. One by one, Florence's mortal enemies had fallen. But the *Decennale* asks the Florentines to study their city's recent history in an honest, self-critical spirit. Examine yourselves, it says, before you start thinking that the fortunate downfalls of a few old nemeses make you any safer. People who say so are like those who, when the sun shines for a day, don't believe that it will ever rain.[1]

And while we Italians tear each other to bits, mightier foreign powers bring their armies here to fight over Italia's poor lacerated carcass. Ten years on:

> *By no means is Fortune yet satisfied,*
> *she has not put an end to Italian wars,*
> *nor is the cause of so many ills wiped out.*
> *And the kingdoms and the powers are not united . . .*[2]

But fortune will never put an end to those wars because bad fortune is not their cause. Though the element of randomness in human affairs that people call fortune can be powerful, contemporary Italians overrate its powers and underrate their own capacities to shape events. The *Decennale*'s political message is that Florentines and other Italians are responsible for their own defences. Their recent failures can't be put down to the bad luck of being exposed to foreign predators, but only to their own bad choices. If they ever face up to this uncomfortable truth, they might have some chance of standing up for themselves.

By the time Niccolò starts to write his poem, he is hard at work on a remedy – and he plans to use the *Decennale* to help promote it among Florentine citizens. Until Italians have their own armies, nothing much would change. Events in the decade since 1494 have convinced him of that, and he wants others to wake up and realize it with him. Until recently a mere pipe dream, his fantasy of forming a Florentine citizen militia now has the support of some of the city's most powerful men. He had often talked of it to Cardinal Francesco Soderini. Inspired by his younger friend's confidence in his project and impressed with his attention to detail, the cardinal had taken Niccolò's idea to his brother Piero.[3]

A series of recent catastrophes in the Pisan campaign persuaded the Gonfalonier to consider the militia project. Once Cesare was gone, the Florentines had hired a string of mercenary captains to try their fortune again. They sent out galleys to block aid sent to Pisa from the sea. They tried to block the flow of supplies to Pisa by pouring vast amounts of money into a project aimed at changing the course of the Arno River, inviting all the best engineering brains in Italy to propose designs; Leonardo da Vinci was among those who entered but failed to win the competition. Secretary Machiavelli was appointed to supervise the project, which, through no fault of his, turned into a fiasco: the architects had badly underestimated the scale of the enterprise and the costs of materials and labour needed to complete it. Florentine money was finite, and popular patience was running out. But Pisan *virtù* – Machiavelli's word of highest praise, which he endows with a wider range of meanings than our 'virtue' – seemed to grow wonderfully with each fresh assault.

For Niccolò, *virtù* can mean spiritedness, especially in battle. But the highest-quality *virtù* includes an aptitude for organization, industry, and far-sighted prudence. It further includes an unclouded knowledge of one's own limits, the wisdom and self-discipline not to overreach them, and the ingenuity to use whatever opportunities and resources one has, however scarce they might be. *Virtù* doesn't need good luck, or even much freedom, to work wonders. On the contrary, it is most admirable, even most effective, where there are obstacles to overcome. Look at Pisa. It has nothing good from fortune: for nearly ten years, its people have been exiled and impoverished, their city reduced to a barracks. Every Pisan family had known extreme material loss, hunger and death. Yet the harsher the necessities they faced, the more they'd stood up for their liberty. Their capacity for virtuous resistance against all odds makes a mockery of fortune's overrated powers. And here was the difference between wealthy Florence with all its dominions and its former subject city, as Machiavelli describes it in the *Prince*: *When cities or provinces are used to living under a prince*, as the Florentines had lived under the Medici, once he is gone *they do not know how to live free* and *are slower to take up arms* in their own defence. *But in republics* like Pisa *there is greater life, greater hatred, more desire for revenge; the memory of their ancient liberty does not and cannot let them rest*.[4] Chroniclers from all over Italy came to Pisa to study the miracle of its resistance and sing its people's praises. Even Florentines praise their enemies' heroism and the most terrible spirit, *terribilissimo animo*, they show in rebuffing every attack. If only, some say, we could be like more them.[5]

In his *Decennale* we first see Machiavelli combining three of his favourite roles: public educator, poetic oracle, and political game-changer. Reformers have to educate as well, since the changes they enact are unlikely to hold fast unless people also change certain ingrained ways of thinking. Like drama, poetry reaches wider popular audiences than dry political treatises, and more vividly illuminates hard-to-digest truths. So here is a poetic history of our times, full of events everyone knows, since they have only just lived through them. Quotable lines, memorable rhymes, a few local heroes and notable villains: Capponi the brave Capon standing up to the French, the divisive Savonarola, the mercenary Paolo Vitelli and his avenging brother, blessed Alexander *slain by Heaven* for inflicting hell on poor Italia. A history of the Florentines' past errors, but not a tirade.

Agostino Vespucci reads drafts, and loves it. He dreams of purchasing a printing press of his own. Let my dream serve yours, Niccolò. If you want your ideas to reach anyone beyond the government palazzo, you'll need a publisher. Together we shall arouse hundreds, thousands, of somnolent brains and realize your *fantasia* of making Roman legions out of Tuscan sheep-shearers and Florentine plebeians. But polish it well; be careful how you put things. *You know the nature of men, their deceptions and secrecy, their rivalries and hatreds, how they creep and slink about behind your back. So look out for yourself, Niccolò mio, and for us all.*[6]

Biagio issues similar warnings. To get his militia project up and running, Niccolò would have to appease his many critics in high places and rein in a tendency to put patronizing superiors in their place. While he was in Rome one magistrate, a certain Messer Agnolo Tucci, had complained to the Gonfalonier that Secretary Machiavelli never answered his letters. Hearing of this from a worried Biagio, Niccolò had written to Tucci: If I did not reply to all your private queries, this was because I'd already addressed them in my official correspondence, at considerable length. But if it pleases you, I'll oblige by reiterating these items. *And I shall write in the vernacular, though I may have written in Latin to the Chancery, though I do not think I did.* The pompous lawyer Tucci flew into a rage, in the presence of the entire Signoria, at the insinuation that he was too uneducated to read Machiavelli's dispatches.[7] *There are malicious minds here,* Biagio tells Niccolò. *And some don't like your friendship with Cardinal Francesco Soderini, who seems to love you particularly.*

*

In October 1504, the cardinal confers further with Niccolò about the idea of a people's army.[8] He had discussed it with other leading men, and while some expressed enthusiasm, others, including Gonfalonier Soderini, remained cautious. They would need strong arguments to accept such a radical innovation.

Niccolò has plenty to hand. Hired troops have no loyalties to the city they're hired to fight for; they care only about their small stipend and saving their necks.[9] And it would not be hard to order things so that neither the Gonfalonier nor any other man could seize tyrannical powers with the help of citizen troops. Divide up the powers that control the militia so that none stand unchecked.[10] Create a new Magistracy of the Militia to command it at home, let the Ten of War command it in war and make the Signoria responsible for paying the soldiers. With a three-way division of authority over the troops, they'd have no clear boss who could lead them into mischief.

Yet the politics of the militia campaign prove as ugly as Niccolò's friends had predicted. Having been persuaded to take up the cause, the Gonfalonier soon faces tidal waves of opposition. Men of quality would have to be insane to arm the plebs within their own walls, some patricians say in private.

But their apprehensions are more personal than any admit in public. A new division had been growing between those who were for the Gonfalonier and those who opposed him. It quickly overshadowed all the city's other factions. The permanency of Piero Soderini's position, so foreign to Florentine republican traditions, makes opposition all the bitterer. The Gonfalonier for Life might have nothing close to the powers of a monarch, or indeed any of the Medici First Citizens; the powers of his office are sharply curtailed by the laws, which oblige him to work through the city's manifold magistracies and the Great Council. Yet from his first days in office, Soderini's enemies had rushed to paint the slightest show of independence on his part as the beginning of tyranny, starting with his decision to take his wife, Argentina, with him when he moved into his apartments in the Palazzo Vecchio, something no fixed-term Gonfalonier had been allowed to do.

Since Piero Soderini tries to sell the militia as a popular enterprise, its opponents need to think how to turn the people against it.
In meeting after meeting, the Gonfalonier and his allies run up
against objections. Secretary Machiavelli takes note of every one.
He ponders how best to answer them, confers with Soderini about
the timing of his answers, fires him up whenever his ardour for the
militia seems to be cooling.[11] You should freely admit, he says, that
the militia, like all great things, needs time to take root and grow,
and must bring some risk in its infancy. Armed with Niccolò's
memoranda, scribbled in the Secretary's small, precise, forward-
racing script, Piero Soderini returns to his daily round of committees
and tells them: the most prudent course is to do this gradually. As
a first step, conscription could be restricted to certain parts of the
countryside around the territories we hold. For now, we'll not form
a citizen army here in Florence or in our subject cities. People need
more time to get used to the idea, and to see the first results of our
experiment. After a year, or several years, if they like what they see,
we can propose that our citizens should be conscripted and trained
like their cousins in the countryside. In the meantime, Niccolò's
notes advise, make sure that the country militias are infused with
a clear notion that their purposes and the Florentines' are one.
There should be only one insignia for all the companies, no matter
where they are based. *They are all banded under one sign of the lion –*
Florence's mascot, known as the Marzocco, is a muscular lion – *to
which all your men are affectionate in the same cause.* And provide *that
no native of a place where there is a militia company may be its constable,*
so that local loyalties cannot crystallize around military leaders.

After more than a year of frustrating deliberations, Piero
Soderini decides to take bold action. Bypassing the usual practice of
consulting with leading citizens at a special preliminary meeting,
he persuades the Signoria and the Ten of War to authorize a first
enrolment of soldiers in the countryside. At the end of 1505, the Ten
send Niccolò to the hilly Mugello and Casentino districts to start
recruiting and training conscripts.

His routine is much the same from one country town to the

next, though local reactions to it are interestingly different. There is always a small central piazza with a church, a town hall, and a market teeming with villagers of all ages selling fruits and vegetables, wine, olive oil, livestock. The Florentine Secretary first meets with local officials, giving them written copies of the new militia orders. Then he or the mayor reads out essential information to as large a gathering as they can muster.

> *Every November magistrates will make a list of the eligible men in their commune between the ages of fifteen and fifty. If an official knowingly leaves anyone out, he will be given two strokes of rope and pecuniary penalties. If someone is conscripted who seems unsuitable to serve because of infirmity, or who has other legitimate reasons for exemption, he will have a month to appeal.*

Prospective conscripts are assured that their military service will not deprive them of their livelihood. They are obligated to make no more than twelve to sixteen manoeuvres per year, and are otherwise free to attend to their own business.

Niccolò spends the first days of January 1506 recruiting in the small town of Borgo San Lorenzo.[12] While most of the men obey the summons to present themselves at enrolment, a fair number fail to show up. People are always suspicious of new things, and not without reason. Give them reasons to trust.

What's the problem? Niccolò asks his newly registered infantrymen. Are they afraid of losing time at work? Do they shy away from bearing arms?

Maybe some, they mumble, not wanting to betray their acquaintances. Then someone speaks up, saying: mostly, they're afraid that when you take their names they'll have to declare their property and be assessed for new taxes.

The Florentine Secretary reassures them: when recruiting for this militia we ask only about a man's age, not what property he possesses.

Worries assuaged, more men start coming forward freely.

Many, Niccolò writes to the Ten, seem eager to take part in a force they hope might bring long-awaited success. He attends public ceremonies held to inaugurate local branches of the militia, a blend of traditional religion and civil devotion, involving both priests and secular authorities. Niccolò had designed the proceedings himself, instructing local officials to repeat the same formalities twice a year. First, all the people of a district – men, women, and children – hear a special Mass of the Holy Spirit. Then a local official reads out a declaration of the conscripts' duties and the penalties incurred if they shirk them, and admonishes them to conserve their union and fidelity. One by one, placing their hand on the Bible in view of the entire populace, they take an oath to observe these commitments as sacred.

Recruitment proves more challenging in some places than in others. The men of the Dicomano district ignore the summons, refusing to train alongside men from neighbouring villages who, someone tells Machiavelli, have been their enemies since the dawn of time, or at least since someone's grandfather committed the first of a long series of hazily remembered yet unforgivable offences. Niccolò uses all his powers of persuasion to overcome their resistance. He meets with village leaders, patiently explaining that good service would be rewarded by special premiums, tax breaks, or amnesties for men charged with crimes, while men who persist in disobeying would be subject to stiff financial penalties. At length, he manages to enlist some two hundred men from Dicomano, writing to the Ten: if anyone back in Florence thinks this job can be done more quickly, he should try doing it himself, and he'll see how hard it is to bring together peasants who fear they'll stop breathing if the precious flame of their ancestral hatreds starts to dim. Nevertheless, Piero Soderini's opponents do their best to magnify these difficulties, saying: what else can you expect from an army of peasants – it's their nature to disobey orders and wallow in petty rivalries. That so-called nature, Niccolò tries to show them, is the product of long-standing habits and customs that can be changed, though not easily. When the countrypeople have some experience of this militia and start to recognize its benefits, their men will enlist more willingly.

But our real problem, Soderini tells him, doesn't lie in the countryside. You might assemble the most spectacular peasant militia the world has ever seen, yet certain great citizens will still mistrust our urban populace to bear arms.

Show them, says Niccolò, that it would be both myopic and disastrous for them to give up on the people. It's no surprise that they seem untrustworthy now, since our so-called great men treat them with such mistrust and contempt. If they give the people good reasons to serve Florence loyally, they might come to deserve that good faith. Give men secure work that allows them to feed their families and win public respect, *in employments that are the nerve and life of the city,* and they'll become its stoutest defenders.[13] The more power and dignity you grant them, the better they'll defend your common safety and freedom. Our sceptics should consult the histories: they'd see that cities have been strongest when the rich weren't afraid to give poorer men equal political rights, including equal chances to stand for high office. In Rome, before *its virtue was turned into arrogance* under the emperors, a reform was made so that worthy men from among the plebs could hold leading positions together with the patricians. So *they were filled with the same virtue as the nobles,* and as a result *that city, by growing in virtue, grew in power.*[14]

These ideas become constant refrains in Machiavelli's later works. A strong army and strong walls are not enough to make a strong state. People's attitudes are the real key to a leader's or a state's power. Therefore, military reforms need to go hand in hand with social and political ones. A well-ordered political economy that ensures a decent living for all a city's people is one of the main foundations of a city's military power. And cities whose people are free, secure in their livelihood, respected and self-respecting, are harder to attack than those that lack such robust arms.[15]

But for now, he holds back from saying too much. Soderini can hardly stand up before his fellow patricians and tell them that to make a strong home army they need to treat men from the artisan and labouring classes as near-equals; nothing would more swiftly kill Niccolò's reformist dreams. Instead, speak of small measures. Say: these popular men might earn your trust if you ensure that they're paid well and promptly. And make this new militia a model of justice, a justice sorely lacking in our city at present, a haven where every man can expect the same rewards or penalties whether he is rich or poor, patrician or plebeian. For *the foundations of any state are arms and justice.*[16] Establish laws that say clearly when and how to punish soldiers' or captains' misconduct. Make punishments strict and apply them impartially to every soldier, regardless of his rank or personal connections. Show them that this new militia will tolerate no bribery or special favours for friends. Where there is justice of this kind, conscripts are more likely to obey commands: *for justice makes the entire army obedient, while where it is not there are no arms.*[17]

In the meantime, Niccolò tells Soderini, we can always do more to sell our project to the people. If the militia becomes a truly popular thing, the patricians won't be able to kill it. Carnival season is approaching. Niccolò sends orders to district captains to prepare their troops for their first major exercise, to be performed before the Florentine public. Show these urban sceptics, he says, what their coarse Tuscan countrymen are made of. Prove that strict discipline and the right motivation can transform woodcutters and pig farmers into top-notch soldiers.

On 15 February, transfixed crowds watch four hundred peasants march into the Piazza della Signoria, accompanied by the beat of drums.[18] Each conscript wears an iron breastplate over a white waistcoat, a white cap, and tights half red, half white. Some carry lances, others muskets. Their faces, young and old, heavy or gaunt, pale or reddened by the elements, are solemn. A few spectators try to provoke them, but their eyes show no flicker of irritation or amusement. Weapons are raised, bodies about-turned, feet tramp-tramped in perfect unison. The effect is mesmerizing, beautiful, with the heart-rending beauty one finds only in things that are man-made, from poor, unlikely materials, but re-sculpted with a fine art that discovers their hidden powers.

This, Niccolò writes later, is the true art of war. It depends on a deeper, more philosophical kind of knowledge than most people associate with military know-how: the knowledge that whatever defects you find in a particular set of men, or in human nature generally, well-designed laws and institutions can hold their defects in check and cultivate virtues you – and perhaps they – didn't know they had. For *men never work any good unless through necessity,* and if *hunger and poverty make men industrious, the laws make them good.* It may be true that men generally are *ungrateful, fickle pretenders and dissemblers, evaders of danger, eager for gain.* But teach them discipline, give them just rewards and instil fear of just punishments, and a skilled military artist can make them into an honest and valiant army that cannot be used to injure the great or create a tyranny, since *arms given by the laws and by order, on the backs of one's own citizens or subjects, never do harm.* Italian princes and Florentine grandees blame the ungrateful, fickle, unruly people for their military weakness. But they *ought to be ashamed of themselves* and realize that the problem is not *a lack of men apt for the military but their own fault,* since they, with their impoverished view of human possibilities, *have not known how to make their men military.*[19]

The humblest onlookers see that nobility can be coaxed out of the roughest granite, that true nobility does not come from names or bloodlines but from human thought and effort. Officials explain how the country militia works. Though these men are soldiers, they do not live in barracks but remain in their own houses with their families and keep their own work, being obliged to appear from time to time when needed. 'It has been ordered that many thousand such men serve in this way, so that we will not have need of foreigners,' Luca Landucci wrote in his diaries. 'This was thought the finest thing that has ever been arranged for Florence.'[20]

The *Decennale* is now in print and, it seems, circulating quite widely. Agostino Vespucci had published it on his new printing press, footing the costs himself. Niccolò's first published work, in the exciting new medium of print, is apt to make his name known throughout Florence and beyond. It is hard to say who is prouder, the author or his publisher. Agostino fusses for hours on end over the choice of typeface, the layout of each page and the folds of the paper.[21] Soon praises start pouring in. Ercole Bentivoglio, Florence's captain-general, is delighted by its elegant composition and density.[22] The author's subtler teachings about the need for self-critical history seem to have gone over the captain's head. But military officials are not the target audience for Niccolò's poem, which speaks above all to the political men, citizens of greater and lesser rank, who will decide whether or not his militia should become a permanent institution. He had dedicated it to Alamanno Salviati, one of the militia's most implacable critics, in the hope of changing his mind. *We trust in the skilful steersman,* the poem ends,

> *in our oars, in the sails, in the cordage;*
> *but the way would be easy and short*
> *if you reopen the temple of Mars.*[23]

But the patrician Salviati and his friends remain unimpressed by Secretary Machiavelli's political versifying and his spruced-up marching peasants. In October, someone tells Biagio that Alamanno was at a dinner where, within earshot of many people, he declared: 'Since I've been one of the Magistrates of the Ten, I've never entrusted a thing to that scoundrel Machiavelli,' going on to call him the son of a bastard, and worse.[24] Machiavelli, he implies, is proof that Gonfalonier Soderini abuses his authority, since he gives such power to a man like that.

'I am so sick and tired of making excuses for you,' Biagio tells him. You take too little account of the opinions of men who can destroy you, you treat them and underlings like your Biagio too coldly, rushing ahead with your plans as if you could never take a wrong step. *Blame falls on me,* since we are friends and the closest of colleagues, *and yet I keep on sticking my neck out. Go and retch. You are a latrine cover, and anyone who wants you can pick you up with a stick.*

Yet Biagio also reports that the militia campaign is gaining momentum, despite endless daily objections. 'Niccolò, my very beloved friend,' Cardinal Francesco Soderini writes, 'we are delighted to learn how well your new military idea is progressing. You write wisely that this idea requires justice above all, and must get no small satisfaction from the fact that such a worthy thing should have been given its beginnings by your hands, backed by all the force of your intelligence and learning.'[25] On 5 December 1506, the Great Council votes to create a new magistracy: the Nine Officers of the Florentine Ordinance and Militia, responsible for overseeing military affairs. Niccolò Machiavelli is appointed as the First Secretary of the Nine, retaining his posts as Second Chancellor and Secretary to the Ten. For now, he has won.

It remains to appoint a captain of the troops. The new law stipulates that he has to be a non-Florentine, from lands at least forty miles distant from the city's dominions. We need a man, Niccolò reasons, who will make rebels and criminals think hard before they flout our orders. New laws need tough enforcers. Florence's enemies ridicule this militia, calling it an army of sheep-lovers. The choice of captain should signal to them that it is a force to be feared.

Piero Soderini proposes Miguel de Corella, Cesare Borgia's former lieutenant. Niccolò had made his acquaintance at Cesare's court. Popularly known as Don Michelotto, Corella is a well-born Spaniard with a terrifying reputation. He was said to have executed the duke's murderous designs with cold-blooded nonchalance, notably strangling Vitellozzo Vitelli and Oliverotto da Fermo in Sinigaglia – at the same time – with a violin string. The Gonfalonier sends Niccolò to discuss the matter with leading members of the government. As they're aware, the name of Michelotto sends shivers up every Italian spine. His name alone would be Florence's best weapon; it will intimidate rebels and help break up vendettas. The magistrates of the Nine and their new Secretary would of course keep a sharp eye on whoever becomes captain of the militia, promptly dismissing any who misbehaved.

The leading citizens oppose the appointment. But the Gonfalonier acts boldly again. In April 1506, he pushes Corella's appointment through the necessary bodies. His adversaries protest loudly; in private, some begin to plot his downfall. None is more enraged than Bernardo Rucellai, who secretly departs to Avignon, remaining in self-imposed exile from Florence as long as Piero Soderini is head of state.[26]

~

In December 1507, Niccolò prepares to go to Germany on a sensitive new mission. Emperor Maximilian I had been making plans to enter Italy to have himself crowned Holy Roman Emperor by the pope and assert his imperial claims in Milan. This would amount to a declaration of war with France, since King Louis currently held that city. With their heavy dependence on the French alliance, the Florentines were worried. Piero Soderini's first choice of envoy, Niccolò Machiavelli, was overruled in favour of a young patrician, Francesco Vettori. But when Pope Julius II threw his support behind the Germans out of hostility towards the French, a collision seemed imminent. And now, against bitter opposition, Machiavelli was chosen to join Vettori at Maximilian's itinerant court with secret new instructions.

Travelling through Lombardy, he is stopped by French officials who subject him to a harsh interrogation about his government's intentions towards the emperor.[27] As a precaution, he destroys all the official letters he carries with him, even those he'd concealed in unlikely places. He finds the imperial court and Vettori in Bozen in the southern Tyrol. After several audiences with the emperor and his intermediaries, they compose dispatches to send home, many of them in code.

The commonest way to code a message is through cipher. A writer first composes his message in everyday language, then encrypts it by replacing every letter with a different letter or symbol. The keys to these codes are held in Florence's Chancery offices, signed by a notary to verify their authenticity, and locked up in safes. Travelling envoys must either commit them to memory or carry the keys in some very secure place on their persons. The writer of cipher can throw skilled decoders off track by throwing in a bit of nonsense or everyday trivia along with whatever he wants to keep secret:

> *Magnificent Magistrates of the Ten, etc.* . . . bu bo bi be ba King of France 15.15000 :. :. :. :. :. 2 0 3. 79.999: . . . This is a stupidity: beating the bean [masturbating] to those who believe that in the world there is any virtue . . . men-at-arms are continually coming here in pairs, and 4 or 6 infantry at a time, and all are sent to Trent in such a way that there are many more troops there than others estimate.[28]

And it does no harm to entertain readers, whether or not you want them to discover the hidden message.

> This says nothing. Ba be bi mo bu ca ce ci co cu da de di do du . . . And there are here certain rascals as big as donkeys that have cocks like my thigh that go about stabbing these poor maids, so that Your Lordships would marvel . . .

Vettori watches as Niccolò bends over the missive and signs his superior colleague's name: Servitor Franciscus de Vectoriis. Its recipients would of course know Machiavelli's writing. When a message is urgent, it may be best to code and convey it by some other means, since obviously encrypted letters are sent off to professional code-crackers, thus delaying delivery. Some people use invisible ink, or write on the inside of the sheath of a sword, or conceal notes in the collar of a dog or in the most private parts of a messenger's body.[29] One message is sent to the two Florentine envoys written in parchment and hidden in a loaf of bread. This method has its disadvantages: the bread had got soaked then dried, so that the letter comes out in pieces, only a quarter of it legible.[30]

Then there are codes that use ordinary language and letters, but substitute the usual meaning of certain words or phrases with some secret meaning known only to one's intended readers. The writer might use 'thrush' to mean weapons, 'velvet mantle' for the King of France, 'enema' for Venice, and so on.[31] Or when he wants to express an opinion while masking it, he may use the ancient method of ambiguous language. When Niccolò was with Cesare Borgia, he often wrote home in this vein: *Duke Valentino exhibits an unheard-of fortune, and a spirit and confidence more than human that he can attain all his desires.*[32] Superficial readers would read this as high praise: agents perhaps reported back to the duke that Secretary Machiavelli is his devout servant. But his friends in the Chancery and Cardinal Soderini knew that when Machiavelli describes some-one as fortune's pet he means his successes are ill-founded, while to have confidence more than human is foolish arrogance, hubris. Or when he remarks on some political man's 'astuteness', this is not the compliment it seems: for Niccolò, as for many ancient writers, an astute politician – unlike a 'prudent' one – is a cunning oppor-tunist who knows little about how to build lasting orders.[33]

Already near-neighbours at home, Niccolò and Vettori form a close friendship during their long German sojourn. They are back home by the middle of June 1508. Having wasted much time and money prevaricating, the emperor had lost his Diet's support for his Italian enterprise and was forced to call it off. Nevertheless, dread of Maximilian's descent into Italy had thrown the Floren-tines into turmoil, encouraging Soderini's enemies to accuse him more loudly than ever. And in May the two envoys in Germany had received shocking news.

In what appeared to be a flagrant violation of laws against asso-ciating with political traitors, a member of one of Florence's richest families, nineteen-year-old Filippo Strozzi, had secretly become engaged to Clarice de' Medici, Cardinal de' Medici's fifteen-year-old niece. One expected such lawlessness from the banished Medici. Cardinal Giovanni often invited young Florentines, among them Vettori's younger brother, Paolo, to dine with them in Rome; and it was well known that his sister-in-law Alfonsina, Piero's widow, wanted to contract a Florentine marriage for her daughter Clarice. But the Strozzi were gambling with high stakes. The penalties for those found to have encouraged the marriage, if it went ahead, could run from heavy fines and the confiscation of property to exile and possibly death.

While the Gonfalonier and his supporters consider what to do next, Niccolò is sent off again, this time to organize the militia to storm Pisa. While he was in Germany a fresh siege had begun under the command of Commissioner-General Niccolò Capponi, Francesco Vettori's brother-in-law and son of the hero of 1494. Machiavelli remains at camp throughout the summer, then off and on into spring. He reviews the militia infantry, sends out men to search the mountains for concealed enemy troops, and supervises the building of a stockade near the mouth of the Arno – three rows of piles bound together with strong iron bands below the water's surface – to block supplies sent to Pisa from Genoa and Lucca. Overall, the troops are well disciplined, fulfilling their duties without complaint. When a number of men from the Pescia company apply for leave to see their families, Niccolò grants it to a few, who all return promptly. As the time of silkworm hatching draws near, he writes home to the magistrates, more and more men will have to be relieved of their duties so they can work on the farms. To keep good order in an army, as in a city, one has to pay close attention to details, not slighting what might seem small matters to great men sitting comfortably in Florence. Keep paying men on time, supply enough straw for them and their horses, punish any officer who abuses his position, *and you'll keep troops in proper obedience; otherwise your orders will be derided by everybody, and everything here will end in confusion.* An envoy from Lucca comes to avow his city's wish for good understanding between that republic and Florence. Niccolò replies that they would have it if the Luccans cease to make their resources available to the Pisans and let their city be an asylum to its warmongers.

By the end of summer, leading citizens are calling to press harder on Pisa than ever. Amid all the uproar over the Strozzi–Medici affair, the one thing different factions agree on is that this drawn-out war should now be fought to the end, with whatever means are deemed necessary. War councils reverberate with strong words.[34] The time has come for rage; generosity can come later. The enemy won't be reduced unless we put a thong around their neck. As to whether the war is just or not: if it is, it's also just to do whatever seems necessary to win, for which no one can reproach you. And even if it isn't just, better to end all these troubles by any means we can.

A few cautious speakers strain to be heard. 'If Pisa is pressed hard and reduced to utter desperation,' says Piero Guicciardini, 'we risk arousing its supporters and making things worse for ourselves. The King of France already complains that our methods of siege by starvation are inhuman, and his words encourage our enemies.'

But Soderini is determined. Success would help boost his government's popularity at this moment of its greatest internal danger. If the Pisans would not capitulate until they are starving and dying inside their walls, then they must be starved. At the end of August, he writes to Niccolò: 'To our group here it seems as if this laying waste is going very slowly. We urge you to press for it to be finished, in such a way that the least possible fodder is left to the enemy and with the greatest possible swiftness, and you will be highly praised for it.'[35]

As Secretary to both the Nine of Militia and the Ten of War, Machiavelli is put in charge of an operation to devastate whatever crops had been missed in earlier attacks on the countryside around Pisa. He shares the general opinion that the time has come to win this seemingly unwinnable war, the source of so many evils for the republic. When he recalls all its travails later – when the republic is no more – he sees more clearly still how much the war with Pisa had weakened its chances of survival. The Florentines had *spent very much in the war, fruitlessly; from very much spending came very heavy taxes; from the taxes, infinite quarrels among the people.*[36] They now had to win swiftly and decisively. The longer Pisa starved, the more hatred Florentines would awaken in the wider world, as if they weren't hated enough already.

Elections are held for new commissioners to head the camps surrounding Pisa. When the first results come in, Niccolò is appalled: his Salviati adversaries, Jacopo and Alamanno, have been selected. Then someone, perhaps in Soderini's camp, digs out a law that prohibits two men of the same family from serving in high military posts simultaneously. So Alamanno takes up the appointment, together with Capponi and a third commissioner, Antonio de Filicaia.[37] These new commissioners don't know how to push a war to its end, Niccolò grumbles. Wait and see, they'll soon be doing what our great gentlemen do best, trying to buy off the Pisans with money and special favours, instead of relying on the force of arms. He coins a maxim that would become the title of a chapter in the *Discourses*: *That in difficult times one goes to find true virtue; and in easy times not virtuous men but those with riches or kinship have more favour.*[38]

His apprehensions are soon put to the test. In an effort to take Pisa by stealth, the Florentines cut a deal with one of their prisoners of war. Alfonso del Mutolo, son of a Pisan blacksmith, had been locked up in Florence's Stinche prison for a year.[39] After befriending one of his gaolers, he promised that if he were released he would find some way to deliver one of Pisa's main gates to the Florentine army. So they'd freed him and sent him back to Pisa, welcoming him quite openly at the camp, together with other Pisans, whom he would leave to one side while conferring with the commissioners and their legates. Niccolò is suspicious: if Mutolo is acting in good faith, he wonders, is it reasonable that he should deal so openly with us in front of his countrymen?

The war commissioners ignore such warnings, as does Soderini. One night, on Mutolo's order, they send a company of about thirty soldiers to climb over Pisa's Lucca gate. After several have gone ahead, one of them looks over the wall and shouts out that his comrades on the other side have been killed or taken prisoner. Mutolo and his compatriots respond with a barrage of artillery against the Florentine camp. *Their desire to have Pisa*, Niccolò would later reproach his countrymen, *blinded the Florentines* to the thinly disguised plot.[40]

Take care, colleagues warn him yet again. Filippo Casavecchia is one of his oldest friends; he has been assisting with the troops in the countryside. 'I'm clear on one thing, Niccolò,' he says. 'You'll get yourself completely excluded from public life one day – enough said.' The Secretary is now approaching forty. His skills as a diplomat to foreign courts have been honed and polished; few men in Florence are better at handling sensitive missions. Yet he still finds it hard to control an urge to snub his own self-important compatriots, however necessary others say it is to humour their airs and graces. He gets on with Antonio de Filicaia, but relations are tense with Alamanno. He and commissioner Capponi soon get up each other's noses, despite – or perhaps because of – their closeness in age: Niccolò is just three years older. Capponi has lodged a formal complaint, Biagio tells him.[41] He claims your letters are too few and insufficiently respectful. You know how it is, *the more powerful must always be right, and one must show respect for them*. His years in the Chancery have toughened Biagio's hide; he grows weary of both patrician power-games and his friend's refusal to play along with them. *Everyone wants to be coddled and esteemed, so that is what someone who finds himself where you are has to do.*

The siege carries on through the winter and spring of 1509. Florentine troops lay waste to Pisan territories, destroying farms and houses and driving countrypeople into the city for protection. This was the strategy: with more mouths to feed inside the city walls and dwindling provisions, famine would force the Pisans either to capitulate or turn in desperation against each other. The poorest, already burying their children by the dozens and barely surviving on dog-meat and rats, would start begging the government to reach terms with the enemy, threatening riots and worse.

If Pisa were like other cities, the strategy would be invincible.

But fourteen years of war had made Pisa a different kind of city altogether. Fighting, privation, enduring long seasons without meat and with little grain, abandoning one's home at a moment's notice, losing children to battle or hunger: all had become a normal way of life. Toddlers grew up expecting to bear hardship. Girls and boys learned how to kill and were undismayed by the thought of their own deaths. When a few bold citizens began to speak of capitulating, gangs of youths used arms to terrify them into silence.[42] For their part, a whole generation of Florentines had been brought up with stories of pitiless Pisan cruelty. Captured Florentine soldiers, according to one leaflet, had been taken into a country church where the Pisans had chopped off their genitals and stuck them in their mouths, then sliced off their ears and carved out their eyes, which they chopped into tiny pieces. The Pisans, knowing that a fearsome reputation can only help underdogs, did not deny such reports.

In March, Niccolò gets an urgent message from the Ten of War requesting that he go to the city of Piombino, south of Pisa.[43] The Pisan authorities had asked that city's lord, Jacopo d'Appiano, to mediate peace negotiations. Now d'Appiano writes that a large number of Pisans are at his court, and urges Florence to send some trusted man to hear what they have to say.

Niccolò posts servants at the door of the audience chamber to count the number of men who come through. Over 160, they later tell him, many of them Pisan citizens, and at least as many peasants. A few well-dressed city men approach Niccolò and Signor d'Appiano.

'We expected at least two or three notable Florentine citizens to treat with us,' says their chief, 'not a mere Secretary.' But now that he is here, they want him to inform the Signoria that the people of Pisa are disposed to seek peace, provided that they are assured of their lives, property and honour.

Niccolò turns sideways to address Signor d'Appiano. 'These ambassadors,' he says, 'have said nothing. If they want a reply, they'll have to make some definite proposition. What kind of security do they require?'

The Pisans confer among themselves. Then one of their leaders speaks up. 'Perhaps the best way to our security is that you Florentines should leave us everything within the walls of Pisa to govern for ourselves, while you take the rest of our dominions, and the surrounding countryside.'

Niccolò notices murmuring towards the back of the throng. He smells discord between the ambassadors – city men, mostly well-to-do – and the deputies from the countryside.

Turning again towards his host, he says, 'It must be evident to you, Signor, that these gentlemen are laughing at us. Negotiations are pointless if they don't mean to put Pisa into our hands with all her territory, on the same terms as before their rebellion.' For the first time, he turns to the Pisans. 'Your security will depend on the loyalty with which you throw yourselves into the arms of my Signoria.'

Then, looking over the heads of the citizens, he addresses the rural deputies behind them. 'I'm sorry for your simplicity,' he says, at last exuding human warmth. 'You're playing a game you can't win, for if these city men get what they want they'll forget all the sacrifices you've made for their city and treat you as slaves, sending you back to your ploughs.'

'That is improper language, Secretary!' one of the velvet-clad ambassadors cries out. 'You are trying to foment division among us.'

Niccolò senses that the country deputies relish his remarks. The wealthy citizens who claim to speak for everyone still have their fathers' houses and bank accounts, and families safely in exile; they don't starve to death or see their homes and harvests destroyed year after year. One deputy pipes up, 'We want peace. We want peace, Secretary!'

Machiavelli has learned a good deal about the concerns of countrypeople in his years with the militia. He knows how to assuage their deep-rooted suspicions of city-dwellers – and how to play on them. Go home and ask for full negotiating powers, he tells them, if you are serious about ending the war.

~

By April, Florence's armies are closing around Pisa. The Ten want to send Niccolò to a safer camp at Cascina, but he baulks at the thought of being so far from the main stage of action. *I know that encampment would be less dangerous and less strenuous but, had I not wanted danger and hard work, I would not have left Florence. So may it please Your Lordships, let me stay here in these camps, where I can be of some good use; there I should be of no use at all and would die of despair.*[44] The blockade is working. With no new bread or grain getting through and stockpiles consumed, hundreds of people start descending on the government palazzo in Pisa crying, 'We are perishing from hunger!'

In mid-May, French troops inflict a hard defeat on Pisa's most formidable allies, the Venetians. Bereft of this key support, the Pisans accept that the game is up. On 2 June, they sign their treaty of capitulation.

With the Pisans reduced, what kind of peace should their conquerors grant them? There is no shortage of Florentines who want to punish a subject city that had proved so disloyal at the coming of the French, costing them so much in money and reputation and inciting other subjects to follow their rebellious example. Now the victors are so strong, these voices say, that we can deal with the losers as harshly as they deserve. Build military garrisons to hold them down so they'll never again think of rebellion. Punish and enfeeble them with high taxes.

Others fear that harshness in victory will fatally weaken any peace agreement. *I have taken marvellous satisfaction in this ceasefire,* Filippo Casavecchia tells Niccolò, *and wept and lurched about and done all those things that dignified men do, in imitation of old sheep. Nevertheless, now that my reason is recovering its power, I remain extremely anxious about it.*[45]

Niccolò agrees. *For prudent princes and republics, it should be enough to conquer,* he would write later. *For most often when it is not enough, one loses; great conquests often give rise to greater ruin because of the insolence that victory gives you.*[46] *Niccolò,* Casavecchia declares, *if ever one was wise, it should be now. I do not believe your philosophy will ever be accessible to fools, and there are not enough wise men to go around. Every day I discover you to be a greater prophet than the Hebrews or any other nation ever had.*

His friend's camp intensity makes Niccolò laugh; Machiavelli's personal letters are usually teasing, and he teases no one more relentlessly than his Casa. Casavecchia's letter does not say what he takes to be Niccolò's prophetic *filosofia*. He may mean no more than his vision for the militia. But something like a philosophy of peacemaking can be found in Machiavelli's later works, its rudiments worked out in several short pieces usually dated to his time as Secretary and Second Chancellor: his *Discourse on Pisa*, 'On the Method of Dealing with the Rebellious Peoples of the Valdichiana', and *De Rebus Pistoriensibus*, a probing analysis of how to deal with factional strife in Pistoia.[47] Having played no small role in reconquering Pisa with his militia, he now wants to teach his city how to maintain what they acquired with such hardship.

His *Prince* and *Discourses* set out peacemaking advice that reflects his and his city's experience with Pisa. *Do not take what you cannot hold.* Though it's natural for men to wish to acquire, it is folly to try to hold down cities like Pisa that make you pay dearly for your conquest.[48] *Peace is faithful where men are willingly pacified.* A clement peace, worked out together with the defeated, is more likely to quell resistance than a harsh or unilateral one; with it, you may hope to make Pisa's former rebels your partners, who will stand side by side with you in your future travails.[49] *Either placate the conquered, or eliminate them.* The easiest way to conquer Pisa would be to destroy every shred of the city's independence, expelling or killing its leaders and reducing the remaining population to poverty and terror. But the Florentines had done this in the past, and look where it had got them. By destroying Pisa's wealth and driving most of its citizens into exile, the conquerors were left with a shrunken populace whose tax payments covered a mere fraction of the costs of occupation – a few thousand souls determined to resist them to the death. *If the people hold you in hatred, fortresses do not save you.*[50] Never underestimate the quality of losers: nothing could be stupider than to imagine that people who have been defeated now have no choice but to endure servitude, especially people like the Pisans, who are *used to being or seem to themselves to be free.*[51] And finally, *victories are never secure without justice.* The Florentines' history with Pisa should teach them that those who covet *others' share usually lose their own, and before losing it live in continual unease.*[52]

Though Niccolò has no say in city councils, his views carry some weight with Piero Soderini and a few other citizens who draft the peace treaty. The document is ratified on the night of 7 June. Niccolò Machiavelli of the Second Chancery is one of the Florentine signatories, along with Gonfalonier Soderini, the First Chancellor Marcello Virgilio Adriani, Machiavelli's coadjutor Biagio Buonaccorsi, the magistrates of the Ten of War and the Priors of Liberty, one of whom is Francesco Vettori.[53] The post-war arrangements do not reflect all of Niccolò's maxims for peacemaking. A new fortress is built at Pisa, and a garrison of some thousand men posted there to guard against subversion from inside or without. But intentions are expressed to diminish the military presence over time. Otherwise, the terms are moderate. All injuries done to either side during the war are pardoned. Confiscated property that had belonged to Pisans or the Florentines before the war is restored to its previous owners. Most taxes and duties are imposed at the same rates as before 1494; others are lifted for the duration of ten years to give the shattered Pisan economy time to recover.

On the following day, 8 June, a horseman gallops from Pisa into Florence, waving the olive branch. Bonfires flare up all over the city. Illuminations burn from every tower, bells peal, fireworks boom. Niccolò is still in Pisa with Biagio, who is overcome with joy. 'Finally,' he sighs, 'all our city's travails are rewarded by the Omnipotent God and his glorious Mother!' Agostino writes on the day of peace: *It is not possible to express how much delight, how much jubilation and joy, all the people here have taken in the news of the recovery of that city. In some measure, every man has gone mad with exultation. If I didn't think it would make you too proud, my Niccolò, I'd say that you with your battalions accomplished so much good work that you*

*restored the affairs of Florence. I swear to God, so great is the exultation
we are having that I would write a Ciceronian oration for you if I had
time.* A no less exultant Filippo Casavecchia throws a celebratory
fishing party. *I wish you a thousand benefits from the outstanding acqui-
sition of that noble city,* he tells Niccolò, *for truly it can be said that your
person was cause of it to a very great extent. I'm saving you a ditch full of
trout and a wine like you have never drunk; if you don't come, you'll be the
cause of my living unhappily ever after.*[54]

While Florentines pulled together to win their war in Pisa, at home
the Strozzi–Medici affair kept tearing them apart.[55] In the autumn
of 1508, Gonfalonier Soderini declared before the Great Council
that the whole business was part of a plot to bring down the republic. The prospective bridegroom Filippo Strozzi inadvertently
fanned public dismay by writing to his brother Alfonso – a staunch
opponent of the Medici and of the marriage plans, who publicized
the letter's contents – that he, Filippo, sought only to make a socially
advantageous alliance by marrying Clarice de' Medici, and cared
nothing for what the Florentine lower classes or their popular
government thought.

Soderini responded by having formal accusations filed against
Filippo and his alleged cohorts. They were charged with crimes
against the state and conspiring to overthrow the government.
Alfonso Strozzi, presumably desperate to spare himself and the rest
of his family the dire fates of expropriation and exile, argued that
the city's grave wounds would be healed only if his younger brother
were severely penalized and the heads were cut off the Rucellai,
Archbishop Pazzi, Filippo Buondelmonti and other conspirators.

No precise record exists of Machiavelli's views at the time. But
another of Filippo's brothers, Lorenzo – whom Niccolò would later
count as a friend, or at least a helpful patron – reports that many
believed the harshest accusation had been penned by Secretary
Machiavelli on Soderini's behalf.[56] In his *Discourses* Niccolò offers
general advice on what the leaders of fragile republics should do to
conspirators who, driven by private or partisan ambitions, seek

to restore a monarchy. Not long after Lucius Junius Brutus and his colleagues expelled the last kings from Rome and founded the republic, a group of young patricians formed a conspiracy to bring back the kingship. Among these men were several sons of Brutus, the founder of Roman freedom. When the plot was discovered and the plotters sentenced, many expected Brutus to plead for mercy for his sons, though the laws he'd helped establish demanded the execution of traitors. But Brutus did not flinch. Putting the sanctity of public laws above his personal affections, he sat on the tribunals and condemned his guilty sons to death. His example, Niccolò argues, should be imitated by all new republics where some people – having grown used to living under princes before – do not know how to live in freedom. For *whoever makes a free state and does not kill the sons of Brutus* in the same manner *maintains himself for little time.*[57]

The phrase 'sons of Brutus' stands here for any friend or relative of those who enforce the laws who conspires to restore princes in a republic. Machiavelli's point is not that, when freedom is at risk, even the most coldly violent means may be used to preserve it. It is, first of all, that new republics need clear legal procedures – like those Brutus helped establish in Rome – to judge and execute conspirators against the state. Florence's lack of such procedures had already fuelled dangerous turmoil in the cases of the five pro-Medici plotters, Savonarola, and Paolo Vitelli. And Machiavelli wants to stress, second, that upright leaders should put public laws above their own or other people's private feelings. They should resist emotional appeals to ties of family or friendship, and punish with Brutus-like severity when this is what the laws and the republic's survival demand.

Being prepared to kill the sons of Brutus, then, means being prepared to use severity – the Roman virtue of *severitas* praised by Sallust and Seneca – in applying the laws, not lawless violence in the name of political necessity. A statesman needs to know when to use clemency and when severity. In making peace with Pisa, clemency was more just, and helped restore lasting order. In the case of the

Medici marriage – here Niccolò agreed with Alfonso Strozzi – the strictest penalties were justified.

But Piero Soderini was no Brutus, as Niccolò would observe sadly in his *Discourses*. The Gonfalonier *believed that he would overcome with his patience and goodness the appetite that was in the sons of Brutus for returning to another government.* In this belief *he deceived himself.* For *besides believing that he could extinguish ill humours with patience and goodness, he judged (and often said so to his friends)* – one of them probably Machiavelli – *that if he wished to strike his enemies vigorously and beat down his adversaries,* he would have had to go beyond his legal mandate to force through tough new laws against conspirators. This he did not want to do. Niccolò praises Soderini's restraint in wanting to stay within existing – though deplorably imprecise – laws. But he implies that, with the republic's survival at stake, its leader should have worked harder to pass rigorous new legislation before the Strozzi trials. If he had, things might have turned out very differently for him, and for the Florentine republic.

As Florentine armies tightened their stranglehold around Pisa in the last months of 1508, the Strozzi camp began to win ever more powerful support inside and outside the city. As a favour to Cardinal Giovanni de' Medici, Pope Julius tried to intervene, ordering the Signoria to accept the marriage. Soderini wrote back tetchily that this was a matter for the citizens of Florence to decide among themselves, as His Beatitude would understand if he were better informed. Filippo Strozzi had stayed well out of Florence during the uproar. He entered on Christmas Day 1508, and went on trial before the magistracy of the Eight in January.

The Eight punished Filippo with a 500-ducat fine and a three-year banishment to Naples. After a year, his sentence was shortened and he was allowed to come home. His lawyers had argued, successfully, that he was not marrying a Medici rebel but only the daughter of one; and existing laws did not explicitly prohibit marriage with female relatives of male rebels. Soderini tried to have Filippo confined to Florentine territory so that he could not travel to Rome and marry Clarice there. But the magistrates refused to comply, and the couple were wed in February 1509. The other accused were fined or given limited terms of exile.

The outcome signalled an ominous shift in the city's political mood. Friends of the Medici saw how easy it was to get around the republic's weak laws against rebels. Soderini's enemies, however they felt about a possible Medici restoration, now have few qualms about using the newly invigorated threat of their return to undermine the Gonfalonier. Meeting with Piero Soderini towards the end of the Pisan war, Niccolò finds him strangely sanguine. It's a bad business, the Gonfalonier concedes. 'But my enemies would have gone for my throat if we'd pushed tougher laws through the Great Council once the case had already blown up. They'd have called me a tyrant for the rest of my days, and used it to scrap the post of life-long Gonfalonier after my death.'

It is too late to dispute with him again, Niccolò realizes. The damage is done, and Piero will not change his ways. He thinks that, once men get to know him, they'll see how absurd it is to suspect him of tyrannical ambitions; he has always insisted that with time, goodness and fortune, he could eliminate envy without any scandal, violence, or tumult. *He did not know*, Machiavelli would later write, *that one cannot wait for the time, goodness is not enough, fortune varies, and malignity does not find a gift that appeases it.*[58] At an unknown date, perhaps while Soderini still lived, Niccolò pens an epigram, affectionate yet exasperated in tone:

> *That night when Piero Soderini died*
> *his spirit went to the mouth of Hell.*
> *Pluto roared: Silly spirit,*
> *Why to Hell? Go up into Limbo with the rest of the babies.*

13

Measure Yourself and Limit Your Hopes

Two years later, Florence and Pisa are at peace, but Italy is on the brink of yet another war of the greater powers. After years of sullen animosity, muffled only by the heroic labours of their diplomats, King Louis XII and Pope Julius II are preparing for what both sides now see as an inevitable clash of armies. A few years earlier, at the end of 1508, optimists had hoped for an improvement in France's soured relations with the Church when Julius invited foreign powers, including the king, to form a League at Cambrai to help him put an end to Venetian conquests in the Romagna and Lombardy. But when French might proved decisive in crushing the Venetians, a worried Julius did a volte-face. In 1510, he reconciled with Venice and launched a new crusade to eject the French from Italy, announcing his enterprise with the battle cry: *Fuori i barbari!* 'Out with the barbarians!'

'And to the pope we are the king's most devoted friends in Italy, and hence his enemies.'[1] Piero Soderini has summoned Niccolò to his quarters in the Palazzo della Signoria to give him orders to go to France; the Florentines need to reassure Louis that the city has not gone over to the pope. 'Though you must also try to avoid committing Florentine troops to the king, as the pope would take this as a sign of our hostility.'

Though he still holds the same official posts, Secretary Machiavelli has grown closer than ever to the Gonfalonier in these embattled times, and more dogged in Soderini's defence. He had heard French envoys complaining that Cardinal Francesco Soderini had not been seen at court for many months. 'They say that the king broods over the meaning of his absence.'

Soderini instructs him to tell Louis that, while his brother had wished to call on him and pay homage, the pope had prevented him from doing so. 'Francesco is bound to obey his first master. And Julius has such a violent temper that even great princes feel they have to treat him with deference.' As soon as he arrives at court, Niccolò should assure the king that both Soderini brothers remain certain that their city's happiness is linked to the prosperity of the French crown. 'I can't see why it has to come to war. But now that everyone says it must, we are in worse straits than before we recovered Pisa.'

Talk of this collision was already in the air when Niccolò went to Rome in 1506. Though the king hopes to humble the pope, a Vatican insider had told him, the pope will most assuredly humble the king.[2]

'Julius wants to make himself and the Church arbiter of Italian affairs,' says Niccolò. 'And the king, it must be said, has made things easy for him.'[3] After taking Naples and Milan a decade ago, Louis had been lord of two thirds of Italy. He'd have remained unassailable if he hadn't helped Pope Alexander and Cesare seize the Romagna. That error, in Niccolò's opinion, cost Louis almost all his Italian allies. And now they have a pope who loves nothing more than himself in a suit of armour, riding at the head of his papal armies. Niccolò recalls Julius declaring to him four years before at an audience in Rome: 'To be able to change Bologna's government by force of arms, I have furnished myself with an army that will make all Italy tremble, let alone Bologna.'[4] This *Papa terribile*, as the people now call him, has a talent for advertising his aims in a stirring slogan. With him, it's always out with someone, Soderini sighs: out with the tyrants, out with the barbarians.

The antipathies between Julius and Piero Soderini run deeper than politics.[5] Soderini is a cautious man who values fidelity to one's allies and principles. The pope, as even his friends admit, is a man of impetuous and choleric temper who had shown more than once that he was no less willing than Alexander to break his treaties as it suited him. At least, Niccolò observes, Julius is transparent in his bad faith. Pope Alexander, he says in the *Prince*, *never thought of anything but how to deceive men*; no man was better at asserting the most sacred oaths, then ignoring them in his actions. But Julius once told the Secretary quite openly, in one of their audiences, that he cared nothing for treaties made by other popes, or even for those made by himself.[6]

'Our greatest fear now is that he'll win support from the King of Spain,' says the Gonfalonier. 'We've heard rumours that the Spanish have a fleet in Sicily with more than ten thousand troops aboard, which King Ferdinand may put at Julius's disposal.' No doubt, Niccolò responds, trying to get a smile out of his dour friend, *the pope's audacity needs to be founded on something besides his mere sanctity.*[7]

In July, he rides to Lyons and Blois. Cardinal d'Amboise had died at the end of May. The multilingual Florimond Robertet, a likeable man of bourgeois origins, now serves as one of the king's chief advisers and the Florentines' main intermediary at court.

'His Majesty feels that your Florentine Lordships have slighted his friendship in various ways,' Robertet tells Niccolò on his arrival. 'You may need to correct this alienation by acts of special kindness.'[8]

When they meet, the king is unexpectedly affable. 'But do not forget,' he tells Secretary Machiavelli, 'how many benefits your city has had from us for many years. Now the time has come for your Signoria to give particular assurance of their feelings towards us.' Louis scrutinizes his visitor's face as if looking for some trace of hypocrisy. Like Florence's tireless Gonfalonier, he has aged in the past few years, grown new furrows between his brows.

'Secretary,' he says at last, 'I have no enmity with the pope, or anyone else. But since every day gives birth to new friendships as well as enmities, I desire that your Signoria declare themselves without delay as to what and how much they would do in my favour were the pope to molest my possessions in Italy. In return I offer them all the forces of my kingdom. If need be, I will come myself to help them.'

Over the next days, Niccolò talks to as many people as he can: French barons, Spanish envoys and the pope's own ambassador. This last he finds a man of great experience and wise judgement who privately laments the current state of things. 'I've left nothing undone to try to preserve peace in Italy,' he tells Niccolò. 'But recent events have robbed me of all hope of it. I see no good that can come of this warmongering. It will harm the poor people in Italy most of all.'

As for the French, Secretary Machiavelli writes to the Signoria, they all seem to think the pope wants to ruin Christianity. They speak of summoning him before a special ecclesiastical council to destroy his temporal and spiritual power. Louis is so enraged by the pontiff's insults that he seems ready to avenge himself even at the risk of losing all his Italian territories. An embassy had come from England, whose king seemed inclined to back the French; his ambassadors departed laden with gifts and promises of new titles for English noblemen. *If you desire not to lose the friendship of the French, O Magnificent Signori,* Niccolò advises them, *you must show them that you really mean to be their friend. For these French do not trust us altogether, and will never trust Your Lordships until you declare yourselves openly in their favour and join with them arms in hand. And you may believe as you believe the Evangely that if war breaks out, you will not avoid declaring yourselves in favour of one party.* Whatever the dangers to Florence of their French alliance – and they are greater now than ever before – the king is infinitely more reliable than the volatile Julius. So take sides now before necessity forces you. *Reflect well, and then take the direct course for the object you aim at.*

In early August, the French start urging the Florentines to act as peace-brokers between the king and the pope. Working with Cardinal Soderini's business agent, Niccolò throws himself into drafting a mediation plan. When they present it to the king, Louis seems irritated. 'What would you have me do?' he demands. 'I shall never be the first to declare myself.' Louis used to be better at masking his feelings; now it is as though he has been infected by his arch-enemy's self-indulgent impetuosity, and vents whatever he feels at the moment. 'But I promise you,' he says at last, 'that if the pope makes any demonstration of affection towards me, be it only the thickness of my fingernail, I'll go the length of my arm to meet him. Otherwise, I won't budge an inch.'

For the next two weeks, Niccolò's dispatches speak of nothing but the merits of peace. A colleague from the Chancery writes that the pope has been trying again to separate Florence from France, and that the Signoria are despairing over the probable costs of this imminent war, saying it will be far more costly than that with Pisa.[9] Towards the end of August, Niccolò has another audience with the king. Louis has a hacking cough; his feverish spirits have spread to his body. His words are like a slap. 'I will not let this pope beat me. If he pushes me any further, I'm resolved to make the most magnificent war ever seen in Italy.'

His latest plan is to convoke a rebel council of the Church somewhere outside Rome. This council would denounce the present pope and relieve all Christians of any obligation to obey him. If Louis could persuade England and the emperor to agree, they would elect a new pontiff. Then, come spring, Louis promises, he will swoop down on Italy with such overwhelming force that no city or village would dream of resisting. 'It will not be war,' he grins, 'but simply a promenade to Rome.' *And in truth*, Niccolò tells his government, if our city were not located right in the line of fire, all this purging of the Church *would be very welcome, so that our priests* – whose lust for temporal power has brought us all so much grief – *might also taste a little of the bitterness of this world.*

Some contagious sickness is rife throughout France, one that makes its monarch cough too hard to speak. More than a thousand people are dying in Paris each day. Niccolò comes down with it as well. Whenever he is sick and far from home and family, the old dread returns, and so haunts his mind that he soon feels worse. He loses his appetite, grows weaker. For five days he stays in lonely confinement, coughing and fretting over things left undone.

When at last he emerges, still quite alive, things have moved nearer to a state of war. Julius has spat on tentative overtures towards peace. King Louis releases all his subjects from obedience to the pope and issues a proclamation forbidding French subjects to go or send anyone to Rome on business with Julius. Louis is a man obsessed: awake or asleep, Niccolò observes, he *thinks and dreams of nothing but the wrong he conceives he has received from the pope.* There is nothing to be done now but implore the king not to mimic his rival, who *has no scales or measuring stick in his house,* but instead to weigh his next actions carefully.[10] Secretary Machiavelli goes to the king with news that papal troops have captured the rebellious city of Modena. This conquest, he points out, brings the pontiff dangerously near to Florentine dominions.

Later, Robertet summons him to his chambers and says, 'His Holiness the pope needs a good thrashing.' He laughs and slaps Niccolò on the shoulder, as if to say: and he'll get one soon enough.

Then, as they are about to raise their glasses, a painter carries in a portrait of the late Cardinal d'Amboise, in all his glorious portliness.

'Oh my master!' Robertet cries out. 'If you were still living, we would now be with our army at Rome.' The Frenchman proposes a toast. 'To our beloved cardinal, may his soul rest in peace, and in everlasting freedom from these earthly toils.'

Niccolò drinks deeply. He, too, has missed d'Amboise's blunt ways and sure judgement, without which the king seems a lost man.

'How keenly we all feel the cardinal's absence,' laments Robertet. 'The king is not used to attending to details, so he neglects them, while those who should remind him of them take no authority on themselves to do so. And so, while the physician gives no thought to the sick man and the servant forgets him, the patient dies.'

In December 1510, Filippo Strozzi, released early from his exile, requests an audience with the Signoria. They are stunned by what he has to say. A woman had come to him who'd heard about a plot to assassinate Soderini.[11] A man from Bologna had proposed it to Medici partisans in Florence, suggesting several different ways of killing the Gonfalonier. After his ordeal of the previous year, Filippo wants to make a display of unimpeachable transparency. He admits that certain Florentines may have encouraged the foreign conspirator, though he is reluctant to name them.

Word soon spreads that, as soon as Filippo heard of the conspiracy, he had gone to see his mother-in-law, Alfonsina de' Medici, and quarrelled with her over what to do. It remains unclear how much she or her brother-in-law Cardinal Giovanni knew about the matter. No Florentines are charged in the case, but Soderini's government proclaims strict new laws against citizens who have dealings with the Medici. Niccolò had long been in favour of such laws; he may never have stopped urging Soderini to pass them in the wake of the Strozzi–Medici marriage.

Meanwhile, the campaign to remove Secretary Machiavelli from his influential position had grown vicious. On 20 December 1509, a masked man, flanked by two witnesses, had knocked on the door of a government notary and handed him an envelope. Niccolò was away from Florence attending to the militia at the time. A week later, he received a letter from Biagio. Its contents were terrifying.[12] What I am about to tell you, wrote Biagio, *is of such great importance that it could not be greater.* The notary had been handed an anonymous statement claiming that Niccolò di Bernardo Machiavelli held all his government posts illegally. *It stated that since you were born of a father, etc., you can in no way exercise the office that you hold, etc.* The allusion may be to Bernardo's status as communal debtor, or to rumours of his illegitimate birth. Whatever the issue, now *the law is being stretched in a thousand ways and given sinister interpretations.* Several of Niccolò's patrician defenders had urged Biagio to warn him of the rising storm. *Your adversaries are numerous and will stop at nothing. The case is public everywhere, even in the whorehouses, and now a great number of people have started to gossip about the matter and shout it about everywhere, threatening that if something is not done, etc.* Stay away from Florence for a few days, his friends had advised; we'll defend you in your absence.

For years, he had trained himself not to care about attempts to tarnish his reputation. The important thing was to be sensitive but not prickly, to register every small offence and stay on guard against larger ones, while showing how hard it is to harm you with either. The best way he knows to rise above his enemies' attacks is to flick them off like flies. To close friends, he vents his ire by ridiculing the Medici partisans who try every dirty trick in the book to trip up the Gonfalonier and his loyal associates. He offers himself up as the butt of his own jokes, a gullible victim of anyone who promises to gratify men's fleeting lusts. *I was in Mantua for three days*, he tells a friend, *losing my discrimination because of conjugal famine, when I came upon an old woman who launders my shirts.*[13] The probably fictional laundress led him into her dank underground house, promising to show him some fine shirts, *and naïve prick that I am, I believed her and went in.* There in the gloom was a woman

> *affecting modesty, with a towel half over her head and face. I, being a shy fellow, was absolutely terrified. Her thighs were flabby and her breath stank. Nevertheless, hopelessly horny, I went to her with it. Having done with it and feeling like taking a look at the merchandise, I took a piece of burning wood from the hearth and lit a lamp above it. Ugh! I nearly dropped dead on the spot, that woman was so ugly. The crown of her head was bald, so that one could make out a few lice promenading about. Her mouth resembled Lorenzo de' Medici's, but it was twisted to one side, and from that side drool was oozing because, since she was toothless, she couldn't hold back her saliva. Her upper lip sported a longish but skimpy moustache, and her long, pointy chin twisted upwards a bit. Assaulted by the stench of her breath, I threw up on her. I shall stake my berth in heaven that, as long as I'm in Lombardy, I'll be damned if I get horny again.*

Though Niccolò may well have had commerce with a few hideous prostitutes in his day, the sick-making details of his description – too long and pornographic to reproduce in full – sound like obvious invention, while the grotesque reference to Lorenzo hints at a possible political allegory. The moral of his high-minded story is that some men, when they can't have what they want all the time – whether sex or power – lose their judgement and settle for whatever cheap means of gratification someone offers them. Afterwards, when they behold what they bought in a moment of pure self-indulgence, it makes them sick. So it was in times past, when Florentines bought Medici promises of salvation. It would be the same if they make the same mistake again.

But now Niccolò's defamers are closing in and want blood. *Do not make fun of this*, Biagio chides him, *and do not neglect it.* The present peril *is so great that it would frighten you*, even you with your habit of laughing off every evil.[14] The scandal over Bernardo Machiavelli's debts or birth is quashed, but a new one threatens when, at the end of May 1510, a denunciation of Niccolò appears in one of the boxes placed around the city for people to make anonymous accusations. His accusers claim that he had committed sodomy with 'a certain Lucrezia, known as La Riccia, a courtesan'.[15] Nothing further comes of this allegation, and Niccolò seems to have remained on familiar terms with the woman. Their relationship may have been sexual or political or both. Courtesans could be excellent spies, and some letters addressed to Machiavelli allude to them passing on confidential messages or holding secret codes. In October that same year, Cardinal Soderini's agent, Giovanni Girolami, mentions a courtesan in Lyons called Jeanne who, he tells Niccolò, 'is devoted to you, and therefore you will leave her a letter for her to give me'.[16]

The winter of 1511 is brutal yet beautiful, with recurrent snowfalls bringing master artists and their apprentices out on the streets, where they make the most exquisite snow-lions in living memory, some of them immense; the piazzas are also filled with finely chiselled sea galleys and nude figures, and a miniature city complete with fortresses.[17] As soon as the snows melt, Niccolò makes a muster of troops in the Piazza della Signoria, three hundred mounted bowmen and musketeers. He spends the spring and early summer riding around Tuscany, buttressing defences.

Then Soderini and the Ten call him home with alarming news.

King Louis has decided to hold his renegade Church Council within Florentine territories – in Pisa of all places, wellspring of so many of this republic's sorrows. If his plan goes ahead, Soderini agrees for once with his adversaries, it will turn Florence into the main battleground for the king's war with the pope.

Under pressure from their protector, the Signoria give their formal consent to the plan. But as cardinals and bishops flood into Pisa, they send Niccolò Machiavelli there as well. Do everything in your power, they instruct him, to persuade the king and his cardinals to call off the council.

He makes a first, failed attempt in September, then returns to Pisa in early November. Shortly afterwards, two soldiers, a Pisan and a Spaniard, get into a brawl over a courtesan. Other men leap into the fracas, and soon the whole town is in full-scale riot. After a French nobleman is injured – and with their enemies telling the king that his good friends the Florentines had deliberately stirred up trouble to stab him in the back – the Signoria send two ambassadors to reassure the French and express their profound regret over the incident; one of them is Francesco Vettori.[18] A French cardinal visiting Pisa, Guillaume Briçonnet, assails the genteel ambassador with a violent diatribe, and storms off. But the tense atmosphere makes the prelates more receptive to Secretary Machiavelli's persuasions. In the middle of the month, the Council moves to Milan.

Too late: the damage is already done. Niccolò had attended early sessions of the Council where churchmen had denounced Julius's sins against the Holy Church and declared null and void all his interdicts against the Council's supporters. The tempestuous pontiff had been quick to vow revenge against Florence for hosting such an outrage. In October, he formed a so-called Holy League with Venice and Spain's King Ferdinand against France and its allies. It soon became known that one of its aims was to change Florence's government. As the pope lost faith in Cardinal Francesco Soderini, he'd turned more and more to Cardinal Giovanni de' Medici for advice on Florentine matters. In mid-December,

Julius excommunicates the whole city, forbidding Mass to be said until the following spring.

War begins in earnest. The Florentines celebrate each French victory with bonfires. In April, they hear that Cardinal de' Medici has been taken prisoner by the French at Pavia; two months later, in June, they learn that he has escaped.

Then the news begins to get worse. Milan has rebelled against the king, forcing the French army to flee from that city; papal troops have seized Bologna. In mid-July, the Signoria receive a letter from His Holiness Pope Julius II, addressed to the Florentine people. It demands that the Gonfalonier of Justice, Piero Soderini, should resign his office. If he refuses, the city will pay dearly for its disobedience.

Papal and Spanish troops, under the command of King Ferdinand's viceroy Cardona, amass around Florentine territories. Niccolò is sent to the Valdichiana region as a military commissioner. On inspecting different companies, all gathered outside Pisa, he is pleased to see that so many of the men who have served before are still keen to fight, even the older ones, who could easily be replaced by youthful new recruits. Moved by the entreaties of these men and their company constables, he decides to keep them on. His masters of the Ten of War might protest that he should have discharged some of these middle-aged soldiers, but *I thought it necessary,* he tells them, *first because it seemed to me cruel to discharge men who have served so long, and then because the constables said they would not know what to do without this good part of their old companies.* He addresses the magistrates and city councils of various towns. A letter from Montepulciano reports that Commissioner Machiavelli exhorted the assembled citizens there with great wisdom, assuring them, with most excellent and efficient reasons, that they had nothing to fear, either on this occasion or under more difficult circumstances.[19]

Nothing to fear. When he later recalls his own hopeful words, intoned in scores of modest town halls and cramped village piazzas, he is unsure how far he believed them. On the one hand, the sheer overpowering might of enemy forces was reason enough to fear. The flight of Florence's French ally, driven out of northern Italy by military losses and dwindling provisions, was another. On the other hand, *if one wishes an army to win a battle, it is necessary to make it confident so that it believes it ought to win. The things that make it confident are that it be armed and ordered well, and that its members know each other.*[20] It is the soldiers' part to be disciplined and brave, and the good captain's part to make them so.

But then again, every prudent captain knows that the best army can lose because of some accident: a tactical miscalculation, a small error of timing, flukes of bad weather, sudden illness. Looking back months later, when the world he had fought so hard to build had fallen apart, he wondered if he should have feared such things more.

Effectively abandoned by the French, the Florentines had few hopes of victory. Their troops were, for the most part, in good condition. The city could perhaps have agreed to raise more of them, and dispersed them more widely. Niccolò and the other commissioners put in requests for extra money. But Soderini wrote at the end of July that the citizens had agreed to fund only a few hundred more infantry. They would have to make do.

Then, on 21 August, they heard the dreaded news: the armies of the Church and Spain were marching against Florence. Hunger had made the Spanish troops desperate. They began to descend on farms and villages with terrible violence, plundering and butchering and raping. Now, and not for the first time, the citizens of Florence regretted their parsimony. An emergency meeting was held. The Gonfalonier pleaded for new funds, and some were granted. Foot soldiers and men-at-arms were conscripted in vast numbers. Countrypeople deserted their land and descended on the city, more of them each day, until they formed a line more than a mile long around the walls, jostling each other to get through the city gates with their overburdened carts and mules. With fleeing, hungry villagers crowding the city in the heat, Soderini and his supporters worried that Medici partisans might take advantage of the panic and ignite a tumult against the government. The Signoria agreed to take extraordinary emergency measures. Some five hundred prominent citizens, suspected of working towards the return of the Medici, were detained in the Palazzo della Signoria.

At around the same time, Niccolò was marshalling two thousand choice men from Firenzuola. The plan was to join with other troops to make a strong stand and try to prevent the enemy from approaching further. The other commissioners were confident, and the men's spirits were firm. Yet both commanders and citizens were in two minds about where to concentrate the troops. Niccolò and a few of his colleagues proposed spreading them over a wide swathe of territory which the enemy would have to pass on its southward movement towards Florence. By deploying troops around Firenzuola, a stronghold between Florence and Bologna, they hoped to lure the Spanish to start besieging that town, giving the Florentines time to reinforce their troops nearer to home. Then they would place a ladder of troops all the way down to the city of Prato, about fourteen miles north-west of Florence, entrenching a mass of troops there in order to drive off the enemy before they reached all the way to Florence.[21]

But most Florentines preferred to post the majority of their soldiers in Florence and its immediate surroundings. This opinion prevailed. Some two to three thousand troops were posted at Prato, while around eighteen thousand men were concentrated around Florence. This, Niccolò later remembered painfully, was the first error that tended towards ruin. The next error was graver.

On 26 August, Spanish ambassadors came to the Palazzo della Signoria. They requested that Florence join the League against France, oblige Soderini to resign as Gonfalonier, and let the Medici return to Florence.

The people resolved not to give in without a fight. Their spirits were further inflamed when the militia captured six Spanish soldiers in the countryside and paraded them, in shackles, through Florence. Terror-stricken peasant refugees took heart when they saw how calmly the citizens prepared for the ultimate defence.

This time, people said, we have our own militia to defend us, not foreign cowards. And there are so many battalions here to protect us, with men eager to fight to the death for their country.

Then an offer had come from Viceroy Cardona, a compromise. If Florence would pay the Spanish a tribute and end their alliance with France, they might be able to keep their republican government. For a sum of 25,000 or 30,000 ducats, the Spanish would consider making an accord whereby the ban on the Medici would be upheld. Florence would still be dependent on a foreign master, one unknown and even less trusted than France. But the city would preserve some hope of maintaining its internal freedoms.

Over the following weeks and months, and even when it was all a bitter but distant memory, Niccolò could not think of what happened next without a nauseating spasm of shame. At first, Soderini had decided to negotiate, sending ambassadors to the viceroy. These men came back brimming over with unexpected optimism. From what they had heard and seen, the Spanish troops were starving nearly to death. Given the enemy's wretched condition, they said, Prato could certainly hold out against an attack.

A few weeks afterwards, Niccolò would write a letter to an unnamed 'Gentlewoman' giving his view of these events. Piero Soderini *and the scores of people with whom he was consulting were inspired with such great confidence,* he wrote, *that despite the advice from the wise for peace on that basis, the Gonfalonier kept postponing matters.* Years later, his judgement was still harsher, against both his friend Soderini and the generality of Florentine citizens. *It should have been victory enough for the Florentine people if the Spanish army yielded to some of their wishes and did not fulfil all of its own.* The Florentines should have compromised, agreeing to pay tribute and to give up their devotion to France in exchange for the thing that mattered most of all: their freedom, which hinged on the survival of the republic and on keeping the Medici out.

But the people, *having become proud,* turned down the Spanish offer of an accord. They committed one of the commonest, most devastating mistakes made in politics and war: when peoples do not know *how to put limits to their hopes* and measure their own capabilities, *they are ruined.* In this way, the *insolence that victory or the false hope of victory* arouses makes men *lose the opportunity of having a certain good through hoping to have an uncertain better.*[22]

The gruesome consequences followed swiftly. On 29 August, a ravenous Spanish army went on the rampage – not against Florence, with its heavy defences, but against Prato. The Florentines' decision to try to starve the enemy into retreat had backfired, for starvation only made the soldiers more violent. Within the day, in Machiavelli's words, *the Spaniards took possession of the city, put it to sack, and massacred the city's population in a pitiable spectacle of calamity. More than four thousand died; the remainder were captured and, through various means, obliged to pay ransom. Nor did they spare the virgins cloistered in holy sites, which were all filled with acts of rape and pillage.*[23]

When the Florentines learn of the sacking of Prato, everyone begins to dread that the Spanish will come to sack them next, despite the many thousands of soldiers posted around the city. Niccolò rides back to Florence in great haste. Writing to his unknown and perhaps fictive 'Gentlewoman' weeks later, he tries to remember his thoughts at that moment for, at the time, shock and helplessness and grief overwhelmed the clarity of his thought.

He finds the silver-haired Gonfalonier strangely calm. 'Whatever happens now,' Piero says, 'I trust that most of the people will stand with me.'[24] The Great Council, it seems, had expressed strong gratitude to him for leading them through the storm and refusing to grovel to popes and kings. Soderini still believes that he might reach some accord with Cardona. He sends ambassadors to the viceroy with offers of fidelity and money, provided the Medici stay out.

Chimeras, Niccolò will call these desperate attempts to stay the fast-swinging axe: false hopes that the Spanish would deal with the republic as moderately as the French. The ambassadors return on 30 August with these terms: the Florentines would join the League;

pay the Spanish 60,000 ducats – they had doubled the original sum; send Soderini home, stripped of his post; and allow the Medici into Florence as private citizens. There would be no more negotiations. A trembling Florentine ambassador to the viceroy, Baldassare Carducci, dismays a large gathering of citizens in the palazzo with his accounts of the massacre at Prato. Blood flowed and still flows in the streets, he says. These Spanish devils will stop at nothing. Niccolò hears his speech and sees the reactions; so does Francesco Vettori. Even the most self-possessed people, both men recall afterwards, went out of their heads with fear.[25]

At this point, in Vettori's words, Soderini is advised *by men affectionate towards freedom* – Machiavelli is probably among them – to accept whatever conditions the Spanish offer. So long as they agree that, if the Medici were allowed to return as private citizens rather than anointed rulers, their authority would be held in check, at least for some time. If they returned by force with the Spaniards' and the pope's blessing, they could do whatever they liked.

But again the Gonfalonier prevaricates. He sends his wife, Argentina, away for her safety, yet cannot bring himself to leave the government palace that has been his home for the last ten years. Niccolò's 'Letter to a Gentlewoman' casts Soderini as the doomed, tragic figurehead of a larger and far more complex tragic hero: the humanly flawed but well-intentioned Florentine republic which both men had done everything in their power to save. When ordered by the Spaniards and the pope to relinquish his office, Machiavelli's Soderini replies that, unlike certain unnamed princes,

he had not come into that office through either fraud or force but had been put there by the people. Therefore, even if all the kings in the world heaped together should order him to relinquish it, he would never do so; but if the people of Florence wanted him to leave it, he would willingly. He assembled the entire council and notified them of the proposal. He volunteered, should it please the people and should they deem his departure might bring about peace, to return home. Everyone unanimously rejected this; they all offered even to sacrifice up their lives in his defence.

On the following morning, 31 August, four young noblemen come to the government palazzo. They stride into the Gonfalonier's quarters and demand to see Soderini.[26]

Paolo Vettori, Francesco's younger brother, is the eldest of the group. He had cultivated a certain intimacy with the Gonfalonier several years before, while at the same time growing suspiciously friendly with the Medici exiles in Rome. Now he addresses Piero Soderini boldly. 'Time and fortune are pressing hard on us. It's necessary to choose the right side now and not leave our city to face terrors like those seen in Prato.' Then: 'Some five hundred citizens, some very noble, are still detained here in the palazzo. It would be well to release them straight away.'

Soderini lets Paolo speak his piece to the end, then replies in the most gracious tones, looking intently at each of his young visitors. 'I thank you for showing such love for our city, and for your concern, which I see is great.' He rises to leave.

Antonfrancesco degli Albizzi – the youngest and most ardent of the four – springs forward and seizes Soderini by his shirtfront. 'Before you go,' the young man shouts in the Gonfalonier's face, 'we demand that you release the men that your government has been holding here.'

Shocked by this laying-on of hands, Soderini's few remaining companions are slow to move. The Gonfalonier gestures to them to stay in place. He remains in his assailant's grip, his eyes steady on Antonfrancesco's quivering features. Finally, he says, 'Secretary Machiavelli. Please call for Francesco Vettori to come here at once.'

Niccolò rides off in person to find his friend, who is serving as commissioner of the city's internal defence forces. Together they find Soderini and, in a room adjacent to the audience chamber, the three men deliberate what to do. The Gonfalonier, if he could still claim that title, admits that he is badly shaken.

'You did not seem so,' says Niccolò.

'Perhaps silent indignation made me brave at the moment when I was assaulted. But now that it has passed, I'm afraid. I fear it will come to blood, not mine alone but that of people in the streets. We all know that these men and many others have been waiting for this moment for many years. Now neither laws nor persuasion nor the will of the people will stop them.'

He searches his younger friends' faces for any last sign of hope. After a long silence, Niccolò asks what he thinks it best to do.

'I'll go willingly from this palace and leave it to their friends, if that will ensure that no offences occur on my behalf.'

Niccolò tries to speak, but cannot.

'For my own part,' Vettori says quietly, 'it seems that you've governed so well in your office that I wouldn't want to be in the company of those who deprive you of it.'

At Soderini's request, Vettori goes to find Paolo and the others and negotiates their guarantee of his safe departure. 'This Gonfalonier,' he tells them sorrowfully, 'is a good and prudent man who has never let ambition or avarice transport him beyond what is just and lawful.'[27] That evening, Francesco Vettori takes Soderini to his own house, across the river in Santo Spirito. The next day he accompanies him out of the city into exile in Siena.

That same morning, 31 August: Giuliano de' Medici, Piero and Giovanni's younger brother, enters Florence. Now thirty-three, ten years younger than Niccolò, Giuliano has spent his adult life in Rome, Venice, and various Italian courts; he even makes a genial appearance in Baldassare Castiglione's *Book of the Courtier*, a dialogue set at the court of Urbino in 1507. Now Giuliano has shaved his Neapolitan-style beard and wears the sober garments of any well-to-do citizen. But his partisans welcome him back as if he were their prince. Soon, armed men surround him wherever he goes.

The city seems on the verge of anarchy. Spanish troops flood into Florence, carrying heaps of booty from Prato, which they hope to sell to rich Florentines. The headless, rump government is powerless to keep them out. To ordinary people still hearing gory tales of Prato, the Spaniards, according to Landucci's diaries, seem crueller than the devil. Local boys taunt them and steal their horses; the bodies of a few foreigners are found floating in the Arno, killed by gangs of youths. Afraid that the Spanish commanders might order revenge, magistrates send miscreants to the gallows, stoking further unrest. A new Gonfalonier is chosen, no longer for life but with a fourteen-month term of office.

For the first few weeks after Soderini leaves, the Medici remain private citizens. But behind the chaotic public stage their partisans – who are called *palleschi* after the *palle* balls on the Medici family crest – are planning their long-awaited coup. On 16 September, Cardinal Giovanni and Giuliano de' Medici are in the Palazzo della Signoria discussing reforms with other leading citizens when an uproar rises from the piazza outside. Moments later, the palace is overrun with soldiers shouting, *'Palle, palle!' The entire city was suddenly up in arms*, Niccolò writes shortly after, *and that name was echoing everywhere throughout the city*. The leader of the siege is a mercenary from Bologna hired, Machiavelli claims, by the Medici. The magistrates are forcibly assembled *and compelled to reinstate the Magnificent Medici in all the honours and dignities of their ancestors*.[28]

A new committee is formed for changing the constitution, its members drawn largely from among from the most fervid Medici partisans. They lose no time in dismantling institutions that have protected popular freedoms. Niccolò's citizen militia is the first casualty. The Nine magistrates of the militia are dismissed and the entire organization abolished just two days after the coup, on 18 September 1512. Soderini and his brother Francesco, the cardinal, are banished. And – for the republic's enemies, this is the critical blow – the Great Council is dissolved. Within a few months, the Great Hall that had been built to house the Council is ruined. The fine woodwork is decimated, the beautiful tapestries that had adorned its walls are ransacked, and the vast room is filled with scores of tiny cubicles to accommodate hired soldiers, turning the bastion of popular liberty into a crude barracks at the heart of the government palazzo. It suits the new Medici-led government to keep Spanish troops at the city gates, lest Soderini's friends or resurgent Savonarolans attempt an uprising. The Spanish stay so long, with so conspicuous a presence, that in November the ever-moody Pope Julius II accuses Cardinal de' Medici of ruling Florence with force and adhering more to the Spanish king than to himself.[29]

A jittery circumspection prevails in the Chancery offices in the first days after the coup. The old Signoria, then the new government, had ordered civil servants to carry on with business as usual. Niccolò, Second Chancellor and Secretary to the Ten, still goes to work every morning and returns home at night. But only a few of the leading magistrates who had been friendly to him and the outcast Gonfalonier remain in their offices. Meetings are stuffed with Medici devotees who shun Niccolò and his closest colleagues. Among them, his trusted friends for fourteen years, there is no more laughter: even if they should laugh only at themselves, someone overhearing might suspect more insidious irreverence.

So, day after day, he carries out whatever business drops on his desk in a strange state of numbness, as if he were a machine moved by some outside force, serving its function without interference from a soul or lively mind or history. His self, whatever parts made him more than a functioning body, suddenly has no place here in the chambers where, mere days before, his acuity, his prudence, his severity and his humour, his loyalty and experience and his fantastical hopes for reform had been so useful to his city.

At the end of September, it is announced that measures will be taken to restore the Medici name and possessions to the prominence they had in 1494: their property is to be recuperated, coats of arms repainted on their palazzo and many other buildings, portraits restored to the temple of Nunziata de' Servi, where lifesize wax effigies of illustrious men and families are displayed on platforms or dangled from the ceiling. As part of the restoration campaign, Piero Soderini's image is to be removed from the temple and his legacy discredited.

On hearing this, Niccolò cannot stay silent. A man's mind, he muses in *The Ass*, can't easily be turned against his nature or habits. Though his brain might warn him of the dangers in honest criticism, his nature forces him to see – and point out – human errors in hopes of correcting them. And in the *present age so grudging and evil*, one *always sees bad more quickly than good.*[30]

So in a last attempt to stand up for his friend and for their crushed republican hopes, he composes an unsolicited memorandum to Cardinal Giovanni de' Medici.[31] *Before Your Eminence follows the advice of those who wish to befoul the name of Piero Soderini or expunge every memory of his deeds*, he writes, *think carefully.* The people pushing for such measures pretend that they will give credit to the new Medici government. But their true motives for disparaging Piero are quite different. Many of them have no desire for a Medici state but want to become heads of state themselves. Some perhaps hope to re-establish the old political order so that they or one of their relatives can become Gonfalonier for Life, thus acquiring the authority they begrudged Soderini. If you, Cardinal de' Medici, let these men expose the defects of Piero, you risk creating a monster that will threaten you soon enough.

Not long afterwards – when he had been stripped of his posts and banished from the offices where for fourteen years he had earned respect, made people laugh, and tried to do some good for his city – he must have questioned his own wisdom in writing so boldly. It is true that he had grown unused to keeping silent before men in power. A short time earlier, his opinion had been valued. Surely, he'd thought, this new government's leaders would want the benefit of his long experience. And he could hardly cringe in the shadows while the vultures pecked away at his absent friend's memory. They wouldn't expect such docility, knowing as they did how irreverent Soderini's lackey could be, how quick to defend his friends and the republic, if not himself.

Or had he stupidly played into their hands, given them the pretext they needed to muzzle him once and for all? Perhaps he thought he had done it well. His defence of Soderini had not been overwarm. He'd written as if he had only Medici interests at heart: *I should like to make friends for your house, not enemies.* But Cardinal Giovanni and his advisers, at least some of them, were not fools. They would have sniffed out the writer's truer motives. Behind the façade of helpfulness, Secretary Machiavelli was doing battle for his fallen mentor's name and legacy, venting a barely stifled fury against his enemies and insinuating that the Medici had few bona fide supporters in Florence. And as if that weren't enough, he'd smuggled in an indirect appeal to return to more popular government, insisting that the Medici's best hope of safety would be to found their state on the people at large, and not on the two-faced patricians who claimed to be their friends.

Niccolò is notified on 7 November 1512 that he is herewith 'dismissed, deprived, and totally removed' from his posts of Second Chancellor and Secretary, and prohibited from entering the government palazzo for the period of one year. He and his coadjutor Biagio Buonaccorsi seem to have been singled out as the only expellees; their other colleagues are allowed to stay on.[32] Poor Biagio had already had more than his share of sorrows. His four-year-old son Filippo, Niccolò's godson, had recently died in a fall while playing; then his wife, Lessandra, had been struck down by illness. He had written to Niccolò then: *I have been brought to such a pass that I desire death more than life, since I see no glimmer of hope for my well-being if I should lose her. Pray God to give you better fortune than He does me, who perhaps deserves it more than you.*[33]

As things transpire, both men's fortunes plummet as those of the Medici soar higher and higher. Three months later, on 18 February 1513, town criers announce that a plot has been discovered to kill Giuliano de' Medici and overthrow the government. Its leaders, Pietro Paolo Boscoli and Agostino Capponi, are in custody. And now a warrant goes out for the arrest of Niccolò di Bernardo Machiavelli, whose name had been placed seventh on a list of twenty potential collaborators that had fallen out of one of the conspirators' pockets.

Guards come to his house and escort him to prison in the Bargello. Marietta is pregnant with their third or fourth child; she could not be sure of seeing him again.

Shirt off, he faces his interrogators, who wear the black garments and caps of their office. His arms are bound behind his back and tied to a torture machine that lifts him by rope on his arms with a violent jerk, tearing them away from his shoulders. Six times they ask: why is your name so high on a list of co-conspirators? He does not know, he answers over and over. Yes, he knows the names of the two young men who have confessed, but he is not in league with them, has never discussed the Medici with them.

Shoulders in pain, for three weeks he waits in the cold of his cell, not knowing what will become of him.

> *I cannot tell you at all how I got there,*
> *nor do I know at all the cause why I fell*
> *in that place where I wholly lost my liberty . . .*
> *And I seemed to see Death*
> *nearby with his scythe.*[34]

Boscoli and Capponi have been beheaded, his gaolers inform him. And only a few days into his imprisonment, he hears bells tolling throughout the city to announce the death of Pope Julius II. He had died, it was said, of fever. A suitable death for the hot-headed pontiff.

As soon as movement returns to his fingers, Niccolò asks for pen and paper and scrawls urgent letters to Francesco and Paolo Vettori, urging them to attest his innocence. No response. So he writes three sonnets to Giuliano de' Medici, more probably to lift his own spirits than with the intention of sending them to their addressee.[35]

> *I have, Giuliano, on my legs a pair of shackles*
> *with six hoists of the rope on my shoulders:*
> *my other miseries I do not want to recount to you,*
> *since this is how they treat poets!*

Giuliano is reputed to be a humane young man with a fondness for poetry and amusements. If he could see how good-naturedly the infamous Machiavelli bears his travails, and what amicable sentiments he shows towards his torturers, he might take pity.

Niccolò beseeches the Muses to go *with their sweet zither and sweet song* to *visit Your Magnificence and make my excuses.*

Two hours before dawn on 11 March, after nearly a month of his incarceration, the prison walls reverberate with the boom-boom-booming of cannon and the shrieks of fireworks. Niccolò hears shouting. The voices gather force and erupt in a joyous roar: *'Palle! Papa Lione! Palle!'*

He struggles awake and understands. Cardinal Giovanni de' Medici has been elected pope, taking the name Leo X. The first Florentine to win such a great honour, as his Magnificent father had wanted. Lorenzo is twenty years dead, but his will still lives, and now reaches far beyond Florence. Everyone rises from their beds and goes to their windows; even well-bred women appear in their nightgowns. For days, the city is ablaze with festivities; anyone who saw it from overhead, one chronicler writes, might think that every church, palazzo, and humble house in Florence was burning down.[36]

The new pope declares a general amnesty in his native city: all political prisoners are to be released. After twenty-two days in prison, Niccolò emerges from his ordeal, thinner than ever, still fighting the pain. Now he will have to find a way to be himself – if there is a way – in this new world where Florence is no longer a republic except in name, and the Medici are princes of both Florence and Rome.

14

Be Like the Fox

It is December 1513, nine months since Niccolò's release from prison. He spends most of his time now at his country house in Sant' Andrea in Percussina with Marietta and their children. At the beginning of August, Marietta had given birth to a baby girl, their third or fourth child, who died after three days. Several of their children die young, including the eldest daughter, Primerana; though the circumstances of her death aren't known, her name disappears from letters that mention the other children. But ten-year-old Bernardo and his younger brother Lodovico are growing up strong, and two other healthy sons, Piero and Guido, are born in the next few years, followed by a girl, Baccina, and a baby, Totto, born in the last year of his father's life.

After he was dismissed from his posts and barred from entering the Palazzo della Signoria, Niccolò had decided to spend less time in Florence. It was better to keep his head low, to avoid further trouble with the new political rulers. I shall buy a few chickens, he tells friends. Stand at the roadside under a walnut tree and beg passing travellers for news from Florence or Rome. *Physically, I feel well,* he wrote in August to his nephew Giovanni Vernacci, Primavera's son, *but ill in every other respect. No other hope remains for me but that God may help me.*[1]

Like his helpless compatriots when they faced Cesare Borgia's army a decade earlier, Niccolò, too, can have last recourse to God when all other hope is lost. To God, and Francesco Vettori. Throughout the hot summer, autumn, and now, the start of winter, he has waited every day for letters from his friend. A few weeks before the election of the new Medici pope, Vettori had been appointed one of Florence's ambassadors to the pontificate. And now he writes from Rome, often and at length, and Niccolò writes back.

These letters keep his spirits from sinking into the depression that has threatened to pull him down since his ordeal. Vettori had been greatly distressed at the news of his friend's arrest and torture. Totto Machiavelli had sent an urgent messenger to him in Rome, but Vettori could do nothing to help. 'These days,' he wrote miserably, 'I'm no use to anyone, even to myself. Though as soon as the new pope was elected, I went and asked him for no other favour than your liberation.'

'You did what you could,' Niccolò had reassured his friend, 'and I thank you for it.' He put on his bravest face. *I hope you'll get this much pleasure from these troubles of mine: I've borne them so straightforwardly that I'm proud of myself for it. It seems I'm more a man than I thought I was.* And don't worry, he told Vettori, from now on I'll be far more careful of what I say or write. 'Surely the times to come will be more generous and less suspicious.'

Vettori was less optimistic. His newly arrived fellow ambassadors were Medici cronies close to Leo X. He, Vettori, was much their junior, and regarded warily by his colleagues and the Medici pontiff. His taxes had suddenly increased because, he suspected, Medici partisans among the new tax authorities wanted to punish him for his part in trying to save Piero Soderini.[2] In Rome, he was pulled from both sides. Men would approach him one day who wanted to depose the new government and considered him their ally. Then his brother Paolo would visit with agents of their new masters, feigning total confidence in Vettori's loyalty, then dropping hints that it would be better for him not to consort with certain suspect men. Vettori told Niccolò this, omitting to say whether his name had come up in these discussions.

Though Machiavelli had suffered much more, he tried to cheer his friend with greetings from their old crowd at home. Agostino Vespucci and Biagio, it seems, were not among them any longer; after 1512, there are no further records of Niccolò's interactions with his office-mates. We all miss your company, he told Vettori, in these happy days of political renewal. *Every day we visit the house of some girl to recover our vigour.*[3] Just yesterday, we were at Sandra di Pero's house to watch the procession of Our Lady of Impruneta, carried in to thank God for giving those cardinals the grace to choose a Florentine pope. To win over her continued benedictions, the ever-liberal Medici had given the Lady offerings of the finest garments she had ever possessed: nine new mantles, seven woven in gold brocade.[4] As ever with these bankers, money buys every-thing. *And so we go on marking time during these festivities, enjoying the remainder of this life, so that it seems to me I am dreaming it all up.*

Between the upbeat lines, each man understood that his friend was shell-shocked, urgently seeking in the other some sense of continuity with their broken former world, though knowing it was irretrievably gone. After living a few months in the country, whenever he returned for a few days to Florence Niccolò scarcely recognized the city he used to call his *patria*, his fatherland. His own father had seen it in worse times, perhaps. But back then, the changes from a free republic towards one-family rule had happened more gradually, not overnight. During the short eighteen-year life of the 1494 republic, people had grown used to carping in the streets about this or that policy, or gossiping about the peccadilloes of certain great men. Sometimes – often – their unshackled tongues went too far. Then people argued at the tops of their voices about whether the laws should allow men to say whatever they pleased, or whether they should be tried and punished for spreading lies and venom.[5] They debated whether the state should protect citizens from any offensive words spoken against them in public or in private, or whether one must distinguish between more and less serious kinds of offence. Since the Medici had returned, these noisy, sometimes badly reasoned, emotionally overboiling arguments had vanished from the piazzas and the taverns. Instead, peace and quiet reigned, as Tacitus said it had under the Roman emperors, once the republic had died.[6] Shortly after the *coup d'état*, a man was banished for ten years and forbidden to approach within two miles of Florence because he had been heard using disrespectful words about the house of Medici.[7] His example served as a warning to others, though Niccolò had been too slow to heed it.

While Niccolò tried to be proud of his fortitude in adversity, Vettori felt no pride in his role in the Florentine republic's sad demise, or in anything he'd done since the coup. I doubt, he said bleakly, that I have the spirit to do other than get used to this new government.[8] As you know, 'I adapt to everything and always strive to do good to every man, come what may. In adverse fortune I lose heart and am fearful about everything.' And if you were here at my side, Niccolò, and we could talk in person, 'I think I'd make you fear, with very good reason.'

Whatever fresh horrors Vettori might have in mind and be unable to write about – their letters would of course pass through the hands of Medici informants – Niccolò lacked the heart to dwell on them for now, with his shoulders still aching and the memory of his own recent dread still a constant, unwanted companion. *Magnificent Lord Ambassador,* he'd replied, *your letter terrified me more than the rope* that greeted me in the Bargello. *'How shall I come if thou art afraid, thou who art wont to strengthen me against doubt?'* – a quote from Dante.

Perhaps Niccolò had been disappointed on hearing how ready Vettori was to bow to the new masters. But Francesco had always sought to fit in with what his world expected of him, even striving to shift his political views to avoid dangerous clashes with the powers that be. In this, their two natures were different as night and day. 'These last months,' he told Niccolò, 'have made me lose my faith in all those political discussions we used to have.[9] Everything I hoped for missed the mark. Sometimes I long to be with you and to talk of these things again, but then I think: why bother, since nothing ever turns out the way we want and expect?' They were getting older now; they had children and wives, and taxes to pay. Maybe the time had come to give up their fond political fancies, their illusions that they could do anything other than try to play the new game of politics as they find it.

Niccolò, too, had been grappling with the question of whether high ideals can do much good if, as the Florentines had just seen, random shifts of power, success and failure can wreck everything at a stroke. The city's new kind of politics made it easy to understand Vettori's readiness to abandon their young men's hopes of working together, alongside Piero Soderini, to forge a stronger and better civil order. Florence's new regime was still officially a republic, as it had been under Lorenzo and Cosimo. But the Palazzo della Signoria was no longer the centre of government, as business had shifted towards the Medici Palace and the Vatican. Now one Medici prince – who is also God's emissary on earth – and a few of his intimates decided everything, far away in Rome. It was unsafe to speak of the Medici now, for *one speaks of princes with a thousand hesitations.*[10] And it was pointless to speak of what should be done in this or that matter of policy, since one's opinion would have no influence.

All the same – Niccolò replied to his fatalistic friend – *if I could talk to you face to face, I couldn't help filling your head with all sorts of castles in the air, because fortune has seen to it that, since I don't know how to talk about either the silk or the wool trade, or profits and losses, I have to talk about politics. I need either to take a vow of silence or to discuss this.*[11] And anyone who knew Niccolò would laugh aloud at the thought of him keeping silent while he has either tongue or pen.

In early spring that year, when he gazed across the stubbly yellow fields behind his garden in Sant' Andrea, in the distance he could see the thin, tall tower of the Palazzo della Signoria and the dome of the cathedral in miniature. Here, outside the city walls, Niccolò felt more at odds with his compatriots than ever. Everyone seemed to be dropping their old allegiances and changing their political tune in hopes that a bit of shimmering Medici fortune might rub off on them. Why shouldn't Vettori be like all the rest *who are busy making a place for themselves through insistent entreaties and cunning rather than by intelligence, merit, and prudence?* Niccolò saw others from their old circle, some of his best friends, currying favour with the Medici, giving them loans, pulling every string in their personal networks.[12] He could hardly blame them. This was now their world, whether they loved it or not. Perhaps it was his, too. They are, he is, nobody – and no use to anyone, or so people keep saying – without a place in this new world. For there is no other world, not one that people can see with their unaided eyes and touch with their hands.

He tried to see things through their eyes while embarking on a new project, a book on princes. He was, after all, writing for people like this, people who care most of all about present successes and failures, thinking little of the longer term; people who think reality is what you see and experience today, not the recurring human needs, inclinations and thoughts that might soon gain strength and impose their far sterner reality on the transient, superficial one. These people say, as at times Vettori comes close to saying: give up your republican fantasies, your dreams of early Rome before inequality and ambition corrupted that city. Embrace the present reality. Speak only when spoken to and say only what will please the prince. Become meek and docile, like an ass among asses. Around the same time, Niccolò started composing his poem *The Ass*, in which he vents his frustration with such attitudes:

> Little asses, as they move around,
> are heard making a noise together
> so that whoever speaks is scarcely heard . . .[13]

That is what he sees and hears when he looks at himself and his fellow Florentines. In the noise they now make there is no exchange of views, no sharing of different thoughts. It is not the glorious, tumultuous sound of diverse minds expressing freely what occurs to them but the servile, attention-seeking braying of beasts desperate to stand out among the herd. It doesn't deserve the noble name of speech; it is the jabbering of poor animals wanting more fodder, or a pat on the snout, from their masters. Please, Your Eminence, Your Holiness, believe me – I'll do or say whatever you want if you give me work, lower my taxes, pardon my too-free speech, anything for your crumbs! The honest language of independent speakers has been driven out of Florence. We lie to each other and start believing our own lies. The ones who come out best are the noisiest babblers and flatterers. They spout platitudes and say nothing. For the herd and their herd-masters only hear what is easy to hear, what they think they already know, keep repeating the same badly reasoned blandness to flatter themselves and their herd-chiefs. Which is why a writer who wants to address them must adopt their perspective, even if his aim is to shift it.

The Ass offers some clues as to why Machiavelli writes how and what he does in the *Prince*. The poem's narrator and protagonist is Niccolò himself, transformed into the titular beast. He has adapted to the strange new world he must inhabit, blending in with the herd for his safety. Now he barely recognizes himself. How can he be who he had always been, someone who could never stop pointing out unpleasant truths? Here among this herd, whoever speaks uncomfortable truths is an outcast, a rebel against the world as it is today, which the herd insists is the only world there is. *The truth often makes war on him who tells it.*[14]

How did he get here? Before his asinine metamorphosis, he was like a boy who could not be cured of his urge to run and run, however indecent his running seemed to others, and however hard they tried to restrain him.[15] Then one day he found himself hurtling, falling into *as harsh a place as I ever saw*, and losing his liberty, unable to see where he was going in the blackness. All his vigour was vanquished and he was seized with terror. Then:

> *a woman of utmost beauty, but breezy and brash,*
> *appeared to me with her locks blonde and dishevelled.*[16]

He stays quiet, afraid of failing to show her suitable reverence. But she greets him as if they'd met a thousand times and calls him by name. 'Tell me,' she asks, 'how did you fall into these broken and barren valleys?'

His pallid cheeks turn fiery red; he shrugs his shoulders in

237

silence. He wants to say: my own small wit and vain hopes made me fall into this wretched place. But, seized by shame and self-pity, his mouth cannot form this speech. He, who before his fall had been a man of many and well-formed words, has become as speechless as all the herd animals snuffling and squeaking around him.

The woman laughs, saying, 'Don't be afraid to speak among these trees.' He has fallen, she tells him, into the place where the goddess Circe fled when Jove seized dominion over her ancient nest. To assert his new principality, the great god had spread such rumours of her infamy that she'd abjured all human society. It seems the humans who were the targets of Jove's propaganda believed it, and persecuted their former governor. Now Circe rules this bleak place and, remembering how men once treated her, turns any who stumble into her realm into animals.

Niccolò's new acquaintance is one of her serving-damsels; her duty is to take these beasts out to pasture. Wishing to protect the fallen poet from her queen's transforming gaze, his guide now tells Niccolò to get on all fours and crawl along in the herd among the man-beasts, *in the midst of that crowd which is worse than death.*

At length they arrive at a magnificent palace. His hands and knees are scraped nearly to the bone. After settling her herd in their stable, the damsel takes him by the hand and leads him to her chamber. And here, alone and in her confidence, he begins to recover his lost power of speech.

'My life seemed to have ended,' he tells her, 'until your kindness began to restore it.'

'I've followed the course of your life,' she replies; it seems she is a long-time fan of his poetry. 'And let me tell you: all the ingratitude and toil you've faced came not from any fault of yours.' But as long as the times and Heaven oppose his city, he will have to disguise himself as one of the herd for his own safety. *You must altogether lose your human semblance,* says his hostess, and move about *covered with a different skin.*

She offers him a well-mixed salad, and a good wine that reminds him of certain Tuscan vintages from Val di Greve and Poppi. They dine together, talking *of a thousand little songs and a thousand loves.* Then she leads him to her bed.

At first, he curls up under the sheets on one side, timid and bashful as a virgin wife on her wedding night. The lady teases him like a newly wed husband. 'Do you think I'm armed with nettles or thorns?'

So he musters his manly courage, stretches a quaking hand beneath the sheets, and then *as it ran all over her body, my lost vigour returned.*[17] The old flame that burned in him is rekindled; he remembers himself. He will do as she says and hide this self, the only one he will ever be able to have, and bide his time in this broken world. His skin will grow thick as an ass's and he will stop caring if people slander or slight him:

> *Bites and blows I do not regard*
> *as I once did, for I have grown*
> *to have the same nature as he whom I sing.*[18]

He will adapt to the times and variations of fortune this far, and no more: by changing his outward form and voice, though not his opinions or his hopes. And perhaps one day,

> *if the heavens do not hurl down fresh angers*
> *against me, a bray will make itself heard*
> *in all places; let it light on whom it will.*[19]

Unlike Vettori and many others, then, he refused to give up his habits of conversation or his *castellucci*, his political castles in the air. But he also wanted to work towards bringing them down to earth, not to retreat into a purely contemplative life like some sallow-faced Roman philosopher forced out of action under the emperors. So he needed a few favours. For a start, could the Magnificent Ambassador Vettori put in a request for Totto to be enrolled in the pope's household? Whether through bad luck or little skill, Niccolò's brother had proved a failure as an international man of business. So he decided to join the priesthood. Since the family's political fortunes had sunk nearly as low as in the days when Bernardo's cousin Girolamo was charged with plotting against Cosimo de' Medici's government, they might as well try to crawl their way up through ecclesiastical channels. *And now that you're in Rome with the pope,* Niccolò had added, *do please mention me to His Holiness, if you can, and see if he or his family might engage my services in some way or other.*[20]

Vettori was taken aback. Niccolò's resilience was admirable; so was his lack of rankling bitterness so soon after his tribulations. But if he was serious – and Francesco realized that, in making this request, he was – then he underestimated the suspicions in which the Medici and their partisans still held him. Though no evidence had been found against Machiavelli in the matter of the conspiracy, it was well known that few men had worked harder to shore up the flailing republic and prevent the Medici from returning.

There should be no doubt about my word, Niccolò pressed his sceptical friend, *for since I've always kept it, I'll not start learning how to break it now. Whoever has been honest and faithful for forty-three years, as I have, is unable to change his nature.*[21] Pope Leo and his relatives are realistic men, not despots who demand unquestioning devotion from all their ministers. They know that, among those who can best help them defend Florence, there are many who will never be zealous Medici loyalists, yet can be trusted to serve their government so long as it keeps the city safe. Tell them, said Niccolò, that former Secretary Machiavelli is such a man. He might wish that Florence were a republic in more than name, but he'd never dream of jeopardizing his city's safety if it were consigned to his care. *If these new masters of ours see fit not to leave me lying on the ground, I shall be happy, and believe that I shall act in such a way that they too will have reason to be proud of me.*

But he wasn't desperate, not yet; much as he'd like a steady salary and an occupation suited to his abilities, he'd survive without either. If they don't want his services, he told his friend, *I'll get on somehow. I was born into a family without wealth to spare, and at an early age learned to scrimp rather than thrive.*[22]

Vettori had tried not to raise his hopes.[23] 'I'll see what I can do for you and Totto,' he said, 'though it might be difficult. My influence is far weaker than you seem to think.'

Then he made a wonderful suggestion. Let us, he proposed, pretend that our opinions still carry some weight. Imagine we're living in happier times, strolling together from the Ponte Vecchio through Via de' Bardi, trying to tidy up this mess of a world in our thoughts.[24] I'll start by giving you my opinions on the great foreign policy questions of the day, then you reply with yours. What do you think – is Spain's King Ferdinand a political genius, as one hears so many saying, or a short-sighted opportunist whose cunning will soon lose him friends? What are the various foreign powers trying to get out of Italy? Whose side should the pope take in quarrels between the French, the German emperor, and the Spanish? Leo has little experience of such matters; he needs good men to counsel him on affairs of state.

A diverting epistolary game to lighten these heavy days, and at the same time a job application, Vettori's strategy for seeking to revive his friend's dead political career. Niccolò wrote back in a way that showcased his deep knowledge of foreign affairs, of the main players' motives and the complicated pressures that shape their decisions. Since *the duty of a prudent man is constantly to consider what may harm him and to foresee problems in the distance*, he wrote, *I have put myself in the pope's place and scrutinized in detail what I might now have to fear and what remedies I might use in his place.*[25] He'd dashed off page after page, then went back to tweak, prune or expand on key passages, changing words, adding caveats. Some of the policy advice he gives in these letters finds its way into his *Prince*.[26] The need to take clear sides in the conflicts of great powers, avoiding what might seem the safer road of neutrality; subtle digs at those who admire King Ferdinand's hyperactive power-games, which Machiavelli's letters insist are empty noise that would soon alienate all his allies.[27] And towards the end of his book, he plays with his and Vettori's very different views about what human beings can hope to accomplish when fortune opposes them.[28] At one moment he says: the virtuous response to bad fortune is to stand firm in one's convictions and work hard, however one can, to bring order back to the world. Then another voice pipes up, recalling Vettori's and those of other self-distrusting Florentines, and says: those succeed best who adapt their ways and beliefs to changing times, who bow to Fortune's command! A test, perhaps, of how well readers of all the earlier chapters have absorbed the book's pre-eminent lesson: that it is always better to rely on your own well-founded arms and *virtù* than to follow the latest ephemeral trends or the fortunes of others.

I'll try, Vettori had promised, to show your letters to the pope or to Giulio de' Medici, who it seems will soon be made a cardinal. Expecting the authorities to read his letters, he'd inserted his own words of recommendation for his unjustly ostracized friend. *I want you to believe one thing that I say without any flattery, Niccolò: the throng is so great that one can't help meeting a great number of people, and among them I have not found any man of better judgement than you.*[29]

As autumn and then winter come to Sant' Andrea, Niccolò waits anxiously for Vettori or God to send some manna to the desert, some sign that all his years of service have not been forgotten, that he might still be of use to his prince-ridden city. Here at his country house, where Bernardo Machiavelli used to spend a good part of each week consulting with tenants and selling lambs and piglets and bottles of wine and oil, Niccolò follows what he learned from his father about the art of small-estate management, and the even more useful art of keeping the world's rot at arm's length. Rising daily with the sun, he tells Vettori in mid-December, he goes to the woods of his estate and kills time with the woodsmen, who are always arguing among themselves.[30] Trudging up the road, he chats with whomever he meets along the way and observes mankind, *the variety of its tastes, the diversity of its fancies.* He carries books of poetry under his arm, especially those by poets who were cast out of their homelands, as he feels he is from his. He reads about their amorous passions and remembers his own, *and these reflections make me happy for a while.* He drifts across the road to the inn and fritters away more time playing cricca or backgammon with the innkeeper and a few other regulars: a butcher, a miller and some kiln workers. These games generate *thousands of squabbles and endless disputes and vituperations. More often than not we are wrangling over a few coins; be that as it may, people can hear us yelling even in San Casciano. Thus cooped up among these lice, I get the mould out of my brain and vent the malice of my fate.* Then, returning to his own house, he dines with his family.

That is one side of this born-again Niccolò, the side that no one in the kingdom of asses will take special notice of. A man who gets on with everyday things without involving himself in them, one whose deeds are mostly trifling and detached from his innermost thoughts and feelings, an existence spiced only with time-wasting games and a few harmless memories of old love affairs. The existence endured by most men of middle age. Nothing to worry ass-keepers who keep an eye out for signs of brazen human individuality among their herds.

But in the evening, after the winter sun has sunk below the tiny silhouette of the Duomo, he reveals the rest of himself, his real life, to a select company of friends. At the threshold of his low, vaulted study, *I take off my workday clothes, covered with mud and dirt, and put on the garments of court and palace.* He is not too proud to pay respects and ask for favours, but his benefactors are not the princes who have overrun his city and are overrunning Italy. The courts he enters nightly through his study are *the venerable courts of the ancients,* of Roman and Greek historians and poets and philosophers and the dead men who populate their pages, from whom he seeks something much more real and more enduring than those other princes can ever give him. And there, *solicitously received by them, I nourish myself on that food that alone is mine and for which I was born; where I am unashamed to converse with them and to question them about the motives for their actions; and they, out of their human kindness, answer me.* In their company he is transported far beyond his humdrum new life and the herd-world that enforces it. Here he finds his true homeland full of fellow citizens, not a homeland that rivals his fatherland of Florence, but one that holds out the hope of joining the best wisdom of the dead with the living and making his downtrodden *patria* stronger, safer, more human than asinine. *And for four hours at a time I feel no boredom, I forget all my troubles, I do not dread poverty, I am not terrified by death. I transfer myself into them completely.* He finds his lost wholeness here, in the company of the dead who care about the same things he cares for: the health of republics, the dangers princes pose to every fatherland worthy of the name. Many of them suffered for these concerns of theirs; some found it safer to conceal their views.

> There was never anyone so prudent or esteemed so wise than Junius Brutus deserves to be held for his simulation of stupidity. Titus Livy expresses one cause that induced him to such simulation, which was to be able to live more securely and to maintain his patrimony. Nevertheless, it can be believed that he also simulated this to be less observed and to have more occasion for crushing the kings and freeing his own fatherland whenever opportunity would be given him.[31]

Though he writes these words a few years later in the *Discourses*, they chime well with his self-exhortation to assume the outward form of an ass to protect his inner integrity – and with the urge expressed in his letters to nourish his own judgement of human affairs, despite the present world's suspicion of independent political thinking. Lucius Junius Brutus was celebrated as the founder of the Roman republic, the man who led the revolt against Rome's last kings – the last, that is, until Julius and Augustus Caesar became de facto monarchs more than four hundred years later. While waiting for the right moment to revolt, Brutus concealed his intentions behind a mask of incompetence so that the king would not see him as a threat.[32] Someone who is discontented with a prince but too weak to challenge him, Niccolò points out, cannot make himself safe by staying quiet. For *it is not enough to say: 'I do not care for anything; I do not desire honours or useful things; I wish to live quietly and without quarrel!'* These excuses won't be believed if they come from *a man notable for his quality,* even when such men choose the quiet life *truly and without any ambition.* Bernardo Machiavelli was such a man. Niccolò is far less fond than his father of the quiet life, but he did not deserve the suspicions that brought him so low. To escape continual danger, then, *one must play crazy, like Brutus, and make oneself very much mad, praising, speaking, seeing, doing things against your intent so as to please the prince.*[33] And because, he tells Vettori, *Dante says that no one understands anything unless he retains what he has understood, I have jotted down what I have profited from my conversations with my ancients and composed a little book,* Of Principalities. *It ought to be welcomed by a prince, and especially by a new prince.*[34]

Writing it helps him hold on a little longer to the lost days of Secretary Machiavelli, prudent adviser to statesmen, before everyone else forgets those days and that Machiavelli for ever. He recalls all the leaders and warriors whose methods, merits and errors he's observed over the past fifteen years, and makes their exploits fill the blank pages before him. Savonarola, Caterina Sforza, King Louis XII, Cesare Borgia, Paolo and Vitellozzo Vitelli. Alexander VI, the double-dealing pope, and Julius II, the impetuous *Papa terribile.* He writes in the quiet of his study, surrounded by ancient companions. Livy, Tacitus, Xenophon, Plutarch: clear-headed witnesses to the death of freedom in Rome and Greece, much more violent than its recent downfall in Florence. As his book takes shape he toys with the idea of humbly presenting it – when it is finished and after his closest friends have checked it for propriety – to one of the new Medici princes. It would remind them how much this Machiavelli they'd banished knows about politics, knowledge that might have great utility for them and the whole city.

But he has learned to avoid lecturing princes on what they should and should not do. Instead, he gives free rein to his old talent for ambiguous writing, so useful when writing diplomatic dispatches.[35] He adopts the persona of a cold-blooded adviser to new rulers, one who teaches them how to use other princes, foreign peoples, and their own subjects to serve their soaring ambitions. Yet his writing turns hot, nearly bursts into flame, when he describes how free peoples avenge themselves on those who attack their freedom. And he delights in playing with his readers, testing their ability to see past first appearances, letting sly wit ooze through some of the deadpan lines. Humour is medicine for his wounded spirits, especially humour at the expense of princes.

His little book is packed with surprising, sometimes shocking, praise for great leaders, no matter how super-ambitious, high-flying, cunning or cruel. On closer scrutiny, though, one begins to notice hesitations and caveats that compromise the praise. Take that paragon of modern princes, the man Niccolò seems to praise more effusively than anyone else in his book: Cesare Borgia. *I cannot think how to reproach him*, our author declares.[36] He laid such good foundations for his power – not without committing a few betrayals and murders – but was brought crashing down by an extreme and malignant fortune. Alas, poor Cesare. Such is the power that cruel goddess Fortuna can wield over human affairs, even those of the greatest princes.

Yet the book's long discussion of Cesare's career teems with insinuations that undercut the praise. Niccolò may not reproach him outright. But he treats him as a prime specimen of an inferior sort of prince, one who depends on the fortune of others – other people's money, family connections, and borrowed forces – not on his own arms and virtue. These men tend to rise to power quickly, then crash just as fast. True, he says that Cesare failed 'only' because of his father's death – a cruel stroke of fortune – and then had another bit of bad luck, that of backing the wrong man to be the next pope. But notice the irony: after all his deceptions, murders and other promising efforts to stand on his own two virtuous feet, this fortunate prince still depends on the papacy – that is, on someone else's arms and fortune – to make or break him! And Niccolò's detailed narration of his career is anything but a story of near-success. It is the story of a series of increasingly desperate ploys to hold on to the state his father handed him on a platter, always using money and 'the arms of others' – first his father's, then the French king's, then those of the Spanish – all of which fail to bring him security. The more one reads about Cesare's exploits, the harder it is to ignore a glaring contrast between our writer's seeming good words about his hero and his account of what the fortune-gifted young man actually did. *I would put him forward*, our writer says, *to be imitated by any prince who comes to power by fortune and others' arms.*[37] Not all princes should imitate Cesare, only the fortune-dependent. Those who come to power by their own virtuous arms need not follow his example.

Niccolò steers clear of the sensitive question: were the Medici princes of fortune or of virtue? If princes of fortune are those who buy their way up the political ladder with money and depend on others' arms, the answer seems obvious – and more so than ever with this newest Medici government, swept into power on the back of Spanish troops. But he lets insinuation do the work, lets deeds speak louder than words. If his book were a painting, it would be one whose bold lines and colours create a powerful impression at first viewing: it seems to be about and for virile, worldly wise, occasionally ruthless princes. But look more closely and you start to notice details that subvert the artist's glowing portrait. A weakness in his subject's grip on his sword, a gleam of mania or flicker of self-doubt in his eyes, an unhealthy swelling at his neck.

Niccolò is eager to show the book to Vettori and seek his advice. Do you think, he asks, it would be a good idea to present it to Giuliano de' Medici? Everyone expects Pope Leo to make his younger brother his regent in Florence. And Giuliano, it seems, is both cultivated enough to appreciate some of the book's double meanings and easy-going enough not to take offence at its riskier innuendoes; Niccolò's sonnets addressed to him from prison suggest as much. And if it is a good idea, he presses Vettori, should I take the book to him myself, or send it to you to give him? He wants some recognition from these new chiefs of his political expertise, which is far superior to Giuliano's. That affable young man looks good at the head of a battalion and knows how to sweet-talk ladies in the palaces of Naples and Rome, but he knows nothing about how to safeguard a vulnerable state. *Anyone who reads this study of mine would see that during the fifteen years I have been studying the art of the state I have neither slept nor fooled around.*[38]

The version that has come down to posterity is dedicated not to Giuliano de' Medici but to his nephew Lorenzo – son of the dead Piero – whom Pope Leo would appoint as ruler of Florence in 1513. Perhaps the entire Dedication as we now know it was written only then, or perhaps Niccolò had already drafted it by 1513 and changed little more than the name of its dedicatee.[39] *It is customary for those who desire to acquire grace from a prince to come to meet him with the things of their own that they hold most dear, or with things that they see please him most.* Our writer desires not just princely grace and to please his prince, but also *to offer myself to Your Magnificence with some testimony of my servitude to you.* He hopes it will not appear presumptuous if a man *of low and mean state* like himself *dares to discuss and give rules for the government of princes.* But having examined these matters for a long time, he has reduced them to a 'small volume' which he now offers as a 'small gift', in the hope that *if Your Magnificence considers and reads it diligently, you will know from it my extreme desire that you arrive at the greatness that fortune and your other qualities promise.*

To judge by first appearances, Machiavelli is simply following the conventional proprieties writers were expected to observe when addressing princes in his day. Other such books open with florid greetings, praise for the – usually young – prince's great fortune and native, if untested, abilities, and expressions of the wish to help him become an excellent ruler. But in insisting on his servitude, his base condition, and his fawning hopes that *Your Magnificence will at some time turn your eyes from the summit of your height to these low places,* Niccolò goes far beyond the usual expressions of deference. While other advice-givers of his times – Erasmus writing to Emperor Charles V or, a few decades before, Bartolomeo Scala to Lorenzo il Magnifico in his dialogue on laws – eulogize their prince's heaven-sent greatness, they do not insist, as Niccolò does, on their own lowly status and desire for servitude. And there is a mock-innocent audacity in his Dedication that would have hit most contemporary Florentines between the eyes. By addressing as 'princes' men who were not officially princes or monarchs at all, but simply leading men in a republic of equals, Niccolò slyly exposes that fiction. His humble professions of servitude are entirely out of place in the republic that Medici Florence still pretended to be. And his implication that the Medici expected such treatment from fellow citizens speaks much more loudly than any direct charge of hypocrisy.

Contemporaries who knew of the author's track record in addressing Medici princes must have been bemused – or amused – by its ingratiating overtones.[40] This was, after all, the same Niccolò who'd been presumptuous enough to send an unsolicited memorandum to Cardinal Giovanni de' Medici before he became Pope Leo X, advising him to distrust the patricians who'd backed his family's return to power and to establish his new government on the people. It was the same Niccolò who, after being tortured on suspicion of plotting against that government, had written cheekily familiar sonnets to Giuliano de' Medici bemoaning his unjust treatment and the stink of his prison cell. Now here he was again, writing to Giuliano, or to Lorenzo, young men with no political experience to speak of, in tones more suitable for addressing a great monarch, a Roman emperor, or a tyrant.[41] Had Niccolò Machiavelli, who until now had never bowed down before money or power, been broken at last? Does his *Prince* show his readiness to change his political colours and abandon his once fearless style of addressing great men, in the hope that the Medici might shed their suspicions and restore him to the fold of Florentine politics?

Francesco Vettori and other friends who knew of Niccolò's love for double-edged writing – a love that shines through in almost everything he writes – might have detected a whiff of parody, and plenty of his old self, between the obsequious lines. *I have found nothing in my belongings that I care so much for and esteem so greatly as the knowledge of the actions of great men, imparted to me through a long experience of modern things and a continuous reading of ancient ones.* For *to know well the nature of princes one needs to be of the people*, as he, Niccolò, says he is. If they read his little book carefully, they will find that this is one of its recurring, subtly argued lessons: any prince who thinks he can rule without taking popular interests seriously will soon lose his state.

When reading the *Prince*, one often has the impression that the book speaks in two different voices, sometimes in the same sentence. One voice is louder, tough, ambitious, impatient to set aside moral scruples for the sake of gaining an advantage. The other is less attention-grabbing and, for readers on the lookout for signature Machiavellianisms, far less intriguing. Yet it is this lower-key voice that recommends the book's most practical measures, the policies that tend to produce lasting power and security, not just dazzling but problematic results. It points out the advantages of working quietly to build 'dykes and dams' for one's defences instead of lashing out when bad fortune strikes, or giving in to the latest powers-that-be. It shows that even the greatest princes need to deal transparently with their allies and share power with their people if they want to maintain their state.[42]

Niccolò keeps dangling both options before readers throughout his book, letting them decide which voice – the hard-headed, amoral pragmatist's, or the other one – offers the more realistic route to lasting safety and a decent common life. His *Prince* is a series of mind-teasing conversations – he calls them *discorsi*, discourses – with his readers, whether they are princes or not. This way of writing, as some of his favourite ancients realized, can be far more persuasive than direct lectures. A high-spirited young prince's eyes might glaze over if he reads, yet again, that he ought to be a lover of justice and resist the temptation to violate moral standards for the sake of greater power. Such middle-aged advice is more likely to sink in if it comes from someone who seems to support the prince's ambitions and who writes in a more beguiling, subversive language than that of preachers and pedants.

If the *Prince* is – as many early readers thought – a masterwork of playful-and-serious political irony through and through, this would explain many puzzles: the impression of different voices, the maddening ambiguities and, above all, how someone who had devoted fifteen years to defending a popular republic against a Medici revival could, only months after his release from prison, turn around and write a brilliant advice book showing his princely gaolers how to strengthen their grip on his city. This last puzzle seems all the more mystifying since the author's next book, the *Discourses*, which he probably started writing very soon after the *Prince*, quite candidly prefers republics to princes.

Then again, readers who aren't fooled by all the author's asinine tricks might smell something fishily republican behind his persona of adviser to princes. Near the beginning of the book he declares that, since he discusses republics elsewhere, presumably in the *Discourses*, he will 'leave out' reasoning about them here. But this is a false promise, for the *Prince* will keep coming back to republics, peoples and freedom. The harder its cold, controlling voice tries to ignore them, the more they keep bursting on to the scene and threatening trouble if the prince doesn't attend to their concerns. And Niccolò does not leave out his hastily disbanded militia, or his older arguments that strong defences depend on justice. Neither money nor sheer numbers of men make strong armies, he tells his readers, but only people who are motivated to fight to the death. And they'll be motivated only when they have a real stake in the government they're expected to defend: when they can make a decent living, feel that they're treated with public respect, perhaps even take part in politics.[43] If the louder voice of the amoral adviser goads princely readers to accumulate more and more power, the *Prince*'s lower-register voice – Niccolò's, perhaps, beneath his bestial disguise – constantly hints that well-ordered republics are stronger, safer, and more natural for the human animal.

15

Simulate Stupidity

By 1516, copies of Niccolò's unpublished *Prince* are circulating among friends, and find their way further afield. We have no record of whether or not he or Vettori carried out the vague plan to present the book to Lorenzo, or whether any of the Medici read it at this stage. Nor, alas, is there any record of what Vettori or Niccolò's other friends thought about the book and its chances of helping to rehabilitate its author.

But considering how little the Medici trusted him at the time, it is hard to believe that anyone who had his best interests at stake would have encouraged him to send it to Florence's rulers. The book takes too many risks with its cunning double-speak. The disgraced Secretary Machiavelli offers aspiring princes advice on how to ascend to great power in a republic. One can find many examples of men who did this with violence and fraud, he admits, and got away with it. But there are other ways that are cleaner, more civil, better for your reputation. Colour your ambitions with decent appearances. Be liberal with your money; bribery is the easiest way to power. Win supporters by exploiting divisions between the great and the people. Soon they'll make you top man and you'll soar towards absolute power. All advice delivered with a straight face. But a bit close to the bone for the Medici, who had done exactly what Niccolò describes.[1]

And then comes the quiet, killer warning: of course, once you reach the top you'll face a host of new problems, since people in stolen republics never forget their former freedom and will start to hate you. But don't worry, says our deadpan adviser: there's a much easier way to hold power, if you're lucky enough to get the kind of princedom that subsists by causes that the human mind cannot fathom. I speak of ecclesiastical principalities. These are always secure and happy, because they need no human prudence to prop them up.

Vettori must have blanched at the thought of Leo or Cardinal Giulio de' Medici reading all this so soon after Niccolò's arrest and torture. If his friend's aim was to write a handbook ingratiating himself with Florence's new princes, his means – exposing the serpentine ways that had brought the Medici to power – were oddly chosen indeed. Niccolò could hardly have expected that family's leading men, eager to cast themselves as defenders of religion and moral rectitude, to shower rewards on him for advising them to steal republics, bribe and violate oaths like the Borgias, cheat their allies, assassinate their rivals, and ignore the laws of war. Perhaps he thought the genial Giuliano, while he lived and seemed likely to be made Florence's lord, would be amused by his book's now-dark, now-light wit and have some sympathy for its sotto voce republican sentiments. Had he claimed that six pulls of the torturer's rope had made him see the true political light and become an advocate of princes, though, no one would have believed him.

And if his friends discouraged him from presenting his *Prince* to the Medici, or if he sent it and they ignored or loathed it, they were unlikely to make his life worse than it already was. Neither Giuliano nor the pope would think it worth punishing him further for a piece of writing that, while awash with impudent innuendo, contained nothing that was outright heretical or treasonous. Whatever others might think of his little book, the acts of writing and polishing it must have cheered Niccolò up no end. He'd known for a long time that irony is an excellent weapon, a way for the powerless to assert a kind of power over their oppressors. Armed with the ironist's skill of producing two voices at once, a writer can look princes in the eye and whisper, 'I see you naked,' while loudly feigning admiration for their fine silken robes. If Vettori warned him that, with all his glowing examples of wicked princes, readers would accuse him of perversity and immorality, he could always reply: 'But if they do, Ambassador, in my defence I'll cite something you wrote in your own hand and showed me in Germany. Responding to your brother Paolo's objections to your literary fancies, you declared: "If someone says that my little stories contain bad examples, I respond that anyone who reasons thus should flee all reading as they would a venomous serpent, for there are very few books that don't present bad examples. Isn't the Bible full of lascivious stories? Isn't the Book of Kings one of love affairs, fornications, adulteries, frauds, rapine and slaughters? Nonetheless, we put it in the hands of every young maiden."[2] My writings show things done badly so that people might avoid falling into the same snares as my characters.'

His contact with Vettori had dwindled. For almost two years after the events that had bound them together in the painful sympathy of shock and regret, they'd still looked to each other for a kind of solace no one else seemed able to give them. 'Come visit me here,' Vettori had pressed his friend. 'I have a cellar full of good wine, and a neighbour – a woman of noble family and reputedly easy morals – whom you'd not find unattractive. You'll have no other business than to see the sights of Rome, then come back home to joke and to laugh with me.'[3]

Niccolò had replied that he'd like to visit, but hesitated because the Soderini brothers were there and he'd feel obliged to talk to them. 'And if I do,' he said, 'I won't be able to count on dismounting at home when I return to Florence. They'd escort me straightaway to prison in the Bargello.'[4] Over a year after promising to intercede with the Medici on his friend's behalf, Vettori told Niccolò that he'd tried again, showing Machiavelli's shrewd letters on foreign policy to the pope and to Cardinal Giulio de' Medici. 'They marvelled at their wit and praised their judgement,' Vettori told him. But nothing came of these efforts to find a place for Niccolò's talents under the new government.[5]

'I don't lose all hope in myself yet,' Niccolò had assured his friend. 'And if I did, I'd have a bone to pick with myself alone.' But sometimes bitterness came spewing out. *I tell you, Ambassador, there are*

nothing but crazies here. Only a few are familiar with this world and real-
ize that whoever tries to act according to the herd will do nothing useful,
because no two men think alike. There were moments of despair at the
thought that all his good works were forgotten or despised. *I am*
rotting away and see that if God does not show me a more favourable face,
one day I shall be forced to leave home and to place myself as tutor or sec-
retary to a governor, or – this was his greatest dread – *to stick myself in*
some deserted spot to teach reading to children and leave my family here to
count me dead. They'll do better without me because I cause them expenses,
since I'm used to spending and cannot do without spending.[6]

But by 1516, Vettori's political star was on the rise, leaving him
little time for supportive, self-revealing letters to Niccolò Machiavelli,
a man without salary or title. In Rome, Vettori had grown close to
Pope Leo's nephew Lorenzo di Piero de' Medici, now Duke of
Urbino as well as leader of Florence. He is always at the twenty-four-
year-old duke's side, acting as his most intimate adviser.[7]

Niccolò hears from their mutual friends that Vettori's new life at
the pinnacle of Medici politics is not easy. The more Lorenzo
trusted his advice, the testier Vettori's relations had grown with
the duke's mother, Alfonsina, who, it seemed to him, recklessly
fanned the flames of her son's ambitions, with little thought for
Florentine sensitivities.[8] Taking charge of government affairs
during Lorenzo's long absences from Florence, she used her
considerable fund-raising skills to attract wealthy sponsors for
new building projects and public spectacles. Instead of watching
peasant troops perform musters in the piazza, the people now witnessed staged mock-battles in expensively built mock-fortresses
erected in front of the government palazzo, and gaped at the
blood-fights of various beasts – lions, bears, leopards, stags, bulls,
horses, buffaloes – that were herded and barricaded together in the
main piazza and set on each other.[9]

The loss of Vettori is compensated by new friends. Most of them
are much younger than Niccolò, men in their very early twenties
and thirties from some of Florence's greatest patrician families.
They meet in the outer gardens of Bernardo Rucellai's villa on the

outskirts of Florence. A beautiful irony of history: in the years of his self-imposed exile from politics when Piero Soderini was Gonfalonier, Bernardo Rucellai had often met his collaborators in these same gardens, the Orti Oricellari. Here they had discussed literature and philosophy, but also how to undermine the popular government and advance their own aristocratic ideals. Now Bernardo is dead and his grandson Cosimo, a diminutive youth in fragile health – the effect of a venereal disease contracted a few years earlier – leads discussions that often have a different kind of subversive edge. Most of the young men in this new generation of Orti Oricellari regulars have fathers or uncles who detested Piero Soderini and the Great Council and were keen supporters of a Medici restoration. They and the sons do not see eye to eye. If the fathers had been afraid of losing their aristocratic prerogatives under a popular government, the sons have the greater fear of losing political power altogether in a Medici quasi-monarchy.

Niccolò's reputation as a political *enfant terrible* seems to increase his appeal to this new generation of patricians. Cosimo and the sons and grandsons of Rucellai's contemporaries had been quick to take this old man of nearly fifty into their midst, making him their intellectual lodestar, confidant and friend. They remember seeing, when they were boys, Niccolò's magnificent peasant militia do its musters in the piazza. Now they read whatever he writes, and implore him to write more. They are tougher and better critics than his contemporaries. They are his muses now; he trusts them more than Clio, Thalia, and Calliope, the goddesses of history, comedy, and epic poetry. His assemblage of 'noontime friends', as those who gather in the Rucellai gardens call themselves, give him fresh hope that all his unorthodox ideas might not die with him.

These gardens are the setting for Machiavelli's dialogue *The Art of War*. Some of the conversations it relates may actually have taken place, while Niccolò invented others. The dialogue opens at the end of a banquet; servants are beginning to clear the tables while full-bellied diners drift about, chattering and admiring the collection of late-Roman busts and Hellenistic statuary that Bernardo had assembled there for his private delectation.[10] Then their host, seated upright in his litter, proposes that they move to the shadier part of the garden.

Cosimo's guests head towards a copse of tall trees that appear to mark the garden's edge. Passing between two thick-trunked palms, they find themselves in an altogether different garden, secluded from any outsider's view. The sun, denied full access by the branches overhead, sends trickles of light between the hedges encircling the sanctuary. The older men sit on benches; the youngest throw themselves on the grass. The guest of honour, a trim elderly gentleman dressed in dark but luxurious fabrics, insists that he is more comfortable on a hard seat, without extra pillows and padding. He is, after all, a military man.

They ply him with questions. First, Cosimo takes the role of lead questioner; then he passes the baton to the youngest of the company, Luigi Alamanni, a budding poet. Then the next youngest, Zanobi Buondelmonti, takes over, showing off his knowledge of ancient Roman battle tactics, but with a genuine curiosity about how the older man would order his own armies for battle, exhort the sagging spirits of his troops and regulate the taking of spoils after victory. The distinguished guest answers them freely. Though nearing seventy, Fabrizio Colonna is still one of the most acclaimed mercenary captains of the day. After commanding armies of mercenaries for many years, he tells them, he has grown convinced that they are useless. 'A truth I learned too late to correct, for I am now an old man,' he sighs, 'and will have no opportunity to create the kind of army that now seems best to me.'[11]

'What sort of army would that be?' asks Cosimo.

'One made from one's own citizens, who fight out of duty and love of their own, not for money.'

If Florence's masters still distrusted Machiavelli's judgements on politics and foreign affairs, they might be more receptive to his thoughts on how to organize armies. But he needs to pitch his ideas in the right way. To persuade the rulers that citizen armies are better than mercenary ones, it was best to avoid making the case in his own name, and to put it in the mouth of someone the Medici could trust and respect. Fabrizio Colonna is such a man. For years, he'd commanded armies that fought against France's Louis XII, the Medicis' enemy. And he is no man of the people like Niccolò Machiavelli, or a former functionary with little military experience, but a seasoned soldier who knows what he is talking about – and a foreigner untainted by Florence's partisan prejudices. Whether or not Fabrizio really held the views Machiavelli ascribes to him, he is the perfect, surprising salesman for his militia project.

Upon publication in 1520, *The Art of War* is well received in Florence and Rome. The dialogue reveals much about the author's political and military hopes in the years after his fall from grace, and about new ways he finds to put forward his unconventional opinions. Encouraged by his young friends here in the Orti Oricellari, he has not given up hope of reviving some version of his old Magistracy of the Militia. The ancients, he has Fabrizio say, held that nothing could be better in a republic *than for there to be many men in it trained in arms.* And Italians everywhere, take note: the most excellent men are found where there are many free republics, not one great state that dominates subject peoples. For *where there are many powers, many valiant men must spring up; where there are few of them, few.* That is why, after the later Roman Empire *extinguished all the republics and principalities of Europe and Africa and the greater part of those in Asia, almost all the world ended up being corrupt* – and soon the Scythians, being less corrupt, came *to prey upon the empire that had extinguished the virtue of others and did not know how to maintain its own.*[12] Whenever one man or one state tries to control too much, they sap the virtue in whatever people they succeed in controlling, so their subjects become a liability instead of the key source of their own security.

So his life begins again, the same life lived with the same purpose, but realized through different activities. He is barred from the political theatre, but here in these gardens he can still practise politics in a less conspicuous way, by writing for and talking to these young men, whose chances of one day doing what he would like to do for their city are better than his. Here of all places, in the garden of his friend Soderini's old enemy, he starts to reassemble some shadow of his old public self. He avoids speaking his mind too forwardly, which is easier to do with much younger men than with one's peers: it is natural for the old, if they are not selfish, to withhold their over-strong opinions so that the young who look up to them have room to form views of their own. He has been writing short discussion pieces inspired by their garden debates on the first ten books of Livy's *History of Rome*. In style, they follow the pattern of the twenty-six chapters that make up his book on princes. Each *discorso* asserts what sound like straightforward opinions and maxims, so that one might think they give you the writer's final views on ancient and modern statecraft. But they are also full of reservations, ambiguities, and doubts, as if mimicking the questions speakers raise in a dialogue. His Orti friends can't seem to get enough of these little pieces. By now he has over a hundred of them; they are urging him to write a preface and collect them in a book.[13]

For some time now, Niccolò has accepted that he should hope for nothing from the new rulers, not even their scraps. He had passed more than two years in the wilderness before he understood that he might never again be permitted to work for his city, never go on another mission or give advice on alliances or defences or peace settlements, never have the chance to rebuild his militia. He'd sworn to Vettori that he'd keep hoping to find some way to stand on his own feet again, though he knew that, whatever he did, he had to avoid offending the new masters again. Still, there is hope for the city while these young friends of his are in it: being spirited, intelligent, and of the right families, they might help and counsel princes for Florence's benefit. When the collection of his *Discourses* is nearly ready for binding – though, like the *Prince*, it remains unpublished until after his death – he writes a dedication quite different from that earlier book's to the young Lorenzo de' Medici:

Niccolò Machiavelli to Zanobi Buondelmonti and Cosimo Rucellai,
Greetings.

I have gone outside the common usage of those who address their works to
some prince and, blinded by ambition and avarice, praise him for virtuous
qualities when they should blame him for every part worthy of reproach.
So as not to incur this error, I have chosen not those who are princes, but
those who for their infinite good parts deserve to be.[14]

He'd withheld some of his more pungent opinions, especially
about his new friends' aristocratic prejudices, when he first joined
their garden salon. But as their mutual affection deepened, he let
some of them seep out from his *discorsi*, following the precept that
no one should take offence at any criticism offered for the sake of
seeking truth. They'd heard him say, more than once, that so-called
gentlemen were more apt to wreak havoc in republics than the
people: convinced of their natural right to command, they resent
sharing power with others, which naturally offends the majority,
whom they hope to exclude from government. Niccolò tries to
express the problem in universal terms, lest he seem to be founding
his views on his personal anti-patrician sentiments.[15] In any city,
ancient or modern, one finds an enmity between the great, whatever they call themselves – nobles, patricians, the rich – and the
people. This arises because the great everywhere want to dominate, while the people want not to be dominated. The people's
desire is more reasonable than the desire of a few to dominate the
many. It follows that governments that seek to satisfy the popular
desire are firmer and last longer than those that let a few command
the rest. If his friends could see the problem of elitism in this ruthlessly logical way, a few of them might begin to step back from
their family and class prejudices and recognize the advantages of
well-ordered popular government.

The literary, political, and philosophical discussions of the Orti
Oricellari are not aimed at producing a common programme or political party. They are tough-minded debates in which participants are

urged to express their independent views and to ply each speaker with doubts and questions. 'I tell you how I understand the matter at hand, and leave it to you to judge whether it's true or not,' Niccolò has Fabrizio Colonna say in *The Art of War. And I'll be grateful for your interrogations, because I'm going to learn as much from your questions as you do from my responses.*[16] Here Fabrizio seems to express Machiavelli's own attitude to intellectual and political conversations, especially with the young.

When he and his Orti companions talk about how to reform the Medici government, Niccolò's seniority does not exempt him from the same tough grilling he gets when defending popular republics in some of his *discorsi*. His young friends remember the days of the 1494 republic as a time of nerve-wracking turbulence, with one crisis following another and their elders muttering about the lunacy of letting the mass of people take part in government. Princely governments may be bad, they say. But some would point out that our recent experience proves that republics, especially popular ones, are no better.

That appears true enough, Niccolò admits, when one looks at Florence's recent history. 'But I prefer to judge these things not just by asking what the experience of certain times or places might teach us – what is or what has been – but also by asking what can reasonably be.'[17] A government's quality, he proposes, doesn't depend only on whether it is government by the people, a prince, or a few purportedly wise men. It also depends on laws that keep any individual or class or party from dominating the others. He makes the case for the rule of laws over that of men in his *Discourses*, arguing there that both princes and popular republics that have lasted long *have had need of being regulated by the laws. For a prince who can do whatever he wishes is crazy; a people who can do whatever it wishes is not wise.* And if you have to choose between a badly ordered multitude and an undisciplined prince, he had told his dubious young hearers and readers, the choice is clear: *a prince unshackled from the laws will be more ungrateful, varying, and imprudent than a people.* Moreover, *to cure the illness* of excessive ambition among the people *words are enough*; while *for curing the prince's, steel is needed.*[18]

His friends are unconvinced, and he enjoins them to prod him hard with their misgivings. Like his *Prince*, the *Discourses* move back and forth from confident-sounding assertions to hesitations, as if the writer is mimicking different voices in a live conversation, perhaps echoing or anticipating doubts voiced by his fellow habitués of the Orti Oricellari. What if a prince is exceptionally wise or good? Aren't such princes better than even the most orderly of peoples? Different opinions contend with each other on Machiavelli's pages.

There are and have been many princes, and the good and wise among them have been few. In general, *a people is more prudent, more stable, and of better judgement than a prince.*

But when a republic has degenerated badly, as Florence's has now, doesn't it take the unified will and force of one princely man to put things in order?

Perhaps: *Where the matter is corrupt, well-ordered laws don't help unless one individual uses extreme force to ensure their observance.*[19]

This bracingly 'realistic' voice seems to be expressing the author's own bottom line. But in the discussion that follows, Niccolò sets out some quite devastating reservations about one-man, extreme-force solutions to corruption.

So, his *Discourses* continue, we'll have to find an individual who can purge the rot single-handedly, with few or no scruples about the means. Then comes a first doubt: *I don't know if this has ever occurred*, or whether it is humanly possible. After all, *no man can live long enough to have time to restore good habits to a city that has wallowed in bad ones for a long time.*

He might do what's necessary, another voice answers this doubt, if he has such audacity and force of spirit as to sweep the city clean at one stroke – though this will bring great dangers to himself and cause much bloodshed. *I grant that few know how or wish to use* such extreme methods. But when corruption is great, there may be no other way.

In that case, the discourse goes on, we'll have to hope and pray that such an extraordinary bold man, one who knows how to take risks and do bad for good ends, will appear among us.

Some might wonder, though, how a man with this type of character would use his power. *For* – here is another doubt – *it very rarely
happens that someone good wishes to become prince by bad ways, even
though his end be good.* And if someone acquires princely power
through bad ways, it's almost impossible *that it will ever occur to his
mind to use well the authority that he has acquired badly.*

Some readers might conclude, then, that it is safest to look for
ways to reform corrupt cities that don't rely on a single man.
Others may try their luck, gambling with very high stakes, and hope
against all odds that their redeemer is that extremely rare man who
will use bad means well. Don't expect me to tell you what to do,
Niccolò seems to say to his patrician friends and future readers. It's
your responsibility to get this thing right that so many of your
fathers and grandfathers kept getting wrong.

When he is not in the gardens discussing history, politics and
poetry, Niccolò lives quietly, often travelling back and forth
between Florence and his country house. He tries to find good
teachers for his sons. Bernardo – his father's namesake – and
Lodovico are almost young men, Piero and Guido still toddlers.
His sister Primavera's son, Giovanni Vernacci, has gone into trade
and now travels throughout the Levant. From time to time, he
sends caviar or other exotic gifts to his uncle and his family, who
had taken him into their house as an orphaned adolescent and
raised him as their own.[20]

Niccolò hopes for all their sakes that Giovanni's business will
thrive. The leases on his farms and his owner's percentage of their
tenants' sales are never enough to cover all the growing Machiavelli
family's expenses. This penury grieves him as it seldom had his
father; Bernardo exemplified the simple Roman virtues better than
his son. *Fortune has left me nothing but my family and my friends,* he tells
his nephew, *and so I make capital of them – and particularly of those who
are closest to me, as are you.* Since he has no talent for making capital
through trade or banking, he will have to make it by begging from
his nearest and dearest. So if Fortune should send some honourable

business affairs your way, Giovanni, *I trust you'll do to my children as I have done unto you.* In the first two years after his torture and imprisonment, he'd suffered bouts of melancholy and retreated into isolation on his farm with his books and his pen. *Since my adversities have reduced me to living on my farm,* Niccolò tells his nephew, *I sometimes go for a month at a time without thinking about myself. So it is no surprise if I neglect you;* don't be angry or surprised if I fail to answer your letters. But in any case, *my house will always be at your disposal, as it has been in the past, humble and wretched though it may be.*[21]

He borrows money from friends, or from friends of friends who have more money than they know what to do with.[22] Perhaps through Vettori's mediations, he acquires a generous new patron, Lorenzo Strozzi, and dedicates his *Art of War* to him. He is the older brother of Filippo Strozzi, whose marriage to young Lorenzo de' Medici's sister Clarice had scandalized Florentines in 1508–9 and caused a fatal crack in the old republic's foundations; the Strozzi family bank is one of Florence's greatest. Encouraged by this support and inspired by his companions at the Orti Oricellari, he now writes every day for hours on end, working on several things at once. By 1518, he is putting his 142 *Discourses* into order. He had finished or was polishing up his eight-part poem *The Ass,* which starts with his own ill-starred tumble into the wilderness of men-turned-beasts, and goes on to discover how many of these pathetic creatures were once great Florentines:

> *How many whom I had once considered Fabiuses and Catos*
> *when I learned there of their natures,*
> *I found to be sheep and rams!*

The epic ends with the poet deep in conversation with a man-beast who looks suspiciously like someone well known to his readers:

> *Then I saw in a low place, when I turned my eyes towards it,*
> *a big fat porker covered with mud.*

I shall by no means tell whom he resembled;
let it suffice to say that he would come to three hundred
or more pounds, if he were hung on the hook.

Pope Leo's corpulence had attracted comment and ridicule since his youth, and recent allegations of his corruption had made porcine comparisons seem more apt than ever. In order to fund a costly war aimed at installing his nephew Lorenzo as Duke of Urbino, Leo had resorted to pawning table silver, jewels and furniture from the papal palace to replenish his war chest and had named thirty-one new cardinals, many of them in exchange for promises that their families would help fund the campaign. Then, in October 1517, a German monk called Martin Luther posted Ninety-Five Theses against clerical abuses on the door of the main church in Wittenberg. Complaints quickly spread against widespread simony, nepotism, and the sale of indulgences in the Church. Before the year was out, a plot to poison Leo was discovered. Cardinal Francesco Soderini, Niccolò's old friend, was one of its ringleaders. He had gone, willingly, into exile from Rome.

And there are the plays. Niccolò had been working on a vernacular translation of *Andria* or 'The Girl from Andros', a comedy by the playwright Terence, and reading other Roman comedies with his young friends. If the Medici can put on theatre trumpeting how they saved the city, they say, why not give them more accolades, but with something a little truer to life? They'd heard that he had dabbled in playwriting many years ago, and had a script lying about somewhere – his comedy of *The Masks*, inspired by Aristophanes' *Clouds*.[23] He'd been discouraged from showing it to the public, for it was full of scorching attacks on Florentines whose pseudonymous identities would be apparent to all. But why not try a different kind of comedy, one with characters that didn't obviously send up this person or that – a comedy of manners, mostly bad ones, set here in Florence but showing things that might be seen in any city? *Look at the scenery now set before you*, he'll have his Prologue say: *this is Florence, another time it will be Rome or Pisa – a thing to make you laugh till you crack your cheeks.*

His new play is first staged in Carnival season, February 1518, at an unknown venue – perhaps the spacious gardens of the Orti Oricellari – probably to a select, invited audience. Its fame soon reaches the ears of the pope and other members of his family, who perhaps have the opportunity to see it performed the following year. Louis XII had died in 1515, and Leo and the new French king, François I, had decided that it would be in both their interests to seal their improved relations by finding a bride for Lorenzo among the king's relatives. Francesco Vettori was sent to France to negotiate with the families of various candidates. At length, an agreement was struck, and in May 1518 Lorenzo marries Madeleine de la Tour, daughter of the Count of Auvergne. The nuptials are held in France, but a second wedding celebration takes place in Florence later that year, so that Florentines would not feel their First Citizen had forgotten them. Machiavelli's play may be among the entertainments on offer at those festivities.[24] Though he adds or rewrites parts of it for later performances, also adding songs to be sung between the play's five acts, here is a taste of what its audiences would have seen.

The actor narrating the Prologue welcomes them, saying: This is a play about deception. I will show you a rich young man, just back from France, deceiving a virtuous Florentine woman whom he loved. Prologue admits that the playwright isn't famous. And if his little piece seems imprudent, forgive our author. For he *strives with these vain thoughts to make his wretched life more pleasant, since otherwise he does not know where to turn his face – having been cut off from showing other powers with other deeds, there being no pay for his toils.* In fact, he's come to expect nothing but spite and scorn in these degenerate times. But be warned

> *that the author too*
> *knows how to find fault, and that it was his earliest art;*
> *and in no part of the world where* sì *is heard* [where dialects of
> Italian are spoken]
> *does he stand in awe of anybody, even if he plays the servant to those*
> *who can wear a better cloak than he can.*

Then a young actor walks on stage, dressed in the latest French style. He is the wealthy Callimaco Guadagni, returning to his native Florence after many years away in France. Having fallen madly in love with Lucretia, a virtuous married woman, he will have no rest until he can get into her bed. Enlisting the help of several accomplices – a maggoty little servant, a greedy, hypocritical priest, a parasite who thrives on other people's dirty schemes, and Lucretia's own mother – our hero concocts a series of elaborate deceptions to gratify his desires, with the help of the root *mandragola*, or mandrake, known both as a cure for infertility and a potent poison.

The object of Callimaco's frenetic desires appears rather late on stage, played by a bewigged youth. Her name would remind the audience of an assault on the virtue of another, more famous Lucretia, the wife of a Roman nobleman who was raped by a son of Rome's last king, Tarquinius Superbus. That Lucretia had thereupon seized a dagger and killed herself, galvanizing her father and his friend Lucius Junius Brutus to conspire against the kings and refound Rome as a republic, an event Machiavelli praises in his *Discourses*.

But the *Mandragola*'s conspirators and their Lucretia are a far cry from those virtuous early Romans. Whereas they had plotted to avenge a woman's virtue, these paragons of Florentine manhood plot to violate it. The Roman Lucretia killed herself rather than live with the shame of her defilement, and became the symbolic founder of a virtuous new republic. At the end of the play, her Florentine namesake decides to trade in her wifely virtue for a life of covert adultery.

Like the *Prince*, the *Mandragola*, with all its inventive deceits, holds up a mirror to its audiences, showing them the truth behind their professions of piety and decency. And a few spectators might wonder if Callimaco, posing as a doctor who claims to wield a poisoned cure, has anything in common with the self-styled saviours of Florence's barren republic. Of course, the similarity between their name and the protagonist's fake profession might be pure coincidence. On first hearing the quack doctor's proposals, Lucrezia's dubious husband, Messer Nicia, retorts:

I talked last evening with several doctors [medici]. One of them said I should go to San Filippo, another to Porretta, another to Villa. And they seem to me like so many vile birds [uccellacci: also a person who brings ill omens]. For to tell the truth, these doctors of medicine don't know what they're fishing for.[25]

If there is a character that sometimes seems to speak in Niccolò's voice, it is the buffoonish, cuckolded Messer Nicia, whose name and complaints resemble those of the playwright:

In this town there's no one who isn't a shitsticks; virtue isn't valued. I've shat out my guts to learn two aitches, and if I had to live by it, I'd be out in the cold, I can tell you. A man who doesn't have the state in this town, even one of my standing, can't find a dog to bark at him. But I don't care about them, I'm not dependent on anybody. All the same, I don't want to be quoted, because I'd certainly get some big tax or some leek in my tail that'd make me sweat.[26]

The comedy is a resounding hit. The writer, a slight, pale man of fifty, a little greyer than he was when he fell out of public grace seven years before but otherwise unchanged, comes on stage, takes a bow. Niccolò can look back on the past seven years and say that he has not wasted his time, though he makes no money by his own labours and cannot act on the public stage. But now at last his *Mandragola* has won him the ear of the public. His play and the playwright's fame soon spread throughout Italy. Pope Leo wants to see the play performed in Rome.[27] Machiavelli and his friends start plotting ways to use his triumph as a stepping stone towards gaining a bit of money and political favour.

In October 1518, a month after his Florentine marriage festivities, Lorenzo de' Medici goes to meet his uncle Pope Leo in Montefiascone, which lies on the road between Florence and Rome.[28] His trip gives rise to heated speculation. Even before the duke's return from his sojourn in France, many feared that he would seek papal permission to make his powers more absolute. There were rumours that King François had agreed to such a plan, now that Lorenzo has a French wife of noble blood and shows himself an eager defender of the king's interests in Florence.

Chroniclers give divergent accounts of what Duke Lorenzo wanted to discuss. According to some, among them Filippo de' Nerli – one of Niccolò's friends from the Orti Oricellari – Lorenzo wanted to get the pope's consent to make Florence a principality in name as well as in practice. Francesco Vettori, on the other hand, would later insist that the young duke had almost the contrary aims: he wanted to turn over his duchy of Urbino to the Church, give up his title of duke and his captaincy of Florence's troops, and govern Florence as a citizen among other citizens, as he and the pope had promised before. It was Alfonsina who harboured despotic ambitions for her son, Vettori claims, though he tried to resist. In a bid to stop Lorenzo from carrying out his good intentions, she sent word to him during his travels that she was sick and likely to die, and that he should return straightaway to Florence. Being a good son, he did so, but took ill himself and never recovered.

In May 1519, less than a year after his marriage, Lorenzo dies. Some reports say the plague or some other illness was the cause of death, others complications from syphilis. His wife Madeleine had died the previous month, after giving birth to their daughter Caterina. Fourteen years later, Caterina de' Medici would marry King Henri II and become Queen Consort of France.

In that same year, Niccolò and his friends from the Orti Oricellari mourn a far greater loss to the city, and to themselves. After much suffering brought on by his ailment, Cosimo Rucellai dies at just twenty-five years of age. *The Art of War* opens with a eulogy to the man who had hosted their garden discussions with such an open mind and such passion for seeking truth.[29] *I will never recall his name without tears*, Niccolò declares. *For I do not know what was so much his – not even excepting his soul – that he would not willingly have spent it for his friends.*

269

16

Imagine a True Republic

Soon after Lorenzo's death comes the opportunity Niccolò had been hoping for since 1512. He had tried all these years, in various ways, to talk politics with the Medici. But they had swatted down, shunned or politely ignored all his overtures. At least their indifference to his opinions had grown milder over the years.

Now, however, Pope Leo appoints his cousin, Cardinal Giulio de' Medici, to act as Florence's new head of government. The pope is anxious to appease a populace that had come to detest Lorenzo's autocratic style of rule; many blame Francesco Vettori for fanning his young master's tyrannical ambitions. Leo now wants the cardinal to invite prominent men, including some known to be unfriendly to the Medici government, to hold private talks about the future of Florence. They will be asked to propose specific reforms, which the pope and his cousin promise to cut up with the utmost diligence. Among the names put forward as possible contributors to this dialogue is that of Niccolò Machiavelli.

He sets to work straightaway on his proposal. His young noon-time friend and co-dedicatee of his *Discourses*, Zanobi Buondelmonti, is asked, or decides, to draft one of his own. Though Zanobi's proposal is lost, it is probably safe to assume that he and Niccolò agree on some points and disagree on others. He is not his friends' teacher, and learning is not a matter of one-way transmission; he admits that he needs their help to test his ideas. He sketches some thoughts, then tries them out on Zanobi, Luigi and others in their circle when they meet. What institutions are most suitable for Florentines with their particular history, prejudices and anxieties? How much power should a reformed Florence give to the patricians on the one hand, the people on the other? What powers should the Gonfalonier have, and how long should his term of office be? And – a most delicate question – should the Medici reopen the Great Council, the symbol and main instrument of a popular republic? Tell me, he entreats his friends, whether I seem too bold in making this suggestion or that, or if my tone might irritate some important personage in the Medici camp. What of his militia: should he smuggle some mention of it into his package of wished-for reforms? In the end, he decides not to. His friends point out that his *Art of War* is almost ready for publication; Lorenzo Strozzi promises to give a copy to Cardinal Giulio. For now, be modest. Don't pique them with your too-daring ideas. Step by step. His travails have taught him that much, even if they failed to cure him of all his hopes.

The more pessimistic of his comrades wonder if he puts too much faith in the laws. You claim that laws are the guarantee of freedom, they say, but aren't all actual laws just rules laid down by whoever is strongest?

Not, he replies, if the strong realize that they and their friends will be safest if they consult with others who are weaker, as Giulio de' Medici says he wants to consult with the likes of us now. We need to show him that the laws which protect his best interests will also protect those of the people, and indeed the other classes of citizens. The Medici want a government that lasts long, keeps them safe, and gives them glory. Everyone else wants one that lasts long, keeps them safe, and gives them a fair hand in the affairs of state. I'm trying to work out a plan that can satisfy all these desires.[1]

He tests some of his more radical ideas on his Orti companions, but leaves them out when writing to the Medici. It is tempting to repeat – this time, of course, putting it more diplomatically – what he'd written to Pope Leo when he was still Cardinal Giovanni in 1512: it would be best for both you and the city if your laws put a rein on the rich and well-connected, or they'll use their wealth and connections to seek boundless power, offending both the prince and the people. He'd amused his young friends by declaring forthrightly in the *Discourses* that *those republics that maintain a political and uncorrupt way of life do not endure that any citizen either be or live in the usage of a gentleman; indeed, they maintain among themselves an even equality.*[2]

He recalls his long mission to Emperor Maximilian in Germany almost a dozen years ago. He and Vettori had chatted through the night, dreaming up a dozen brilliant schemes for reforming Florence and Italy. Luigi and Zanobi, now even younger than he'd been then, deserve to hope that they might make some mark, do some good for their city. So far they, and Niccolò's less well-born sons, have had no chance even to dream. It was in Germany, Niccolò tells them, that I saw with my own eyes what many ancient writers say: that the firmest republics are those where there is more equality in how people live.[3] The rich there live almost like people we call poor here. They aren't constantly building bigger and bigger palaces and villas, or throwing their money about on the latest fashions in clothes or new furnishings. Instead of losing sleep over what they lack by comparison with others, they conserve their energy and use it to secure what they need. So though individual citizens might seem poor next to our wealthy men, the public is rich. Taxes and sumptuary laws are used to check extremes of wealth and poverty. And even the rich agree to give up a good part of their wealth to the state – as it used to happen in Sparta and in Rome before things went bad – because they see how this makes them safer and freer. Look at the Germans and the Swiss: they live more simply than we do, and are free and well-armed. Our rich Italians live lavishly and aspire to live even more lavishly, but what freedom we have is constantly threatened by unrest from the poor. And then we're terrified of arming the poor because they might use arms against the rich!

Some of our spendthrift relatives might not understand your sense of 'freedom', his friends point out. How can you call it freedom if people aren't free to keep whatever money they make, or to live as luxuriously as they please? To certain Florentine merchants and bankers, your equality-making laws would seem like a revenge of the envious poor against the wealthy.

I'd tell them, Niccolò responds, that the freedom I speak of isn't private licence to do whatever one chooses.[4] If anyone says that there is no true freedom where the laws leave no room for individuals to choose what work they do, whom to marry, how many children to have, or what opinions to hold and speak short of calumny, I'd agree with them. But when I say *libertà* I mean public freedom, which can only be preserved if I accept laws that set bounds on my choices, and on everyone else's. In a world I'm forced to share with others who have their own equally stubborn desires, what could be less realistic than the notion that I should have licence to do whatever I want? Our natural freedom leads to chaos unless we use our brains to order it with political art. Public freedom is the highest product of that art; it is not natural, but the finest of human creations. And once established, it has to be tended to like the most sensitive garden – you need to prune bad weeds here, water dry patches there, spot sicknesses before they flare up and spread. Freedom doesn't maintain itself. God does not maintain it. It is up to you.

Now his proposal, which he calls a *Discourse on Remodelling the Government of Florence*, is ready to be sent to Cardinal Giulio de' Medici, though it is formally addressed to the pope. He had taken great care to work out the right approach. Even if they ignore most of his advice, he needs to make a good impression so that they won't block him from any future public service. So like his *Prince*, the *Discourse* avoids lecturing its addressees on how to make their government conform to the common good, since that might seem presumptuous. The writer's sole concern, he insists, is to show the Medici how to preserve their family's reputation and to keep themselves and their friends safe, now and in the future. Yet his point – cast, as usual, in studiously non-moralizing language – is that the Medici can only secure their own safety and glory if they take steps to promote the common good.[5]

He begins by declaring that no firm government can be devised if it is neither a fully fledged princedom nor a republic. *All the*

constitutions between these two are defective, whether they are aristocratic republics or mixes of principality and republic. But since to
set up a princedom where a republic might do well *is a difficult thing,
and thus inhumane and unworthy of whoever hopes to be considered
merciful and good,* Machiavelli will *pass over further reasoning about
princedoms and speak of the republic.*

Then he addresses the Medici pope directly. *I know that Your Holiness is much inclined to one* – that is, to a republic – and believe *that
you postpone establishing it because you hope to find an arrangement by
which your authority in Florence may continue to be great and your
friends live in security. Since I believe I have discovered one,* he continues
modestly, *I hope Your Holiness will pay heed to my thoughts, so that if
there is anything good in it, you can make use of it and learn how great is
my wish to serve.*

The only way to preserve the Medici reputation, he now tells
Leo, is to establish a *vera repubblica,* a true republic, instead of trying to mix princely practices with republican forms. A true republic
will never be 'perfect' in the sense of flawless, blissful, or immune
to corruption. It is still a human artefact, subject to human frailties.
But it can be perfect in the sense that its laws and institutions match
the best standards of government that we flawed human animals
can hope to live up to. Widely shared power is the most important
of these standards: all classes of citizens, from the least to the greatest, must have their fair share of authority. Consent is another:
magistrates should be given their authority by willing citizens, not
be granted or stripped of powers at a prince's will. The laws should
treat everyone equally, regardless of poverty or wealth or party and
family connections; no man may stand above the laws. The Court
of Appeal must be reformed and strengthened. Citizens should not
lack the courage to punish important men. But anyone accused of
serious crimes must have a clear right to appeal his case.

All these ideas also appear in his *Discourses,* and between the
foxy lines of the *Prince.* Bernardo Machiavelli would have approved;
his son's opinions concur with the main thrust of his own arguments in Bartolomeo Scala's dialogue on the laws.[6]

Last but not least, the pope must realize that the most important class in a republic is not the patricians, but the people. *Without satisfying the generality of the citizens*, Niccolò stresses, *to set up a stable republic is always impossible.* If he longed to throw in a snide quip about the great gentlemen whose appetite for lording it over others makes them *altogether hostile to every kind of civilization*, he restrained himself.[7] The so-called great men, too, must have their share of power; otherwise they will always make trouble. Niccolò's true republic, like Plato's and Aristotle's ideal *politeia* – the Greek word is usually translated in Latin as *res publica* – is emphatically not what the ancients called democracy, direct rule by the people over the patricians and the very poor. It is the rule of laws that stand above the entire demos and regulate relations between its 'parts', as he calls them, so that no class or part can dominate the others. But once the basic laws are strengthened to ensure that no group feels excluded, the best way for the Medici to win safety and honour would be to reopen the Hall of the Great Council and distribute substantial powers to the general body of citizens. The office of Gonfalonier should be held for at least two or three years. Florence had always had too many different magistracies, each with too-short terms. Niccolò would abolish some of them and put senatorial powers in the hands of sixty-five citizens over forty-five years of age, chosen from the city's various professional guilds.

Ingeniously, he maps out a way for the Medici to make these reforms without jeopardizing their safety or that of their partisans. In the pope's and Cardinal Giulio's lifetimes, the Medici may continue to rule as de facto monarchs. But he advises them to make provisions for a peaceful transition to a true republic on their passing. Surely, he says, Your Holiness can do nothing more glorious or pleasing to God than to undertake these reforms for the good of your native city. They are also in your own best interests. For now that Niccolò has been invited to play the role of doctor of state – his favourite of all the roles he has played in his life – he must, at least for a moment, be brutally frank. This Medici regime, he tells Leo, is headed for disaster if the pope and his cousin fail to apply his remedies to a sickened political body. He can now say outright what he could only hint at, through thick veils of irony, in the *Prince* and in his comic play. *By holding the city of Florence under these present conditions you risk a thousand dangers; and before they come, Your Holiness will have to endure a thousand vexations unbearable by any man.* Florentines are exasperated with matters as they stand. For years he has heard the frustration grating in his young friends' voices, the voices of the future. The city hovers on the brink of civil war. And if it erupts *Your Holiness can imagine how many deaths, how many exiles, how many acts of extortion will result, enough to make the cruellest man – much more Your Holiness, who is most merciful – die of sorrow.*

The Medici can only hope to escape utter ruin if they *give the city institutions that can stand firm by themselves,* without the prop of princes. For *they will always stand firm when everybody has a hand in them,* and when *no class of citizen, either through fear for itself or through ambition, will need to desire revolution.*

His *Discourse* sheds a corrective light on Machiavelli's reputation as an arch-realist who scoffed at all sorts of ideal or 'imagined' republics. Some ideals are detached from realities, some grounded in them. Some 'realities' are whatever is done here and now, by whoever seems to be at the top of the latest political or military or profiteering game. Other realities run deeper in human nature. Natural tendencies towards duplicity and violence are among them. But so is the ability to find ways to hold those tendencies in check, to design institutions that future generations will want to imitate. The human ability to think up – to imagine – such institutions, drawing on past experience but also considering what *could* be done by human beings as we know them, even if it has not yet been done: this is the most basic reality behind Niccolò's art of politics. Near the end of his proposal, he compares his own motives with the aims of ancient philosophers who, like him, found ways to carry on their own more deeply realistic kind of politics when the world around them lost its bearings:

No man is so exalted as are those who have with laws and institutions reformed republics and kingdoms. And so much has this glory been esteemed that when unable to form a republic in reality, they have done it in writing, as Aristotle, Plato, and many others, who have wished to show the world that if they have not founded a civil way of life, they failed not through their ignorance but through their impotence in putting it into practice.

He sends his proposal to Cardinal Giulio de' Medici. When he was younger, he would have expected some strong response to his efforts. Even if his suggestions went unheeded, someone would have read his words – vigorous, profound and moving, full of hope and brooding fear for the future – and recognized a man whose first-rate brain should be put to the service of his country. Now he is over fifty; he has maintained his good spirits for many years by expecting nothing from the world of great men and their politics. A man who expects nothing from others does not resent them, or not too much. And he tells himself to keep expecting nothing but formal expressions of thanks, the same words Giulio would offer Zanobi – almost like a son to Niccolò – who has worked so hard on his own memorandum, and who, being young, hopes for much more. But Niccolò, too, cannot help hoping.

~

A year later, spring 1521: he finds himself on the road to Carpi, a town near Modena in the Romagna. For the first time in nearly a decade, he is carrying letters of credence from the government of Florence. At long last, the thing he has wished for: to represent and serve his city again as an envoy. *Niccolò*, says his letter of appointment, *you will proceed to Carpi, and on arrival present yourself before His Reverence the Father-General of the Order of the Minorite Brothers and his assistants.*[8]

When he told them the good news, Zanobi and the others had practically rolled about on the ground laughing. Finally, Niccolò gets his mission – and what a mission! The cardinal couldn't have found a more fitting use for his talents. His brief was to persuade the Franciscan monks at Carpi to form a separate organization within the Florentine dominions, apart from the rest of Tuscany. Having received complaints that some of the brothers had strayed from the exemplary life expected of monks, the Florentine authorities want to put them on a tighter leash. Machiavelli's instructions do not mention Pope Leo's worries about Martin Luther's firebrand followers in Germany: Church leaders are terrified that heresy might sprout up close to home.

So, his friends say, you're to go and lecture a few friars about sanctity? Don't underestimate my hidden talents, he retorts. And he has another, parallel mission: the Consuls of Florence's Wool Guild have engaged him to recruit a friar to preach at the Duomo during Lent. 'It's like asking Ser Sano or Pachierotto,' both well-known homosexuals, 'to find a beautiful and graceful wife for a friend.'[9]

This comes from Francesco Guicciardini, brother of one of his oldest friends, Luigi Guicciardini. Francesco, fourteen years younger than Niccolò, had already enjoyed a precocious career as a lawyer and high-ranked diplomat. Now he works for the papal administration as governor of Modena. Perhaps at his brother Luigi's prompting, for the sake of old neighbourly ties, he had invited Niccolò to stay with him on the way to Carpi. Guicciardini is known in Florence as an aloof, ambitious sort who had little time for pleasures or pleasantries, even in his youth. 'When I was young,' he'd later admit, 'I used to scoff at dancing, singing, riding and knowing how to dress – all those things that seem decorative rather than substantial. But later,' he says drily, 'I understood that skill in this sort of entertainment paves the way to the favour of princes.'[10] While pursuing his fast-rising political career, he'd written a sharply observed history of the Florentine republic from the times of Lorenzo to the end of the wars with Pisa. Piero Soderini and his government come off particularly badly in its pages.

'I suppose I must do penance for my sins before they'll entrust me with anything else,' says Niccolò. It wasn't as if Cardinal Giulio, or whatever joker had recommended him for this particular job, might not have known what he was doing – sending the writer of the *Mandragola*, with its ferocious barbs against clergymen, into the boglands of bleakest friardom. Was it a test of his eagerness to serve his country and its ecclesiastical Medici masters, a humiliation, both at once? Would Machiavelli treat these churchmen with the decorum he failed to show when dealing with popes and friars in his writings?

Or perhaps they wanted to see if he could turn his satires about the bad customs of priests to some practical use. Maybe Giulio wanted him to use his famous scalpel wit to upbraid these Minorites for their deficient sanctity. Starving beggars, in any case, take whatever scraps they can get, and he'd been begging in vain for many years, raising his children in the strictest frugality. Marietta must have helped ensure that the modest proceeds from their farms were spent prudently; she may have urged him to put aside his pride and accept whatever work came his way. He'd vowed to his friends that he'd behave himself, while savouring the delicious irony of his long-awaited embassy.

But on arriving at the monastery, he is overwhelmed with gloom. A humourless little monk shows him to a dreary cell where he is to sleep. The food is bad, in equal parts bland, stale, and nasty; the company is much the same. His impulse is to ridicule it all, but there is no one there to laugh with him.

How clever of the cardinal and his friends to dream up this way to slap him on the wrist, beaming with smug magnanimity as they promised to put him back to work at some task worthy of his experience. 'When I behold your titles as Ambassador of the Republic and of Friars,' Guicciardini had said, 'and consider how many kings, dukes and princes you've negotiated with in your day, I'm reminded of Lysander, the brilliant Spartan general whose alleged pride and ambition made him unpopular with his peers. After winning so many victories and trophies for the Spartans, he was given the task of distributing meat to the same soldiers he'd so gloriously commanded.'[11]

He could never wallow in humiliation for long. Now, instead, he'll try to make fun of his plight, his hosts, himself. After a long day of wrangling with his prolix, painfully tedious hosts, he writes to Guicciardini. *Magnificent Governor. I am turning over some way in which I might stir up strife among these friarhoods so that they might start going after each other with their wooden clogs.* His advanced age and outsider status have made him freer than most men he knows, or than his younger self, to indulge in pure silliness. Send me a servant, or a messenger, whose attentions would cause my reputation among these friars to swell. Bugger decorum.

The next day a crossbowman arrives, bearing a letter addressed to *His Magnificence M. Niccolò Machiavelli, Florentine Nuncio, etc.* That 'M.' is good, he thinks. He is neither a Messer – a qualified doctor of laws or medicine – nor a Monsignor, but these monks are vulgar enough to be agog at the faintest hint of a title. On seeing the martial-looking messenger and hearing whispers, 'To His Magnificence!' the friars spring up from their seats and swarm around their visitor, asking him what the news was. *And I,* he tells Guicciardini later that day, *to heighten my prestige, said that the emperor was expected at Trent, that the Swiss had convened fresh embassies, that the King of France wanted this and that.* Thinking he must be a diplomat of very great stature, *they all stood around with their mouths hanging open.*

Send a flurry of further dispatches, he implores Guicciardini. If those friars see dispatches arriving thick and fast, my shabby conditions here might improve.

Francesco, good man, gladly obliges. 'Though I'm not,' he writes, 'in the habit of performing such services without pay.' He promises to send a fresh crossbowman to Niccolò the following day *with his shirt flying behind his hips, so that everyone will believe you are an important personage.*

Their plot works wonders. Within hours, Niccolò has been given a better bed and much better meals. *I gobble up enough for six dogs and three wolves,* he reports to his co-conspirator. He revels in his new-found status. Even as I write this, he tells his friend, I have a ring of monks about me; *they marvel and gaze at me as at one inspired. And I, to make them marvel even more, sometimes pause writing and breathe deeply. Then they absolutely begin drooling.* The next day, though, he is almost caught out. *Cazzus!* he curses, coining a word of his own from *cazzo* ('prick') and the Latin ending *-us* to mock the ponderous Latinity of his friars. *This host of mine is as crafty as thirty thousand devils.* He'd got his hands on Guicciardini's letter and suspects their little prank. *So now my arse is all a-gurgle: I live in fear that he'll take a broom and pack me off to the inn.* He begs his accomplice to take the next day off so that everything he's gained from the joke – *solid meals, splendid beds, and the like – is not yanked out from under me.*

Having read Guicciardini's history of Florence and meeting him alone in Modena, Niccolò knew he'd find a man who'd share his own eye for self-destructive human follies but not perhaps one who could appreciate a good prank, let alone invent a few of his own. Now Francesco says he's written to Niccolò's host in Carpi, telling him *that you were a very exceptional person. His reply begged me to inform him what this exceptionalness of yours consisted of. I didn't feel I should answer him, so that he may be kept in suspense and have reason to show you full respect. So make good use of this repute while it lasts.*

I believe I shall, replies the ambassador to the friars, and I dearly hope that after this sojourn among Their Friarhoods, I'll have occasion *to spend another night with Your Lordship, may he live and reign for ever and ever.*

Irksome though this mission was, the opportunity it afforded to make this excellent new friend more than outweighs its absurdities. More than almost any man Niccolò knows who'd long been immersed in the world of politics, Francesco Guicciardini has been careful to preserve a mind of his own. He shows its full scope and qualities to few, but is quick to identify the rare men he trusts without reservation. Niccolò, it seems, is one of them. Over meaty Romagna cooking and numerous bottles of local wine, they discover a shared glee in puncturing all sorts of pretensions, especially those of clergymen.[12]

'I compliment you on your good works in Carpi,' Guicciardini tells him when Niccolò visits again on his way back home. 'I've had my share of business with those friars. If you managed to sow some discord among them – or at least left a seed that might take root later on – it would be the most outstanding deed you ever accomplished. Of course,' his friend goes on, 'that wouldn't be difficult, given their ambition and ill will. I trust those holy men didn't pass on some of their talents for lying to you.'

'Great governor,' Niccolò replies, 'I can easily outdo the lies of all the citizens of Carpi. For some time now, I've never said what I believe, or believed what I said. And if I do sometimes tell the truth, I hide it behind so many lies that it's hard to find. I've become a true doctor of this art.'

He is curious to hear more about how a man who works for the papacy sees the present crisis of Christendom. With the Lutheran heresy spreading throughout Germany, Leo has been trying to enlist the new German emperor, Charles V, to crack down on the apostates in the Holy Roman Empire.

Guicciardini minces no words in his response.[13] 'My position under His Holiness forces me, for my own good, to further the pontificate's interests. Were it not for that, I'd love Martin Luther as much as myself. Not to free myself from the laws of Christianity, but to see that pack of scoundrels get their just desserts. I doubt there's a man alive who loathes the clergy with its avarice, its ambition, its sensuality, more than I do. Those vices are bad enough in themselves, but they're hardly suited to those who profess to live a life devoted to God.'

Guicciardini's long, heavy-jowled face somehow maintains the same expression whether he is joking or in earnest: an expression of brooding intensity held in check by a slow-moving body and a fiercely self-disciplined mind. The contrast with Niccolò's sharp cheekbones, lightweight frame, and eyes that keep acting out his words is stark. Yet their temperaments go together very well.[14]

'Ever since they appointed me to hunt down a friar to send to Florence,' Niccolò confides, 'I've been having wicked thoughts about the style of preacher I'd like to choose. When your fleet-footed messenger arrived the other day, I was sitting on the toilet among those monks, mulling over the absurdities of the world and imagining the man I'd like to find –'

'I think those Lord Consuls of the Wool Guild expect you to bring back some friar unlike any to be found on this earth,' his host says. 'After all, people have always considered you exceedingly extravagant in your opinions, and the inventor of new and outlandish things.'

'And I'm resolved to be as pig-headed about this idea as I am about my other ideas, though I know I'm at variance with the ideas of most Florentines.' Niccolò says this as if he is taking a vow of holy chastity. 'They'd like a preacher who would teach them the way to Paradise. I want one who will teach them the way to go to the devil. Not, as you've said of yourself, because I want to liberate anyone from a life of true virtue. But I do believe the following would be the true way to go to Paradise: instead of praying for some new holy man to save you, learn the way to Hell in order to steer clear of it yourself.'

He had tried to show how Italians and Florentines had made their own earthly hell in his *Decennale*. In a less obvious way, his *Prince* had shown how political hells are made by unwary princes and empires, with the help of fatalistic peoples – or corrupted ones – who help or let them grow too great for anyone's good. His favourite ancient historians did this: they retrace the steps that led to humanity's greatest disasters so that later generations may learn how to avoid the same, or worse. Sallust, Livy, Tacitus show how once virtuous Rome became a prison under the emperors. Thucydides shows, with a subtly critical art, how a rich and brilliant Athens went mad with desire to dominate all Greece and destroyed itself in the process. Niccolò has recently started writing his own history of Florence; he hopes it will teach similar lessons to his compatriots and anyone else who reads it. Though his host's face remains impassive, he sees that Guicciardini understands him completely.

When their conversation turns to Florentine politics, they have different opinions about how the government should be reformed. Like so many of his class, Guicciardini mistrusts what his friend calls the 'generality of people'. He wants Florence to have an aristo-cratic republic similar to the Venetian. But he agrees with Niccolò that oligarchy is not aristocracy: the government of the few is no good if it is not the government by the best. And the best are not always found in the same hundred or so families, or among the wealthy. Guicciardini's true aristocracy would be a meritocracy.[15] Niccolò wants a government where those who prove their merit hold the highest posts, but where important powers are given to a wider council, though not perhaps as wide as in Savonarola's day. They both take a grim view of their city's turn towards an undisguised principality. Niccolò describes the proposal he had sent to Giulio and Leo. He had heard nothing further about their vaunted plans for reform.

His host, though younger, is far more cynical than his friend. 'The world and princes are no longer made as they should be,' Guic-ciardini says, 'but as they are.'[16] But now tell me, how did you come to think of writing this new history?'

'I had need of money,' says Niccolò. His young friends of the Orti Oricellari had grown excited by his early ideas of a Florentine history, and someone – possibly the keen networker Battista della Palla – had the thought that he might be able to get a stipend to write it. Battista had taken the idea to the pope and to Giulio in Rome.[17] 'He claims he found the pope very well disposed towards me,' Niccolò tells Guic-ciardini. They'd spoken of his *Mandragola*, which Leo had ordered to be staged in Rome; Battista assured him that it was all ready, learned in entirety by its players, and that it would doubtless give great pleasure. Soon afterwards, Niccolò was invited to draft his own contract for a commission, leaving the amounts to be deter-mined by his new employer, the Studio (University) of Florence.

Florence, 10 Sept.–7 Nov. 1520
Honoured Sir. The substance of the contract should be as follows.
He is to be hired for — years at a salary of — per year with the condition that he must be, and is to be, held to write the annals or else the history

*of the things done by the state and city of Florence, from whatever time
may seem to him most appropriate, and in whatever language – either
Latin or Tuscan – may seem best to him.*

Nic. Machiavelli

He had signed his contract on 8 November 1520, six months
before his present conversation with Guicciardini and his stay with
the friars, accepting a modest salary of a hundred fiorini di studio –
a little over half what he'd earned in the Chancery. More recently,
he'd had offers of serious political employment from Piero Soderini, who was now exiled in Rome under papal protection and
treated very well by the pope and his family. The former Gonfalonier had spent the first period of his exile in the republic of Ragusa
on the Adriatic. It was now a protectorate of the Ottoman Empire
but had large Florentine and Italian colonies of merchants, and was
an important shipbuilding and commercial centre. The republic
needed a chancellor, and Soderini had recommended his old friend
for the job. Niccolò turned down the offer; it was too far from
home, and his family needed him here. Then, in April 1521, Piero
had urged him to take up a position as secretary to Prospero Colonna, a member of the noble Roman clan and cousin to Fabrizio,
the guest of honour in *The Art of War*. 'I judge it,' Soderini had written, 'much better than to stay there and write histories for a few
petty florins.'[18] The salary had been tempting: 200 gold ducats and
additional expenses. But again he'd decided to stay at home. He
wants to put his political knowledge to use, but for his native city,
not for a faraway one or a great foreign lord.

Guicciardini offers warm congratulations. 'Whoever gave you
the task of writing these annals, whether it was the pope or the
cardinal, is greatly to be commended. And I don't believe this legation to our friars will prove completely useless for your purposes.
In these three days' idleness, you've imbibed the entire Republic of
Clogs, and you will no doubt make use of that model of government for some purpose.'[19]

So far, Niccolò feels freer in his writing than he has since he was expelled from politics nine years ago. No one will mind what he says about popes who died four hundred years ago, so his first chapters are full of comical, low-key parodies of posturing pontiffs and their useless crusades. 'But once I reach the times of Cosimo and more recent governments,' he tells Guicciardini, 'I may need you to tell me if I'm being too offensive, either in my exaggerating or in my understating of certain facts. And since life has taught me the value of caution, I shall continue to seek advice from myself and do my best to arrange it so that – while still telling the truth – no one will have anything to complain about.'[20]

Back from his mission and ensconced with his books in the countryside, Niccolò hears snatches of news from travellers who stop at his tavern, or from friends who write. The Ottoman Sultan Selim I had made a truce with Hungary in 1519. His successor, Suleiman the Magnificent, renews war in June 1521, just after Niccolò's embassy to his friars. At the end of August, Suleiman captures the Christian citadel of Belgrade. Leo's response to the threat is to issue thunderous calls for a crusade against the infidel.

The hysteria over this latest assault from the east makes Niccolò long to pour cold water over its instigators. And since his new employers are the chief instigators and he wants to keep being paid, how convenient that the first chapters of his histories deal with rather similar popes and crusades in the past! As Guicciardini had remarked to him, in writing histories you can comment indirectly on present follies, and more freely than if you speak outright of your own times. For names and details change, but not basic human motives and errors, which one sees are much the same in every time and place; and *changing the names and forms of things means that only the prudent recognize them* – recognize, that is, that in narrating the past you are also discussing the present.[21]

So he goes back to the earlier Church, to earlier crusades and pontiffs long dead. Nearly five hundred years ago, Niccolò writes in his histories, Pope Urban II found himself hated by the Roman

people, and realized that Italy's disunities made him insecure.²²
Hoping to save his own skin and preserve the Church's precarious
rule in Rome, Urban made an inflammatory speech against the
infidels, which for a while distracted people from their much worse
troubles at home. These are some of the coolest deadpan tones
found in any of Machiavelli's works; he is now a true doctor of
deadpan. In the following century, Emperor Frederick Barbarossa,
frustrated because Pope Adrian IV had taken away his power and
titles in Rome, joined the great enterprise in Asia so as *to vent against
Mohammed the ambition that he had not been able to vent against the
vicars of Christ.* The Crusaders fought for a long time, with exceedingly varying fortunes, until they were trounced by the Saracen
leader Saladin. Our author attributes their defeat to *Saladin's virtue* –
a word he almost never uses in connection with churchmen – *and
to the discords of the Christians, which in the end took from them all the
glory they had acquired in the beginning.*

Like so many of its precursors, Pope Leo's crusading plan fizzles
out, leaving the Turks stronger than ever and Christendom's internal rifts ever deeper. Then, in December 1521, news reaches Florence
that sends the city into a ferment of uncertainty. At the age of
forty-six, Leo has died of malaria. Death came so suddenly that the
last rites could not be administered.

For weeks, Florentines speculate: might Cardinal Giulio de'
Medici become the next pontiff? He certainly had hopes of being
elected, and more than fair chances, as one of the preferred candidates of Emperor Charles V. On 9 January 1522, however, the
election of Pope Adrian VI, a surprise compromise candidate from
the Netherlands, is announced. He promptly embarks on a bold
path of reform, issuing strong denunciations against the sale of
indulgences and seeking to stem the tide of Lutheran revolt in
German lands.

But Adrian is old, Florentines point out. Giulio would soon have
other chances. In the meantime, though the cardinal is now head
of the Medici family and Florence's leader, he spends too much
time politicking in Rome to deal with Florentine affairs, and lets

unpopular Medici clients run the city. All the high hopes for reform he'd raised after Lorenzo's death had come to nothing.

It pains Niccolò to see his Orti companions' dejection. For a while, Zanobi Buondelmonti seethes with anger. These princes of ours are all humanity, liberality, and hot air, he'd mutter together with Luigi, and many others. Giulio invites us to talk and give him counsel, listens patiently and answers with such soothing words – then insults us by doing the opposite of all the advice he praised. Does he think we're so stupid that we don't notice? Or such cowards that we'll stay quiet? Even Battista della Palla, who had expected Leo and Giulio to help him pursue a great career in the Church, is bitterly disappointed. The aspiring young historian Jacopo Nardi, another member of the old garden circle, says of Giulio that no other Medici had 'concealed the principate with more accomplished appearances of civility and freedom'.[23] Over the past few years – too late for their own good – Florentines had become more accomplished decoders of the realities behind such super-smooth appearances.

Between his histories and family matters, Niccolò has less time than before to see his friends. When he does see the Orti Oricellari crowd, they vent their outrage less and less, seeming to busy themselves with trips to Rome and Siena, and other places. At home, he and Marietta agonize over his nephew Giovanni Vernacci, whose business affairs are in a shambles. Since Giovanni is abroad and refuses to come home to Florence, his creditors have started to chase Niccolò, demanding immediate payment. 'Come back and show yourself to the people you've done business with,' he orders his nephew through letters. *If you don't look into your affairs squarely and sort them out, harm and disgrace will ensue.*[24]

Then, at the end of May 1522, he receives heart-stopping news. A conspiracy has come to light. It seems a number of Florentine men have been plotting to assassinate Cardinal Giulio de' Medici on 19 June, the day of Corpus Christi. A courier carrying messages between the conspirators was apprehended and tortured until he revealed the entire plot. Its main instigators were the King of France and Niccolò's old friend Cardinal Francesco Soderini. French troops and galleys had already been sent to several places in and around Florence's dominions. Local conspirators, once news went out that the cardinal had been poisoned, were meant to arouse the Francophile Florentines to change their government, ideally to a Venetian-style aristocratic republic. The courier also confessed, or carried on him, the names of the Florentine plotters. At their head was Zanobi Buondelmonti. Other young men from the Orti Oricellari circle, including Battista della Palla and Luigi Alamanni, were among his cohorts.

These three manage to save themselves by fleeing into exile. Others are less lucky. A cousin of Luigi's is caught and imprisoned; so is their friend Jacopo Diaceto, who confesses the plotters' intentions. They are sentenced to death and beheaded on 7 June. Zanobi and Luigi are ordered to report to the magistrates within three days or be declared rebels. When they do not obey, they are found guilty of sedition and murderous intentions. Penalties are ordered against anyone found to have furnished money or otherwise helped them.

At just this time, early June 1522, Totto Machiavelli is lying on his deathbed.[25] Of all the sorrows Niccolò has known, these are altogether the heaviest: the death of a beloved brother, for years his only surviving sibling and his rock through many trials, and the loss and imperilment of his noon-time friends. Despite his closeness to them and his former closeness to Cardinal Soderini, this time he is not arrested or suspected of involvement. Four years later, one of the conspirators, Niccolò Martelli, would testify that Zanobi had wanted to invite Niccolò Machiavelli to join them. He'd been dissuaded when others pointed out that he might attract too much suspicion to their cause since, unlike the rest of them, Machiavelli was known 'not to be a friend of the illustrious House' of Medici.[26]

Though he seems to have known nothing of their plans, certain chroniclers who attended the Orti Oricellari discussions in his time there suggest that his ideas were an important influence on the conspirators' actions. He'd tried to make them see the advantages of republics and hinted, more discreetly, at the shortcomings of all principalities. Had he also helped to plant the idea of a conspiracy in their young heads? He had, it is true, discoursed at length on conspiracies; they are the subject of the longest chapters by far in both his *Prince* and his *Discourses*.

But the writer's own views are often hard to pin down in those books, and his views on conspiracies are no exception. Machiavelli never quite tells his readers whether secretive plots are useful or useless; he leaves it to them to judge their utility from his numerous examples. And the upshot of almost all of them is that such plots are so fraught with dangers, so unlikely to succeed, and so prone to provoke repressive backlashes that they are best avoided. He recalls his own father's cousin Girolamo, exiled then killed for conspiring against Cosimo de' Medici, and the ambitious Cola Montano in Milan, who had recklessly fired up his young students to risk their lives in a plot against the duke of that city. If one wants to get rid of a hated government, he'd told his friends, there are better ways than secretive plots carried on by a few men who have no popular authority. Popular uprisings are more likely to succeed, and have some chance of leading to stable government, if the generality of people remains involved.[27] Or if the people are too cowed, whoever has the prince's ear must try to show him that it is in his own interest to change his methods of rule, or to step down. Talk to him, whenever and however you can. Warn him of the imminent dangers to himself and his cronies and his dreams of leaving behind a glorious reputation.

He and they had tried, and failed, to get a real hearing, and now the princely government would be even worse. In 1522 and 1523, after a long hiatus in the records, he and Vettori strike up a fresh correspondence. Perhaps Niccolò had heard something surprising that would come out in the conspirator Martelli's later confession: Martelli claimed that Francesco Vettori had been considered as a possible sympathizer with the anti-Medici plot, perhaps because of his discomfort with Leo's anti-French policies. Some said that King François had contacted him personally to find out where he would stand if the plot succeeded.[28]

Vettori may never have stopped trying to use his contacts to help his old friend when he could. He and Niccolò quickly fall back into their old style of banter, in letters that pass from serious political matters to family problems to risqué stories about mutual friends. In their earlier exchanges, Niccolò had often been the one trying to cheer up his melancholic friend; now, after all his recent blows, it is Vettori's turn to do the cheering up. Their letters never mention the conspiracy or Niccolò's worries about his exiled friends. But while seeming to discuss Niccolò's problems with his sons and nephews – writing, unusually, in Latin – it almost sounds as if Vettori might be offering him veiled consolation about his lost intellectual children of the Orti Oricellari. 'You get too upset about our sons' habits, my Niccolò,' he writes – though Vettori has only daughters. 'As we grow old, we become too morose and finicky, and we do not remember what we did when we were young. Don't torture yourself with what you cannot change.'[29] In one line he speaks of 'your son, Lodovico', in the next of 'your sister's son, Lodovico' – though Niccolò's sister had only a Giovanni. A later letter from another friend of the Orti circle, Filippo de' Nerli, tells Niccolò not to use 'the code about sons'.[30] Whether or not Vettori's letter uses such a code and whatever its message, its Latinity and other peculiarities are suspect. *One must remember what pleasures, what advantages are derived from sons, and not always complain if they fail in some duty or do something against the rules; for if you act that way,* Vettori tells his friend, *you will live in too great torment and anxiety.*[31] Zanobi, Luigi and Battista are now on the road, sometimes together in one place, usually in different places: Lucca, the poet Ariosto's home in Garfagnana, then Venice, then France. King François pays them to make various anti-Medici contacts; sometimes they are arrested and in danger. Their families and friends in Florence have reason for concern.

17

Never Give Up

In January 1525, a crowd gathers at a villa outside Florence. The host is Jacopo Falconetti, known to his friends as *il Fornaciaio*, 'the brick-maker', a rich plebeian who boasts one of the most fashionable banquet tables in Tuscany. Some years before, having somehow offended the men in power, he had been exiled outside the city's walls. But now his banishment has been lifted, and to celebrate his liberty Falconetti wanted to throw the best party Florentines had seen in over a decade, since the days of the republic. He could think of no better way to attract a wide cross-section of guests and, once he had them there, to conjure up the right mood, than to advertise as his party's main attraction the new comedy by his friend, the author of *La Mandragola*, Niccolò Machiavelli.

Now in his fifty-sixth year, the playwright can hardly believe his own good fortune. Never in his life has he had so much admiring attention, not even after his militia and diplomatic efforts helped Florence recapture Pisa in 1509. Falconetti has spared no expense to make this new play the most impressive spectacle anyone in the audience has ever seen. He'd brought in workmen to level off his garden so it can serve as a stage. He'd hired the famous sculptor and painter Bastiano da Sangallo, known as Aristotele because of his affected gravitas, to design the stage set. He'd sent out hundreds of invitations to Florentines, high and low, from fellow men of the people all the way to the city's top ranks, not excluding a few Medici. After the event, one of Niccolò's friends tells him that *the fame of your revelries has spread and continues to spread not only throughout all Tuscany but also throughout Lombardy.* Everyone, he says, has heard how Machiavelli and his play were the star attractions at that gathering, how the host put all his wealth and house and lands at your disposal. *These are things that are usually done only for princes.*[1]

The play enacts a battle over a girl, the *Clizia* who gives the play its name, who since infancy has been the ward of Nicomaco and his wife, Sofronia. Their son now wants to marry the fair Clizia, but his father has fallen madly in love with her as well, setting parent against child, husband against wife. Though Niccolò draws the main plot from an ancient comedy by the Roman dramatist Plautus, he infuses it with his own deep-cutting wit. And spectators would laugh at the eponymy between the playwright's name and his pathetic, besotted Nicomaco, whose attempts to consummate his passion achieve no victory, but are frustrated by the far cleverer machinations of his wife. Sofronia wins the battle and restores the natural order of things, where grizzled old men, especially married ones, do not chase after young girls, bringing shame to themselves and their families.

At this moment, Niccolò and his Nicomaco have more in common than their names. The character's lovelorn torments, his lost self-control, are the writer's own. And the whole world seems to know. One of his friends writes to another, behind Niccolò's back: *I can't help saying how aggrieved I am about what daily reaches my ears concerning our Machia.* If Italy weren't wracked with so many other troubles just now, *I'm certain that people would talk about nothing else but him, seeing that a paterfamilias of such character is galloping off – I do not want to say with whom –*[2]

Barbera Salutati. She is in her early twenties and makes her living as a courtesan, letting men like Falconetti pay for her company. She and Niccolò had met a year earlier, at Falconetti's house. And now the ageing father of five surviving children floats about in a haze of infatuation. His friends tease him. Take care, says Guicciardini: if you spend so much time in the company of that courtesan, professional charmer that she is, she'll spoil your appreciation of true feminine virtues. I fear you're getting too *used to your Barbera, who strives, as does her kind, to please everyone and seeks rather to seem than to be.*[3] Machia, other friends write to one another, is getting too attached to this Barbera. Someone should take measures to end this affair before hell breaks out for him at home.[4]

He mocks himself in public to show that he knows what a buffoon he looks. But it is not just her soft skin that captivates him, her laughter at his jokes, her art of stirring an old man's dried-up juices with a brush of white fingers on his sleeve. Barbera is a talented musician; she sings like an angel, and writes poetry. She and her troupe perform songs between the acts of Niccolò's play – his lyrics, written with her in mind, sung to music by the famed madrigal composer Philippe Verdelot. After they became close, she'd confided in him: she dreamed of having a stipend to support her music so that she might live independently, as an artist, without having to entertain men with those other arts she now knows so well.

Niccolò had sympathized. Before securing his present contract for his *Florentine Histories*, he'd received no money for his writings, and for a decade had supported his family with proceeds from the family farms. He promises to tell one of the most powerful financiers in Florence about her plans. Filippo Strozzi is a close friend of Francesco Vettori, and has helped Niccolò with other financial matters. Though Strozzi agrees to meet her, and flirts with her when he does, his offers don't amount to much.[5]

Still, miraculously, Barbera lets Niccolò get closer to her. He cannot get away. Ten years earlier, he'd written to Vettori about some other passing fancy, back when 'love' meant lust and was all just a game, but now it seemed much more. *You will realize how far that little thief, Love, has gone to bind me with his fetters. Those bonds are so strong that I am in absolute despair of my liberty and am unable to conceive of any means of unfettering myself; they make such a tangle that I believe I cannot live happily without this kind of life.*[6]

Age has not chastened him. Even in late middle age he is like the untameable boy in his poem *The Ass*, who could not stop himself *running though the street, and at any time, without any heed*; even after the boy's family lock him indoors for months and send doctors to wave perfumes under his nose and drain blood from his head, no sooner had he stepped outside than

his hair began to stand on end.
And, everything else abandoned, there returned to him the fancy for
  running,
which goes on working and is never quiet.
And after that he always ran, as long as he lived.

In the city at large, he now has a reputation to live up to, not any more as a man who carries the burdens of state security on his shoulders, but as a comic writer. His comedies confront human errors in the opposite way to that of Savonarola's followers, who still secretly pray for a new era of theocratic reforms. Niccolò would indulge the same pleasures they would persecute and push his compatriots to the edge of hell – hell being nothing more than what you get when you overstep the limits of natural and civil orders, or fail to stop those who do. The city needs him. He is its best-loved warning voice, its most entertaining oracle.

His standing with the Medici is better than ever, thanks to his hugely popular plays and widely read *Art of War*, and to the good offices of well-placed friends: Francesco Guicciardini, Filippo Strozzi and his brother Lorenzo, Francesco Vettori. The first eight books of his *Florentine Histories* are nearly completed. He'd done most of the writing at his house in Sant' Andrea, cutting himself off from the distractions of city life for weeks on end; I'll send your regards to the chickens, he wrote to his brother-in-law in Florence.[7] He writes to Guicciardini about his struggles to describe the ascent of the Medici to power in the old republic. I'd pay ten soldi – no more than that, mind – *to have you by my side so that I might show you where I am, since I am about to come to certain details* and don't want to offend the men who pay my salary.[8]

His apprehensions are justified. The second half of his histories is a masterpiece of subtle, sotto voce criticism of the present Medici rulers' forebears, in the style of ancient historians who could not write freely about the emperors.[9] While giving Cosimo and Lorenzo due credit for their merits, Machiavelli shows how their family grew great by cultivating networks of friends with lavish lending and spending, and by straining the laws to breaking point. His histories are not partisan: they don't pretend that Florence's early years as a republic were a golden age of liberty and justice, or blame the Medici for stealing the government from the people. They hold up a brutally honest mirror to all Florentines. Each episode springs to life like a scene in a play. In one generation after another, citizens struggle for freedom but soon get dragged down by their own human weaknesses – their desire to dominate others, their unwillingness to share power with rival parties, their failure to see behind good appearances, their yearning for God, or some extraordinary man, to save them. Like the greatest ancient histories, Machiavelli's carry warning lessons for all times. He treats history as a medicine used to purge its readers of arrogance, naivety about human nature, and the fatalistic belief that the course of human affairs cannot be regulated by our intelligence, but has to be left to nature or to God.

Now he can sign a letter to Guicciardini: *Niccolò Machiavelli, historico, comico, et tragico* – Historian, Comic Author, and Tragic Author.[10] For there is a great deal of tragedy in his histories up to the death of Lorenzo il Magnifico, as there is in the events that moved him to write the comic *Mandragola* and in the seemingly cold-blooded advice in the *Prince*. Once he puts the finishing touches to this instalment, he proposes to start writing about the troubles that followed Lorenzo's death: the coming of the French in '94, Savonarola, the Borgias, Pisa, Piero Soderini.[11] Events he witnessed with his own eyes and ears. He thinks he deserves a rise in salary to write these next parts. He'd ask Filippo Strozzi to help him get it from the man who commissioned this work: Giulio de' Medici, who is now Pope Clement VII.[12]

For despite their growing unpopularity in Florence, the Medici have continued to have unbelievable good fortune in the Vatican. Less than two years after Pope Leo's death, following the short-lived pontificate of Pope Adrian VI, the conclave had elected Leo's cousin Giulio as his successor. But instead of multiplying Florence's blessings, Pope Clement gave the city one of the worst governments anyone could remember. In February 1524, he'd invited prominent citizens to a sumptuous banquet.[13] There he proposed that his guests should ask for Ippolito de' Medici, the illegitimate thirteen-year-old son of the pope's cousin Giuliano, to be declared eligible for all public offices. Their formal request would make it appear as if the Florentine people wished for a Medici prince, lending the gloss of legitimacy to the boy's blatantly unconstitutional position.

Francesco Vettori was among the new pope's guests. In the past, he had tried to avoid conflicts with the Medici. One had better adjust to the facts of power, he'd told Niccolò all those years ago; we get nowhere with our pipe dreams of making the world more reasonable. But this time he had protested. The mood of frustration in Florence was already threatening enough. The poor and middling were getting poorer, the rich angry at being deprived of their share of power. Vettori reminded Clement of how things had gone after Lorenzo died. People who'd kept quiet until then began to cry out against Piero de' Medici's government of spoilt, power-hungry boys and yes-men, though Piero was not a child like Ippolito, or born out of wedlock, or granted such extensive powers and privileges as the pope wanted to give his pubescent relation. Then came Savonarola's prophecies, and French armies, and Medici exile. His Holiness should take care lest history repeat itself.

But Clement and his cronies managed to win the support of the majority of men present. Henceforth, Ippolito was to be prince in all but name, ruling under the guidance of a non-Florentine cardinal, Silvio Passerini, whom the pope appointed as governor of Florence in May 1524. In a gesture of reconciliation towards the family responsible for his banishment, Niccolò's friend Falconetti had invited the new leaders to his gala production of Machiavelli's comedy; the dark-haired boy could be seen in the audience, one of the youngest people there. And there is another Medici youth, a year older than Ippolito, whom the pope is quietly grooming for future greatness. Though the official story says that Alessandro de' Medici is the second Lorenzo's illegitimate son, others suspect that his father is Pope Clement VII himself.

*

A few weeks after the grand premier of his *Clizia*, Niccolò consults Vettori, now special envoy to the Vatican, about when he should go to Rome to present his histories to the pope. 'His Holiness enquired after you just the other day,' his friend replies, 'and asked whether you'd finished the great work. When I told him I'd read part of it and said it would surely give satisfaction, the pope said: he ought to come here, and I feel for certain that his books are going to give pleasure and be read willingly. But wait a bit before you come. Clement has many worries now; his state of mind is hard to read from one day to the next. I wouldn't want you to go away empty-handed.'[14]

Vettori knows that Niccolò wants to negotiate a higher salary for his labours as Florence's semi-official historian. And there is another matter he wants to discuss with the pope. He has never given up on his citizen militia project, never stopped believing that it is the best hope for Florence's security. If he does nothing else in what remains of his life, he must try to do this for his city – persuade Clement to revive the institution that Leo had abolished.

In May, at last, Niccolò delivers his histories into Pope Clement's hands in Rome. The pontiff receives him warmly, rewarding him with a bonus of 120 gold ducats in addition to his salary. The money is soon gone. Niccolò pays a large part of it into a dowry bank for his young daughter Baccina, and a larger portion for back taxes, leaving a meagre sum for Marietta's household expenses.

When he broaches the subject of his militia, the pope listens intently. For all his self-possessed cordiality, Clement has a long memory. He won't have forgotten the conspiracy against his life only a few years before, plotted by Machiavelli's friends from the Orti Oricellari. On the other hand, he knows all too keenly his family's present weakness in the city; and hostilities between France's King François and the Habsburg Emperor Charles V are threatening to unleash a storm over Italy. Florentines can only benefit, Niccolò urges, from having well-trained troops to defend their interests, which are inseparable from the pontiff's own.

Perhaps, Clement replies, we might make a start with this militia somewhere other than Florence. There is no need to say what

Niccolò knows well: it is too dangerous for the Medici to arm dissatisfied citizens there. But they might put it to the test in the Romagna, a region particularly vulnerable to foreign invaders. Francesco Guicciardini is governor there, and Clement has recently appointed him lieutenant of his papal forces. Confer with him, the pope suggests, then we can speak again.

Niccolò goes to the Romagna in July to try to persuade his friend to back his plans. They drink, visit courtesans, talk of Barbera and discontents in the city. All the old laws have been flouted; ordinary councils no longer meet; foreign ambassadors deal only with Ippolito and his cardinal at the Medici Palace, who impose whatever taxes they please. And Clement's foreign policies have made matters worse, far worse. Emperor Charles V's troops had seized Milan from the French earlier that year; they now control that city, as well as Naples in the south. King François had pressed the pope to enter a league against the Habsburg emperor, together with England, Venice, and the Duke of Milan. Instead, Clement had signed a treaty with Charles's viceroy on 1 April 1525. This treaty, in effect, made the emperor master of Tuscany and set Florence's Medici government against France, the city's old ally.

Leading men in Florence, including Francesco Vettori, had advised Clement to side with the empire as the safer, though less honourable, course. Since Florence's dominions have no forces of their own, they pointed out, the massive imperial army would quickly bring the city to ruin. Necessity forces us to submit to the emperor.[15] Niccolò rejects this fatalistic logic. If the problem lies in our lack of forces, he tells Guicciardini, let us make some. His old friend Vettori means well, he wants to save what he can of his city's independence; but he has spent all these years over-cautiously adapting to others' rising fortunes instead of making his own. Niccolò's book on principalities had tried to persuade fatalistic pragmatists that an individual's or state's present weakness should not stop them from taking bold, independent measures to try to save themselves on their own terms. He knows that *many have held and hold the opinion that worldly things are so governed by fortune and by*

God that men cannot correct them with their prudence – indeed that they have no remedy at all. Men who hold this opinion think they are being wise when they bow before fortune's current favourites and follow their commands. *When I have thought about this sometimes,* Machiavelli admits, *I have been in some part inclined to their opinion. Nonetheless, so that our free will not be eliminated, I judge that it might be true that fortune is arbiter of half our actions, but also that she leaves the other half, or close to it, for us to govern.*[16]

We can't measure these things precisely; fortune and free will are not empirical data that can be seen or calculated by their mass or motions. But even if someone could prove that fortune had ninety-nine per cent influence and free will only one, or less, that minuscule percentage would still leave room for us to act or not to act – to exercise the modest powers we call freedom and prudence to put ourselves in better order. Human freedom doesn't need to be vast in order to be effective. In fact, the most praiseworthy human works – such as the building of great cities, or their preservation over time – have come forth where there was less room for choice, where people had to think and work all the harder to overcome obstacles.[17] So *they should indeed never give up. They have always to hope and, since they hope, not to give up in whatever fortune and whatever travail they may find themselves.*[18]

Guicciardini agrees that Clement's policy risks selling out Florence's – and Italy's – last scraps of freedom. But he nurses the usual patrician prejudices against Machiavelli's people's militia, and has too many pressing worries to discuss idealistic projects. His new appointment as Pope Clement's military lieutenant depresses him. If the pope stays on the path he's taking now, he tells Niccolò, there'll be nothing for me to do but try to make our inevitable demise less agonizing. 'You can call me Illustrious Lord Lieutenant, I'll honour you with Your Excellency,' he says, 'and with these reciprocal titles we shall renew each other's pleasure. But it will soon be turned into mourning when we find ourselves with our hands full of flies at the end. I believe that we're all walking in the shadows here in Italy, with our hands tied behind our backs.'[19]

Niccolò had never heard his friend, normally stone-cold under pressure, express such despair. 'But let's speak of happier things,' says Guicciardini. He has thought of the perfect distraction from his worries: a plan to stage Machiavelli's *Mandragola* during the next Carnival season in the Romagna, here in Faenza. 'At least,' he says, 'it is a discussion that is within our power.' And besides, 'recreation is more than ever necessary amid so much tumult.'

So Niccolò returns to Florence and sets about improving his Comedy of the Mandrake, but not before he has sent Guicciardini twenty-five stomach pills to relieve his anxieties, and the recipe he uses to treat his own frequent episodes of discomfort.[20] Mix one and a half drams of bitter aloe with one dram of germander and half a dram each of saffron, myrrh, betory, pimpernel, and Armenian bole. *I can tell you that they have revived me. Start by taking one after dinner; if that causes a movement, do not take any more; if it does not, take two or three – at most, five. But I never took more than two, once a week, when I felt heaviness in my stomach or in my head.*

At the end of summer, he hears excellent news: his name has been put on the list of citizens eligible to be selected for certain public offices.[21] After thirteen years in the political wilderness, he is back. He takes it as a signal from Clement that his militia plans are still pending, that his city needs him more than ever, and not just as its comedic and historical conscience. Through the bleak autumn months, he often dines with Barbera and other friends and they discuss the forthcoming production in Faenza. He composes lyrics for some new *intermezzi*, songs sung between the acts. Barbera and her troupe will perform them, the composer Verdelot will create sweet harmonies to offset the play's caustic wit. *So you see*, he writes to Guicciardini, *we are applying ourselves diligently so that this celebration will have all it needs for perfection.* Get ready to roll out the carpets for us, Magnificent Governor of Romagna. *For once, let us have a merry Carnival; arrange a room for Barbera with those friars, and if they don't go crazy over her, I shall not want any money for it.*[22]

But politics kills their plans. In January 1526, a month before the scheduled performance, Pope Clement recalls Guicciardini to

Rome on urgent business. He is to lead the latest initiative in Clement's dangerously fickle foreign policy: to negotiate a league against his signed and sworn ally, Emperor Charles V.

The beginning of 1526 finds Niccolò deep in discussions with Guicciardini, Filippo Strozzi, and other friends close to the pope. After Clement's sudden shift of allegiance, they all fear that this Medici pope is taking Florence and Italy straight to the graveyard. True, Machiavelli and Guicciardini thought he was wrong to throw in his lot with this all-conquering emperor in the first place. But no policy, as Niccolò had been arguing for years, is less prudent than to make an agreement one day and break it at the first inconvenience. There is no safety in vacillation. Now no one would ever trust this Florentine pope, not the emperor, nor the French and their allies. While he shifts about without any steady compass, alienating everyone, all of Italy lies exposed, disunited, and friendless. Guicciardini is Clement's chief negotiator; he pours out his desperation to Niccolò. 'I've lost my bearings,' he admits. 'I have never seen anyone who, when he sees bad times coming, didn't seek in some way to try to protect himself – except for us, who await them unprotected in the middle of the road.' If the vultures soon swoop down on Italy, the two men agree, Italians won't be able to say that sovereignty was taken away from them, only that it fell shamefully from their hands when they chose not to fight for it. 'We have hung up our brains,' says Guicciardini, 'no less than our weapons.'[23]

Though he has no official post, Niccolò begins to offer his friend detailed foreign-policy advice, telling him what Guicciardini should advise the pope to do. Clement had egregiously violated one of Machiavelli's key political maxims: avoid sitting on the fence when you are caught between two powerful rivals. Instead, one should take clear sides and stick with allies through thick and thin. Even if they sometimes lose, your loyalty will win their trust, and they'll return the favour when you are in trouble. Firm friends are always one's best hope of security. As to which side Italians should choose, clearly both French and imperial alliances carried risks and humiliations. But *prudence consists in knowing how to recognize the qualities of inconveniences, and in picking the less bad as good.*[24] Machiavelli has never trusted the ambitions of emperors. Charles V's empire, he tells Guicciardini, is *an odious, alarming, and dangerous power.* The safer gamble is to work night and day to recover the trust of our old allies, the French. King François is now being held prisoner in Madrid, having been captured in battle a year before by his mortal enemy Charles. *We should arrange it*, says Niccolò, *so that as soon as the king gets out he has someone close by who, with his authority and eloquence, can make him forget about the things of the past* – that is, the pope's perceived betrayal – *and to demonstrate Italy's unanimity against this empire.*[25]

And if Florence and the pope cannot regain French goodwill, Machiavelli sees just two choices. We could try to buy our way out, he tells Guicciardini – the usual Florentine way. *But I personally don't believe that we can, because either I'm completely blind or the King of France will first take your money, and then your life.* There is a better course: *We can arm ourselves in earnest and help our own cause.* The pope and the Florentines can seize the initiative and exhort other Italians to form militias of their own citizens. With so formidable a common enemy, they might at last have some chance of cooperating in Italy's common defence. We should get moving with this plan without delay, he tells Guicciardini, not wait for a French commitment. *Whether overtly or covertly, we must assemble a military force or one morning we shall wake up completely lost.*[26]

Throughout the spring of 1526, he lobbies as hard for his militia as he did twenty years earlier, with the energy of a much younger man. At the end of April, Pope Clement summons him to Rome. He approves Niccolò's new plans to overhaul Florence's fortifications and authorizes the creation of a new magistracy, the Curators of the Walls. Machiavelli is appointed supervisor and secretary. His eldest son, Bernardo, will be his assistant.

No time to savour his triumphant rehabilitation, no time to squander on comedies, histories, amorous longings, anything but walls and armies. He and Bernardo meet with engineers from morning to dusk, discussing various proposals. *My head is so full of ramparts that nothing else could enter it*, he tells Guicciardini. But walls are useless without armed men and firm allies. Allies depend on diplomacy and trust, arms on discipline. Both are sorely lacking. Together with Guicciardini, he inspects a contingent of the pope's troops near Milan in July. A travesty of an army – no one knows where they're supposed to set up camp, with the officers heading one way and the troops going in the opposite direction, their leaders having failed or disdained to give them proper orders. *Had the enemy known about the disarray*, he writes to another friend, *there is absolutely no doubt that they would have caused us grief, and we risked the danger of having them instantaneously become masters of Italy.*[27]

Guicciardini is amused by Niccolò's reactions. As you're aware, he writes to a mutual acquaintance, Machiavelli's standards of good order are higher than most of ours. 'He came to reorganize the militia, but seeing how rotten it is, he has no hope of having any respect from it. Since he is unable to remedy the faults of mankind, he will do nothing but laugh at them.' The friend replies: 'I'm glad Machiavelli gave the orders to discipline the infantry. Would to God that he might put into action what he has in mind, but I doubt whether it is like Plato's Republic.' So he'd better return to Florence and carry out his duty of fortifying the walls, 'because the time when we'll need them is fast approaching'.[28]

By laughing at rottenness, the decay of human order, he might help destroy the rot. And then the world could start afresh, good men build new and better institutions. It cheers him to hear that Vettori now sees how dangerous it would be to support the emperor's designs in Italy. 'Men have come to Florence from Milan and Cremona,' he writes to Niccolò at the anti-imperial camp, 'with such tales about the imperial troops that no one would rather have them come here than the devil. I'd call it good news if we should hear that the sultan of Turkey had taken Hungary and was heading towards the emperor's capital at Vienna, and that the Lutherans were coming out on top in Germany, and that the Moors, whom the emperor wants to drive out of Aragon and Valencia, were going on the offensive.'[29]

On the same day in early August 1526, a letter arrives from Jacopo

Falconetti. He'd gone to see Barbera, Falconetti reports, after Niccolò had lamented that she didn't write often enough. 'I could not help giving her a good piece of my mind; so she answered that there was no man whom she esteemed more highly and at whose orders she was more completely, but also that she did you some occasional discourtesies to see if you love her.'[30] Love, however, was only part of the matter. Barbera had taken on the task of mediating highly secretive communications between Vettori, Filippo Strozzi and Machiavelli, evidence of how much they all trusted her discretion. In his letter Vettori writes that he'd just received two long letters from Niccolò, in code. He had sent them on to Strozzi in Rome, urging him to *handle them with his usual care; I am certain he will, if only he can get them deciphered,* which won't be easy. When Vettori received them, he'd gone straight to a friend of Niccolò's, who took him to Barbera's house. But *although she showed me the code, my age, my worries, my infirmities have so weakened my body and my imagination that I could not decipher it properly* until he consulted another trusted friend, *with a thousand remonstrances not to talk.*[31]

These letters probably conveyed military information that Niccolò wanted to keep from falling into enemy hands. But later events suggest another possible topic, almost as sensitive. Sometime in 1526, Vettori, Filippo Strozzi, and other leading citizens had begun to make secret plans for a change of government in Florence. It seems likely that his friends included Machiavelli in their discussions. Given his closeness to Guicciardini and his new office as Curator of the Walls, no one was better placed to report on the state of defences in Florentine and papal dominions, ensuring that their plans would have solid military intelligence. And no one had wanted changes for as long as Niccolò had.

Their opportunity soon arrives. At the end of August, after the emperor's supporters in Rome went on a violent rampage through the Vatican, Clement swerves his policy around again and makes a truce with his League's imperial enemies. One condition of the truce is that the pope would hand over his banker and relative, Filippo Strozzi, as hostage. Having already lost patience with Florence's government, and harbouring certain political ambitions for himself, Strozzi proves useful to his imperial gaolers. They offer him a deal: they will give him his freedom if he, in exchange, will spearhead an uprising against Medici rule in Florence.

Strozzi's associates make contact with the younger generation of anti-Medici resistance fighters. Zanobi Buondelmonti and Battista della Palla had gone into exile in Siena after their failed 1522 conspiracy against the Medici. The new conspirators, led by Strozzi, with Vettori as his closest collaborator, now recruit the young men to run their propaganda operations. They spread rumours among the Florentines about their present government's errors and treacheries, and promise the Signoria much-needed grain and other benefits if they would cast off the Medici yoke.[32]

Towards the end of March 1527, the pope is obliged to accept another truce with Charles V. Naively trusting in the eight-month ceasefire and its terms, which stipulate that imperial forces would leave Italy, Clement makes another rash decision: he disbands the papal army. Niccolò is horrified. Surely the emperor's next moves are obvious: he would take advantage of the pope's credulity, rip up the agreement, and send his troops south to rape and plunder their way through the Romagna and Tuscany. By early April, the emperor's general Charles de Bourbon, heading an imperial army of 14,000 German lansquenets, is assailing the area around Bologna. The pope does nothing to stop the relentless march towards Florence, even though, as Machiavelli tells Vettori, these enemy troops have no discipline to speak of; they know how to pillage but not how to fight. But the greatest threat we face, he despairs, comes not from them but from ourselves, from our Italian inertia.[33]

Yet even now Niccolò enjoins his friend and the Florentines to resist. *You Florentines can still save yourselves*, he writes, *if you surprise the enemy by arming yourselves and putting up a fierce defence of Pisa, Pistoia, Prato, and Florence*. You might then persuade the enemy to come to terms. They'll most likely be painful terms for you, you'll have to make concessions – *but not absolutely fatal*.[34] The same advice he'd given Piero Soderini fifteen years ago, in 1512, before the Spanish attacked Prato. Don't push your luck when you're clutching at your last desperate hopes, compromise to cut your losses, save what you can; what you lose now you can recover later. Soderini had refused to compromise, and Florence had fallen into the hands of princes. This time, things might go another way.

He is still in the Romagna with the anti-imperial troops, but writes every day to friends in the city, anxious to hear what is being done to prepare for the expected enemy attack. Bernardo, his eldest son, with a cool, well-organized head like his grandfather Bernardo's, is supervising extensions of the city walls in Niccolò's absence. But the citizens are starting to panic. They send petitioners to the Medici Palace demanding that the city should be able to arm itself. Marietta manages to keep their household calm, with Bernardo's help. Lodovico, their second son, is off in the Levant, testing his fortune as a merchant. Perhaps just as well: his letters suggest a self-centred, ill-disciplined youth, not the sort one would expect to hold steady in a crisis.[35] With the four younger children, Marietta tries to carry on as if these were normal times, though she can't always hide her fears, for them and for her absent husband; she'd grown used to having him at home all these years, and now he is nearly fifty-eight years old, and they have a new baby, called Totto after his father's brother, who has an eye infection that the nurse can't seem to cure. The children keep demanding: will the Spanish and Germans come here? Piero is thirteen, Guido a year or so younger, Baccina eight or nine. Guido writes to his father in Forlì:

We learn from your letter that you have bought such a beautiful chain for Baccina, who does nothing else but think of this beautiful little chain and pray God for you, that He should make you come back soon. We are not worrying about the lansquenets any more because you have promised us to try and be with us if anything should happen. We pray you to write to us if ever the enemy should think of coming and harming us.

I shall begin this Easter to play and sing and do three-part counterpoint. In Latin, I am getting to participles today. Ser Luca has read me almost all the first book of Ovid's Metamorphoses. *I want to recite it all to*

*you by heart as soon as you get home. Madonna Marietta gives you her
regards and sends you two shirts, two towels, two caps, three pairs of
hose and four handkerchiefs. She prays you to come back soon, and so do
all of us. Christ be with you, and keep you in prosperity.*[36]

Though the present makes exhausting demands on his strength,
Niccolò still thinks of his children's future. *To my dear son Guido
Machiavelli,* Niccolò writes from Imola. *I've had a letter from you
that has given me the greatest pleasure. If God grants you and me life,
I believe that I may make you a man of good standing, if you are willing to
do your share.* But you must study hard and take pains to learn letters and music – *for you know how much distinction is given me for what
little ability I possess. Thus, my son, if you want to please me and to bring
profit and honour to yourself, study, do well, and learn, because everyone
will help you if you help yourself.* He has not always been the best of
breadwinners, though the generosity of friends and his father's
example helped bring his family through the hardest times. Bernardo Machiavelli had shown his son that one can get by with little
and yet preserve one's independence, and that a frugal inner freedom is better for cities and souls than a well-paid servitude,
especially when one serves people or practices that are thoroughly
corrupt.

Guido has asked his father's advice about an unruly young mule
on one of their farms in Sant' Andrea. It seems Niccolò had assigned
him the task of checking with tenants about any problems they
might have and reporting back to his father, whose reply recalls the
fate of his alter ego in *The Ass*, the boy who wouldn't stop running, despite all the quack cures the *medici* poured down his throat.
*Since the young mule has gone mad, it must be treated just the reverse of
the way other crazies are; for they are tied up, and I want you to let it loose.*
Give it to Vangelo, tell him to take it to Montepugliano and then
take off its bridle and halter, and let it go wherever it likes. *Let it
regain its own way of life and work off its craziness. The village is big and
the beast small; it can do no one any harm.* And tell your mother that
I've never longed so much to return to Florence as I do now. *Just tell*

her that, whatever she hears, she should be of good cheer, since I shall be there before any danger comes.[37]

He confers constantly with Guicciardini, who, burdened with the thankless task of trying to command the pope's ungovernable troops, seems ready to give up hope of doing anything that might help save his master or his city. Though he keeps asking Clement for reinforcements around Florence, the bewildered pope does nothing, as if he were in a state of paralysis. The emperor's troops are getting closer, starving, terrorizing the countryside. Refugees crowd in from the countryside. There is not enough grain to feed everyone.

Then, on 16 April, Guicciardini decides to takes matters into his own hands. He orders all the papal troops at his disposal to go and defend Florence. Ten days later the people of Florence, too, take independent action.[38] The first spark comes from an accident: a man selling caps on a crowded square, a soldier shouting that his prices are too high and making as if to strike him, causing a nearby mule to bolt and stampede through the frightened throng. Then cries go up of *'Popolo e libertà!'* and people stream into the Piazza della Signoria. Young men seize control of the government palace. Niccolò's friend Luigi Guicciardini, Francesco's elder brother, tries to pacify the rioters from the rostrum. Together with Vettori, he summons an emergency meeting of the chief magistrates. Though most of these men are Medici clients, Vettori persuades them to vote unanimously in favour of ending Medici rule and banishing Ippolito, Alessandro and their associates from Florence.

This unplanned uprising takes Vettori, Filippo Strozzi, and their co-conspirator friends by surprise, scuppering all their carefully laid plans for an organized revolt. It all happens so fast that no guard is placed at the city gates or in the magistrates' palace. And whatever his frustrations with the Medici pope, Francesco Guicciardini is still Clement's lieutenant; he had sent troops to defend the city from outside attackers, not to provoke an anti-Medici rebellion. No one stops him from entering the city shortly after the uprising, together with a contingent of papal infantry who escort the underage Medici boys back to their family palace. Instead of the usual harsh reprisals taken against rebels, Guicciardini negotiates very moderate terms with Vettori. All those who took part in the rising are pardoned and Medici government is restored, after a brief respite.

But not for long. Instead of attacking Florence, imperial forces rapidly move to Rome. On 6 May, they sack the Holy City, the bloodiest attack in living memory, with famished German troops shouting, '*Vivat Luther Papa!*' as they smash sacred relics and plunder houses, shops, banks. Florentine merchants and bankers suffer terrible losses. Blaming the pope, now held captive by the emperor's troops, even the Medicis' stalwart friends turn against the unpopular government.

Filippo Strozzi had been released from his captivity at the end of March. Arriving in Florence during the sacking of Rome, he sets to work with Vettori, Vettori's brother-in-law Niccolò Capponi, and Luigi Guicciardini on plans for a second attempt to expel the Medici. Since they already have the people on side, their next most powerful weapon is Strozzi's wife. The last time Clarice de' Medici Strozzi found herself at the centre of a political storm, nearly twenty years before, she had been a mere girl whose controversial marriage helped pave the way for her family's return from exile. Now she is thirty-four, the mother of ten children, and she goes, carried by litter, to her old home, the Medici Palace, to request a peaceful end to Medici rule in Florence. After enduring her robust reproaches, Cardinal Passerini, guardian of the two Medici boys, agrees to leave the city. Filippo Strozzi arrives soon afterwards. His leadership of the coup is embraced by young patricians who have long waited for the chance to get rid of the Medici.

There is no record of Niccolò Machiavelli's movements during this latest Florentine revolution. We know only that Guicciardini sent him on 22 May to Civitavecchia, near Rome, where he was to discuss defences with the commander of the French fleet that had been called up to oppose the emperor; Niccolò may have been outside the city while his friends began negotiating a new republican constitution. The greatest challenge would be, as it had been after '94, to make a republic that had some chance of being accepted by both patricians and the wider populace. Niccolò surely hoped that the well-nigh bloodless coup might lead to the creation of a government resembling the one he'd sketched in his *Discursus* seven years before: one where power is shared among different parts of the citizen body, with the largest share held by a revived Great Council, the voice of the people.

Instead he returns, at the end of May, to a city almost as divided as it had been in the last days of Savonarola. Disagreements had flared up among its new leaders about how fast or far to move towards a broad-based popular government. Niccolò Capponi, son of the celebrated Piero who defied the French king in '94, is elected Gonfalonier for a year, backed by a wing of Savonarolan-party republicans. The new government passes sumptuary laws that regulate luxury in dress, prohibit gambling and ban certain books, provoking a backlash from more secular-minded republicans. Punitive taxes are imposed on some patricians more than others, according, many complained, to their political allegiances; men like Francesco Guicciardini who had held prominent posts under the Medici are hit particularly hard. As for Machiavelli, when elections come up for the reformed Chancery, he puts his name up for his old post. But another man with no experience is chosen, the candidate of the rejuvenated Savonarolan faction. The revenge of history: Niccolò had first entered the Chancery in '98 after his anti-Savonarolan supporters had pushed a Savonarola partisan out of his office.

Lacking any sources that tell us what he thought or did in the wake of this disappointment, most biographers, one borrowing from another, are apt to repeat the following speculations. The rebuff to his hopes of a return to political life, they surmise, must have thrown Machiavelli into a profound depression. He was a political man through and through, a man in love with the *vita activa*, whose passion had been thwarted for fifteen years. And now, even with the Medici gone, his dreams of recovering his old place in the Palazzo Vecchio had been crushed almost as soon as they'd been dreamt. Realizing that he had probably lost his last chance to become a political player again, able to serve his city in deeds and not mere words, his spirits sank lower than they'd ever been, fatally damaging his health.

But it is hard to fit this version of events with the resilience Niccolò had shown through far more painful setbacks in his life. For *strong republics and excellent men retain the same spirit and their same dignity in every fortune.*[39] In his *History of Rome*, Livy has the great general Furius Camillus say, 'Holding great honours and powers did not exalt my spirits, nor did exile depress them,' and Niccolò has made these words a rule for himself. Not one he could always live up to, to be sure – he has endured many bouts of dejection – but a standard nonetheless that described how he wished to live his life. In one way or another, under different guises, he'd never stopped expressing essentially the same, firm judgements about politics, republics, freedom, and free speech. Whatever the obstacles set before him, he had always found ways to do or to say what he thought needed to be said or done. When he could not write freely, he wrote even more. If one way of serving the new republic was now closed to him, he could discover others.

And no one knew better than he did that there is more than one way to do politics, and that the right kind of words – words bearing truths that cut through appearances to the heart of things – can be as powerful as deeds, are themselves deeds. Whether he was scribbling down notes of emergency meetings in the government palazzo, talking to kings, popes, and popes' sons on his missions, or reading his Livy and Plutarch in the quiet of his study and composing books and comedies, Machiavelli had never stopped doing politics, never stopped trying to form a republic that had better chances of lasting and thriving than the one he had served. He'd always striven to do what he could for his city, he'd written to Guicciardini a few years back, *whenever I was able to help her out – if not with deeds, then with words; if not with words, then with signs.*[40]

It seems unlikely, then, that despair over the loss of an election was the main cause of his subsequent illness. His exertions of the past year with the new militia and preparations for war, riding up and down Italy as much as he'd done in his thirties, taking little care of what he ate or drank, worries about his family's safety while they waited for the Spanish and Germans to descend on Florence, a prehistory of recurring stomach troubles, mentioned in his letter to Guicciardini, which he treated with some rather dodgy pharmaceuticals: all this might have wrecked his ageing body even if he'd won the election and returned in triumph to his old post. On 20 June, he feels a terrible clawing in his guts, perhaps from a perforated ulcer or peritonitis. The medications he takes only make it worse. Marietta sends their boys to summon doctors, relatives, friends, a priest. Zanobi Buondelmonti and Luigi Alamanni are back in Florence after five years of exile; they rush to his bedside, together with other friends from the Orti Oricellari, and Filippo Strozzi.

In the *Prince*, he speaks of his own *great and continuous malignity of fortune* in the dark times that followed the fall of the republic.[41] Now, at his deathbed, Fortuna seems to have given him a last savage kick up the backside. Just when he was starting to be someone in the rotten Medici world, that world was overthrown – probably with his complicity – and replaced by a new one where he is no one, again. He leaves behind next to nothing to support his large family. And after all his life's work to found a true republic in Florence, he will end life in a republic as badly ordered as the one that had collapsed in 1512, a republic at war with itself.

Then again: he has always said that there are different paths to glory, and different kinds of glory.[42] Most people start out measuring their life's success by how much acclaim they win from their contemporaries. But as they grow older they think ever more about whether they have done anything that will be worth remembering after they die. And what better way to achieve immortality among one's fellow humans than to write books, poems, plays full of powerful truths – works that speak to people in all times and *in any city whatever*?[43] Those who write such books can hope to carry on conversations with others long after their bodies have gone to dust. If people cannot act on or do not value Machiavelli's truths in Florence during his lifetime, they might do so in another city, at another time. He is not the first man who, finding himself *unable to form a republic in reality* because the times were hostile to his ideals, tried to show how to do it through printed or handwritten words, words that might be copied over and over and keep acting on future readers long after he is gone, as had *Aristotle, Plato, and many others.*

Fra Matteo comes to give him the last rites, to which he duly submits, while Marietta and his friends stand by. Vettori cannot be there, or Guicciardini. But the latter had said to him a few years before: 'Your honour would be stained, Niccolò, if you started worrying about your soul at your age. Since you've always lived in a contrary belief, your worries would be attributed rather to senility than to goodness.'[44] An apocryphal story relates that, before he made his confession, Niccolò told his grieving friends about a dream he'd had. In it he saw a crowd of people, emaciated and in rags. When he asked who they were, he was told that they were the blessed souls of Paradise, because it is written, 'Blessed are the poor, for they shall reign in heaven.'[45] These vanished; then he saw a gathering of people in royal and courtly robes, deep in conversation about politics and philosophy. Among them he recognized Plato, Plutarch, Tacitus, and other famous men of antiquity. Asking who these were, he received the answer that they were condemned to Hell, because it is written: 'Knowledge of sacred things is inimical to God.' Asked which group he would like to join, he answered: 'I'd rather burn in Hell for all eternity with the second lot than suffer in Paradise with the first.'

He dies the next day. Marietta asks their thirteen-year-old son, Piero, to convey the news of Niccolò's death to his maternal uncle Francesco Nelli in Pisa.

I have the lamentable duty of informing you that our father, Niccolò, died on the 22nd of this month, from pains in the belly caused by some medicine that he took on the 20th. He allowed Brother Matteo, who kept him company until his death, to hear the confession of his sins. Our father left us in the deepest poverty, as you know.

Aftermath

The 1527 republic survived for three unhappy years after Machia-velli's death. It ended after the ten-month-long Siege of Florence by Imperial and Spanish troops, from October 1529 to August 1530, which put an end to Florentine independence and republican gov-ernment for over three hundred years. Alessandro de' Medici, now twenty years old, was installed at the new pro-imperial govern-ment's head; in 1532, the emperor gave him the title of Duke of Florence. Other than the short-lived republic of 1494–1512, the Med-ici had dominated the city for a hundred years, but until now without holding the official rank of nobility. Henceforth they were nobles, not of free Florence but of the Habsburg Empire.

The new era of Medici rule did not usher in an era of tranquillity and good order. Rivalries between Alessandro de' Medici and his cousin Ippolito, nominal head of Florence's previous Medici government, turned bitter after Clement chose Alessandro as head after 1530 and made Ippolito a cardinal instead. When Ippolito died five years later, it was widely rumoured that Alessandro had ordered his murder, fearing that his cousin was about to expose his corruptions. In 1537, Alessandro was murdered by another relative, Lorenzino de' Medici. Charles V appointed seventeen-year-old Cosimo, from another branch of the Medici family, as Florence's new duke.

Machiavelli's friends tried to weather these changes of govern-ment, but soon gave up, first on the turbulent new republic and later on the Medici regime. Thanks to his years of service to Popes Leo and Clement, Francesco Guicciardini was seen as an enemy to the 1527 republic. Vettori's long-standing connections with the Medici also made him suspect, notwithstanding his leading role in the revolution. By the summer of 1527, both men were living in their villas outside Florence, for their safety. They and their families soon faced financial ruin from forced loans and punitive taxes. Filippo Strozzi, who had led the coup, found himself in similar straits. He went into voluntary exile in France in 1528.

When the republic was toppled in 1530, Strozzi, Vettori, and Guicciardini returned to Florence as key men in the restored Medici government. But within a few years they all fell out with their masters, accusing Duke Alessandro and his cronies of tyrannical rule. Niccolò Machiavelli would not have been surprised. He had always said that there were no middle ways between a true republic and a principality; you have to choose one or the other, since a prince who comes to power in a republic won't rest until he has risen to absolute authority.[1] So if you choose princes, expect them or their progeny to start seizing more powers than you willingly gave them, until they become tyrants.

After Alessandro de' Medici's death, Filippo Strozzi and other Florentine exiles tried to foment another uprising in the city, with backing from King François. Vettori supported the revolt; so, more reluctantly, did Guicciardini. All of them hoped to restore an oligarchic government. But their hopes were crushed when Cosimo de' Medici sent his best troops to oppose the exiles' army. In another case of history coming back to bite, the commander of these troops that dealt the final death blow to Florence's republican hopes was Alessandro Vitelli – son of Paolo Vitelli, the captain whose summary execution had caused such a scandal when Machiavelli was Second Chancellor to the Republic. Incarcerated in the Bargello, Strozzi was found dead one day beside a bloody sword and a scrap of paper with some lines from Virgil; he was declared a suicide, though many doubted it.[2] Both Vettori and Guicciardini died within the next three years.

Nothing more was heard of Marietta after her husband's death, and little is known about their children. Guido Machiavelli took priestly orders and, perhaps inspired by his early studies of Ovid and his father's example, continued his literary studies; he is thought to have written at least one comedy, though it is not extant.

Confounding the singularly unheroic impression he gives in his letters, Niccolò's difficult second son, Lodovico, died fighting for the republic in the Siege of Florence.[3] Baccina's son, Giuliano de' Ricci, became the custodian of his grandfather's writings.

In 1557, in its efforts to deal with the outbreak of heresies encouraged by the Reformation, the Catholic Church under Pope Paul IV established an Index of Prohibited Books. All of Machiavelli's works were soon put on the list. Giuliano de' Ricci fought hard to persuade the Vatican's censors to allow publication of an expurgated version of his grandfather's works, with the offending passages cut.[4] His efforts were in vain. Machiavelli's books remained on the Index until 1890.

In one of several passages in the *Discourses* that must have helped seal this fate, Niccolò observes that the Christian 'sect', as he called it, had always declared war on ideas and writings that it could not control – and especially on those that presented ordinary human reasoning, not priestly authority, as the best source of guidance in private and political life. Early Church zealots had ruthlessly *persecuted all the ancient memories* of pagan sages and religions, *burning the books of the poets and the historians, ruining images, and spoiling every other thing that might convey some sign of antiquity*.[5] Now, his own works, which seek to revive the pre-Christian wisdom and moral standards of the ancients he loved best, would suffer a similar fate.

But he always had a few defenders, though they had to be careful how and how far they defended him, even when they lived in realms that had rejected the supreme authority of the Church of Rome. In 1594, Alberico Gentili, a Protestant exile from Italy who became Regius Professor of Civil Law at Oxford, declared that 'in that branch of philosophy which deals with morals and politics' Machiavelli was among modern writers 'the most distinguished of his class'. His notoriety had already spread beyond Florence and Italy, with both Catholics like Reginald Pole and Protestants such as Innocent Gentillet publishing invectives charging him with impiety and immorality. But 'if I give a just estimate of his purpose in writing,' countered Gentili, 'and choose to reinforce his words by a sounder interpretation, I do not see why I cannot free from such charges the reputation of this man who has now passed away. If our purpose is to interpret authors favourably, we shall palliate many faults in this man also, or we shall at least tolerate in him those that we tolerate in Plato, Aristotle, and others who have committed offences not unlike his.'[6]

Notes

Preface

1 Pole, *Apology*.
2 Among Machiavelli's defenders were the English philosopher and statesman Francis Bacon; Alberico Gentili, an Italian Protestant who took refuge in England and became a professor of law at Oxford; the political theorist James Harrington and his friend Henry Neville, a publisher and translator; the Dutch-Jewish philosopher Baruch Spinoza; and a long line of writers associated with the French Enlightenment.
3 Gentili, III.ix.
4 See Gentili, II.9.
5 Italics are used throughout this book for most quotes in Machiavelli's original words, while paraphrased Machiavelli quotes are given in quotation marks. Where his words are presented as dialogue, however, I have given the original and paraphrases together without italics.
6 Rousseau, III.5–6; Amelot, Bayle and Diderot in Soll, 102.
7 Spinoza, *Tractatus Politicus*, V.7.
8 Neville (1691) remarks that 'If Machiavelli was "a little too punctual in designing these Monsters" by drawing them "to life in all their Lineaments and Colours", his purpose was to exhibit their stratagems "to all mankind",' so that they might steer clear of them. Neville adds that the *Prince* is both 'a Satyr' of princes' tyrannical tendencies 'and a true Character of them'.
9 I set out these ideas in Benner, *Machiavelli's Ethics* and *Machiavelli's Prince*.
10 Machiavelli to Guicciardini, 17 May 1521.
11 Machiavelli to Vettori, 26 August 1513.
12 We can't be sure, of course, that everything reported was actually said. But most of the exchanges I turn into dialogues are probable

enough, and always revealing of Machiavelli's or his contemporaries' views on the subjects at hand.

13 Machiavelli to Guicciardini, after 21 October 1525 (date unknown).

1. *The Importance of Good Faith*

1 Dialogue closely follows Bernardo Machiavelli's *Ricordi*, 15–23.
2 On Bernardo's library, see Atkinson, *Debts, Dowries, Donkeys*.
3 According to Bartolomeo Scala in his *Dialogue on Laws*, 167–9.
4 Legation to Baglioni, 11 April 1505.
5 Bernardo Machiavelli, *Ricordi*, 26–31.
6 *Discourses*, I.45.

2. *Take Nothing on Authority*

1 *Discourses*, I.59. On Romulus, I.16–18.
2 *Discourses*, I.53, III.9–10.
3 'Sonnet to Messer Bernardo his Father', translated in Gilbert, ed., Vol. 2, 1012.
4 Scala, *Dialogue on Laws*, 212–13.
5 *Discourses*, I.58.
6 Machiavelli to Vettori, 5 January 1514.
7 Machiavelli to Vettori, 10 December 1513.
8 *Discourses*, I.39.

3. *Do Not Be Deceived by False Glory*

1 *Florentine Histories*, VII.28.
2 *Discourses*, I.10.
3 *Florentine Histories*, VII.24, 29–30.
4 Brown in Connell and Zorzi, eds., *Florentine Tuscany*, 43–5.
5 Below based on *Florentine Histories*, VII.2–4.

6 Following a common usage among historians, I use 'patrician' for what Florentines called the *ottimati* or optimates, members of the wealthy upper strata of Florentine society.

7 On Girolamo Machiavelli's political views and activity, see Raffaela Zaccaria, 'Girolamo Machiavelli', in *Dizionario biografico degli italiani*, Vol. 67 (2006). Treccani: online resource (www.treccani.it).

8 *Discourses*, III.6.

9 Atkinson, 39; Ricci, *Priorista*.

4. Beware of Doctors

1 Below from *Florentine Histories*, VIII.6–9.

2 *Florentine Histories*, VIII.9; account of Jacopo Pazzi's posthumous treatment: Landucci, 18–19.

3 *Florentine Histories*, VIII.1.

4 *Florentine Histories*, VIII.11.

5 Some examples of folk wisdom: Landucci, 152, 155, 173, 220; poor people and plague: Trexler, 362–4.

6 *Prince*, 21.

7 Ficino, *Consiglio contro la pestilentia*.

8 Shaw and Welch, *Making and Marketing Medicine in Renaissance Florence*, 248.

9 *Florentine Histories*, VIII.22.

10 *Discourses*, I.53.

11 *The Ass*, 49–60.

5. Have No Fear of Giants

1 Trexler, 448–9.

2 Plutarch, *Moralia*, I.

3 *Discourses*, I.10.

4 See Benner, *Machiavelli's Ethics*, Ch. 4.

5 *Prince*, Dedication.

6 *Discourses*, I.58.

7 *Prince*, 22 and 23.

8 Machiavelli to Cardinal Lopez, December 1497.

9 Especially in *Prince*, 5; *Discourses*, II.4.

6. How to Speak of Princes

1 Landucci, 50.

2 *Florentine Histories*, VIII.36; Guicciardini, *History of Florence*, 74.

3 'Snake-charmers', trans. Gilbert, ed., Vol. 2, 881–2.

4 To Lorenzo from Petrus Bonus Avogarius, medical doctor, Ross, 301–2 (11 February 1489); Piero Leoni to Lorenzo, 19 August 1491.

5 *Florentine Histories*, VIII.36.

6 Lines in bold are quotations from Savonarola's sermons in *Selected Writings*; here, 157–8, xix–xxi, 36, 60–62.

7 *Florentine Histories*, VIII.36.

8 Festivities: Vasari, *Lives*, 4; Plaisance, 21.

9 Machiavelli, 'Pastorale', trans. based on Gilbert, ed., Vol. 1, 97–9.

10 *Discourses*, I.17.

11 From the final chapter of the *Florentine Histories*, VIII.36.

12 Guicciardini, *History of Florence*, 73.

13 *Discourses*, II.24; *Prince*, 20.

7. Recover Your Freedom

1 Guicciardini, *History of Florence*.

2 Machiavelli, *A Discourse on Remodelling the Government of Florence*.

3 *Discourses*, I.20.

4 *Discourses*, I.2.

5 Savonarola, *Selected Writings*, 69.

6 *Florentine Histories*, I.1–5. Machiavelli himself avoids the word 'barbarians' here and describes the invaders as impressively well-ordered, unlike their shambolic Roman prey.

7 See Herodotus, Book VIII; and the end of *Cyropaedia* by Xenophon, after Livy the author Machiavelli most often cites by name. For Machiavelli's views on conspiracies, see *Discourses*, III.6; *Prince*, 19.

8 Popular reports: Landucci, 56; Guicciardini, *History of Florence*, 86–7.

9 Guicciardini, *History of Italy*, 34–7.

10 Landucci, 58.

11 *Prince*, 3.

12 On the following events: Guicciardini, *History of Florence*, 88–96.

13 Landucci, 60.

14 Plaisance, 47–8; Landucci, 65–6.

15 *Decennale* I, lines 25–30.

16 *Decennale* I, lines 112–16.

17 *Prince*, 13.

18 *Decennale* I, lines 34–6; Guicciardini, *History of Florence*, 99–100.

19 'The Natures of Florentine Men', trans. Gilbert, ed., Vol. 3, 1436.

20 *Decennale* I, lines 37–9.

21 *Discourses*, II.2.

22 *Discourses*, I.20.

23 *Discourses*, II.2.

24 *Florentine Histories*, II.34.

25 *Discourses*, II.2.

26 Guicciardini, *History of Italy*, 94–5; Luzzati, 23–32.

27 *Decennale* I, lines 22–4.

8. The Way to Paradise

1 *Discourses*, I.16.

2 Landucci, 73.

3 Savonarola, *Treatise on the Constitution and Government of Florence*, in Watkins, trans. & ed., *Humanism and Liberty*, 254.

4 Landucci, 90–92.

5 Guicciardini, *History of Italy*, 76–83.

6 Savonarola, *Treatise on the Constitution*, 236–57.

7 Landucci, 88.

8 Machiavelli, *A Discourse on Remodelling the Government of Florence*; see Ch. 16.

9 Savonarola, *Treatise on the Constitution*, especially 250–57.

10 *Discourses*, I.3.

11 Machiavelli, *Articles for a Pleasure Company*, trans. Gilbert, ed., Vol. 2, 865–8.

12 See Henderson, *Piety and Charity in Late Medieval Florence*.

13 *Mandragola*, III.9; *Belfagor*, trans. Gilbert, ed., Vol. II, 869–77.

14 On Adriani and Machiavelli see Godman, *From Poliziano to Machiavelli*, especially 144–51.

15 Biagio Buonaccorsi and Andrea di Romolo to Machiavelli, 23 August 1500.

16 *Exhortation to Penitence*, trans. Gilbert, ed., Vol. 1, 170–74. Lightly paraphrased.

17 Petrarch also gets the last words in the *Prince*.

18 On Christ see *Discourses*, I.12, III.1.4.

19 *Discourses*, I.56.

20 I say more about Machiavelli's religion in *Machiavelli's Ethics*, 386–406.

21 Machiavelli to Giovan Battista Soderini, 13–21 September 1506.

22 *Discourses*, I.11.

23 *Florentine Histories*, IV. 1.

24 Their letters are in Savonarola, *Selected Writings*, 275–9.

25 Landucci, 80, 99–100.

26 Savonarola, *Selected Writings*, 59.

27 Processions and bonfire: Pseudo-Burlamaqui in Plaisance, 68–9.

28 Quoted in Martines, *Scourge and Fire*, 135.

29 Discussion of conspirators' right to appeal is based on Guicciardini, *History of Florence*, 129–36.

30 *Discourses*, I.45.

31 Landucci, 136–8; Guicciardini, *History of Florence*, 137; Plaisance, 18–26, 68.

32 Machiavelli to Ricciardo Becchi, 9 March 1498.

33 Savonarola, *Selected Writings*, 332.

34 On the war of friars and the trial of fire see Parenti, 65, note 1; Landucci, 133–6.

35 Fachard, ed. *Consulte e pratiche*, 30 March 1498.

36 *Prince*, 6.

37 *Decennale* I, lines 154–65.

38 Landucci, 137.

39 *Discourses*, I.54.

40 Fachard, ed., *Consulte e pratiche*, 27 March–8 April 1498. Also see Guicciardini, *History of Florence*, 142–5.

41 This and below from *Florentine Histories*, III.5.

9. So Blinded Are You by Present Greed

1   *Mission to Piombino*, 20 November 1498.

2   Biagio Buonaccorsi to Machiavelli, 19 July 1499.

3   Biagio Buonaccorsi to Machiavelli, 19 and 27 July 1499.

4   On Biagio's background see Fachard, *Biagio Buonaccorsi*, 11; Guidi, *Un segretario militante*, 113–15; Biagio's own *Diario dall'anno 1498 all'anno 1512*.

5   Agostino Vespucci to Machiavelli, 20 October 1500.

6   Agostino Vespucci to Machiavelli, 20 October 1500.

7   *Florentine Histories*, VII.22.

8   *Florentine Histories*, VIII.34.

9   Caterina Sforza is one of two female 'princes' discussed in Machiavelli's *Prince*; he uses the same word for male and female rulers. The other is Dido, Queen of Carthage.

10 Based on *Legation to Caterina Sforza*, 16 July 1499.

11 *Prince*, 9, 19.

12 Below from *Legation to Caterina Sforza*, 17–24 July 1499.

13 *Prince*, 21; *Discourses*, II.15.

14 *Prince*, 18.

15 *Discourses*, II.24; *Prince*, 20.

16 My account of the Vitelli episode draws especially on Guicciardini, *History of Florence*, 152–73.

17 *Prince*, 12.

18 *Prince*, 12.

19 Machiavelli, *Discorso sopra Pisa (Discourse on Pisa)* in *Opere*, I, 3–4; *Prince*, 5.

20 Connell and Zorzi, eds., *Florentine Tuscany*, 71–3.

21 Developments in Pisa: Luzzati, 119–20.

22 *Prince*, 5.

23 *Discorso sopra Pisa (Discourse on Pisa)* in *Opere*, I, 3–4.

24 Fachard, ed., *Consulte e pratiche*, 13 August–1 October 1499.

25 Landucci, 159–60.

26 Biagio Buonaccorsi, *Diario*.

27 Machiavelli to a Chancery Secretary in Lucca, early October 1499.

28 *Discourses*, I.8.

29 *Discourses*, I.31.

30 *Discourses*, I.45, I.34.

10. *Build Dykes and Dams*

1 'Sonnett to Messer Barnardo His Father', trans. in Gilbert, ed., Vol. 2, 1012.

2 Burchard, 180–81.

3 Fachard, ed., *Consulte e pratiche*, 7 December 1499.

4 Fachard, ed., *Consulte e pratiche*, 20 March 1500.

5 *Legation to the Army in the Field against the Pisans*, 8–28 July 1500.

6 See *Prince*, 17; *Art of War*, 127–9.

7 From *Notula per uno che va ambasciadore in Francia (Notes for One Going as an Ambassador to France)*, in *Opere*, I, 52–6.

8 Below based on *Legations to the Court of France*, July–November 1500.

9 Machiavelli's remarks on the French: 'The Nature of the French' (*De natura Gallorum*) and 'An Account of the Affairs of France', in Detmold, ed., Vol. 4, 404–20.

10 *Discourses*, II.15.

11 'Confidential Instructions', in Detmold, ed., Vol. 4, 421–5.

12 *Prince*, 26.

13 *Tercets on Ambition*, trans. Gilbert, ed., Vol. 2, lines 122–3.

14 *Prince*, 24.

15 *Prince*, 3, 4, 5.

16 *Prince*, 25.

17 Totto Machiavelli to Niccolò, 27 August 1500; Biagio Buonaccorsi and Andrea di Romolo to Machiavelli, 23 August 1500.

18 'The Nature of the French', in Detmold, ed., 419–20.

19 *Legations to the Court of France*, 26 September, 2 October, 25 October 1500.

20 Florentine Italian, which Machiavelli and others sometimes call 'Tuscan'.

21 Agostino Vespucci to Machiavelli, 20–29 October 1500.

22 'Confidential Instructions', in Detmold, ed., Vol. 4, 421–5.

23 Machiavelli would expand on these thoughts in *Prince*, 3.

24 Landucci, 174.

25 Burchard, 189–90.

26 Landucci, 178–83.

27 *First Legation to Valentino, Opere*, II, 623–4.

28 Guicciardini, *History of Florence*, 258–9.

29 Agostino Vespucci to Machiavelli, 25 August 1501.

11. Fortune Loves Impetuous Young Men

1 Fachard, ed., *Consulte e pratiche*, 10 September 1502.

2 *First Legation to the Duke of Valentinois*, 26 June 1502.

3 'A Description of the Method Used by Duke Valentino in Killing Vitellozzo Vitelli, Oliverotto da Fermo, and Others [at Sinigaglia]', trans. Gilbert, ed., Vol. 1, 163–9.

4 See *Prince*, 7, on 'the vulgar'.

5 'Confidential Instructions', in Detmold, ed., Vol. 4, 421–5.

6 Cicero, *De officiis*, I.xiii.44–7.

7 *Prince*, 18; 'Method Used by Duke Valentino'.

8 All dialogue below based closely on *Second Legation to the Duke of Valentinois*, 5 October 1502–21 January 1503.

9 *Prince*, 7.

10 *Tercets on Fortune*, trans. Gilbert, ed., Vol. 2, lines 106–11.

11 *Florentine Histories*, I.24.

12 *Prince*, 7.

13 *Prince*, 1. Machiavelli plays with the contrast throughout his book. See Benner, *Machiavelli's Prince*.

14 *Prince*, 6 and 7.

15 *Discourses*, III.31.

16 *Tercets on Fortune*, lines 160–62, 166–8.

17 *Prince*, 7.

18 *Prince*, 12 (laws and arms), 9 (hostile people), 17 (cruelty).

19 *Prince*, 9, 21.

20 *Discourses*, I.18.

21 'On the Method of Treating the Rebellious Peoples of the Valdichiana', in Gilbert, ed., vol. 1, 161–2.

22 Biagio Buonaccorsi to Machiavelli, 21 October 1502.

23 *Prince*, 19.

24 *Prince*, 16.

25 *Prince*, 9.

26 Little is known about him beyond Machiavelli's somewhat opaque remarks.

27 *Prince*, 7.

28 Burchard, 216.

29 Fachard, ed., *Consulte e pratiche*, 6 May–August 1503.

30 Burchard, 225–6.

31 *Decennale* I, lines 442–7.

32 This and below from *Legations to Rome*, October–December 1503.

33 *Decennale* I, lines 472–4.

34 Letters from Totto Machiavelli, 17 November 1503; Piero del Nero, 16 November; Luca Ugolini, 11 November; Biagio Buonaccorsi, 17 November and 4 December.

35 Marietta to Machiavelli, 24 November 1503 (shortened).

12. How to Win

1 See *Discorso sopra la provisione del dannaio* ('Discourse on the Provision of Money'), in *Opere*, I, 12–16.

2 *Decennale* I, lines 523–26.

3 On Machiavelli's influence on the militia see Guidi, *Un segretario militante*.

4 *Prince*, 5.

5 Luzzati, 16–19.

6 Agostino Vespucci to Machiavelli, 13 October 1502.

7 Machiavelli to Agnolo Tucci, November–December 1503; Biagio Buonaccorsi to Machiavelli, 4 December 1503; Cardinal Soderini's praise in a letter to the Florentine Signoria, December 1503 (*Mission to the Court of Rome*, 387–8).

8 See letters from Cardinal Francesco Soderini to Machiavelli, 26 October and 29 May 1504.

9 *Prince*, 12.

10 *La Cagione dell'ordinanza* ('Discourse on the Organization of the State for Arms'), in *Opere*, I, 26–31 (untranslated).

11 Militia arguments: from *Cagione* and *Provisione dell'ordinanza*, in *Opere*, I, 26–43.

12 Machiavelli to the Ten of War, 2 January and 5 February 1506.

13 *Prince*, 10.

14 *Florentine Histories*, III.1.

15 *Prince*, 10.

16 *Cagione dell'ordinanza*, in *Opere*, I, 26–31.

17 *Frammento di discorso sulla milizia a Cavallo* ('Fragment of a Discourse on the Cavalry Militia'), *Opere*, I, 43.

18 Details in Landucci, 218.

19 *Discourses*, I.3; *Prince*, 17; *Art of War*, Book I; *Discourses*, I.21.

20 Landucci, 218.

21 Agostino Vespucci to Machiavelli, 14 March 1506.

22 Ercole Bentivoglio to Machiavelli, 25 February 1506.

23 *Decennale* I, lines 547–50.

24 Biagio Buonaccorsi to Machiavelli, 6 and 11 October 1506; *Legazioni. Commissarie. Scritti di governo*, xi.

25 Cardinal Francesco Soderini to Machiavelli, 4 March 1506, 15 December 1506.

26 Guicciardini, *History of Florence*, 258–9.

27 See *Legations to the Emperor of Germany*, 25 December 1507–14 June 1508.

28 *Ba be bi*, numbers, etc., are undeciphered symbols; most words are deciphered 'decoys'. These were written by Machiavelli and Vettori in Bolzano/Bozen on 25 January and 14 February 1508, published in *Leg.Com.Scritti*. Machiavelli's correspondence often refers to codes

used in personal letters, as when Biagio writes: 'Do not answer concerning the code above, or use the style that I have, that is, write in code.' 15–18 October 1502, 5 November 1502.

29 These methods are set out in Machiavelli's *Art of War*, VII.123–9.

30 *Legations to the Emperor of Germany.*

31 These apparent code words appear in letters in Machiavelli's private correspondence and have not been decoded. The specific meanings suggested here are purely speculative.

32 *Second Legation to the Duke of Valentinois*, 8 January 1503.

33 See Benner, *Machiavelli's Prince*, Ch. 9.

34 Words verbatim from Fachard, ed., *Consulte e pratiche*, summer–autumn 1508, 222–6 (no precise date given).

35 Piero Soderini to Machiavelli, 26 August 1508.

36 *Discourses*, I.39.

37 Guicciardini, *History of Florence*, 304.

38 *Discourses*, III.16, I.53.

39 Guicciardini, *History of Florence*, 311–13.

40 *Discourses*, III.48.

41 Filippo Casavecchia to Machiavelli, 30 July 1507; Biagio Buonaccorsi to Machiavelli, 21 February 1509.

42 As recounted in Luzzati.

43 *Third Commission to the Army before Pisa*, 15 March 1509.

44 *Legations*, 16 April 1509.

45 Filippo Casavecchia to Machiavelli, 17 June 1509.

46 *Discourses*, II.27.

47 All in *Opere*, I.

48 *Prince*, 3; *Discourses*, II.20.

49 *Discourses*, II.32.

50 *Prince*, 20; *Discourses*, II.24.

51 *Discourses*, II.23.

52 *Prince*, 21; *Florentine Histories*, IV.27, IV.16.

53 Text of the peace treaty: in Benvenuti, 129–46.

54 Biagio Buonaccorsi in Fachard, *Biagio Buonaccorsi*, 18–19; Agostino Vespucci to Machiavelli, 8 June 1509; Filippo Casavecchia to Machiavelli, 17 June 1509.

55 Guicciardini, *History of Florence*, 298–303; Bullard, 45–59.
56 Lorenzo Strozzi, *Vita di Filippo Strozzi*.
57 *Discourses*, III.3 and I.16.
58 *Discourses*, III.30.

13. *Measure Yourself and Limit Your Hopes*

1 Based on *Third Mission to the Court of France*, 2 June 1510.
2 *Second Mission to the Court of Rome*, 28 September 1506.
3 *Prince*, 3.
4 *Second Mission to the Court of Rome*, 3 October 1506.
5 Machiavelli contrasts the two men in *Discourses*, III.9.
6 Alexander. *Prince*, 18; Julius to Machiavelli: *Second Mission to the Court of Rome*, 3 October 1506.
7 *Third Mission to the Court of France*, 7 July 1510.
8 Below from *Third Mission to the Court of France*, 2 June 1510–24 September 1511.
9 Della Valle to Machiavelli, 25 August 1510.
10 Machiavelli to Giovan Battista Soderini, 13–21 September 1506.
11 Landucci, 242; Lorenzo Strozzi, *Vita di Filippo Strozzi*.
12 Biagio Buonaccorsi to Machiavelli, 28 December 1509.
13 Machiavelli to Luigi Guicciardini, 8 December 1509; shortened and lightly paraphrased.
14 Biagio Buonaccorsi to Machiavelli, 28 December 1509.
15 Trexler, 'La prostitution florentine au XVe siècle'.
16 Giovanni Girolami to Machiavelli, 21 October 1510.
17 Landucci, 243.
18 Devonshire Jones, 45–6.
19 *Commissions to Pisa*, 7 May 1512, in Detmold, ed., Vol. 4, 304–5.
20 *Discourses*, III.33.
21 Machiavelli, 'Letter to a Gentlewoman', in *Machiavelli and His Friends*, 16 September 1512. Also see Guidi, 'Machiavelli al tempo del Sacco di Prato'.
22 *Discourses*, II.27.

23 'Letter to a Gentlewoman', in *Machiavelli and His Friends*, probably September 1512.

24 'Letter to a Gentlewoman', in *Machiavelli and His Friends*, probably September 1512.

25 Vettori, *Sommario*.

26 Vettori, *Sommario*.

27 A note on this version of events, which comes from Vettori's *Sommario*: that text was written in 1527, when Vettori had reason to present himself as pro-republic. But his account is not improbable, given the trust Machiavelli and Soderini placed in him.

28 'Letter to a Gentlewoman', in *Machiavelli and His Friends*, probably September 1512.

29 Vettori, *Sommario*.

30 *The Ass*, I.88–90, 97–99.

31 *Ai Palleschi*, in *Opere*, I, 87–9.

32 Ridolfi, 130.

33 Biagio Buonaccorsi to Machiavelli, 22 August 1510.

34 *The Ass*, II.22–4, 31–3.

35 Sonnets to Giuliano de' Medici, trans. Gilbert, ed., Vol. 2, 1013–15.

36 Landucci, 267–8.

14. Be Like the Fox

1 Machiavelli to Giovanni Vernacci, 4 August 1513.

2 Vettori to Machiavelli, 21 April 1513.

3 Machiavelli to Vettori, 18 March 1513.

4 Landucci, 268.

5 *Discourses*, I.8.

6 Tacitus, *Dialogue on Oratory*.

7 Landucci, 265–6.

8 Vettori to Machiavelli, 30 March 1513.

9 Vettori to Machiavelli, 30 March, 12 July 1513.

10 *Discourses*, I.58.

11 Machiavelli to Vettori, 9 April 1513.

12 Machiavelli to Vettori, 9 April 1513; Vettori to Machiavelli, 15 March on Casavecchia; Machiavelli to Vettori, 25 August on Donato del Corno.

13 *The Ass*, II.10–13.

14 *The Ass*, IV.83–4.

15 *The Ass*, I.31–90.

16 Here and below: *The Ass*, III–IV.

17 *The Ass*, IV.132–5, 137–41.

18 *The Ass*, I.16–18.

19 *The Ass*, I.25–7.

20 Machiavelli to Vettori, 13 March 1513.

21 Machiavelli to Vettori, 10 December 1513.

22 Machiavelli to Vettori, 18 March 1513.

23 *Machiavelli and His Friends*, 515, note 21.

24 Vettori to Machiavelli, 21 April 1513.

25 Machiavelli to Vettori, 20 June 1513.

26 For a wonderful study of the relationship between his letters and the *Prince*, see Najemy, *Between Friends*.

27 Both in *Prince*, 21. On Ferdinand see Benner, 'Machiavelli's Ironies', and *Machiavelli's Prince*, Ch. 21.

28 *Prince*, 25.

29 Vettori to Machiavelli, 23 November 1513.

30 Quotes below from Machiavelli to Vettori, 10 December 1513.

31 *Discourses*, III.2.

32 Livy, I.56–9.

33 *Discourses*, III.2.

34 Machiavelli to Vettori, 10 December 1513.

35 See Benner, *Machiavelli's Prince*.

36 *Prince*, 7.

37 *Prince*, 7.

38 Machiavelli to Vettori, 10 December 1513.

39 *Prince*, Dedication.

40 It was published only seven years after Niccolò's death, but gained some notoriety in his lifetime.

41 See Benner, *Machiavelli's Prince*, Ch. 1, on the absence of the word 'tyranny' in the *Prince*.

42 *Prince*, 25, 21, 10, 19.

43 *Prince*, 10.

15. *Simulate Stupidity*

1 He describes the Medicis' ascent in detail in the *Florentine Histories*, VI–VII.

2 Vettori, *Viaggio*, Book 2.

3 Vettori to Machiavelli, 23 November 1513.

4 Machiavelli to Vettori, 10 December 1513.

5 Vettori to Machiavelli, 24 December 1513; Machiavelli to Vettori, 30 December 1514.

6 Machiavelli to Vettori, 19 December 1513, 5 January 1514, 10 June 1514.

7 Devonshire Jones, 109.

8 Vettori, *Sommario*; Tomas, *Medici Women*.

9 Landucci, 274–6.

10 Based on *Art of War*, I.1–34.

11 *Art of War*, VII.245–6.

12 *Art of War*, II.18, 284–8, 303–4.

13 The *Discourses* as we know it has 142 chapters (separate *discorsi*) divided into three parts. Exact dates unknown; probably composed between 1514 and 1519.

14 *Discourses*, Dedication; shortened and lightly paraphrased.

15 *Discourses*, I.5, *Florentine Histories*, III.3.

16 *Art of War*, I.21–2.

17 Machiavelli to Vettori, 26 August 1513.

18 *Discourses*, I.58.

19 *Discourses*, I.17–18.

20 Giovanni Vernacci to Machiavelli, 26 October 1516.

21 Machiavelli to Giovanni Vernacci, 19 November 1515.

22 Machiavelli to Vettori, 25 August 1513.

23 See Radif, *Le Maschere di Machiavelli*.

24 Ridolfi, *Mandragola*.

25 *Mandragola*, Act I.2.

26 *Mandragola*, Act II.3.
27 Battista della Palla to Machiavelli, 26 April 1520.
28 Devonshire Jones, 136–9; Najemy, *History*, 433.
29 *Art of War*, I.1–7.

16. *Imagine a True Republic*

1 Ideas expressed in *Discourse on Remodelling the Government of Florence*; see below.
2 *Discourses*, I.55.
3 See Machiavelli's two 'Reports on Germany' in Detmold, ed., Vol. 4, 384–401; and *Discourses*, I.55.
4 Arguments based on *Discourses*, II.2., I.2, I.16, I.3.
5 Below from Machiavelli, *Discourse on Remodelling the Government of Florence*.
6 Ch. 3.
7 This line about gentlemen is from *Discourses*, I.55. What follows is still from the *Discourse on Remodelling the Government of Florence*.
8 Legation to Carpi, 11 May 1521.
9 Guicciardini to Machiavelli, 17 May 1521.
10 Guicciardini, *Maxims and Reflections*, 86.
11 This and below: Machiavelli–Guicciardini exchange, 17–19 May 1521.
12 Based on letters 17–19 May 1521.
13 Guicciardini, *Maxims and Reflections*, 48.
14 Below based on Machiavelli–Guicciardini exchanges, 17–19 May 1521.
15 See Guicciardini, *Dialogue*.
16 Guicciardini, *Maxims and Reflections*, 86.
17 Battista della Palla to Machiavelli, 26 April 1520.
18 Piero Soderini to Machiavelli, 13 April 1521.
19 Guicciardini to Machiavelli, 18 May 1521.
20 Machiavelli to Guicciardini, 30 August 1524.
21 Guicciardini to Machiavelli, 18 May 1521.
22 *Florentine Histories*, I.17–19.
23 Nardi, quoted in Najemy, *History*, 433.

24 Machiavelli to Giovanni Vernacci, 9 October 1519, 15 April 1520.

25 See Roberto Pucci to Machiavelli, 8 June 1522.

26 Martelli trial 1526: *Documenti della congiura*, 244.

27 *Discourses*, III.6; *Prince*, 19.

28 Devonshire Jones, 157.

29 Vettori to Machiavelli, 16 April 1523.

30 De' Nerli to Machiavelli, 6 September 1525.

31 Vettori to Machiavelli, 16 April 1523.

17. *Never Give Up*

1 Filippo de' Nerli to Machiavelli, 22 February 1525.

2 Filippo de' Nerli to Francesco del Nero, 1 March 1525.

3 Guicciardini to Machiavelli, 7 August 1525.

4 De' Nerli to Del Nero, 1 March 1525.

5 Filippo Strozzi to Machiavelli, 31 March 1526.

6 Machiavelli to Vettori, 31 January 1515.

7 Machiavelli to del Nero, 26 September 1523.

8 Machiavelli to Guicciardini, 30 August 1524.

9 See Benner, *Machiavelli's Ethics*, Ch. 1.

10 Machiavelli to Guicciardini, after 21 October 1525 (specific date unknown).

11 These parts were never finished, and we have no record of any drafts.

12 Machiavelli to Guicciardini, 21 October 1525.

13 This and below: see Devonshire Jones, 162–4.

14 Vettori to Machiavelli, 8 March 1525.

15 Letter to Roberto Acciaiuoli, 6 March 1525; Acciaiuoli to Vettori, 12 March 1525, discussed in Devonshire Jones, 171–6.

16 *Prince*, 25.

17 *Discourses*, I.1.

18 *Discourses*, II.29.

19 Guicciardini to Machiavelli, 7 August 1525.

20 Machiavelli to Guicciardini, 17 August 1525.

21 De' Nerli to Machiavelli, 6 September 1525.

22 Machiavelli to Guicciardini, 16–20 October 1525; after 21 October 1525.

23 Guicciardini to Machiavelli, 26 December 1525.

24 *Prince*, 21.

25 Machiavelli to Guicciardini, 15 March 1526.

26 Machiavelli to Guicciardini, 15 March 1526.

27 Machiavelli to Bartolomeo Cavalcanti, 13 July 1526.

28 Exchange between Guicciardini and Roberto Acciaiuoli, in *Machiavelli and His Friends*, 376.

29 Vettori to Machiavelli, 5 August 1526.

30 Falconetti to Machiavelli, 5 August 1526.

31 Vettori to Machiavelli, 5 August 1526.

32 Devonshire Jones, 184–8.

33 Machiavelli to Vettori, 5 April 1527.

34 Machiavelli to Vettori, 5 April 1527.

35 Lodovico Machiavelli to Niccolò, 14 August 1525; Vettori to Machiavelli, 16 April 1523.

36 Guido Machiavelli to Niccolò Machiavelli, 17 April 1527.

37 Machiavelli to his son Guido, 2 April 1527.

38 On below, see Devonshire Jones, 189–97.

39 *Discourses*, III.31.

40 Machiavelli to Guicciardini, 17 May 1521.

41 *Prince*, Dedication.

42 *Discourses*, I.10.

43 *Discourses*, I.1.

44 Guicciardini to Machiavelli, 17 May 1521.

45 Ridolfi, 249–50, 330 note 24.

Aftermath

1 *Prince*, 9.

2 Devonshire Jones, 266–79.

3 Ridolfi, 326, note 23.

4 Godman, 303–35.

5 *Discourses*, II.5.

6 Gentili, III.ix.

Bibliography

Primary sources

When citing Machiavelli, his contemporaries, or other authors who wrote in languages other than English, I have based citations on English translations when they were available, sometimes making my own minor revisions. Otherwise, all translations are my own.

Machiavelli

Complete works in the original Italian

Machiavelli, Niccolò. 1997–2005. *Opere*. Vols. 1–3. Turin: Einaudi-Gallimard.

'LEGATIONS' (DIPLOMATIC MISSIONS) IN ENGLISH TRANSLATION
Machiavelli, Niccolò. 1882. *The Historical, Political and Diplomatic Writings*. Vols. 3–4. Trans. and ed. Christian Edward Detmold. Boston: James R. Osgood and Co.

PERSONAL CORRESPONDENCE IN ENGLISH TRANSLATION
Machiavelli and His Friends: Their Personal Correspondence. 1996. Trans. & ed. James B. Atkinson and David Sices. DeKalb, IL: Northern Illinois University Press.

OTHER WRITINGS IN ENGLISH TRANSLATION
Macchiavelli, Niccolò. 2003. *The Art of War*. Trans. & ed. Christopher Lynch. Chicago: University of Chicago Press.
——. 1989. *The Ass (Asino)*, in *Machiavelli: The Chief Works and Others*. Trans. Allan Gilbert. Durham, NC: Duke University Press. Vol. 2, pp. 750–72.

——. 1989. *Decennali* I and II, in Gilbert, ed. *Machiavelli: The Chief Works*. Vol. 3, pp. 1444–62.

——. 1989. 'A Description of the Method Used by Duke Valentino in Killing Vitellozzo Vitelli, Oliverotto da Fermo, and Others [at Sinigaglia]' in Gilbert, ed. *Machiavelli: The Chief Works*. Vol. 1, pp. 163–9.

——. 1989. *A Discourse on Remodelling the Government of Florence*, in Gilbert, ed. *Machiavelli: The Chief Works*. Vol. 1, pp. 101–15.

——. 1996. *Discourses on Livy*. Trans. Harvey C. Mansfield and Nathan Tarcov. Chicago: University of Chicago Press.

——. 1988. *Florentine Histories*. Trans. Laura F. Banfield and Harvey C. Mansfield, J. Princeton: Princeton University Press.

——. 1989. *The Life of Castruccio Castracani of Lucca*, in Gilbert, ed. *Machiavelli: The Chief Works*. Vol. 2, pp. 533–60.

——. 1989. 'On the Method of Dealing with the Rebellious Peoples of the Valdichiana', in Gilbert, ed. *Machiavelli: The Chief Works*. Vol. 1, pp. 161–2.

——. 1998. *Prince*, 2nd edn. Trans. & intro. Harvey C. Mansfield. Chicago: University of Chicago Press.

——. 1989. *Tercets on Ambition (Dell'ambizione)* and *Fortune (Di fortuna)*, in Gilbert, ed. *Machiavelli: The Chief Works*. Vol. 2, pp. 735–9, 745–9.

——. 1989. 'Two Sonnets to Giuliano' and 'A Third Sonnet to Giuliano', in Gilbert, ed. *Machiavelli: The Chief Works*. Vol. 2, pp. 1013–15.

Collections of sources

Fachard, Denis, ed. 1998–2002. *Consulte e pratiche della Repubblica Fiorentina, 1495–1512*. Geneva: Droz: Faculté des lettres de l'université de Lausanne.

Chiappelli, Fredi, and Jean-Jacques Marchand, eds. 1971–85. Niccolò Machiavelli: *Legazioni. Commissarie. Scritti di governo*. 4 Vols. Bari: Laterza.

Marchand, Jean-Jacques, and Denis Fachard, eds. 2002–11. Niccolò Machiavelli: *Legazioni. Commissarie. Scritti di governo*. 7 Vols. Rome: Salerno Editrice.

Works by Machiavelli's contemporaries

Buonaccorsi, Biagio. 1999. *Diario dall'anno 1498 all'anno 1512 e altri scritti.* Ed. Enrico Niccolini. Rome: Istituto Storico Italiano per il Medio Evo.

Burchard, Johann. 1963. *At the Court of the Borgia.* Ed. & trans. Geoffrey Parker. London: The Folio Society.

Cambi, Giovanni. 1785–6. *Istorie,* in *Delizie degli eruditi toscani.* Ed. Ildefonso di San Luigi. Vol. XX–XXIII. Florence: Cambiagi.

Castiglione, Baldassare. 1976. *The Book of the Courtier.* Trans. George Bull. Harmondsworth: Penguin.

Cerretani, Bartolomeo. 1994. *Storia fiorentina.* Ed. Giuliana Berti. Florence: Olschki.

Ficino, Marsilio, *Consiglio contro la pestilenzia,* in Katinis, Teodoro, *Medicina e filosofia in Marsilio Ficino: Il Consilio contro la pestilenzia.* Rome: Edizioni di lettura et letteratura, 2007.

Guicciardini, Francesco. 1932. *Dialogo e discorsi del reggimento di Firenze.* Ed. Roberto Palmarocchi. Bari: Giuseppe Laterza e figli.

———. 1994. *Dialogue on the Government of Florence.* Trans. & ed. Alison Brown. Cambridge: Cambridge University Press.

———. 1970. *The History of Florence.* Trans. & intro. Mario Domandi. New York: Harper Torchbooks.

———. 1969. *The History of Italy.* Trans. & ed. Sidney Alexander. Princeton: Princeton University Press.

———. 1965. *Maxims and Reflections (Ricordi).* Trans. Mario Domandi. Philadelphia: University of Pennsylvania Press.

Landino, Cristoforo. 1974. *Scritti critici e teorici.* 2 Vols. Rome: Bulzani.

Landucci, Luca. 1927. *A Florentine Diary from 1450 to 1516.* Trans. Alice de Rosen Jervis. London: J. M. Dent.

Machiavelli, Bernardo. 2007. *Libro di ricordi.* Ed. Cesare Olschki. Rome: Edizioni di Storia e Letteratura.

Nardi, Jacopo. 1842. *Istorie delle città di Firenze.* Ed. Lelio Arbib. Florence: Società Editrice delle Storie del Nardi e del Varchi.

Nerli, Filippo de'. 1728. *Commentarj de' fatti civili occorsi dentro la città di Firenze dall anno MCCXX al MDXXXVII.* Ed. David Raimondo Mertz and Gio. Jacopo Maier. No city given.

Parenti, Piero. 2005. *Storia fiorentina*. Ed. A. Matucci. Florence: Olschki.

de' Ricci, Giuliano. *Priorista*. MS Palatino E. B. 14.1, in the Biblioteca Nazionale Centrale di Firenze.

Savonarola, Girolamo. 2006. *Selected Writings of Girolamo Savonarola: Religion and Politics, 1490–1498*. Trans. & ed. Anne Borelli and Maria Pastore Passaro. New Haven: Yale University Press.

Scala, Bartolomeo. 2008. *Dialogue on Laws and Legal Judgments*, in *Bartolomeo Scala: Essays and Dialogues*, trans. Renée Neu Watkins. Cambridge: MA: I Tatti Renaissance Library, Harvard University Press, pp. 158–65.

Strozzi, Lorenzo di Filippo. 1851. *Vita di Filippo Strozzi il vecchio*. Ed. Giuseppe Bini and Pietro Bigazzi. Florence: Tip. della Casa di Correzione.

Vettori, Francesco. *Sommario* and *Viaggio in Alamagna*, in *Scritti storici e politici*. Printed electronic edition; no date or editor given.

Other classic works

Aristotle. 1894. *Ethica Nicomachea*. Ed. Ingram Bywater. Oxford: Clarendon Press.

Bacon, Francis. 2001 [1605]. *The Advancement of Learning*. New York: Random House.

——. 1985 [1597–1625]. *The Essays*. Ed. & intro. John Pitcher. Harmondsworth: Penguin.

Cicero, Marcus Tullius. 2005. *On Duties (De officiis)*. Trans. Walter Miller. Cambridge, MA: Loeb Classical Library, Harvard University Press.

Dante Alighieri. 1991. *La divina commedia*. Ed. Giuseppe Villaroel, revised commentary Guido Davico Bonino and Carla Poma. Milan: Mondadori.

Fichte, Johann Gottlieb. 1971 [1807]. 'Über Machiavelli', in *Fichtes Werke*. Ed. Immanuel Hermann Fichte. Berlin: Walter de Gruyter & Co. Vol. 11, pp. 400–453.

Gentili, Alberico. 1924 [1594]. *De legationibus libri tres*. Vols. 1–2. Trans. Gordon Laing, ed. James Brown Scott. New York: Oxford University Press.

Hegel, G. W. F. 1986 [1800–1802]. 'Die Verfassung Deutschlands', in *Werke: Frühe Schriften*. Frankfurt: Suhrkamp. Vol. 1, pp. 451–60.

Livy, Titus. 2000–2002. *History of Rome (Ab Urbe Condita)*. Vols. 1–45. Cambridge, MA: Loeb Classical Library, Harvard University Press.

Neville, Henry. 1691. *Nicholas Machiavel's Letter to Zenobius Buondelmontius, in Vindication of Himself and His Writings*. London: s.n.

———. 1681. *Plato redivivus: or, A Dialogue Concerning Government*. London: Printed for S. I. and sold by R. Dew.

Nifo, Agostino. 2008 [1523]. *De regnandi peritia/L'Art de régner* (Latin and French parallel). Ed. & trans. Paul Larivaille. Paris: Les Belles Lettres.

Petrarch, Francesco. 2004. *Canzoniere*. Ed. Marco Santagata. Milan: Mondadori.

Plutarch. 2000–2005. *Moralia*. Vols. 1–13. Cambridge, MA: Loeb Classical Library, Harvard University Press.

———. 1998–2002. *Lives*. Vols. 1–11. Cambridge, MA: Loeb Classical Library, Harvard University Press.

Pole, Reginald. 1997 [1539]. *Apology*. Selections in Jill Kraye, ed. *Cambridge Translations of Renaissance Philosophical Texts*. Cambridge: Cambridge University Press. Vol. 2: *Political Philosophy*, pp. 274–86.

Rousseau, Jean-Jacques. 1964 [1762]. *Du contrat social* in *Oeuvres complètes*. Paris: Bibliothèque de la Pléiade, Gallimard. Vol. 3, pp. 348–470.

Spinoza, Benedict de. 1958 [1677]. *Tractatus politicus* in *The Political Works*. Ed. & trans. A. G. Wernham. Oxford: Clarendon Press.

———. 2007 [1669–70]. *Theological-Political Treatise (Tractatus theologico-politicus)*. Ed. Jonathan Israel, trans. Michael Silverthorne and Jonathan Israel. Cambridge: Cambridge University Press.

Tacitus, Cornelius. 1979. *Works*. Vol. 1. Cambridge, MA: Loeb Classical Library, Harvard University Press.

Thucydides. 2003. *History of the Peloponnesian War*. Vols. 1–4. Cambridge, MA: Loeb Classical Library, Harvard University Press.

Secondary sources

On the history of Florence and Italy

Atkinson, Catherine. 2002. *Debts, Dowries, Donkeys: The Diary of Niccolò Machiavelli's Father, Messer Bernardo, in Quattrocento Florence*. Berlin: Peter Lang.

Benvenuti, Gino. 2003. *Storia della Repubblica di Pisa*. Pisa-Rome: Biblioteca dell'Ussero.

Biow, Douglas. 2002. *Doctors, Ambassadors, Secretaries: Humanism and Professions in Renaissance Italy*. Chicago: University of Chicago Press.

Brown, Alison. 1979. *Bartolomeo Scala, 1430–1497, Chancellor of Florence: The Humanist as Bureaucrat*. Princeton: Princeton Legacy Library, Princeton University Press.

Bullard, Melissa Merian. 1980. *Filippo Strozzi and the Medici: Favor and Finance in Sixteenth-century Florence and Rome*. Cambridge: Cambridge University Press.

Devonshire Jones, Rosemary. 1972. *Francesco Vettori: Florentine Citizen and Medici Servant*. London: The Athlone Press.

Fachard, Denis. 1976. *Biagio Buonaccorsi: sa vie, son temps, son ouevre*. Bologna: M. Boni.

Gilbert, Felix. 1949. 'Bernardo Rucellai and the Orti Oricellari'. *Journal of the Warburg and Courtauld Institutes*, Vol. 12, pp. 101–31.

——. 1977. *History: Choice and Commitment*, Cambridge, MA: The Belknap Press.

Godman, Peter. 1998. *From Poliziano to Machiavelli: Florentine Humanism in the High Renaissance*. Princeton: Princeton University Press.

Guasti, Cesare. 1859. Ed. *Documenti della congiura fatta contro il cardinal Giulio de' Medici nel 1522*, in 'Giornale Storico degli Archivi Toscani', Vol. III.

Guidi, Andrea. 2006. 'Machiavelli al tempo del sacco di Prato alla luce di sei lettere inedite a lui inviate'. *Filologia e critica*, Vol. 31, May–August, pp. 274–87.

——. 2009. *Un segretario militante: Politica, diplomazia e armi nel Cancelliere Machiavelli*. Bologna: Il Mulino.

Henderson, John. 1994. *Piety and Charity in Late Medieval Florence*. Chicago: University of Chicago Press.

Landon, William J. 2013. *Lorenzo di Filippo Strozzi and Niccolò Machiavelli: Patron, Client, and the Pistola fatta per la peste/An Epistle Written Concerning the Plague*. Toronto: University of Toronto Press.

Luzzati, Michele. 1973. *Una guerra di popolo. Lettere private del tempo dell'assedio di Pisa (1494–1509)*. Pisa: Pacini.

Martines, Lauro. 2007. *Scourge and Fire: Savonarola and Renaissance Italy.* London: Pimlico.

Molho, Anthony. 1994. *Marriage Alliance in Late Medieval Florence.* Cambridge, MA: Harvard University Press.

Najemy, John M. 2006. *A History of Florence, 1200–1575.* Oxford: Blackwell.

——, ed. 2004. *Italy in the Age of the Renaissance, 1300–1550.* Oxford: Oxford University Press.

Plaisance, Michel. 2008. *Florence in the Time of the Medici: Public Celebrations, Politics, and Literature in the Fifteenth and Sixteenth Centuries.* Trans. & ed. Nicole Carew-Reid. Toronto: Centre for Reformation and Renaissance Studies.

Ridolfi, R. 1965. Ed. *La Mandragola di Niccolò Machiavelli: Per la prima volta restituita alla sua integrità.* Florence: Olschki.

Rocke, Michael. 1996. *Forbidden Friendships: Homosexuality and Male Culture in Renaissance Florence.* New York: Oxford University Press.

Ross, Janet, trans. and ed. 1910. *Lives of the Early Medici as Told in their Correspondence.* London: Chatto Windus.

Shaw, James, and Evelyn Welch. 2011. *Making and Marketing Medicine in Renaissance Florence.* Amsterdam: Rodopi.

Tomas, Natalie R. 2003. *The Medici Women: Gender and Power in Renaissance Florence.* Farnham: Ashgate.

Trexler, Richard C. 1981. 'La prostitution florentine au XVe siècle', in *Annales, Économies, Sociétés, Civilisations.* Vol. 36, no. 6, p. 995 and n. 79.

——. 1991. *Public Life in Renaissance Florence.* Ithaca: Cornell University Press.

On Machiavelli, his writings, and their literary contexts

Baron, Hans. 1955. *Humanistic and Political Literature in Florence and Venice at the Beginning of the Quattrocento.* Cambridge, MA: Harvard University Press.

——. 1988. *In Search of Florentine Civic Humanism.* Princeton: Princeton University Press.

Benner, Erica. 2012. 'Das eigene Herr und die *virtù*', in *Niccolò Machiavelli: Der Fürst.* Ed. Otfried Höffe. Berlin: Akademie Verlag.

——. 2014. 'Las ironías de Maquiavelo: Estándares generales y el consejo irónico en *El Príncipe*', in *El Príncipe de Maquiavelo: Desafíos, legados y significados*. Ed. Jorge Andrés López Rivera. Bogotá, Colombia, Pontificia Universidad Javeriana.

——. 2009. *Machiavelli's Ethics*. Princeton: Princeton University Press.

——. 2014. 'Machiavelli's Ironies'. *Social Research: An International Quarterly*, Vol. 81, no. 1, Spring, pp. 61–84.

——. 2013. *Machiavelli's Prince: A New Reading*. Oxford: Oxford University Press.

——. 2014. '*Questa inconstante dea:* Machiavelli's amoral Fortuna', in *Spazio filosofico*, No. 12, October.

Berlin, Isaiah. 1981 [1958]. 'The Originality of Machiavelli', in *Against the Current: Essays in the History of Ideas*. Oxford: Oxford University Press, pp. 25–79.

Bock, Gisela, Quentin Skinner and Maurizio Viroli, eds. 1990. *Machiavelli and Republicanism*. Cambridge: Cambridge University Press.

Booth, Wayne C. 1975. *A Rhetoric of Irony*. Chicago: University of Chicago Press.

Chabod, Federico. 1960. *Machiavelli and the Renaissance*. Trans. David Moore, intro. A. P. d'Entrèves. London: Bowes and Bowes.

Connell, William J., and Andrea Zorzi, eds. 2000. *Florentine Tuscany: Structures and Practices of Power*. Cambridge: Cambridge University Press.

Dietz, Mary G. 1986. 'Trapping the Prince: Machiavelli and the Politics of Deception'. *American Political Science Review*, Vol. 80, no. 3, pp. 777–99.

Fachard, Denis, ed. 2013. *Niccolò Machiavelli: Teatro*. Rome: Carocci Editore.

Garin, Eugenio. 1965. *Italian Humanism: Philosophy and Civic Life in the Renaissance*. Trans. Peter Munz. Oxford: Basil Blackwell.

——. 1993. *Machiavelli fra politica e storia*. Turin: Einaudi.

Gilbert, Felix. 1965. *Machiavelli and Guicciardini: Politics and History in Sixteenth-century Florence*. Princeton: Princeton University Press.

Höffe, Otfried, ed. 2012. *Niccolò Machiavelli: Der Fürst*. Berlin: Akademie Verlag.

Knox, Norman. 1961. *The Word Irony and Its Context, 1500–1755*. Durham, NC: Duke University Press.

Kraye, Jill, ed. 1997. *Cambridge Translations of Renaissance Philosophical Texts*. Vols. 1 and 2. Cambridge: Cambridge University Press.

Langton, John, and Mary G. Dietz. 1987. 'Machiavelli's Paradox: Trapping or Teaching the Prince'. *American Political Science Review*, Vol. 81, no. 4, pp. 1277–88.

Mattingly, Garrett. 1958. 'Machiavelli's *Prince*: Political Science or Political Satire?' *American Scholar*, Vol. 27, no. 4, pp. 482–91.

Najemy, John M. 1993. *Between Friends: Discourses of Power and Desire in the Machiavelli–Vettori Letters of 1513–1515*. Princeton: Princeton University Press.

——, ed. 2010. *The Cambridge Companion to Machiavelli*. Cambridge: Cambridge University Press.

——. 1990. 'The Controversy Surrounding Machiavelli's Service to the Republic', in Gisela Bock et al. eds., *Machiavelli and Republicanism*, pp. 101–17.

——. 2013. 'Machiavelli and Cesare Borgia: A Reconsideration of Chapter 7 of the *Prince*'. *Review of Politics*, Vol. 75, 4, pp. 539–56.

Patterson, Annabel. 1987. *Pastoral and Ideology: Virgil to Valéry*. Berkeley and Los Angeles: University of California Press.

Radif, Ludovica. 2010. *Le Maschere di Machiavelli*. Imperia: Ennepilibri.

Sasso, Gennaro. 1958. *Niccolò Machiavelli: Storio del suo pensiero politico*. Naples: Istituto italiano per gli studi storici.

——. 1987–97. *Machiavelli e gli antichi e altri saggi*. 4 Vols. Milan: R. Ricciardi.

Soll, Jacob. 2005. *Publishing the Prince: History, Reading and the Birth of Political Criticism*. Michigan: University of Michigan Press.

Villari, Pasquale. 1912–14. *Niccolò Machiavelli eisuoi tempi*. Milan: Hoepli.

——. 2011 [1888]. *Life and Times of Girolamo Savonarola*. Trans. Linda Villari. Charleston, SC: Nabu Press.

Watkins, Renée Neu, trans & ed. 1978. *Humanism and Liberty: Writings on Freedom from Fifteenth-century Florence*. Charleston: University of South Carolina Press.

Zaccaria, Raffaella. 2006. 'Girolamo Machiavelli'. *Dizionario biografico degli italiani*, Vol. 67. Treccani: online resource (www.treccani.it).

Acknowledgements

Writing this book was a new departure for me. Many people helped keep it on track and steer it toward publication. Rosamund Bartlett inspired me to venture beyond political philosophy and try my hand at a more biographical book about Machiavelli. My agent, Catherine Clarke, is simply the best. My editors at Allen Lane, Tom Penn and Josephine Greywoode, deserve a large share of the credit for making the book as readable as I hope it now is; I take full responsibility for its remaining flaws. Thanks to Ian Shapiro, grants from Yale University's Macmillan Center funded fruitful periods of research in Florence. Richard Duguid's eagle eye and indexing skills improved the final version. I also thank Sarah Day and Isabel Blake at Allen Lane, my editor Maria Guarnaschelli at W. W. Norton and her assistant Nathaniel Dennett, my superb Italian translator Lorenzo Matteoli, Ilana Bet-el, Amy Bloch, Andrea Guidi, John Najemy, Gretchen Benner and Reed Benner. And Patrick, as ever, with love.

Index

Index